AF262771

"In this urgent and necessary book, Gelman uncovers the complex and troubling history of a once admired—now deeply contested—organization. Drawing on rich archival evidence and propelled by incisive analysis, *The Anti-Defamation League and the Racial State* shows that the ADL was never the steadfast defender of civil rights it claimed to be. For much of its history, it has been dedicated to suppressing Jewish political dissent and assimilating Jews of European ancestry into American white supremacy and the broader liberal racial order that undergirds US and Israeli state power. This history runs through the organization's attacks on Jewish labor, its embrace of McCarthyism, its opposition to legal remedies for racial inequality, and its unwavering support for Zionism— even amid Israel's worst human rights atrocities. The ADL's Trump-era alliance with the far right, Gelman demonstrates, is no rupture with its past but the culmination of a long-standing project: to appropriate the language of civil rights while entrenching the very hierarchies it professes to oppose."

—BARRY TRACHTENBERG, author of *The Holocaust and the Exile of Yiddish*

"An indispensable analytical history of an organization that continues to play an outsized role in shaping, politicizing, and policing the popular common sense. This relentlessly documented, rigorously researched book will indelibly alter understandings of the Anti-Defamation League and its historical relation to liberationist, antiracist, and decolonizing movements."

—DYLAN RODRÍGUEZ, author of *White Reconstruction*

"It is impossible to overstate the importance of this book for these times. Well-researched and deeply informed, *The Anti-Defamation League and the Racial State* shows how the ADL leads the way in undermining abolition and other anti-violence and redistributive efforts by making policing and lawfare appear as socially good violence."

—JODI MELAMED, author of *Represent and Destroy: Rationalizing Violence in the New Racial Capitalism*

"A bold and bracing history of the ADL's century-long campaign to enforce and depict a nonexistent Jewish American hegemony around Israel, capitalism, and US state-building. Gelman deftly traverses Jewish class differences and the divergent range of Jewish commitments to civil rights and Black power, while courageously confronting the ADL's overstating of antisemitism as a tactical reaction to growing anti-Zionism among US Jews. This is a paradigm-shifting must-read."

—SARAH SCHULMAN, author of *The Fantasy and Necessity of Solidarity*

"This compelling book provides *the* indispensable history of an organization that claims to defend equal rights and civil liberties while actually working to secure the foundational logic of the racial and carceral state at home and a genocidal project of apartheid overseas."

—SAREE MAKDISI, author of *Tolerance Is a Wasteland*

"Gelman gifts us a stunningly urgent study that helps us counter the most pernicious myths the ADL's ideological machinery has constructed over decades. What we are left with is an airtight road map to both the concrete historical details and the structural knowledge needed to refuse the Zionist warfare that is intent on reshaping our reality."

—LARA SHEEHI, author of *From the Clinic to the Streets*

"Presenting a remarkable archive of sources, Gelman illustrates how the ADL became a normative force in American racial liberalism, offering anti-hate and anti-bias school curriculum. In doing so, Gelman shows that the ADL has assisted the state in limiting, reframing, and opposing Jewish, Black, queer, and Palestinian demands for justice throughout the twentieth century. *The Anti-Defamation League and the Racial State* is both necessary and important."

—ALEX LUBIN, author of *Never-Ending War on Terror*

"The backlash to pro-Palestinian campus protests in 2023 and 2024 quickly consolidated around anti-liberation, pro-state rhetoric, directly continuous with the manufactured panics aimed at the Black Lives Matter and LGBTQ movements. Gelman here explains why this was not a coincidence but the ADL's institutional logic working as designed. This revelatory book is well-researched, superbly written, elegantly argued, theoretically powerful, and morally just."

—ISAAC KAMOLA, coauthor of *Free Speech and Koch Money*

"Meticulously researched and persuasively written, Gelman's book blows the lid off a household name in the human rights field, revealing the ADL's long-standing record of racial profiling and discrimination."

—ANDREW ROSS, author of *The Weather Report*

"Now, at last, we have something approaching the full story. Gelman deserves the heartfelt praise of progressives and scholars of Jewish life as well."

—PAUL BUHLE, editor of *Jews and American Popular Culture*

"Those hoping to understand the ADL's current far-right alignment must read Gelman's *Anti-Defamation League and the Racial State*. Based on prodigious archival research, this book pulls back the curtain on the ADL's history of so-called 'anti-hate' work, revealing the organization's active role in shaping domestic and foreign policies that marginalized, indeed silenced, efforts to redistribute power and resources most justly. *The Anti-Defamation League and the Racial State* forces a new reckoning with the question of who speaks for the interests—and real safety—of American Jews and indeed of all of us."

—MARJORIE FELD, author of *The Threshold of Dissent*

"As Gelman demonstrates in this indispensable history, throughout a century of ever-changing racial discourses and politics, the ADL has remained consistent in its service to capitalism, whiteness, and settler colonialism. This book is essential reading for scholars and activists working to dismantle the complex systems of oppression insidiously baked into US liberalism and its institutions."

—JEFF SCHUHRKE, author of *No Neutrals There*

"You'll never think of the ADL in the same way."

—A. J. BAUER, author of *Making the Liberal Media*

"Going forward, it will be impossible to understand US political culture without taking this book into account."

—C. HEIKE SCHOTTEN, author of *Queer Terror*

"Gelman helps us make sense of why the ADL is still seen as an authority on civil rights while it continues to drift rightward, accommodating and excusing some of the most racist right-wing antisemites. For parents, educators, and students in schools where ADL materials are still ubiquitous, this book is a call to action. For Jewish leftists, this book challenges us to build alternative institutions to fight for racial justice and to better understand how class and race shape Jewish politics."

—ADAM SANCHEZ, Managing Editor of *Rethinking Schools*

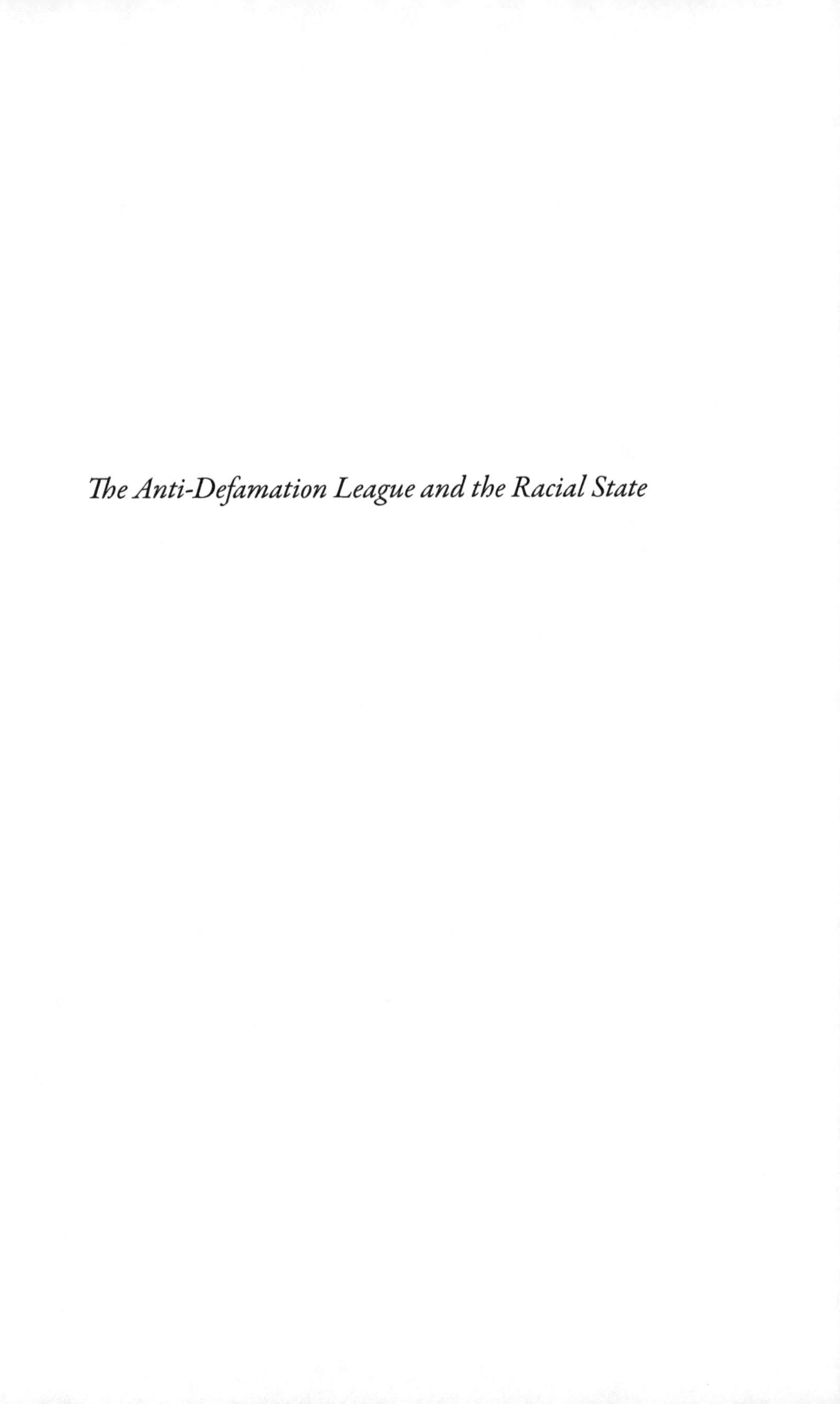

The Anti-Defamation League and the Racial State

The Anti-Defamation League and the Racial State

Emmaia Gelman

UNIVERSITY OF CALIFORNIA PRESS

University of California Press
Oakland, California

Cataloging-in-Publication data is on file at the Library of Congress.

ISBN 978-0-520-41044-2 (cloth : alk. paper)
ISBN 978-0-520-41045-9 (ebook)

Manufactured in the United States of America

GPSR Authorized Representative: Easy Access System Europe, Mustamäe tee 50, 10621 Tallinn, Estonia, gpsr.requests@easproject.com

35 34 33 32 31 30 29 28 27 26
10 9 8 7 6 5 4 3 2 1

For my brilliant kids.
For those who did not survive racism and colonialism, and for
those who are trying.

CONTENTS

Introduction

ON APRIL 9, 1993, newspapers from San Francisco to Baltimore blared variations on a stunning headline: "Anti-Defamation League Offices Raided by Police, Spy Data Sought in San Francisco."[1] The Anti-Defamation League (ADL) was considered a venerable organization, nearly synonymous with civil rights: It was a veteran of the civil rights movement of the 1950s and '60s, an authority on white nationalism in the 1970s and '80s, and a vociferous foe of antisemitism. It was a trusted advocate in politics and law, provided curriculum in schools across the United States, and frequently partnered with the FBI as a watcher of right-wing groups. Now, stunningly, the FBI had found it spying on civil rights groups and antiracist organizers. The ADL's agents had rifled through trash, acquired black market dossiers, surveilled license plates outside political meetings, and run records checks through unauthorized channels at the Department of Motor Vehicles. The following month, the *Village Voice* carried a scandalous follow-up investigation, "How the Anti-Defamation League Turned the Notion of Human Rights on Its Head, Spying on Progressives and Funneling Information to Law Enforcement."[2] Confoundingly, the targets of its spying were groups that advocated for minority rights and freedoms: the American Civil Liberties Union, labor unions, anti-Apartheid groups, LGBTQ groups, community-based organizations opposing wars and dictatorships, and (least surprising)

---

1. Ken Hoover, "Anti-Defamation League Raided by S. F. Cops," *San Francisco Chronicle*, April 9, 1993; *Baltimore Sun*, "Anti-Defamation League Offices Raided by Police Spy Data Sought in San Francisco," April 9, 1993.

2. Robert I. Friedman, "How the Anti-Defamation League Turned the Notion of Human Rights on Its Head, Spying on Progressives and Funneling Information to Law Enforcement," *Village Voice*, May 11, 1993.

Arab and Palestinian organizations. The *New York Times* noted that these revelations had caused "confusion for some liberals." If the ADL's work was to oppose discrimination and fight white nationalists, why was it spying on groups that defended civil rights?[3]

The question seems to have been abandoned as soon as it was asked. Despite the initial shock, the ADL spying scandal was almost instantly forgotten in the press; most activists and advocacy groups also let the matter drop. It played virtually no role in the public's longue durée perception of the ADL as a US institution. Also forgotten are many other dissonant episodes in the ADL's history: its participation in anticommunist witch hunts alongside Senator Joe McCarthy, support for Israel's collaboration with the South African Apartheid regime, and efforts to overturn affirmative action policies, among others. The ADL is a household name in the United States, but its history is a vague, mostly empty bracket, and its reputation cannot seem to take solid shape.

It might seem odd, then, that in Jewish communities the Anti-Defamation League was understood as a conservative organization for much of its existence: an organization of and for the elite classes, protective of the arrangements of political and economic power in which they were dominant, and resistant to ideas and movements that challenge those arrangements. This is settled history in Jewish Studies literature. Until the 1950s, most of US Jewry was working-class and far to the left of the ADL, and the ADL was anxious to distinguish itself from them. No one would have mistakenly thought that the ADL represented the Jewish masses or advocated substantive change, much less liberation. By the time I started researching this history, the opposite was true. Instead of being understood as representative of a specific sector of the Jewish community, the ADL was taken to represent all Jews. Rather than an institution of the upper economic and political classes, it was often described as a civil rights institution. By the 1990s, when the ADL's advocacy for hate crimes legislation placed it at the center of US identity politics, not only Jewish communities but US populations in general perceived the ADL as a progressive institution. After all, hadn't it fought the quotas that once kept Jewish students out of universities? Hadn't it won important cases and helped pass laws against employment and housing discrimination, and hadn't its leaders marched alongside Dr. Martin Luther King Jr.? It was this reputation that briefly made the spying scandal "confus-

3. *New York Times*, "A Dealer in Art and, Some Say, a Dealer in Secret Police Data," April 25, 1993.

ing." It has continued to confound people when the ADL endorses right-wing or racist politics—as when, for instance, Elon Musk made a Nazi salute from the 2025 presidential inauguration stage, and the ADL shocked the world by dismissing it as "an awkward gesture."[4] How do we account for these apparent contradictions?

Part of the problem is that the ADL's reputation is tied to major historical events around which US morality itself is constructed: The Nazi Holocaust as paramount evil and the US civil rights movement as triumph of democracy are often read as the backdrop for its activities. These urgently compelling events substitute vaguely sketched histories for details about the ADL itself. Another part is that *liberal* and *conservative* are confusing terms, often misconstrued as opposites. They are especially mixed up in US conversations about the Cold War and anticommunism, which is exactly where the ADL's story is anchored. Liberalism is often used to mean "being for rights and against discrimination" because the foundational framework of US rights is liberalism. But, as Lisa Duggan explains, both liberal *and* conservative movements in the twentieth-century United States were grounded in liberal capitalism.[5] Therefore, positions generally called conservative, like requiring people to work to qualify for welfare (grounded in the idea that individuals are responsible for their success or failure under capitalism) and opposition to affirmative action (grounded in the claim that it is unfair to white people), both fall under the rubric of liberalism, and were adopted by self-identified liberals. Another problem is that *race*, *racism*, and *antiracism* are themselves unstable and contested terms, used to mean different things.[6] This book attempts to clarify how those confusions have shaped perceptions of the ADL.[7]

4. ADL (@ADL), "This is a delicate moment. It's a new day and yet so many are on edge. Our politics are inflamed, and social media only adds to the anxiety. It seems that @ elonmusk made an awkward gesture in a moment of enthusiasm, not a Nazi salute, but again, we appreciate that people are on," Twitter (now X), January 20, 2025, https://x.com/ADL /status/1881474892022919403.

5. Lisa Duggan, *The Twilight of Equality? Neoliberalism, Cultural Politics, and the Attack on Democracy* (Beacon Press, 2003), 14.

6. On the instrumentalization of the instability of *race*, *racism*, and *antiracism* in discourses of rights, see Daniel Martinez HoSang, *Racial Propositions: Ballot Initiatives and the Making of Postwar California* (University of California Press, 2010), 14.

7. Larry Ceplair, historian of anticommunism, offers this explanation of the confusion over liberalism: "Harry K. Givertz lamented that the term, as currently used (in 1950), 'has come to have contradictory meanings. Everywhere men are dividing into camps over issues raised by liberalism, with only the haziest knowledge of the ground upon which they have pitched their tents.' Raymond English, a 'confessed conservative,' wrote in a 1952 essay that . . .

Most importantly, this study reads the ADL as a political and ideological institution. To do that, this history places the ADL's civil rights activities in the context of its other work—seeing them not in opposition to its overarching conservatism, but illuminating its broader aims. This helps make sense of seeming contradictions and shifts. The ADL has consistently worked to shape carceral aspects of life—including policing and surveillance, foreign policy and global militarization, and the conjuncture of technology and society—and it has helped unmake and remake hegemonic ideas about race, queerness, and citizenship within those spheres. At the same time, the ADL has pursued these projects through the logic and discourse of rights, especially *race* and rights, and those ideas are not static. The ADL has come to embrace norms that would have surprised its past leaders, including racial integration and queer citizenship. Public perceptions of the ADL have also been shaped by shifts in the political landscape. The post–World War II global reckoning with the Nazi Holocaust imbued organizations that address antisemitism with a special place in conversations on racism, and has often (not always) insulated white Jewish voices from moves to decenter white leadership in racial justice work. In the 1970s, the rise of neoliberalism normalized single-issue identity politics as the basis for social justice. Broad, grassroots movements that addressed race, capital, class, sex/gender, militarism, and other intersecting structures together were displaced, and instead identity groups were increasingly represented by nonprofit organizations in a top-down model, as Duggan has historicized.[8] Such shifts have sometimes miscast the ADL as a progressive organization participating in popular social movements. But even as the terms of rights have changed, this history clarifies that liberalism, and the settler colonialism that structures US liberalism, has remained the ADL's frame, closely tied to the project of US racial state-building.

At the ADL's founding—a scant two decades after colonization had enclosed the Indigenous land of North America, just one year after New Mexico and Arizona became the forty-seventh and forty-eighth states, and a decade before the United States extended citizenship to Indigenous people—building out the settler state was a primary undertaking of US civil society.

every person in the United States claims to be a liberal, 'with as large a capital "L" as possible.' The result, English concluded, was 'almost perfect political confusion,' with people thinking and talking about themselves as liberals, while acting and subconsciously believing they were conservatives.'" Larry Ceplair, *Anti-Communism in Twentieth-Century America: A Critical History* (Praeger, 2011), 153.

8. Duggan, *The Twilight of Equality?*, 7.

It was a moral, political, capital, and social project to be carried out by Europeans who were "civilizing" the land, turning it to industrial and profitable purposes, populating it themselves, and becoming the subjects of a liberal regime of rights. Leaning into those terms of nationhood, ADL leaders made the case that Jews were model citizens: motivated by capitalist-aligned notions of individual freedom and advancement, devoted to building the state, and intrinsically "civilized" Euro-Americans. When the ADL eventually began to address anti-Black discrimination in the 1940s (and much later and reluctantly, anti-queer discrimination in the 1990s) it continued to make the case for equality using the same terms. In fact, its advocacy did not only call for rights, it also defined the *subjects* of rights in ways that supported liberal state-building.

The meanings of race and racial identity have been interrogated and theorized in movements and scholarship aimed at dismantling racism. Black sociologists in the early part of the twentieth century articulated racism as an aspect of colonialism. The concept of institutional racism, articulated by Kwame Ture and Charles Hamilton and entrenched in US political culture by the early 1970s, identified whiteness as a state structure. That meaning invoked group histories of accumulation and inheritance, migration, and relationships to power as well as present access to resources, safety, and political voice. Later theorists expanded on the structures conditioning and producing race. Cheryl Harris detailed the function of whiteness as a form of property, and Blackness as exclusion from that ownership; Cedric Robinson articulated race and capitalism as co-constituted structures, identifying racialization as the procedure for producing an inescapable class of dominated labor; Ruth Wilson Gilmore has defined racism as "the state-sanctioned or extralegal production and exploitation of group-differentiated vulnerability to premature death."[9]

The ADL did not follow these developments in the understanding of structural race, but stuck instead to a post–World War II race liberalism that viewed (or perhaps pretended to view) *Black, white,* and other racial identities

---

9. See Penny M. Von Eschen, *Race Against Empire: Black Americans and Anticolonialism, 1937–1957* (Cornell University Press, 1997); Stokely Carmichael and Charles V. Hamilton, *Black Power: The Politics of Liberation in America* (Vintage Books, 1967), 32; Cedric J. Robinson, *Black Marxism: The Making of the Black Radical Tradition* (University of North Carolina Press, 2021 [1983]); Cheryl I. Harris, "Whiteness as Property," *Harvard Law Review* 106, no. 8 (1993): 1707–91; Ruth Wilson Gilmore, *Golden Gulag: Prisons, Surplus, Crisis, and Opposition in Globalizing California* (University of California Press, 2007), 28.

as different flavors of the same dish.[10] For instance, it affirmed the right of Black consumers to buy homes without racial restriction, defining consumers as correct subjects of race fairness. But when Black and brown communities in the Ocean Hill-Brownsville district of Brooklyn sought to educate children outside of mainstream—white-dominated—frameworks, the ADL denounced them as unreasonable and racist. As various popular movements challenged colonial and capitalist-oriented conceptions of rights, from the early Jewish labor movement to the anti–Vietnam War movement, the ADL resisted such changes and moved to restore settler colonial liberal framings. In 1979, as the ADL and major Jewish organizations were again contesting Black political organizing on multiple fronts—affirmative action, anti-Apartheid campaigning, and support for Palestinian human rights—Jesse Jackson bitterly remarked on the limits of solidarity: "When there wasn't much decency in society, many Jews were willing to share decency. The conflict began when we started our quest for power."[11]

It has often been the ADL's conflicts with antiracist movements that have thrown its ideological underpinnings into relief. The ADL is not an outlier in that sense: Civil rights advocacy has been the site of enormous contestation between groups who view the liberal state as a framework for justice, and others who contest it as foundationally racist. As scholars from David Levering Lewis to Olúfẹ́mi O. Táíwò have argued, liberal civil rights work has been driven and captured by elites, including elites within relatively marginalized groups, as a means of exercising power.[12] As such,

10. At times the ADL seemed poised to adopt structural approaches to antiracism. A 1966 ADL study, *Equality and Beyond*, warned that non-discrimination was no longer enough to overcome structures of inequality like residential segregation, which in practice limited access to the exercise of rights. The authors proposed material interventions like direct housing subsidies and affirmative action, alongside liberal non-interventions like "complete freedom of choice in place of residence without respect to racial barriers." Similarly, the ADL's 1967 study on Black political attitudes found Black radicalism to be a reasonable call for substantive change. These pathways, suggested by ADL researchers and viable enough to reach publication under the ADL's imprint, were not adopted by ADL leadership. George W. Grier and Eunice S. Grier, *Equality and Beyond: Housing Segregation and the Goals of the Great Society* (Quadrangle Books, 1966), 8, 83–94; Gary T. Marx, *Protest and Prejudice: A Study of Belief in the Black Community* (Greenwood Press, 1967).

11. Paul Delaney, "Leaders Try to Halt a Black-Jewish Rift," *New York Times*, August 19, 1979; *Time*, "Nation: With Sorrow and Anger," September 3, 1979.

12. David Levering Lewis, "Parallels and Divergences: Assimilationist Strategies of Afro-American and Jewish Elites from 1910 to the Early 1930s," *Journal of American History* 71, no. 3 (1984): 543–64; Olúfẹ́mi O. Táíwò, *Elite Capture: How the Powerful Took Over Identity Politics (And Everything Else)* (Haymarket Books, 2022).

much of US mainstream rights discourse, including that led by institutions ostensibly representing Black, queer, and other groups, has been organized in alignment with liberal and settler colonial framings. What has perhaps made the ADL in particular seem "confusing" is that, as it took up projects like Zionist advocacy and Cold War anticommunism, its settler liberalism became more legible as a rationale for repression. And at moments when the US governing regimes have ratcheted up authoritarianism—as against the New Left in the late 1960s, during the "War on Terror," and in the Trump era—the ADL has made the case that more repression is necessary to protect rights.

The ADL's part in producing ideas about rights and its infrastructure of enforcement has had an enormous impact on US politics and life, and on the globe. Expanding from its anti-defamation and anti-discrimination work, it moved into the era of the War on Terror as a key producer of three Western discourses of state and security: *hate, terror,* and *antisemitism.* These terms have come to evoke a broad threat to liberal rights and democracy from—depending on who is speaking—the political right or left, domestic and global. The terms *hate* and *terror* are so familiar that they are almost always used without definition and without attention to their ideological undercarriage. In fact, as Darryl Li writes, ADL advocacy produced the first US anti-terrorism law, which drew momentum from outrage over the white nationalist violence, but ultimately criminalized material support for foreign designated "terror organizations" explicitly to delegitimize Palestinian anti-colonial resistance. It has continued to drive anti-Muslim, anti-Palestinian, and anti-anticolonial "terrorism" discourse in its role as an authoritative national voice on extremism.[13] The ADL has also driven the popular understandings of *hate* in the United States that have been adopted throughout the West, and underwritten an intense focus on policing hate rather than redressing the racist, gendered, often anti-queer violence of institutions like law enforcement itself, or the racist violence of economies built on corporate profit and scarcity models. Although hate crimes policies initially responded to anti-Black and anti-immigrant violence in the United States in the 1980s, subsequent decades of ADL-driven advocacy redefined a vast and very

13. Darryl Li, "The ADL and the Anti-Palestinian Origins of US Terrorism Law," in *The Anti-Defamation League: A Critical Reader,* ed. Heike Schotten and Emmaia Gelman (Pluto Books, 2026).

different set of activities as *hate*, including *resistance* to racist violence, political and class conflict, and teaching uncomfortable histories.[14]

In parallel, the ADL mobilized definitions of *antisemitism* that describe opposition to racial state regimes as "hatred of Jews," and made *opposing anti-semitism* a rationale for allocating political and capital resources to shore up those regimes. That campaign launched in earnest with the publication of Arnold Forster and Benjamin Epstein's 1974 book *The New Anti-Semitism*, which sweepingly denounced US movements for racial and economic justice, the anti–Vietnam War movement, and Third Worldist anticolonialism.[15] It continued throughout later decades, eventually producing the campaign of the ADL and allied organizations, launched in 2016, for governments and institutions to adopt the International Holocaust Remembrance Alliance working definition of antisemitism ("the IHRA definition"), which labels criticism or even factual historical discussion of Israel and Zionism as "antisemitism."[16] In October 2023 these discourses became the backdrop against which the Israeli state escalated a campaign of genocide and mass expulsion against Palestinians under its colonial control. In the United States, facing waves of public outrage over US military and monetary aid underwriting the onslaught, President Joe Biden framed it as a moral necessity inextricable from national security. Repeatedly invoking *hate, terror,* and *antisemitism* as entwined strands of a moral and security threat, he cast Palestinians struggling against Israeli colonial domination—and others around the world who opposed Israeli colonization—as its agent.[17]

In the era of the Gaza genocide, the ADL quickly became central to a discursive push to turn attention away from Palestine to an ostensible "crisis

14. Christina Hanhardt's analysis of hate crimes policy as a project obscuring power, and primarily benefiting white people, has animated this research. See Christina B. Hanhardt, *Safe Space: Gay Neighborhood History and the Politics of Violence* (Duke University Press, 2013), 163–65; Darryl Li, *Anti-Palestinian at the Core: The Origins and Growing Dangers of US Antiterrorism Law* (Center for Constitutional Rights and Palestine Legal, 2024), 16.

15. Arnold Forster and Benjamin R. Epstein, *The New Anti-Semitism* (McGraw-Hill, 1974).

16. The International Holocaust Remembrance Alliance (IHRA) working definition of antisemitism is discussed in the epilogue.

17. Biden, "Remarks by President Biden on the Terrorist Attacks in Israel"; Joseph Biden, the White House, "Remarks by President Biden at the US Holocaust Memorial Museum's Annual Days of Remembrance Ceremony," the White House, May 7, 2024, https:// bidenwhitehouse.archives.gov/briefing-room/speeches-remarks/2024/05/07/remarks-by-president-biden-at-the-u-s-holocaust-memorial-museums-annual-days-of-remembrance-ceremony/; Ussama Makdisi, "Beyond the Palestine Exception," *Critical Times* 8, no. 1 (2025): 1–32.

of antisemitism" in the United States. It declared virtually all who resisted Israeli violence—Hamas, Palestinian people, anti-genocide protesters, Jewish groups calling for ceasefire, and scholars and journalists discussing Israel's settler colonial history—to be "supporters of terror," hate, and/or antisemitism, labeling them antidemocratic and anti-American, and concatenating them with Nazis.[18] Whether or not policymakers were actually convinced by the ADL's mischaracterizations, they echoed the claims in legislatures and university boardrooms, often citing the ADL by name. The imperative to condemn Palestinian resistance and center the "crisis of antisemitism" narrative, expanding on the compulsory Zionism that already prevailed in US politics, became a form of compulsory patriotism and opposition to the nation's attackers.[19]

At the same time, however, the security rationales of *terror*, *hate*, and *antisemitism* were stripped of some of their commanding social power. A new discourse, shaped by mass movement against the Gaza genocide, reframed the relation between Palestinians and the Israeli state in terms of settler colonialism and resistance, indigeneity, and political Zionism; indeed, in terms of power.[20] In that context, the ADL was increasingly identified as a political institution that leveraged "civil rights talk" for more vulgar political projects.[21] This was a remarkable destabilization of the ADL's position and the

18. Tom Perkins, "Anti-Defamation League Ramps Up Lobbying to Promote Controversial Definition of Antisemitism," *The Guardian*, May 16, 2024. In primary sources, see, for instance, the ADL's "backgrounders" on Hamas and groups organizing ceasefire/anti-genocide marches. "Hamas," https://www.adl.org/resources/backgrounder/hamas, accessed December 1, 2023; "Who Are the Primary Groups Behind the US Anti-Israel Rallies?," October 20, 2023, https://www.adl.org/resources/blog/who-are-primary-groups-behind-us-anti-israel-rallies, accessed November 14, 2023.

19. Umayyah Cable, "Compulsory Zionism and Palestinian Existence: A Genealogy," *Journal of Palestine Studies* 51, no. 2 (2022): 66–71; Lara Deeb and Jessica Winegar, "Resistance to Repression and Back Again: The Movement for Palestinian Liberation in US Academia," *Middle East Critique* 33, no. 3 (July 2024): 313–34.

20. See, for instance, the widely circulated *Los Angeles Times* interview with Israeli historian Avi Shlaim. Stuart Miller, "The Author of 'The Iron Wall' Sees a 'Sinister' Precedent Behind Israel's Actions in Gaza," *Los Angeles Times*, November 27, 2023.

21. See, for instance, Jeet Heer, "Why the Anti-Defamation League Loves Certain Bigots," *The Nation*, November 20, 2023; Najwa Mayer and Randa Tawil, "Palestine and the Asian American Question," *The Margins*, February 3, 2025. On "civil rights talk" (or simply "rights talk"), see Emmaia Gelman, "The World Upside-Down: Zionist Institutions, Civil Rights Talk, and the New Cold War on Ethnic Studies," *Critical Ethnic Studies* 8, no. 2 (2023). For further reading, see *The Anti-Defamation League: A Critical Reader*, ed. Heike Schotten and Emmaia Gelman.

consuming, fear-based collective identity that Joseph Masco describes as War on Terror "national security affect."[22]

This bottom-up rethinking of key political ideas organizing US life expanded on a long decade of intense contestation of meanings of race, racism, rights, and justice that had already made deep shifts in US political culture, brought about by social movements. When I began contemplating this project in 2014, the Black Lives Matter (BLM) movement had just risen up nationally around the murders by police of Eric Garner and Michael Brown, and the 2013 acquittal of Trayvon Martin's killer. BLM sparked a mass, public, ongoing reckoning with meanings of race and marginalized identity, antiracism and social justice. Within a few years, it had grounded popular racial justice movements in demands for police and prison abolition and critical assessments of the carceral state.[23] The analysis that BLM organizing brought to dinner-table conversation was decidedly transnational: It drew links between US and Palestinian experiences of racialized, colonial, dispossessive state violence, and the ways that both had been explained away as keeping the nation secure and protecting (some) people's rights. As BLM overlapped with Indigenous protest against dispossession, settler violence, and fossil fuel capitalism, popular conversations about racist state violence expanded to indigeneity and settler colonialism, and traced US and Israeli settler colonialism as interconnected violent structures.[24]

In 2016, the first Trump presidential campaign opened an era of permissive incitement for white nationalism, including antisemitism. The violence produced by Trump's relentless rhetoric was largely anti-Black, anti-immigrant, and anti-Muslim, including escalated racist action by police. Trump's policies while in office harmed primarily the same groups, along with poor and transgender people.[25] At the same time, many of his erratic pronounce-

22. Joseph Masco, *The Theater of Operations: National Security Affect from the Cold War to the War on Terror* (Duke University Press, 2014).

23. Charmaine Chua, "Abolition Is a Constant Struggle: Five Lessons from Minneapolis," *Theory & Event* 23, no. 5 (2020): S127–47.

24. Noura Erakat, "Geographies of Intimacy: Contemporary Renewals of Black–Palestinian Solidarity," *American Quarterly* 72, no. 2 (2020): 471–96.

25. Center for American Progress, "52 Harms in 52 Weeks," January 10, 2018, https://www.americanprogress.org/article/52-harms-52-weeks/; ABC News, "'No Blame?' ABC News Finds 54 Cases Invoking 'Trump' in Connection with Violence, Threats, Alleged Assaults," https://abcnews.go.com/Politics/blame-abc-news-finds-17-cases-invoking-trump/story?id=58912889; Pauline Grosjean et al., "Inflammatory Political Campaigns and Racial Bias in Policing," *Quarterly Journal of Economics* 138, no. 1 (2023): 413–63; National Center

ments fueled antisemitic action, including his endorsement of conspiracy theories (for instance, he claimed billionaire George Soros was paying anti-Trump protesters) and his claims that Jews were disloyal to him, and to the United States, because they were insufficiently loyal to Israel.[26] The spectacle of Trump-inspired marchers in Charlottesville in 2017 chanting anti-Jewish slogans, and catastrophic acts of violence, including synagogue shootings in Pittsburgh and Poway in 2018 and 2019, triggered a sense of emergency around Jewish vulnerability.[27] Policymakers, media, and many civic institutions turned for leadership to institutions like the ADL: institutions that had reliably supported police and rejected social justice movements' challenges to racism, state violence, and colonialism.[28]

Through the ADL's lens on rights, concerns about white nationalists' antisemitism became a platform for demanding increased police presence and militarization and for accelerating US support for Israel. *Opposing antisemitism* became a rationale for many institutions—including police, legislatures, colleges, and corporations—to repress the Black-, brown-, and Jewish-led antiracist movements that challenged them from the left, despite the fact that those movements were directly engaged in fighting antisemitism. Framed in these conservative terms, antisemitism discourse superseded attention to racism and white nationalist violence, and perversely framed social justice movements themselves as a central threat to tolerance and democracy. Indeed, a steady ramp-up of policies ostensibly aimed at protecting against antisemitism served to expand racist policing, pulled essential resources out of Black, immigrant, queer, and other communities, and transferred power upward. In this ferment, institutions like the ADL were now themselves identifiable as conservative: forces for insulating a racial, carceral order against calls for change.

Far from succeeding, this weaponization of concerns about antisemitism galvanized a powerful resistance from the social movements it attacked, and clarified the importance of understanding racism and colonialism together.

---

for Transgender Equality, "The Discrimination Administration," https://transequality.org/the-discrimination-administration, accessed February 7, 2024.

26. David Klepper and Lori Hinnant, "George Soros Conspiracy Theories Surge as Protests Sweep US," AP News, June 21, 2020; Louis Keene, "Every Time Donald Trump Has Accused American Jews of Disloyalty," *The Forward*, March 19, 2024.

27. David Smith, "Donald Trump's Rhetoric Has Stoked Antisemitism and Hatred, Experts Warn," *The Guardian*, October 29, 2018.

28. See, for instance, "Envisioning Solidarity," *Jewish Currents*, January 6, 2020. https://jewishcurrents.org/envisioning-solidarity.

One key moment of recognition came in 2016. The Movement for Black Lives (M4BL), a coalition arising from BLM protest to offer a concrete program of solutions, had just released a policy platform titled *A Vision for Black Lives: Policy Demands for Black Power, Freedom, & Justice*. Understanding the United States as a transnational actor and racial capitalism as a global structure, it cited US investments in Israeli genocide against Palestinians as a project that diverted public funds from US communities and fueled an apartheid state.[29] ADL leader Jonathan Greenblatt decried M4BL as "irresponsible and completely over-the-top" and "distract[ing] us" from legitimate civil rights work. Adding insult to injury, he attacked with language from a Black spiritual historically sung by civil rights marchers: "So let's work to keep our eyes on the prize," Greenblatt wrote.[30] The ADL continued to hit back against antiracist organizing through the Trump era. As the term *intersectionality* entered the popular lexicon, signifying the imperative to recognize the interleaving of state, capital, and cultural systems of violence (if not always used with precision), organizers of the Women's March and the Chicago Dyke March used it to explain why Zionism was not welcome in feminist- and queer-organized liberatory spaces. The ADL charged them with "rejecting Jews," bypassing the challenge to Zionism (and obscuring that both events were organized by and included Jews).[31]

The increasing popular rejection of the ADL's civil rights authority built on a groundwork of earlier, often quieter (and risky) opposition by Arab, Muslim, queer, and Jewish leftist organizations. In August 2020, that resistance had produced #DropTheADL, an open letter initially signed by more than one hundred progressive/antiracist movement organizations calling on others to reevaluate the ADL as a partner in social justice work, accompanied by a primer on the ADL's history. "Even though the ADL is integrated into community work on a range of issues," it read,

29. Movement for Black Lives, *A Vision for Black Lives: Policy Demands for Black Power, Freedom, & Justice* (2016), https://web.archive.org/web/20160801231434/https://policy.m4bl.org/platform/; Movement for Black Lives, "Invest-Divest," 2016, https://web.archive.org/web/20160801231555/https://policy.m4bl.org/invest-divest/.

30. Jonathan Greenblatt, "Eyes on the Prize: In Pursuit of Racial Justice, Stick to the Facts and Avoid the Fiction," *Medium*, August 4, 2016, https://jonathan-g.medium.com/eyes-on-the-prize-in-pursuit-of-racial-justice-stick-to-the-facts-and-avoid-the-fiction-5a5486a5cb4e.

31. Sharon Nazarian, "By Rejecting Jews, Intersectionality Betrays Itself," Anti-Defamation League, January 25, 2018, https://www.adl.org/news/op-ed/by-rejecting-jews-intersectionality-betrays-itself.

it has a history and ongoing pattern of attacking social justice movements led by communities of color, queer people, immigrants, Muslims, Arabs, and other marginalized groups, while aligning itself with police, right-wing leaders, and perpetrators of state violence. More disturbing, it has often conducted those attacks under the banner of "civil rights." . . . Given the destructive role that it too often plays in undermining struggles for justice, we believe that we cannot collaborate with the ADL without betraying our movements.[32]

In the years following its release, the call to "#DropTheADL" was increasingly taken up in social justice movements and adopted in independent campaigns by Jewish, Muslim, Palestinian, Asian, HIV/AIDS, education, labor, and peace organizations.[33]

The ADL's conflicts with popular movements from below have not been based on differing approaches to civil rights. Rather, they point to the work the ADL has performed to strengthen systems of capital, policing, and political culture primarily in support of the US and Israeli states and their imperial expansion. Rather than a Jewish organization, a civil rights organization, or an Israel advocacy organization, it is a US political institution. Its projects have been to expand state authority, and discipline structural and epistemological resistance to the state, in a much broader sphere—Jewish, Black, Arab, Muslim, queer, and other. In other words, the ADL's conflicts with organizing from below can be understood through its own work as part of a social movement from above, as Alf Gunvald Nilsen and Laurence Cox theorize. As part of the fabric of state-supporting institutions, its role has been to marginalize movements for rights that challenge existing power arrangements—

32. "Open Letter to Progressives: The ADL Is Not an Ally," DropTheADL.org, August 2020, www.droptheadl.org. The author was a member of the working group that produced the #DropTheADL letter and primer.

33. See, for instance, Jewish Voice for Peace, "Fight Antisemitism, Reject the ADL," https://www.jewishvoiceforpeace.org/resource/reject-the-adl-landing/; American Muslims for Palestine, "Drop the ADL," https://www.ampalestine.org/organize/campaigns/drop-adl; US Campaign for Palestinian Rights, "The ADL Is Not An Ally! #DroptheADL," https://uscpr.org/campaigns/drop-the-adl/; 18 Million Rising, "TAAF: Drop the ADL! Community Letter," https://www.18millionrising.org/2024/dropadl-letter/; Kayla Kumari Upadhyaya, "ACT UP NY Calls on GLAAD to Oppose Genocide, Drop the ADL," *Autostraddle*, May 13, 2024, https://www.autostraddle.com/act-up-ny-calls-on-glaad-to-oppose-genocide-drop-the-adl/; Drop the ADL from Schools, "Open Letter to Educators: The ADL Is Not a Social Justice Partner," https://droptheadlfromschools.org/; Sonia Chajet Wides, "In Monumental Vote, NEA Teachers Join Chorus Against ADL," *In These Times*, August 21, 2025, https://inthesetimes.com/article/in-monumental-vote-nea-teachers-join-chorus-against-adl; Code Pink, "Drop the ADL Action Guide," https://www.boughtbyzionism.org/expeladlguide.

and to naturalize commonsense ideas about race and rights that preserve them.[34] As this book clarifies, its Zionism is an integral element of that overarching project, rather than a focus on a foreign matter.

At the same time, it is impossible to disentangle the ADL's state-oriented work from the ways it references and relies on Jewish identity to situate itself: as a political representative of US Jewry, a purveyor of claims about "Jewish values," and a definer of and defender against antisemitism. It would also be inaccurate and short-sighted to hold it separate from US Jewry as a community or polity, even though the ADL's claim to represent US Jews has always been severely troubled. The ADL has existed as a Jewish institution and worked in partnership with major Jewish and Zionist organizations even as it has attacked other sectors of Jewish life. It has cultivated Jewish supporters through what Melvin Urofsky has termed "campaign Judaism," which supplants religious and cultural identity with an identity based on heeding calls to action on Israel- and antisemitism-related emergencies.[35] Its integration into powerful political circles, and its development as a right-wing ideological force, are a function of an elite, conservative sector of the Jewish communal sphere that itself was forged in the particular confluences of European Jewish migration with US and imperial histories.

As such, this is a study of the ADL's role in structures of power: a critical history in the sense that *critical study* sets out to discern how power produces the seemingly natural conditions in which it operates, and to comprehend and resist the violence of those operations. It is not a study of how the ADL's advocacy has had good effects as well as bad, although we can say with certainty that some people have benefited from its work—in the same way that, for instance, police have certainly prevented violence in one given situation or another, even though policing is in fact "violence work," as Micol Seigel terms it: a state violence–*producing* structure.[36] This is certainly not a full history of the ADL, partly because it focuses on the organization's confronta-

<hr>

34. Laurence Cox and Alf Gunvald Nilsen, "'At the Heart of Society Burns the Fire of Social Movements': What Would a Marxist Theory of Social Movements Look Like?," in *Tenth International Conference on Alternative Futures and Popular Protest: A Selection of Papers from the Conference*, ed. Colin Barker and Mike Tyldesley (Manchester Metro. Univ., 2005), 3. Hil Aked's work on Zionism as a social movement from above led me to Cox and Nilsen. Hil Aked, *Friends of Israel: The Backlash Against Palestine Solidarity* (Verso, 2023).

35. Melvin I. Urofsky, "American Jewish Leadership," *American Jewish History* 70, no. 4 (1981): 415.

36. Micol Seigel, "Violence Work: Policing and Power," *Race & Class* 59, no. 4 (2018): 15–33.

tions with popular movements, because its work is far too extensive to take up in one project, and because I did not have access to the ADL's in-house archives. (Among many topics inadequately covered here, I want to call attention to three especially. They are the ADL's organizing of public and private resources for militarist projects, its minimization of genocides and outright denial of the Armenian genocide, and its attacks on scholarship and campus organizing on Palestine and against Zionism, apartheid, and colonialism.)[37] This is also not a book about the people who have worked for the ADL, apart from its leaders. As #DropTheADL rolled out across social media in 2020, one reader posted a distressed Facebook query asking whether it meant they should reevaluate their family history.[38] Their grandmother had pounded the pavement in segregated neighborhoods in Chicago in the 1950s, gathering tenant stories and plaintiffs for the ADL's housing anti-discrimination campaign. The story of her work to end anti-Black as well as anti-Jewish discrimination was an important memory defining her as a righteous and strong person, and a touchstone for the family's multigenerational commitment to social justice. If the ADL was not what it seemed, was the grandmother's work still an honorable legacy? Questions like this haunt US histories with particular force as liberal mythologies unravel: Zionism as a liberation project, minority identity as an indicator of progressive political positions, US institutions as defenders of democracy.

As we look critically at these histories, it is essential to separate the projects of institutions and their leaders from the stories of most of the people who worked within them—especially since institutions purposely construct appealing narratives to recruit community supporters, funders, and political allies. Uncovering the history and ideological underpinnings of the ADL does not suggest that all of the work of staff and volunteers has been disingenuous or toxic. From challenging housing discrimination to infiltrating White Citizens Councils, some people working for the ADL have taken risky stands and made substantial dents in material injustice. Others who worked for the ADL because they wanted to contribute to civil rights have been misused or stymied. (In a 2021 investigative report, for instance, the organization's staff lamented that the ADL was pursuing the interests of

37. For a discussion of these issues, see Steven Salaita, *Israel's Dead Soul* (Temple University Press, 2011), 41–70, and Abena Ampofoa Asare, "The Silencing of Fred Dube," *Boston Review*, January 18, 2024.

38. This Facebook post has since been deleted by its author. The account here is my recollection.

right-wing donors in projects that directly contravened and "made impossible" the work of its Civil Rights Division.)[39] On the other hand, some people who worked for the ADL *have* acted as "white saviors" and overt racists. Sifting through the meanings of individual people's work in the ADL is a detailed, specific endeavor that this book does not take up.

This project began with two questions, at first glance unrelated. As part of Jewish- and Palestinian-led organizing to shift US discourse on Palestine in the early 2000s, I had struggled with the ways that Zionists pointed to historic Jewish liberalism and participation in the US civil rights movement to claim that Israel was a moral endeavor. The ADL was the leading US voice making these claims. An ADL poster series presented some of them in 2007: "Which of the Middle East nations protects and encourages freedom of the press?," asked one poster. "Which . . . protects the legal rights, safety & freedom of the LGBT communities?," asked another. "Only Israel," they answered, mysteriously eliding military censorship of the Israeli and Palestinian press as well as anti-queer violence, denials of rights in the Israeli state, and relentless militarized violence against Palestinian queers that targets them as queers and as subjects of occupation and apartheid.[40] I wanted to understand why the ADL invested so heavily in civil rights and at the same time advocated obviously racist and violent projects, including colonial violence in Palestine and also US-based projects like supporting blanket surveillance of Muslims by the New York City police department, claiming that they advance Jewish safety and protect democracy.[41] Rather than construe

39. Jacob Hutt and Alex Kane, "How the ADL's Israel Advocacy Undermines Its Civil Rights Work," *Jewish Currents*, February 8, 2021.

40. This ADL poster series is archived at the Palestine Poster Project. See Anti-Defamation League, "Freedom of Press," 2007, https://www.palestineposterproject.org/posters/freedom-press-0, and "Only Israel," 2007, https://www.palestineposterproject.org/posters/only-israel-1. On censorship, see Orayb Aref Najjar, "'Dear Israeli Chief-Censor . . . Sincerely Yours, the Palestinian Editor-in-Chief': Censorship, Negotiation and Procedural Justice," *Studies in Cultures, Organizations and Societies* 5, no. 2 (1999): 297–330. On the mythologies of queer rights and their imbrication with colonial enclosures, see Nada Elia, *Greater Than the Sum of Our Parts: Feminism, Inter/Nationalism, and Palestine* (Pluto Press, 2023).

41. Ali Gharib, "Abe Foxman Rationalizes Blanket Spying on American Muslims," *Daily Beast*, April 29, 2013, https://www.thedailybeast.com/abe-foxman-rationalizes-blanket-spying-on-american-muslims/.

these as contradictions, it seemed important to look for the logic that threaded them together.

Later in the decade came the US campaign to legalize gay marriage, led by queer groups that were influenced by or even directly modeled on the ADL's advocacy. I was struck by the extent to which white, wealthy gay and lesbian marriage advocates narrated their campaign by comparing marriage restrictions to historic anti-Black discrimination, and demanded Black voters' support for "the new civil rights movement." Their insensibility to their own privileged position, and to their articulation of marriage as a means of securing the benefits of racial and economic *in*equality, seemed to run in parallel to the ADL's civil rights discourse. Learning from community organizers and queer scholars, particularly Dean Spade, Kay Whitlock, and Christina Hanhardt, I came to see that these interconnected tracks had been laid over the course of at least twenty years. In an earlier period, the queer campaign for hate crimes laws, intended to intervene in anti-queer violence, had been heavily shaped by the ADL.[42] Queer antiracist critiques of the *hate frame* had already begun to theorize how the idea of policing individualized *hate* shores up the racial state, and how it intersects with the political exigencies of Zionism.[43] Investigating the hate frame and Zionism together unlocks an extensive, multifaceted, and frankly enormously creative conservative project of rewriting ideas at the heart of the liberal state: race and identity, vulnerability and injury, protection and rights, and democracy.

As these entry points suggest, historicizing the ADL has turned out to be not just a matter of tracing its advocacy or "following the money." (Following the money, often an important way of mapping political work, misses the dense field of personal relationships and moral authority that underwrite the ADL's work.) Instead, it calls for mapping an epistemological terrain bounded by particular understandings of race and rights, and building other concepts on and around them. To make its epistemological intervention, the ADL has leaned on the notion of the *civil rights movement*, not in its historical meaning but as a political-cultural conceptual field, as Jodi Melamed has elaborated it—the simplified and sanctified story that a great collective effort was made, and now the United States is defined by a

---

42. See Morgan Bassichis and Dean Spade, "Queer Politics and Anti-Blackness," in *Queer Necropolitics*, ed. Jin Haritaworn et al. (Routledge, 2014); Kay Whitlock, "Reconsidering Hate: Policy & Politics at the Intersection," Political Research Associates, June 1, 2012, https://politicalresearch.org/2012/06/01/reconsidering-hate.

43. See Hanhardt, *Safe Space*, chapter 4, "Visibility and Victimization," 155–84.

national commitment to "being against" racism and "standing up for" racial and like-race identities.[44] Although simple, this is a powerful interpretive technology through which racialized and marginalized identities are first defined (and often negated through "colorblindness" or the claim that they are "no different" from a presumed norm), then attached to notions of rights, and then made subjects of state/public obligations to provide remedies for rights that are unfulfilled: Dylan Rodríguez terms this constellation of ideas *the Dream*, and its subject the *Civil Rights Citizen*.[45] Organizing political identity around demands to redress histories of group marginalization, made by levying demands for group inclusion and rights, makes marginalization an essential and powerful aspect of people's identities, as Wendy Brown theorizes.[46] The ADL's history demonstrates how asserting a marginalized identity can—if the marginalized group holds enough power, ironically—become a lever for mobilizing enormous resources.

Running alongside the ADL's interest in the *civil rights movement*, if more quietly, is its anticommunism. The ADL was an active participant in the mid-century Red Scare and viewed anticommunism as an essential part of its work to contain antisemitism. To some extent this is an expected feature of the ADL's identification with liberal capitalism and the US state. But as Charisse Burden-Stelly writes, anticommunism has been an essential technology for racial control: a mode of governance, drawing on law and culture to "penalize, regulate, censure, and criminalize ideas and beliefs that challenged US racial oppression, economic inequality, and class antagonism by labeling them 'communist.'"[47] Indeed, anticommunism is full of ideas about race. Anticommunist discourse, including the ADL's, has portrayed "communists"—a sweeping category for people and movements seeking more equitable distribution of power and resources—as foreign agents

44. On "official antiracisms," see Jodi Melamed, *Represent and Destroy: Rationalizing Violence in the New Racial Capitalism* (University of Minnesota Press, 2011), 54. The term *like-race* is drawn from Janet E. Halley's theorization of gay and lesbian rights advocacy that emerged in the 1980s and '90s. See Halley, "'Like Race' Arguments," in *What's Left of Theory? New Work on the Politics of Literary Theory*, ed. Judith Butler, John Guillory, and Kendall Thomas (Routledge, 2000).

45. Dylan Rodríguez, *White Reconstruction: Domestic Warfare and the Logics of Genocide* (Fordham University Press, 2020), 28.

46. Wendy Brown, *States of Injury: Power and Freedom in Late Modernity* (Princeton University Press, 1995), 73–74.

47. Charisse Burden-Stelly, *Black Scare/Red Scare: Theorizing Capitalist Racism in the United States* (University of Chicago Press, 2023), 147.

polluting the nation, nonwhite immigrants, and Jews. (Dissonantly, the ADL's approach has been to insist that *no* Jews are communists, while also opposing Jewish communists.) Borrowing from liberalism's moral lexicon, the ADL and other anticommunists have also characterized leftists as racists: hostile to white people (as the ADL denounced Black liberation movements), and villains who slyly pretend to care about racism to dupe Americans into supporting communism (as detailed in the ADL's 1951 primer for schoolteachers, *How You Can Teach About Communism*).[48] As such, anticommunism has been pitched as the defense of white workers, Jews, immigrants, Black people, and other "others," soliciting marginalized groups to ally with elite power. The ADL has continually marked political movements as good/democratic or bad/totalitarian through a lexicon of race and anticommunism. Casting its enemies as racially intolerant and totalitarian, the ADL has used those terms to mean Nazism, Soviet communism, white nationalism, anti-Zionism, Palestinians, and US social justice movements.

Anticommunism has also been a tool for curating the notion of Jewish community and, perhaps more importantly, Jewish polity. Early on the ADL and other major Jewish organizations sought to marginalize and distance themselves from the immigrant Jewish left, but with the fervor of the Red Scare in the 1950s, they developed a more robust approach: directly purging leftists from Jewish service organizations and community groups. This collaboration circumscribed Jewish political identity—quite literally, it left no place for Jewish leftists in the institutions structuring much of Jewish life. Within those institutions, anticommunism was installed as a centerpiece of Jewish identity. This in turn allowed the ADL and other major Jewish organizations to advocate for conservative, anti-left policies in the national political sphere as "Jewish interests." The association of Jewish ethnicity and anti-left positions persisted from the 1952 execution of Jewish communists Ethel and Julius Rosenberg, to the 1983 blacklisting of largely Arab and Jewish advocates for Palestinian rights as "antisemites," to the 2021

48. For examples of the ADL's messaging on Black liberationist organizing and thought, see Anti-Defamation League of B'nai B'rith, "Anti-Semitism in the New York City School Controversy: A Preliminary Report of the Anti-Defamation League of B'nai B'rith," January 1969, and Forster and Epstein, *The New Anti-Semitism*; Ryland W. Crary and Gerald L. Steibel, *How You Can Teach About Communism* (Anti-Defamation League of B'nai B'rith, 1951).

denunciation of ethnic studies scholars as "fringe activists."[49] Tying Jewishness to the anti-leftist "vital center" of US politics allowed the ADL and its allies to begin casting leftist movements as inherently antisemitic, despite long Jewish traditions of support for leftist politics.

Beyond ideology, the ADL's ties to the state are structural. Its leadership has been drawn from what Melamed has termed the *state-capital formation*: the ecosystem of political and corporate actors, individuals and institutions, who leverage laws, militarism, and other aspects of state authority to preserve and expand their power.[50] Even as the ADL has adapted to changing framings of rights, it has remained committed to preserving capitalism and the racial colonial structure of the US state, not the counterhegemonic struggles whose rhetoric the ADL has often deployed in communicating with the public. That is not to say that the ADL has never changed; it has responded to the changing content of Jewishness, race and ethnicity, gender, economic formations, and other building blocks of political culture. Instead, the ADL's history shows that it has often absorbed those shifting terms while working steadily to preserve core state-capital interests. Additionally, in the midtwentieth century the ADL moved from *supporting* the white supremacy, capitalism, and colonialism of the US state to being a *producer* of its infrastructure of laws and hegemonic ideas; from an upper-class German Jewish institution to a quasi-state institution, carrying out the work of governance, empire, and repression, first at home and later abroad.

This sets the stage for a last idea that is central to this history: *subjects of remedy*. Beginning in the 1970s—ironically, just as its leaders noted that endemic anti-Jewish discrimination had ended—the ADL shifted away from arguing that Jews should be treated exactly the same as anyone else and began to articulate Jewishness as a marginal identity that, in the interest of egalitarianism, was owed protection. At the same time, it argued for *excluding* Arabness from the discourse of ethnoracial civil rights. *The New Anti-Semitism,* published in 1974 by ADL national director Benjamin Epstein and lead counsel Arnold Forster, made the case that the problem arose because Jewish economic, social, and political *inclusion* in US society meant that

49. Lauren Gilbert, "'A Very Ticklish Problem': The AJC Response to the Rosenberg Trial & Execution," *The Word: The CJH Blog*, April 27, 2023, https://blog.cjh.org/index .php/2023/04/25/a-very-ticklish-problem-the-ajc-response-to-the-rosenberg-trial-execution/; Anti-Defamation League of B'nai B'rith, *Pro-Arab Propaganda in America: Vehicles and Voices. A Handbook* (January 1983); Gelman, "The World Upside-Down."

50. Melamed, *Represent and Destroy,* 1.

Jewish interests were now aligned with those of the state. Epstein and Forster argued that a new kind of antisemitism arose when leftist political movements opposed "establishment" interests—particularly Israel—either without concern for Jewish interests or viewing them as "part of the problem."[51] Being included in and represented by the state, in other words, was reformulated as a kind of marginalization.

The reconstruction of Jewish marginality and vulnerability evolved as the ADL undertook antisemitism audits, national anti-bias education, and hate crimes laws throughout the 1980s. As it did, it remained anchored in the idea that being fully integrated and empowered in political, capital, and social structures did not demarginalize US Jewry ("Success is not the test," Epstein and Forster contended in their 1962 book, *Some of My Best Friends . . .*) and attached to calls for US state and popular support for Israel as a remedy.[52] To denote this abstracted, leveraged Jewish identity and its call for state protections, I use the term *subjects of remedy*. Although initially a call for non-Jews to attend to what the ADL defined as Jewish interests, the ADL also used calls for state protection to remake Jews' own identity, centering it on antisemitism, detaching it from antiracist allegiances to the left, and producing "consensus" support for Israel. The ADL's reporting on antisemitism—from diagnosing resistance to racist schooling as a crisis of "Black antisemitism," to peremptory counting of "antisemitic incidents" that pushed against Jewish communities' efforts to reckon with the complexities of class, race, and power—served both to set up claims for *remedy* and to instruct Jews that their allegiances lay with the political right.

In parallel, the ADL and its partner institutions sought to quash Arab American efforts at ethnic political organizing by rejecting them as *subjects of remedy* and portraying them instead as agents of Arab states surreptitiously trying to influence US politics. When Arab American communal leaders became targets of racial violence at the hands of US Jewish supremacists, that violence was deemed political rather than racial. These moves were produced by the ADL against the field of *civil rights*, holding Jewishness as like-race (occupying the same role as Blackness in a civil rights lexicon) and Arabness

51. "Establishment" is used in the original text with quotation marks where the authors are pointing to "radical leftists'" use of the term, and without quotation marks where the authors are referring themselves to dominant institutions. Arnold Forster and Benjamin R. Epstein, *The New Anti-Semitism* (McGraw-Hill, 1974).

52. Benjamin R. Epstein and Arnold Forster, *Some of My Best Friends . . .* (Farrar, Straus and Cudahy, 1962), 34.

not as like-race but as foreign. Additionally, conflating Jewish and Black subjectivities greatly diminished the meaning of anti-Blackness—just as "colorblindness" elided both the productive, generative histories of Blackness and its history of compounded exclusions. That procedure aligned well with racial liberalism, against Black Power, and against antiracist/anticolonial calls to redistribute power. Through the medium of hate crimes law advocacy, the ADL embedded it in racial discourse and displaced the possibility for more transformational antiracist measures.

The ADL accumulated ideological force through periods when the state faced crises of authority over race matters, and the ADL took up its defense. In the aftermath of World War II, the United States faced a new need to project global authority against fascism, which in turn produced an imperative to dismantle prejudice in the United States.[53] The ADL reorganized itself to become the anticommunist knowledge-production agency demanded by the moment, as Stuart Svonkin documents in an earlier history of Jewish defense organizations.[54] It became an essential provider of public relations and education materials on prejudice, developed a network of experts and resources, and produced scientific literature. In the late 1970s and early '80s, a surge in white nationalist organizing and violence again made the ADL indispensable. Responding to the urgent desire for police to forcefully stop the violence, the ADL took up leadership of the state-by-state campaign for hate crimes laws. As schools struggled to respond to the crisis, the ADL developed an anti-bias education program that became ubiquitous across the United States within a few years. Both efforts enshrined conceptions of race and rights that limited antiracist challenges to the state, firmly established a cultural notion that Jewish identity was marginalized, and elevated the ADL as an indispensable resource for addressing social problems.

The ADL's engagement with neoconservatism helps make sense of the "confusion" in which its conservative work was mistaken as progressive. In the late 1960s, students, anti–Vietnam War organizers, women's and gay liberation movements, and other streams of counterculture were breaking with traditional ideas, including ideas about the United States itself. They eroded presumptions that the US was a bastion of freedom, and that capitalism was necessary and moral. As these changes gathered momentum, a cadre of social-

---

53. See Mary Dudziak, *Cold War Civil Rights: Race and the Image of American Democracy* (Princeton University Press, 2000).

54. Stuart Svonkin, *Jews Against Prejudice: American Jews and the Fight for Civil Liberties* (Columbia University Press, 1997), 65–70.

ist leaders began to split from the left, first as dissenters and then as full-fledged opposition. Some had played substantial roles in the civil rights movement but were now displeased by what they viewed as immoderate Black nationalism and gender liberation; additionally, they were intent on opposing communism and still sold on US and foreign interventionism as a vehicle for democracy. Rather than adopting the old language of conservatism, they maintained that they were the real supporters of liberal civil rights and often talked about their work in terms of racial and economic justice.[55] Beginning in 1967 the ADL hired several of those leaders, and over the next twenty years it became part of a network of labor, policy, and government organizations collaborating on neoconservative projects. (These events appear obliquely in histories of the left and right, documents from the ADL's 1993 "spying scandal," and records of AFL-CIO collaborations with the CIA in Central America, the Philippines, and South Africa.) Like the ADL, neoconservatives supported civil rights demands that they deemed "responsible"—those that remained colorblind and did not disrupt state order—while opposing Black liberation and anticolonial movements as "extremist." Their deployment of the language of civil rights, and the fact that some prominent neoconservative figures had strong civil rights movement credentials—most notably Bayard Rustin—meant that their conservatism was often overlooked.

Ironically, although its currency has been its claims to represent civil rights, the ADL has relied in parallel on another currency: the proximity of its leaders to wealth and political power. In keeping with the "great men" model of politicking favored by the institutions of the upper classes, its modus operandi has been to intervene in problems at the top by speaking as a peer to the newspaper publishers, institutional bosses, and government leaders who hold the executive authority to work by fiat. To do that, it has depended heavily on its leadership's overlaps with corporate, legal, and political moguls. The advancement of Eastern European Jewish immigrants from poverty and marginality to relative wealth and inclusion in the post–World War II era grew the state-capital class through which the ADL worked. The rise of neoliberalism in the 1970s, which ramped up collaborations between corporate capital and government, greatly expanded its potency. These changes are reflected intimately in ADL leaders' oral accounts of the personal relationships that enabled their work. Increasingly wired to the "great men"

---

55. See, for instance, Murray Friedman, *The Neoconservative Revolution: Jewish Intellectuals and the Shaping of Public Policy* (Cambridge University Press, 2005), 196–203.

at the same time as its interests expanded in Israel and Cold War policy, the ADL became a different kind of "establishment" political organization—one closely connected to US efforts to steer the Cold War global order, and whose remit far exceeded the sphere of rights.

As these chapters show, though, the ADL's history is also one of constant encounter with resistive ideas and movements that have not accepted its terms. Reading it as a political organization rather than an ethnic or rights organization means turning our gaze to what it has fought *against* and who has resisted it. Far from hegemonic, the ADL has been forced to continually defend its propositions about race and rights, as well as capitalism, democracy, and the imperial state, and to try to marginalize or destroy the social movements whose very existence challenged the claim that its values were universal.

A note on sources and approaches: This has been a magpie's project, bringing together archival fragments and arranging them onto an array of frameworks, including movement, labor, and Jewish communal histories, and theories of race, queerness, and colonialism. The ADL is a sprawling organization with a vast set of publications, an enormous footprint in media, and relationships with hundreds of major organizations and public figures whose histories—most much better documented than the ADL's—help draw the map. All manner of ADL materials are archived in many places. Jewish archives are a rich source, since the ADL's behind-the-scenes work appears in the records of other organizations. Collections from sources as disparate as the NAACP, the National Gay and Lesbian Task Force, the American Jewish Archives, Amistad Research Center, San Francisco's GLBT Historical Society, the AFL-CIO, War Resisters League, the Education Resource Information Center (ERIC), the National Security Archive, the Reagan administration, public libraries, YouTube film preservation accounts, and others have all yielded pieces of the puzzle. The ADL's own oral histories, published in 1986 and reflecting on more than forty years of its leaders' thinking, are candid and insightful. Since the ADL has widely rankled and transgressed, the archives are also filled with critiques, often by organizers who preserved ADL meeting materials, sometimes richly (and tartly) annotated. The ADL has been the subject of a good deal of FBI investigation, as well as public records requests making those documents public. Additionally, although this book is not centered in Jewish Studies, it leans heavily on the work of Jewish Studies scholars. It has been grounding to follow the ADL through those histories and understand that these findings are not a controversial reading of Jewish history. Similarly, histories of neoconservatism, including views from within the movement, helpfully clarify that we are all observing the same processes of contention over race, rights, and state power. This book is indebted to research by activists and movement researchers in labor, antiracist, and queer organizing circles who have combined their experiential insights with rigorous, detailed historical study of ideas, institutions, and states. I hope this work lives up to the high standard they set.

Drawing on Jewish Studies literature, newspapers and archival documents, and political theory, chapter 1 follows the ADL's first decades. It situates the ADL's founding community, loosely called German Jews, in the context of US colonial settlement, formation of the US racial regime and white identity, and the Progressive Era. Looking at the ADL alongside the other Jewish institutions taking shape at the same time highlights their shared project of disciplining the Eastern European Jewish immigrant left and urging the new immigrants toward whiteness and liberalism, alongside the ADL's efforts to combat Christian and nativist anti-Jewishness. The final section follows the ADL's transformation from an ethnic uplift organization to a site of Jewish sociality and fundraising, where Jews were brought into the US state-capital class and performed its rituals.

Chapter 2 maps the ADL's efforts in the early Cold War period to chart out a morality that attached its heroes to Americanism and its bogeymen to racism. It draws on the ADL's published books, pamphlets, and advertisements of the period, exposés, and an extraordinary 1953 live television event with President Harry Truman and a host of Hollywood stars. The chapter follows the ADL's conversion in the 1950s and '60s into an education and intergroup relations organization, and its work in those fields to suture liberal anticommunism to the notion of racial tolerance. It traces the ADL's simultaneous work to popularize the notion that Arabs advocating for Palestinian rights were partners of the white Christian Right, and to designate the Jewish and Black left as "extremist." Finally, the ADL's work to situate itself as a model of Americanism appears in two areas of mass media: one, the 1953 television spectacle, and the other, the anticommunist productions of the Walter Winchell radio show and the McCarthy hearings. These fuel the ADL's rise, through Cold War politics, as a quasi-state organization.

Chapter 3 traces the ADL's negotiation of crises in its relationship to the "civic religion" of civil rights, just at the moment when it took up advocating for Zionism in earnest using the civil rights movement as its analogy and rationale. Using writings by ADL leaders, Black and Jewish organizers, and scholarship in critical race and ethnic studies, this chapter traces the "whitening" of US

Jewry, and the break between Jewish institutions and Black-led civil rights organizing, as catalysts for the ADL's moves to reclaim moral authority on racism as leverage for its other work. The *ADL Bulletin* and other ADL reports limn its conception of the rising threat to domestic order and the US-led global order that was posed in the 1970s and '80s by the New Left, Black Power, Marxist/leftist revolutions abroad, and transnational solidarities against racism and colonialism. The ADL's responses appear in two opposite-direction engagements with Blackness. In one, centered on school integration battles and the Ocean Hill-Brownsville conflict, it constructed a new menace of "Black anti-semitism" that portrayed Black liberation as intolerant and dangerous, while beginning newly to claim Jewishness as a marginalized identity. In the other, it reconstructed its connections with Black leadership—however thin—through an alliance with Bayard Rustin, the establishment of an urban affairs department, and programming aimed at Black entertainers and journalists. This section previews the events and relationships that flowed into neoconservatism, bringing the ADL, many Jewish organizations, and many "white ethnics" along with them.

Chapter 4 takes up the 1993 ADL spying scandal and, pulling its thread, investigates it as a palimpsest of projects far afield from civil rights and Zionism. At the heart of the spying scandal is Irwin Suall, the ADL's fact-finding director. Constructing Suall's political biography finds him at the center of not only the ADL, but also the "right-wing socialist" history of Social Democrats USA, a major wing of the neoconservative movement and authors of Reagan-era soft power interventions in Central America, Asia, and Africa. Tracing the connections between the ADL, Central America, and organizations like the National Endowment for Democracy and the AFL-CIO's Free Trade Union Institute, this history places the ADL's adventures on the right—including the 1993 "ADL spying scandal"—in the context of neoconservative projects to undercut leftist movements around the world. This chapter makes use of FBI files, archived federal documents, and the deeply researched histories of organizations and community structures written by organizers within them, including labor organizers, socialists, Jewish anti-Zionists, and neoconservatives.

Chapter 5 historicizes the ADL's national anti-bias education empire, launched in the mid-1980s. Reading archival accounts of conflict over the ADL's core school programming, titled "A World of Difference," this chapter follows the ADL's move into space opened by a crisis of urban racial tensions and the decline of transformational, redistributive social movements. In the

San Francisco Bay Area, the rise of Arab American community organizing and solidarity with Palestine appears as the context for the ADL's interventions in school curriculum there. Queer archives provide the story of efforts by community-based queer, Arab, Japanese, and Jewish organizers to negotiate with the ADL, and ultimately to oppose it. The ADL's demands of queer and BIPOC communities reveal anti-bias education as a project of constraining and curating knowledge on racism. At the same time, this history traces the ADL's development of a strategic alliance with emerging queer political power.

Chapter 6 follows the ADL's construction of neoconservative logics of race, identity, and rights, including "the new antisemitism" and *hate* and *terror* frameworks, and its *de*recognition of both anti-Arab racist violence and Arab American politics. Drawing on Jewish/left critiques of the ADL's *Annual Audit of Anti-Semitism*, this chapter historicizes their emergence in the 1980s as a "white grievance" project—constructing white, middle- and upper-class Jewish identity as a *subject of remedy*—linked with Jewish/neoconservative opposition to affirmative action and rifts with Black political leaders over their recognition of Palestinian rights. This history becomes the backdrop for dissonant developments: the ADL's rise as a national authority on white nationalism and its simultaneous embrace of the Christian Right, and its leading role in responding to racist and anti-queer violence—as an architect of hate crimes law—while opposing Black, brown, and queer communities' framings of violence. To trace these as ideological and epistemological projects, this history looks to the personal writings and oral histories of ADL leaders, accounts of community organizers, and congressional testimony.

The epilogue takes a turn to events after 1990, including the advent of the IHRA definition of antisemitism, the rise of anti-Zionist and antiracist movements in the context of Israeli escalations of genocide, and the wave of US repression that sets the context in which this book has made its way to print. It considers the concatenation of *hate*, *terror*, and *antisemitism* frameworks and the proliferation of anti-antisemitism watchdogs that extend the ADL's model.

As these histories cross borders between cultural studies, critical race and ethnic studies, and political and communal history, they highlight the crucial importance of analyzing the Anti-Defamation League as an institution that has been key to producing the liberal racial state and the US-led global order of rights. Its history is not quite, or not only, a Jewish communal history, but an artifact of the deployments and redeployments of identity as the fields shift in which they confer power. Although the ADL presents too much history for a single work to take in, reading it across history is the move that reveals these adaptations. Threaded together, these chapters situate the ADL's long project as one of racecraft, uncovering the ADL's close interconnection with the settler racial state as its animating force. Elaborating the *civil rights movement* as a conceptual field, they illustrate the ways that Black, Arab, queer, and Jewish subjectivities have been triangulated to mask the operations of power behind "rights talk" and to secure the material power of remedy that the racial progress narrative produces. They help expand the view of neoconservatism to include the ADL and its anti-extremism work. Finally, they demand, and begin to offer an accounting of, the turn during the 1980s and '90s in which political will to stop white supremacist violence, spurred by failures of the civil rights movement and the rise of queer and Palestine liberation movements, was co-opted and rearticulated as "standing against hate." The epistemological racial meanings worked through the projects traced here continue to set terms for movements to redistribute power and end state violence—movements from Black Lives Matter, to queer and anti-Zionist Jewish efforts to reclaim flattened identities, to Palestinian decolonial resistance and beyond.

ONE

White Settlers and Immigrant Riffraff

BEFORE WORLD WAR II

IN EARLY DECEMBER 2022, the head of the Anti-Defamation League joined hip-hop radio personalities Charlamagne tha God and DJ Envy on their morning show *The Breakfast Club* and gave their eight million listeners a short history of his organization.[1] The appearance was an important public relations event for the ADL, which had been engaged in pitched public battles over antisemitism and anti-Blackness. Several weeks earlier, pro-basketball player Kyrie Irving and rapper Ye (Kanye West) had each made social media posts referencing antisemitic conspiracy theories. ADL CEO Jonathan Greenblatt was leading a demand for their apologies. It was not going smoothly. The public had accepted that the messages were antisemitic, but it had also accused the media and the ADL of anti-Black racism: Social media buzzed with the charge that Black public figures, including Irving and West, were regularly subjected to far more censure than white figures, while anti-Black racism did not cause much outrage. Further, Irving had pledged half a million dollars to the ADL and agreed to undergo ADL anti-bias training, but he was still being pressed for more renunciation and apology. In one exchange with Greenblatt, TV personality Nick Cannon likened the insistent pressure on Irving to the "buck-breaking" practices of enslavers, intended to dominate strong, resistant Black men and teach others to fall in line. Greenblatt had not known the term.[2]

---

1. Breakfast Club Power 105.1 FM, "Jonathan Greenblatt on Combatting Anti-Semitism, Anti-Black Racism, Kanye West, Kyrie Irving + More," posted December 7, 2022, YouTube, 1:03:46, https://www.youtube.com/watch?v=wVXcIcIBtTU.

2. Jon Blistein, "Kyrie Irving Boosts Antisemitic Movie Peddling 'Jewish Slave Ships,'" *Rolling Stone*, October 29, 2022; NBA, "Joint Statement from Kyrie Irving, Brooklyn Nets and Anti-Defamation League," https://www.nba.com/news/joint-statement-from-kyrie-irving-

29

In the midst of these tensions, Greenblatt's appearance on *The Breakfast Club* was a chance to make some repair to the ADL's reputation as a civil rights agency. In telling the ADL's origin story, he recounted a parable that tied together Black and Jewish experiences of marginalization. The ADL was founded in 1913, he said, after Leo Frank was lynched in Georgia. Frank was not only a Jew, but a Yankee industrialist in the South, and therefore a symbol of many local resentments. He was charged with raping and murdering a child, convicted on shaky evidence, and jailed. A white mob abducted him from his cell and murdered him in a public hanging, where the crowd gathered "as if at a holiday barbecue."[3] As intended, Greenblatt's retelling of this horrifying story evoked the lynchings that have stalked Black communities throughout US history. "Sounds familiar," Charlamagne tha God nodded. Greenblatt moved on to deliver the moral: Springing from that pain, the ADL's mission statement was remarkable—"securing justice and fair treatment for all"—because it transcended race. Even more poignant, it was a gesture from one "vulnerable . . . weak" community to another. "A hundred years ago Jews did not have, you know, economic resources to speak of. They did not have much social capital," Greenblatt explained. "The idea that they would fight for *themselves* made sense. The idea that they would also fight for others? That was an audacious, outrageous idea." Jews had a familial bond with Black people, Greenblatt was saying, and the ADL embodied it.[4]

Greenblatt's account of the ADL's founding was mostly untrue, though. While most US Jews were indeed poor and marginalized at the time of Leo Frank's murder in 1915, the ADL's founders and their community were not. Although the ADL's founders were interested in rights, they were white men who shared in the prevailing racist notions of their time. Nor did they sug-

---

brooklyn-nets-and-anti-defamation-league, accessed August 10, 2025; ESPN, "Kyrie Irving: I Can Dismiss Any Label You Put on Me | SportsCenter," posted November 3, 2022, YouTube, 6:32, https://www.youtube.com/watch?v=_aakf4_gEHU; Nick Cannon (@ nickcannon), "NICK CANNON on Instagram: 'THE CONVERSATION EVERYONE IS AFRAID TO HAVE . . . Comment Below. #2HATEorNOT2HATE,'" Instagram, November 8, 2022, https://www.instagram.com/nickcannon/reel/CkrvVqyu5AN/. See also C. Vernon Coleman, "Nick Cannon Compares Kyrie Irving's Suspension Conditions to Buck-Breaking in Slavery," *XXL*, November 8, 2022, https://www.xxlmag.com /nick-cannon-kyrie-irving-suspension-buck-breaking/.

3. Leonard Dinnerstein, *The Leo Frank Case* (University of Georgia Press, 2008), 143–45.

4. Breakfast Club Power 105.1 FM, "Jonathan Greenblatt on Combatting Anti-Semitism."

gest that Jewish and Black people shared the same position; rather, as Jeffrey Melnick writes, they saw "that Jews would naturally be the first 'whites' to suffer the fate normally reserved for African Americans once the floodgates were opened."[5] Even the story that the ADL was founded in response to Leo Frank's lynching stretched the truth: It had been established two years earlier. Catalyzed by Frank's sensationalized trial, it was the culmination of a longer project of anti-defamation protests.[6]

The ADL's actual origin story is nonetheless a tale of race in the United States. The organization was formed in 1913 by midwestern German Jews of the fraternal lodge B'nai B'rith. Its founders, well assimilated into the white upper classes, were concerned that the arrival of poor, unassimilated, laboring-class Jewish immigrants—Eastern European Jews—was changing the perception of Jewishness. Tracing this early history, historian Deborah Dash Moore writes, "In Chicago one B'nai B'rith lodge 'explained that it declined to accept Polish and Russian Jews as members because, as Polish and Russian Jews, they were not yet civilized, were inclined to Orthodoxy and not fit to belong to a respectable organization of American Jews.'"[7] Although the ADL's principles announced its aim "ultimately to put an end to unfair discrimination against all citizens," the term "unfair" did not refer to all discrimination.[8] Anti-Black, anti-Indigenous, and anti-immigrant policies were pervasive, but the ADL did not address them. It did not take the part of Jewish workers as they struggled against exploitative bosses. While its leaders opposed anti-Jewish discrimination, they did so as white citizens. But Greenblatt's tale is instructive, too. It gestures to the ways that the ADL has shaped and deployed ideas about race and rights across its long century—and poses the question: To what ends? The history of advocacy that the ADL *did*

5. Jeffrey Melnick traces the multiple ways that Jewish organizations navigated the racial politics of an anti-Jewish lynching. Rather than embrace the implied connection between Jewishness and Blackness, Frank's defenders invoked anti-Black racism to focus blame on the other possible suspect, and compared anti-Jewish attacks to violence in tsarist Russia rather than anti-Black violence in the United States. Discussions of the scourge of lynching and the Frank case slipped across contexts that made racial meaning: US anti-Blackness, Russian anti-Jewishness, German Jewish wealth and whiteness, Russian Jewish poverty and racialization, North/South class divides, and more. See Jeffrey Melnick, *Black-Jewish Relations on Trial: Leo Frank and Jim Conley in the New South* (University Press of Mississippi, 2000), 109–30 and chap. 5. Quoted text at p. 123.

6. Deborah D. Moore, *B'nai B'rith and the Challenge of Ethnic Leadership* (State University of New York Press, 1981), 106–9.

7. Moore, *B'nai B'rith and the Challenge of Ethnic Leadership*, 29, 55.

8. Anti-Defamation League, *Report of Anti-Defamation League* (1915).

undertake, and its conflicts with antiracists and social movements that *countered* its claims about race and rights, make the ADL legible as an institution of the longue dureé US settler colonial project and its expansion into empire.

In US schools, on television, and in the literature of Jewish organizations, the rich iconography of US Jewish history is presented in grainy images from the turn of the twentieth century. Crowds disembark from boats at Ellis Island, long-bearded peddlers push their carts among tenement buildings, clothes-lines are strung high above Yiddish shop signs. Between the 1880s and 1920s, around two million Jews fled the violence and repression of tsarist Russia for the United States. They crowded into cities where they scraped together a living, often as sweatshop labor. (My own grandmother, her parents, siblings, aunts, and uncles trickled into Cleveland during this period, where everyone worked in my great-uncle's bakery.) As Jewish immigrants organized to improve their conditions, they helped build mass movements for labor and tenant rights, establishing a legacy of radical dissent against elite power. These vignettes animate stories about Jewish marginalization as a precursor to citizenship and inclusion: "the Ellis Island whiteness" narrative, as Matthew Frye Jacobson has described it.[9] Indeed, most Jewish immigrants did arrive in that period—overwhelming the quarter-million Jews who were already settled across the United States—and the struggles of Eastern European Jewish refugees have been a moral compass for later generations of Jews.[10]

Ellis Island is not the origin story of the Anti-Defamation League, though. The ADL and other major Jewish institutions arose from the Central European immigrants, loosely called German Jews, who had arrived earlier.[11] The history of German Jewish migration from 1820 to 1880 is largely missing from popular narrations of the US Jewish past. The Jews who arrived in the decades before the 1880s came from a range of class backgrounds, even if they came with little capital, rather than as a destitute mass. As a group they attained wealth fairly quickly. Those who made their fortunes in the United

9. Matthew Frye Jacobson, *Roots Too: White Ethnic Revival in Post-Civil Rights America* (Harvard University Press, 2006), 7, 64–65.

10. Howard Morley Sachar, *A History of the Jews in America* (Vintage Books, 1993), 117. On Jewish labor and tenant organizing, see pp. 182–89.

11. On the complex geography of "German Jews," see Hasia R. Diner, *The Jews of the United States, 1654 to 2000* (University of California Press, 2006), 82–88.

States were quickly absorbed into the US middle and upper classes, becoming central to business, banking, and politics.[12] Entering a racial order defined by settlement and slavery, German Jews were generally if not exclusively received as white, and identified themselves as such.[13] Whiteness was not a singular category. German Jews' experience of racial and political inclusion naturally differed from other groups', and their position certainly shifted as a group and as individuals; race is relational, dependent on differentials between groups.[14] (For instance, historian Howard Sachar notes that in the mid-1800s, even as Jews were welcomed as white settlers in the South, insurance rulebooks asserted that Jewish shopkeepers were *not* white and therefore riskier to insure.) However, German Jews *expected* to be white and politically included, and they additionally understood that higher class status meant more inclusion. The luminaries of German Jewish communities were the business elite whose role in trade and finance also made them political elites. To the extent that the ADL's history is documented, its chroniclers recognize the organization as a product of this leadership and its racial/social class

12. Hasia R. Diner, *A Time for Gathering: The Second Migration, 1820–1880* (Johns Hopkins University Press, 1995), 63–65.

13. See, for instance, Sachar on the "Germanization" and "nativization" of US Jewish populations in *A History of the Jews in America*, 53, 72. Eric Goldstein writes that German Jews themselves used the terminology of "race" with varying meanings, in keeping with its shifting significance in different periods. In the mid-1800s it described a communal bond, shared culture, and origins, and was also used as a way of claiming positive Jewish group characteristics, "emphasizing their thrift, their commercial success, and their community mindedness" as well as Jewish women's performance of domesticity and European feminin-ity. Using "race" to describe Jewishness did not mean they were describing themselves as nonwhite, nor did others perceive them as such—despite the existence of cartoons and other materials that used the idea of racial features to convey antisemitic meanings. At the turn of the century, mass immigration produced a nativism and nationalism that made "race" a less neutral term, and at that point Jewish leaders stopped using it. In short, racial meaning was heavily specific to the time period, linguistic turns, and the ways that people understood themselves and others as groups and in relation to the emerging state. Eric L Goldstein, "'Different Blood Flows in Our Veins': Race and Jewish Self-Definition in Late Nineteenth Century America," *American Jewish History* 85, no. 1 (1997): 37, 44, 54.

14. George Lipsitz provides this succinct description of the relationality of race: "It's the life of the party; it never goes anywhere alone. Because race has to do with differen-tial citizenship, lesser citizenship, premature death, disproportionate exposure to violence, it makes you look at more than one group." See Lipsitz, "Race as a Relational Theory," in *Relational Formations of Race: Theory, Method, and Practice*, ed. Natalia Molina, Daniel Martinz HoSang, and Ramón A. Gutiérrez (University of California Press, 2019), 23.

orientation.[15] Even where the whiteness of upper-class German Jews was not completely durable, it was the framework for their ideology, political engagement, and institution-building.

Recentering German Jewish migration as the ADL's historical framework requires, also, recentering settler colonialism. In marked contrast to the Ellis Island arrivals, German Jews arrived to a United States in the throes of new settlement. Under Andrew Jackson's presidency, the state was enthusiastically engaged in "extinguishing" Indigenous land claims through the Indian Removal Act of 1830, mass expulsion and death-making on the Trail of Tears, and cataclysmic brutality against Indigenous resistance.[16] As the state emptied territory and laid it at the disposal of settlers, large and small business interests were furiously pushing through the Midwest and the South. These were the same conditions that animated German Jewish settlers' aspirations. Allen Tarshish writes about the Jewish settler experience, that "new immigrants were not attracted to a region which was more or less static" but to sites of novelty and expansion.[17] Accordingly, as the white occupation of Indigenous land pushed forward, the work of settling it, building its social and political infrastructure, and making it "American" were key features of the German Jewish experience. Wealthy people and strivers alike were closely entwined with colonization processes. Some of the most fabled German Jewish tycoons—Meyer Guggenheim, Levi Strauss, William Haas—built banking and mercantile businesses on prospecting and provisioning westward settlement.[18] Jewish immigrants of all classes traveled to the growing cities of the Midwest and beyond, where small enterprises, often as informal as peddling, grew exponentially as the manufacturing economy took off.[19]

15. For histories that closely cover the ADL, see Joseph M. Kirman, "Major Programs of the B'nai B'rith Anti-Defamation League: 1945–1965" (PhD diss., New York University, 1967); Stuart Svonkin, *Jews Against Prejudice: American Jews and the Fight for Civil Liberties* (Columbia University Press, 1997); Moore, *B'nai B'rith and the Challenge of Ethnic Leadership*; Cheryl Lynn Greenberg, *Troubling the Waters: Black-Jewish Relations in the American Century* (Princeton University Press, 2010).

16. See Roxanne Dunbar-Ortiz, *An Indigenous Peoples' History of the United States* (Beacon Press, 2014), chap. 6 and 100–118.

17. Allen Tarshish, "The Economic Life of the American Jew in the Middle Nineteenth Century," in *Central European Jews in America, 1840–1880: Migration and Advancement*, ed. Jeffrey S. Gurock (Routledge, 1998), 274.

18. Sachar, *A History of the Jews in America*, 60, 92.

19. Tarshish, *Central European Jews in America*, 276.

The frontier was a workshop for Jewish identity. Hasia Diner notes that peddling, in particular, "functioned as the nearly universal American Jewish male experience" from the 1840s to the 1870s. Itinerant peddling meant that a portion of the German Jewish population was constantly moving to the conflictual edges of territorial expansion, where new markets were appearing and supplies were needed. Even at the frontier, German Jews were not cut off from communities in bigger cities. Rather, peddlers linked the settled parts of their communities to the frontier, through business ties that ran along the same pathways as immigrant social ties. Diner explains: "This pattern played itself out all over America. As new interior cities such as Cincinnati, St. Louis, Chicago, Pittsburgh, Nashville, Sioux City, Omaha, Milwaukee, Kansas City, Atlanta, and Chattanooga developed, Jews arrived early. Among the first Europeans to arrive in these places ... each peddler functioned in a long Jewish economic chain linking shopkeepers to Jewish wholesalers in the larger cities on whom they depended for credit."[20] A network of Jewish fraternal lodges, B'nai B'rith, was founded in 1843 and grew from these conditions to a wide-reaching national organization. It formed threads of connection among the settled and itinerant, constructing an enthusiastic Americanism tied to Jewish ethics, as well as business and social networks. Over the next two decades, as the organization's leaders avoided taking positions on slavery and the Civil War that might cause trouble for Jews, they emphasized instead the patriotic role of Jews in the effort to build a nation on Western, modernist, industrialist ideals.[21]

The process of settlement and state-building forged a national identity bound in contradictions, and American Jewish identity mirrored those tensions. The embrace of freedom was central to the sense that diverse groups were bound together as Americans—but not all groups. The conquest, dispossession, and subjugation of Indigenous people that underlaid that national belonging posed a thorny challenge. Roxanne Dunbar-Ortiz writes that "reconciling empire and liberty," two competing rationales of US state-building, was achieved in part by re-narrating brutal, largely state-enacted military conquest as the story of immigrant strivers sweating to build a wondrous place and a free political structure.[22] Jewish settlers did the same re-narration,

20. Diner, *Jews of the United States*, 99–100.
21. Moore, *B'nai B'rith and the Challenge of Ethnic Leadership*, 25, 28. On the contributions of Jewish soldiers to settlement and colonial defense, see also the 1895 publication by Simon Wolf, who would become president of B'nai B'rith in 1903: Simon Wolf, *The American Jew as Patriot, Soldier and Citizen* (The Levytype Company, 1895).
22. Dunbar-Ortiz, *An Indigenous Peoples' History of the United States*, 10.

portraying their role in conquest and settlement as a way to affirm their American identity. "Suggestions about Jewish credit and responsibility for American land acquisitions dotted the popular Jewish press throughout the nineteenth century into the early twentieth," David Koffman writes. "They 'won' the land upon which to settle from Native Americans despite settlers' selective and strategic conviction that the land had been unoccupied. . . . Jewish ambitions for expansion were articulated as great surges of forward movement for modernity and of expansion in nation-making terms."[23] German Jews perceived themselves as white in the particular sense conferred by Europeanness and settlement and embraced the US colonial undertaking as a moral, civilizing engine. In opposition, they viewed Indigenous people as dangerous *because* they rejected the seizure and industrialization of land and resisted state control. In other words, beyond enacting settlement, settler colonialism was the value system underpinning German Jewish immigrant life just as it pervaded the rest of US life. Accordingly, in the 1890s, when upper-class Jews encountered new currents of anti-Jewish exclusionary sentiment, they pointed to Jewish military service in the Indian Wars as proof that they belonged: that they were white, properly masculine settlers. For Jews, Koffman writes, this "meant membership in one of the central dramas of the American metaphysic: taming the land and 'pacifying' its 'wild' inhabitants."[24] These self-portrayals harmonized with the European nationalisms and colonialism of their sending culture. As Koffman writes, their development in the United States mirrored, too, the contemporaneous European vision of the "muscle Jew," a masculine, defensive ideal that merged European eugenics and Zionist colonial nationalism.[25]

Settlement was not the only field on which German Jews constructed a white-coded Americanism. Like other groups, they made their racial, economic, and political identification with the state in myriad ways: from facilitating the transnational marketing of slavery-produced goods (as the Lehman and Seligman family empires did) to building a Grecian-style statue to liberty

23. David S. Koffman, *The Jews' Indian: Colonialism, Pluralism, and Belonging in America* (Rutgers University Press, 2019), 55–56.

24. In the same spirit, as Diner recounts, the American Jewish Historical Society was created by Oscar Straus, Cyrus Adler, and other "notables" to provide for the need to show Jewish contributions to the establishment of the US state. Diner, *Jews of the United States*, 173; Koffman, *Jews' Indian*, 61.

25. Koffman, *Jews' Indian*, 51; Todd Samuel Presner, "'Clear Heads, Solid Stomachs, and Hard Muscles': Max Nordau and the Aesthetics of Jewish Regeneration," *Modernism/Modernity* 10, no. 2 (2003): 269–96, 270.

and the US Constitution (as B'nai B'rith did in 1867).[26] As Michael Rogin has argued, Jewish entertainers and audiences used blackface performance to emphasize their own not-Blackness and to construct white ethnic identity, as did other immigrant groups.[27] German Jewish commentators argued that Jews, as bearers of European Enlightenment thought, were natural Americans: "Remember that the true Jewish spirit has ever fostered free thought; has ever been against despotism and for individual liberty," exhorted the editors of the *B'nai B'rith Messenger* in 1907.[28] In parallel, they affirmed the centrality of European whiteness to the US national project, including its defense of rights. Over the span of decades, these ideas anchored B'nai B'rith's resistance to anti-Jewish sentiment and its support for the progress of nation-building. One such instance was a 1916 speech to the North Dacotah B'nai B'rith lodge by Tracy R. Bangs, a political figure who had overseen settlement as a Land Office clerk, US attorney, and banker. Under the heading "The B'nai B'rith: Its World Mission," the national *B'nai B'rith News* circulated his remarks to its members as an enlightened call to civil rights. "We all belong to the great white race," Bangs told the gathered lodge members. "We are, or at least should be, brothers of the human family, and the only problem is that of equal rights and justice to all."[29]

In short, German Jews' communal identity in the United States was shaped by the structures into which they arrived. Settler colonialism was one such structure, and so was anti-Blackness. Sixty years of German Jewish migration from 1820 to 1880 spanned slavery, the Civil War, Reconstruction, and the sharp retrenchment of Black freedoms through Black codes and white supremacist violence. As German Jewish institutions were established, and patterns of leadership emerged that reinforced racial and national identity, they too became a structure that shaped the community. In these

26. Elliot Ashkenazi, "Jewish Commercial Interests Between North and South: The Case of the Lehmans and the Seligmans," in *Central European Jews in America*, ed. Gurock, 28; Wolf, *American Jew as Patriot, Soldier and Citizen*, 65–66.

27. Michael Rogin, *Blackface, White Noise: Jewish Immigrants in the Hollywood Melting Pot* (University of California Press, 1996), 56.

28. *B'nai B'rith Messenger*, "Editorial," November 29, 1907.

29. *B'nai B'rith News*, "The B'nai B'rith Its World Mission, Address by Hon. Tracy R. Bangs, Ex US Attorney for North Dakota, Delivered Before Dacotah Lodge, Concluded from Previous Issue," vol. 7, no. 5 (1916): 4. On Tracy R. Bangs, see W. B. Hennessy, *History of North Dakota, Embracing a Relation of the History of the State from the Earliest Times Down to the Present Day, Including the Biographies of the Builders of the Commonwealth* (Bismarck Tribune Company, 1910).

contexts, members of the community would not have particularly recognized themselves as choosing a politics or producing whiteness. Indeed, that is the point: Identification with whiteness, hand in hand with enthusiasm for settler conquest, was naturalized in German Jewish immigrants' communal construction of Americanness. The institutions that grew from their sociality, their largesse, and their vision of the United States naturally reflected their presumptions.

B'nai B'rith, the secular institution that would eventually launch the ADL, took up some of the function of Jewish community infrastructure that religious organizations did not provide.[30] Between 1843 and 1878, B'nai B'rith accumulated twenty-one thousand members, about 9 percent of Jewish men in the United States.[31] Its members spoke German and English rather than Yiddish, and some lodges communicated only in English. The leadership, if not all members, viewed Jewishness as a religion and a communal bond rather than racial difference.[32] Although some had arrived without money, German Jews were upwardly mobile as a group, and by 1880 "represented a fairly solid phalanx of comfortable, middle-class merchants."[33] The community's leading lights had entered into US political life as appointees to public office, elected officials, or owners of infrastructure like newspapers or philanthropic funds. The membership of a German Jewish state-capital class was clearly emerging. Some of that upper-class stratum was included in B'nai B'rith's membership along with the middle classes. Against the backdrop of other Jewish organizations run solely by elites, B'nai B'rith considered itself relatively democratic, "not an aristocracy of brains or virtue. . . . It unites all classes to the end that the good may improve the evil and the best the good."[34] However, that openness found its limits with the arrival of new immigrants who seemed incommensurably different.

It was the arrival of Eastern European Jewish immigrants that threw B'nai B'rith's elitism into relief. Previously, members had seen themselves as forging

30. Moore, *B'nai B'rith and the Challenge of Ethnic Leadership*, 87.

31. Three smaller lodges accounted for another twenty-two thousand Jewish men. Moore, *B'nai B'rith and the Challenge of Ethnic Leadership*, 43; Samson D. Oppenheim, "The Jewish Population of the United States," *American Jewish Year Book*, 1917, 31.

32. Heeding Hasia Diner's caution against treating Jewish immigrants of this period as an ideological monolith, I focus here on organizations and leadership, which both represented communal thought and produced its ideological frameworks. Diner, *A Time for Gathering*, 232; Moore, *B'nai B'rith and the Challenge of Ethnic Leadership*, 86.

33. Diner, *A Time for Gathering*, 65.

34. B'nai B'rith president Leo N. Levi, as quoted in Moore, *B'nai B'rith and the Challenge of Ethnic Leadership*, 78.

community ties rather than bounding others out. But Eastern European Jews defied German Jews' sense of belonging to European modernity. The *Ostjude*, as Eastern European Jews were called in German, was "a beggar and a loafer," a bumpkin, and backwardly religious. Additionally, the US frontier was now closed, and along with it the opportunities that had helped German Jews forge both fortunes and identities through settlement. As Eastern European Jews amassed in the United States, "the vocations at hand were now mainly toiling in needle-trade shops or other trades, and selling merchandise in small stores."[35] These jobs did not invite the admiration that entrepreneurship and frontiersmanship had conferred on earlier immigrants, nor did they portray Eastern European Jews as civilizers (although, half a century later, the same jobs would be nostalgically recalled as a sign that Jews had worked hard and raised themselves up by their bootstraps). B'nai B'rith members' realization that they did not want to admit the immigrants "transform[ed] it de facto into an exclusive sociability," writes Moore.[36] That exclusivity was not just social, but structured in capital. When the Eastern European Jewish throngs arrived to work in sweatshops, German Jews were far more likely to own the factories than labor in them.[37]

The vast new wave of immigrants to the United States began in 1881, as Jews in Russia were subjected to rampaging pogroms. The pogroms were precipitated by the assassination of Tsar Alexander II and subsequent efforts by Russian leaders to disorganize the anti-tsarist revolutionary movement by fomenting nationalist violence against Jews. "'Barefoot brigades' of lumpenproletariat and peasants now set about rampaging through some 160 Jewish communities in the southern Pale, looting, burning, maiming—killing," Howard Sachar writes. "By year's end, twenty thousand Jews were left homeless and destitute. Scores of thousands of others fled." Following the pogroms, Russian law banned Jews from living in rural areas, buying land, and joining professions like law and medicine. Packed into cities, unable to support themselves, sick from malnutrition and unlivable conditions, they fled. Two million Jews emigrated to the United States between 1881 and 1914.[38]

35. Hyman B. Grinstein, "The Efforts of East European Jewry to Organize Its Own Community in the United States," *Publications of the American Jewish Historical Society* 49, no. 2 (1959): 73–89.
36. Moore, *B'nai B'rith and the Challenge of Ethnic Leadership*, xiii.
37. Sachar, *A History of the Jews in America*, 86.
38. Sachar, *A History of the Jews in America*, 117–18.

In contrast to German Jews' collective enthusiasm for business, state-building, and bourgeois European culture, all of which had helped their assimilation, the refugees' unruly politics and desperate origins cast them as especially intrusive foreigners.[39] German Jewish leaders themselves viewed the new immigrants as racially "other," uncivilized, and dangerously disloyal to state order. Some of the new immigrants had been involved in revolutionary movements before emigrating; others were radicalized by their experiences of violence and exploitation. In the US, they responded to racism and labor exploitation by forming organizations around resistive ideals, mobilizing mass protest, and articulating the value of working-class communities over elite capitalist society. They also continued to support anti-tsarist resistance at home, including armed resistance. (Alarmed, in 1903 B'nai B'rith's president Leo N. Levi urged Jews not to irritate the Russian government by blaming it for anti-Jewish pogroms.)[40] One Milwaukee newspaper editorialized around 1915: "We must keep in mind that we are dealing with people who do not belong to European civilization," clarifying that "they are the most ignorant and useless element of Russia."[41] Accordingly, even as German Jewish community leaders set up immigrant aid organizations, they were animated by their hostility toward the newcomers. Hoping to defend against the sense that Jews on the whole were foreign and unhealthy, they funded Progressive Era uplift organizations to teach English, Americanization, and physical development.[42] To help the new immigrants find jobs and lessen urban overcrowding, they marketed Eastern European Jews as cheap, docile labor and often sent them to places where German Jewish businesses needed strikebreakers.[43]

As Eastern European Jews developed institutions around labor and revolutionary politics, the upper-class leadership of German Jewish society was naturally concerned. The socialist Workmen's Circle formed in 1900 and the

39. Rischin describes such characterizations of "Russians" (Jews) in German Jewish newspapers, among them "wild Asiatics" speaking "piggish jargon." Moses Rischin, "Germans Versus Russians," in *The American Jewish Experience*, ed. Jonathan D. Sarna (Holmes and Meier, 1986), 121.

40. Philip Ernest Schoenberg, "The American Reaction to the Kishinev Pogrom of 1903," *American Jewish Historical Quarterly* 63, no. 3 (1974): 275.

41. Melech Epstein, *Jewish Labor in USA: An Industrial, Political and Cultural History of the Jewish Labor Movement* (Ktav Publishing House, 1969), 45.

42. Sachar, *A History of the Jews in America*, 157.

43. Epstein, *Jewish Labor in USA*, 50.

Labor Zionist Farband in 1910.[44] The Workmen's Circle grew quickly, and by 1910 it had more members than the B'nai B'rith lodges.[45] Labor historian Melech Epstein records one report of an immigrant aid worker: "The rich, older Jews were quite upset by the strange mixture that was pouring in upon them from Eastern Europe and which by giving a generous sum of money they were trying to make American. There were Socialists of several varieties who, far from consenting to be made over, were resolved to help make America over.... These Socialists were most embarrassing to the bountiful German Jews ... what would the neighbors say?"[46] Beyond their feelings of embarrassment, the older leadership understood Eastern European Jews as a threat to their social and political positioning. The sheer number of immigrants, their inescapable visibility, and their condition of mass crisis linked Jewishness to foreignness and poverty. It elicited anti-Jewish vitriol and revulsion in Jewish and non-Jewish press, civic institutions, and bourgeois circles, tainting presumptively white upper-class Jews with racialization.[47] In 1887, the elites' anti-immigrant fears were realized when a shocking story rippled across newspapers. Financier and politician Joseph Seligmann had been refused a room at his usual luxury hotel, the Grand Union in Saratoga, New York, which had suddenly adopted a "no Israelites" policy. More exclusions "spread like wildfire" at exclusive resorts and civic clubs.[48]

It was against these combined threats to whiteness, bourgeois identity, and the emerging settler state that German Jewish leaders founded new institutions to retake control. They classed these institutions as *Jewish defense*. The major Jewish defense organizations that emerged in response to these shifting circumstances were the American Jewish Committee (AJC), the Anti-Defamation League, and the shorter-lived American Jewish Congress. They joined a fleet of Jewish charities created in the same period by German Jewish upper classes to address the needs of refugees, which in turn reflected the larger wave of Progressive Era institutions established for "social hygiene": to socially uplift immigrants and the poor and to improve their immediate

44. Now renamed as the gender-neutral "Workers' Circle" throughout the United States, through the organizing efforts of students of the Boston Workers' Circle shule. Boston Workers' Circle, "History," n.d., https://circleboston.org/history/, accessed June 2, 2025.

45. Moore, *B'nai B'rith and the Challenge of Ethnic Leadership*, 87–89.

46. Epstein, *Jewish Labor in USA*, 51.

47. Leonard Dinnerstein, *Uneasy at Home: Antisemitism and the American Jewish Experience* (Columbia University Press, 1987), 34.

48. Sachar, *A History of the Jews in America*, 98–101.

living conditions. Defense organizations and charities of the period were concerned with the depredations of poverty, inducements to crime, and lack of refined cultural tastes that they saw in the chaotic underclass of cities. The organizations created by Jewish leaders in particular mixed their sense of responsibility for poor kin—the need to address the desperate conditions of Jews in the United States and the Russian empire—with the eugenicist impulse to fight racial "degeneracy."[49] The Jewish defense organizations' interest in uplifting Jews was not only a matter of defending against antisemitism, but defending the upper classes as well. In 1891, a *Detroit American* editorial explained: "Our great duty, therefore, is to raise our race. . . . The Jew . . . must elevate his lowest type, if the highest classes are to attain their legitimate place in the popular estimation. . . . It has become a question of self-defense."[50]

The elite concerns that produced the ADL in 1913 had first produced an earlier defense organization, the American Jewish Committee. The committee was founded in 1906 to advocate where it perceived Jewish rights being denied and to address Jewish poverty. The approach of the luminaries who led this community relations effort was to work from the top: As former staffer Steven Windmueller describes, to "penetrate the thinking and behavior of the general society by accessing elite and principal institutions . . . public officials, press and media elite, the intellectual and academic sector, and the leadership of business and labor."[51] This *shtadlan* (intercessor) approach, also called the "great men" model, had historical roots in European and Asian Jewish communities where representatives were appointed to communicate with rulers. In the US context, it meant using the personal connections of Jewish leading lights with the most powerful actors of state to bring the community's needs to their sympathetic attention.[52]

The impetus for creating the American Jewish Committee was also a thoroughly elite project: Its leaders aimed to keep poorer, more radical

49. For an overview of the eugenicist groundings of Progressive Era "uplift" social work, see Angie C. Kennedy, "Eugenics, 'Degenerate Girls,' and Social Workers During the Progressive Era," *Affilia* 23, no. 1 (2008): 22–37.

50. Quoted in Sachar, *A History of the Jews in America*, 156.

51. Steven Windmueller, "'Defenders': National Jewish Community Relations Agencies," in *Jewish Polity and American Civil Society: Communal Agencies and Religious Movements in the American Public Sphere*, ed. Alan Mittleman et al. (Rowman and Littlefield, 2002), 23.

52. Melvin I. Urofsky, "American Jewish Leadership," *American Jewish History* 70, no. 4 (1981): 412.

Eastern European Jews from establishing their own institutional voice.[53] At the turn of the century, popular organizing was gathering force. Pogroms in Russia were continuing, and Jews urgently sought ways to leverage US power to intervene. Between 1903 and 1906, mobs rained down unthinkable violence on Jews in the Russian empire. "Nails were driven through heads; bodies, hacked in half; bellies, split open and filled with feathers. Women and girls were raped, and some had their breasts cut off," writes Monty Noam Penkower.[54] In Russia, the Jewish Bund organized self-defense and protest strikes, linking resistance to pogroms to the larger program of socialist resistance to the tsar.[55] US Jews, including German Jews, led the collection of relief funds and petitioned the president to intervene. Some raised money to arm the self-defense groups. Tens of thousands of Jews marched in the street to demand US intervention. The crisis of pogroms, the rise of popular movements, and the chaotic shape of Jewish political life demanded some structure. "Organization was in the air," in the words of Louis Marshall, attorney and chairman of the Jewish Theological Seminary.[56] The danger was that the leftists, mass marchers, and labor organizers might be the ones to organize. "In order to avoid mischief we should take the initiative," Marshall told B'nai B'rith president Adolph Kraus.[57]

The event that finally pushed German Jewish leaders to set up the American Jewish Committee was, simply, the launch of other plans for a Jewish organization that would give voice to the marching class. Reform rabbi and anti-imperialist Judah Magnes had been working with leftists to organize mass demonstrations and fundraising to arm the self-defense groups. In 1905, feeling the urgency of establishing a more coordinated approach, Magnes began organizing toward a national, participatory Jewish association to take up representational politics. The idea of a popular Jewish political organization was too much for some of the community elites. Defensively, they moved to form an institution under their own control: the American Jewish Committee, a closed, nonmembership body that would

<hr>

53. Daniel P. Kotzin, *Judah L. Magnes: An American Jewish Nonconformist* (Syracuse University Press, 2010), 102.

54. Monty Noam Penkower, "The Kishinev Pogrom of 1903: A Turning Point in Jewish History," *Modern Judaism: A Journal of Jewish Ideas & Experience* 24, no. 3 (2004): 187.

55. Louis Harap, "The Bund Revisited: III," *Jewish Life*, April 1974, https://www.marxists.org/subject/jewish/harap-bund-3.pdf.

56. Naomi W. Cohen, *Not Free to Desist: The American Jewish Committee, 1906–1966* (Jewish Publication Society of America, 1972), 8.

57. Kotzin, *Judah L. Magnes*, 102.

defend Jews by leveraging the social relationships among "great men" and powerful institutions. Its founders enticed Magnes to join their executive committee, and he accepted, reasoning that the relationships and resources of the political class might be a more efficient way to intervene in the Russian crisis.[58] Their intention was explicitly not to be a popular or democratic organization, whose "rabble-rousing" might interfere in "the efforts of individual intercessors deploying the tried methods of backstairs diplomacy," historian Naomi W. Cohen writes. Instead, they cultivated a group of thirteen luminaries as the executives, and sixty delegates from around the United States, all highly placed peers in business and politics.[59] Over the next decade, Eastern European Jewish immigrants, leftists, and Zionists would all continue to demand representation. In 1922, the American Jewish Congress was established by more democratically minded German Jewish leaders Stephen Wise, Louis Brandeis, and again Judah Magnes, deliberately including Eastern European Jewish members.[60]

Shortly after the American Jewish Committee's founding, the B'nai B'rith lodge of Bloomington, Illinois, launched its own intervention in the new landscape presented by Eastern European Jewish immigration. In 1908, the lodge established a publicity committee to push back on negative portrayals of Jews in newspapers, stage and film, and textbooks, and to educate the public on Jewish thought and life.[61] This reflected growing concern among Jewish leaders at the moment that Jews were being associated with criminality—partly through unfair stereotyping, but also through factual reporting on organized crime, including sex commerce. Several Jewish organizations set out to disentangle discussion of crime from discussion of Jews, and at the same time pursued the "moral hygiene" projects common to Progressive Era social uplift work: They set out to correct the behavior of those Jews who had strayed. The National Council of Jewish Women created

58. Kotzin, *Judah L. Magnes*, 100–2.

59. Cohen, *Not Free to Desist*, 8, 16.

60. In this history, I mostly set aside the American Jewish Congress, never as powerful as the ADL and American Jewish Committee, and shorter-lived. The American Jewish Congress included some socialists and "radicals," and it advocated Zionism long before the other defense organizations. The ADL and American Jewish Committee perceived it in dramatic opposition to their own positions. However, it was similarly liberal and anticommunist, and maintained a leadership mostly drawn from the same sphere. On the American Jewish Congress, see David Verbeeten, *The Politics of Nonassimilation: The American Jewish Left in the Twentieth Century* (Cornell University Press, 2017), chap. 2.

61. Kirman, "Major Programs of the B'nai B'rith Anti-Defamation League," 52–53.

programming for the education and health care of the lower classes and "cultivated the 'instinctive shrinking from the vulgar' among Jewish women."[62] In New York and Chicago, Jewish dignitaries, including banker and philanthropist Jacob Schiff and B'nai B'rith's president, Adolph Kraus, joined mayoral investigative committees to stamp out gambling, sex work, and the sex trafficking "white slave trade."[63]

In 1913, that B'nai B'rith committee was transformed into an organization: the Anti-Defamation League of B'nai B'rith. Sigmund Livingston, the lodge president and attorney who had pioneered the publicity work, became its chair. As Livingston saw it, his project was to preserve the "high regard in which the Jew is held by the American public." Historian Jack Wertheimer describes the particular upper-class dread to which the ADL was an answer: "The fears of 'native' Jews: A new immigrant group had brought 'obnoxious' characteristics to America that threatened the reputation of all Jews."[64] The Harmonie Club, a German Jewish social club in New York City, made the calls for exclusion plain, calling for "more polish and less Polish." Isidore Straus, philanthropist and cofounder of the American Jewish Committee, described his horror at Eastern European Jewry: "Let me assure you that in case nothing is done to eradicate the innate principles of these people, they will, by their superior numbers, in time bring so much injury to our children that I shudder to think about it."[65] To Livingston and his peers, solving this problem meant quelling negative representations in newspapers, theater, and demagoguery, as well as reining in Jews who sullied the brand with immoral or ungentrified actions.

Livingston's main concern was with lower-class Jews, even though some of the tropes that concerned him correlated to middle- and upper-class men. Populist antisemitic images often caricatured Jews in relation to money and business ethics, for instance, combining Christian religious hostility to Jews with resentment of Jewish upper-class wealth. The ADL campaigned to have such images removed or to prevent their production: In 1915 it successfully organized film executives to stop using Jewish characters "whenever [they]

62. M. Alison Kibler, *Censoring Racial Ridicule: Irish, Jewish, and African American Struggles over Race and Representation, 1890–1930* (University of North Carolina Press, 2015), 127–28.

63. American Social Hygiene Association, *Social Hygiene Volume IV* (1918), 146.

64. Livingston and Wertheimer quoted in Moore, *B'nai B'rith and the Challenge of Ethnic Leadership*, 105.

65. Joseph Dorinson, "Jewish Politics: The Art of Survival," in *America's Ethnic Politics*, ed. Joseph S. Roucek and Bernard Eisenberg (Greenwood Press, 1982), 236.

. . . desired to depict a hard-hearted money lender, a blackmailer, a firebug, a depraved gambler, a swindler, a grafter, or a white-slaver."[66] But Livingston viewed uncouth immigrants as the *cause* of that antisemitic attention, and he perceived that their objectionable ways encouraged antisemitism among bourgeois Jews themselves. Livingston wrote: "A Jewish immigrant from 'X' is uncultured and unethical. We have the same experience with one or more immigrants from the same country or locality. Then we conclude that all Jews from 'X' are unethical and uncultured." In that case, Livingston saw an ethical obligation to fix Jews themselves rather than battling the stereotypes. "It is our duty both as citizens of this country and as Jews, if the immigrant from 'X' does not measure up . . . to the highest standard required by American citizenship, to elevate him to that standard," he concluded.[67]

Although the ADL's form of defense work was less rarified than the American Jewish Committee's, it nonetheless conceived of a bourgeois, patriotic polity as the moral material for its work. Accordingly, it banked on associating Jews with commitments to individual freedoms, industry, and European reason as the natural framework for arguing against antisemitism. The ADL intended to guide mainstream political culture by reaching the managers of civic life: editors, theater producers, school administrators. By 1916, Livingston reported, the ADL had already made "hundreds of appeals" to movie executives not to use malign Jewish characters in their films, called on publishers not to print "unjust articles," and urged schools not to use nursery rhymes that villainized Jews.[68] In one sense, appealing to managers reflected the familiar *shtadlan* model of working at the top as well as an effort to interrupt tropes that ran through Christian and nativist discourse. Additionally, though, it was a means of circumventing working-class Eastern European Jews who were, in many cases, the performers and writers who drew stereotypical comedic characters from their own lives, and the Jewish audiences who found them heimishly hilarious.[69]

The ADL's organizational structure reflected the same desire to impose discipline on Jewish life. Intending to present a contrast to the American

66. Anti-Defamation League, *Report of the Anti-Defamation League of the Independent Order B'nai B'rith: Together with Principles of the League and Correspondence* (1920), 12.

67. Anti-Defamation League, *Report of the Anti-Defamation League of the Independent Order B'nai B'rith* (1920), 5–6.

68. *B'nai B'rith Messenger*, "What Our Lodges Are Doing," February 1918, http://www.archive.org/details/nationaljewishm0101bnai.

69. Moore, *B'nai B'rith and the Challenge of Ethnic Leadership*, 112.

Jewish Committee's small clique of leaders, B'nai B'rith appointed an executive committee of 150 of its members and announced that ADL membership was open to "any reputable person, regardless of sex or creed," and without any dues.[70] In practice, though, it reproduced a broader-based elitism. The executive committee was a roster of notables including attorneys, politicians, bankers, businessmen, and rabbis, and the ADL never became a mass membership organization. While Livingston "spoke of a membership of 'a hundred thousand,' B'nai B'rith leader Adolph Kraus preferred the 'representative and high class' Jews of America."[71] Even the middle-class German Jewish vision of moral, upstanding Jews did not extend to the immigrant poor, or to Jews resisting capital and empire in Russia and the United States, or to those who eschewed the demure sociality of the upper classes.

The ADL's effort to curate a collective Jewish reputation while simultaneously asserting that Jews were not a group immediately produced contradictions. For instance, the ADL opposed the emergence of Jewish political clubs: loose social organizations that had begun to organize the Jewish electorate in the mid-1910s, as other communities were similarly organizing. Deeming such organizing to be racializing of Jews and contrary to Americanism, the ADL roundly denounced it in a 1915 resolution. "Neither religion nor race should be appealed to in American politics. . . . There never has been and never will be such a thing as the Jewish vote," the resolution pronounced.[72] At the same time, the ADL forthrightly claimed authority to speak on behalf of Jews, especially when addressing the business and political class about Jewish communal matters. Claiming that role was a strenuous task since, among Jews themselves, the ADL's authority was not a given. In 1920, Livingston called for it in an imperious passive tense, writing: "One of the principal reasons for the organization of the Anti Defamation League was the recognized desirability of a central office representing American Jewry which could act authoritatively." To his frustration, discipline was not tight. Instead, Jews had been caused "considerable embarrassment through the more or less officious action of individuals who take it upon themselves to speak on behalf of American Jewry."[73]

In his plea for an ADL-administered order, Livingston offered an example of this embarrassment. In 1920, the Mohawk Valley Cap company had

70. B'nai B'rith News, "Anti-Defamation League," vol. 4, no. 2 (October 1913).

71. Moore, *B'nai B'rith and the Challenge of Ethnic Leadership*, 114.

72. *Chicago Examiner*, "Use of 'Jewish' by Politicians Assailed," January 27, 1915.

73. Anti-Defamation League, *Report of the Anti-Defamation League of the Independent Order B'nai B'rith* (1920), 27.

published a racist cartoon with the caption "The Evolution of a Bolshevik." As the B'nai B'rith newsletter described, it showed "in three drawings the evolution from a donkey to a most disgusting caricature of a Jew." The ADL had quietly taken up the matter, writing to the company's executive. But a Mr. Stein of Utica, New York, had also sent a spicy letter of complaint to the business. It arrived and caused a stir just at the hour when the ADL's representative, businessman Charles Strauss, was visiting the office. Strauss was upset both by the letter's tone and at the pained reaction of the company's manager, with whom he had a collegial relationship. In an outraged report to the ADL, Strauss decried Stein's letter as "lacking in tact and good judgment" and damaging to the ADL and to Jews. By contrast, Strauss wrote, the manager was "a man of high standing in the business world" and not an antisemite. Strauss asked the ADL to make Stein apologize.[74] The ADL saw fit to reprint Strauss's call in its annual report, along with his moral: that Jews who violated genteel rules of engagement should be kept under control—the ADL's control—for their own good. "A matter of this kind," Strauss wrote, "should not be handled by narrow-minded individuals who do not represent the best example of the people whom we are trying to protect." Livingston added his own moral to the story in the annual report: Instead of members of the uncouth public taking it upon themselves to respond to antisemitism, they should report incidents to the ADL to be documented and *appropriately* addressed.[75] This last aspect of the ADL's pitch regarding the "necessity for centralization" turned out to be enormously important. Six decades later, the ADL would launch its *Annual Audit of Anti-Semitic Incidents*, which did just what Livingston called for—gathering reports and complaints from community members and allowing the ADL to translate them into a centralized, carefully calibrated set of demands for redress. That practice would become a key factor in the ADL's authority to define and quantify antisemitism, underwriting its enormous leverage as a US political actor.

It is also important to note what the ADL did *not* do in its founding period, as it set the terms for its later work. Its remit was the defense of Jews, even if its mission statement called somewhat abstractly for "justice and fair treatment for all." The ADL did not draw connections between Jews' experiences of antisemitism and Black communities' experiences of racism. This

74. Anti-Defamation League, *Report of the Anti-Defamation League of the Independent Order B'nai B'rith* (1920), 27–29.
75. Anti-Defamation League, *Report of the Anti-Defamation League of the Independent Order B'nai B'rith* (1920), 29–31.

was due partly to the fact that its leaders and members were not necessarily opposed to anti-Black discrimination or to discrimination on the whole, even as they spoke of egalitarianism. When its leaders and their peers responded to the particular outrage of hotel advertisements that discouraged Jewish guests, they were quite specific about only objecting to *advertising* that they saw as defamation.[76] The same leaders defended businesses' right to discriminate and expressed sympathy with the idea that establishments catering to upper-class Jews would want to exclude Jews who were "objectionable" on the basis of class.[77] Jewish leaders also did not perceive discrimination against Jews in racial terms, as if parallel to anti-Black or anti-Indigenous marginalization, but as a stew of religious and nativist hostility. Some saw that when anti-Jewish discrimination mirrored elements of anti-Blackness, the comparison itself worked to erode their whiteness. Rather than inviting linkages, though, this moved them to further distinguish Jewishness from Blackness. "American politics was organized around antiblack racism rather than anti-Semitism," Michael Rogin writes, which allowed Jews and other ethnic groups to use their own anti-Blackness to both expand whiteness and to place themselves within it.[78] Although the ADL's legislative advocacy did challenge advertising that rejected guests on the basis of nationality, race, and creed, it did not challenge the wholesale anti-Black exclusion and segregation that "did not need to be advertised."[79] Similarly, the ADL advocated movie censorship laws that banned "maligning" nationality, race, and creed, but it sat out efforts in the same period to oppose showings of the inflammatory anti-Black film *Birth of a Nation*. ADL leaders' views were in keeping with white upper-class notions of the period and cannot be painted with a backward brush as liberatory, certainly not as antiracist.

To read the ADL's ongoing history, then, we begin with its origins in the particularly German Jewish communal experience of six decades of imbrication in settler colonialism, followed by the immigration shock that challenged German Jews' social identities. There was nothing exceptional about

76. Moore, *B'nai B'rith and the Challenge of Ethnic Leadership*, 109.

77. Kibler, *Censoring Racial Ridicule*, 120. In primary sources, see, for instance, *New York Times*, "Hotel Affronts Senator's Sister: Mrs. Frank of Baltimore, Sister of Isidor Rayner, Told That Jews Are Not Wanted. Sought Rooms for Nieces. She Resents the Affront by Leaving the Marlborough-Blenheim at Atlantic City," May 18, 1907.

78. Eric L. Goldstein, *The Price of Whiteness: Jews, Race, and American Identity* (Princeton University Press, 2019), 67–68; Rogin, *Blackface, White Noise*, 165.

79. Kibler, *Censoring Racial Ridicule*, 120–21.

the ADL's merger of settler liberalism and whiteness, elitist approaches to egalitarianism, and efforts to wield disciplinary authority over those whose interests it claimed to represent—to the contrary, it was a fairly standard Progressive Era institution. As these chapters show, the ADL's ideological foundations remained strong even as overt elitism fell out of favor in US politics and as race consciousness became central to US discussions of rights and democracy. They are evident decades later in the ADL's moves to marginalize and dismantle the Jewish left during the 1950s Red Scare, its antagonism toward Black liberation politics beginning in the 1960s, and its mid-twentieth-century adoption of Zionism as an extension of Western influence and imperial capital. In the twenty-first century, the same foundations appear in the ADL's advocacy for the expansion of US militarized policing and Israeli genocide as necessities for a settler construction of "Jewish security," and the assertion that Jewish security, so conceived, was key to protecting Western democracy. As anti-Zionism and a concomitant anticolonialism have become an increasingly *Jewish* mode of US politics since the Palestinian Second Intifada (2000–2005), the ADL's approach is also evident in its efforts to discipline those Jewish movements, or simply disappear them.

Adjacent to the development of the ADL and the defense organizations as "a department of state" for US Jewry, charitable and philanthropic organizations formed a second site of elite leadership.[80] Fundraising for social welfare and defense was the purview of local Jewish federations, which had been created to coordinate community work beginning in 1895. By the time the ADL was founded, they reflected the beginnings of what Lila Corwin Berman has termed the American Jewish philanthropic complex, an ecology of institutions and leaders that was at once a Jewish communal structure and a US capital structure, shaped and produced by the flows of communal wealth and political power and by the US policies that supported their expansion. Together, the federations "organized a larger portion of American Jewish collective life than any other institution."[81] The federation system brought a form of homogeneity and centralization to Jewish institutional politics and at the same time made federation-funded institutions ubiquitous

<hr>

80. Svonkin, *Jews Against Prejudice*, 2.
81. Lila Corwin Berman, *The American Jewish Philanthropic Complex: The History of a Multibillion-Dollar Institution* (Princeton University Press, 2020), 11, 25.

in Jewish communal life. As they did so, the federations' leadership, drawn like the defense organizations' from the state-capital class, exerted substantial control over the content of that life. In addition to raising money, federation leaders determined how to distribute it.[82] Sectors of the community that were not agreeable to them, whether leftists, anti-Zionists, or other, could not access the federations' wealth to develop Jewish institutions.

The federations were established as a paternalistic, Progressive Era structure by German Jews to minister to Eastern European immigrants. As their work stretched into the 1930s and '40s, even as they admitted a more diverse generation of leaders, the federations preserved that moneyed ethos. A rarified inner circle rewarded high-dollar donors with leadership positions. This practice persisted over long decades. A 1979 study by historian Marc L. Raphael examined the workings of the Jewish Communal Fund in Columbus, Ohio. There, he wrote that prestigious top campaign roles were "'passed around' amongst a relatively small group of 'deserving' or 'safe' businessmen (recruited in such a way as to ensure homogeneity and minimize conflict) as rewards for either services rendered or large sums given." Doing so allowed the organizations to keep control of communal work.[83] Anyone considered a "firebrand," "controversial rabble-rouser," "dissenter," "troublemaker," or "hot-head" would be filtered out, even if they were a major donor.[84]

One effect of this plutocratic structure was to invest Jewish communal infrastructure with the political conservatism of the wealthy class. In 1931, as the Depression intensified the need for relief services, the federations were gathered under the umbrella of the Council of Jewish Federations and Welfare Funds (CJFWF, later shortened to CJF). On the one hand, as Diner writes, it was a move to "make their operations more sophisticated and rational" as they studied and responded to communal needs.[85] On the other hand, it dramatically centralized funding and decisions about what work could be pursued under the auspices of Jewish institutions. The biggest donors could effectively approve or veto projects. Kenneth D. Roseman offers an example: In the mid-1960s more than 60 percent of one large federation's

---

82. Berman, *American Jewish Philanthropic Complex*, 89.

83. Marc Lee Raphael, ed., *Understanding American Jewish Philanthropy* (Ktav Publishing, 1979), 28.

84. These pejoratives are taken from Roseman's interviews with federation leaders. Kenneth D. Roseman, "The Men of the Power Structure," in Raphael, *Understanding American Jewish Philanthropy*, 63–64.

85. Diner, *Jews of the United States*, 232.

funds raised came from 4 percent of donors. No major project could be funded without the support of the thirty to forty biggest donors, who constituted the top 1 percent; groups were defunded when they allowed dissidence.[86] Donor control was so complete that researchers investigated whether Jewish communal infrastructure could be controlled by a single person. They concluded that it probably could not, but that "effective control over policy formation in the Jewish community . . . is maintained by a loose coalition of members of the power structure." Their perspectives were known and anticipated, could not be opposed. Despite the appearance of various centers of power, Roseman found that the leading figures were closely connected. "The practical result of this high degree of interrelatedness is that . . . these men constitute a massive and powerful group."[87]

The strict discipline of Jewish institutional life intensified as it became more centralized. Initially, the federations worked alongside the defense organizations in the same communal environment. However, they soon overlapped. By the 1920s, communal concerns had shifted from uplifting the poor to addressing antisemitism. Fewer immigrants were in need of uplift and relief, and fewer were arriving as new laws restricted immigration. At the same time, populist antisemitism escalated. The defense organizations sought to expand their work. Between the 1920s and 1930s they increased staff, opened new local offices, and called on federations to direct funding to defense. When federations themselves were slow to adopt defense work as a new funding priority, the ADL, American Jewish Committee, and American Jewish Congress recruited the federations' donors directly to support their requests, adding them to their boards as advocates. "Federations could not turn down the big donors' requests, for fear of losing their gifts," writes J. J. Goldberg, former editor of the Jewish *Forward*. "The three agencies grew and grew."[88]

In 1944 the defense organizations, the Jewish Labor Committee, and the CJF were further consolidated under the National Community Relations Council (NCRAC).[89] (Goldberg writes that this was the federations' response

86. Kenneth D. Roseman, "The Men of the Power Structure," in Raphael, *Understanding American Jewish Philanthropy*, 64.

87. Roseman, "The Men of the Power Structure," 57, 62.

88. J. J. Goldberg, *Jewish Power* (Addison Wesley Publishing Company, 1996), 105.

89. Jewish Council for Public Affairs, "JCPA: 1944–2019, Celebrating 75 Years of Community Relations & Advocacy," 2019, https://www.jewishpublicaffairs.org/wp-content/uploads/sites/10/2015/09/75th-Anniversary-History-and-Timeline.pdf.

to the defense groups' "blackmail" tactic of organizing major donors to strong-arm the federations' funding decisions.)[90] Within a decade, NCRAC included many more groups and began producing a joint program plan that guided the funding of communal work: a formal agenda for Jewish institutional priorities. Even though the American Jewish Commitee and the ADL formally withdrew from NCRAC for a time (1952–64), chafing at efforts to control them, in practice they stayed close.[91] In 1954 another body, the Conference of Presidents of Major American Jewish Organizations (Presidents' Conference) formed to coordinate Israel-related work among the groups, bringing together the leaders of many of the same Jewish communal organizations in yet another powerful member structure.[92] The overlapping circles formed a powerful exclusion of dissenters that was self-sustaining and durable. Three decades later, in 1982, ADL director Nathan Perlmutter wrote about interlocking boards as a feature of the ecosystem of Jewish organizations: "B'nai B'rith, Hadassah, Mizrachi, National Council of Jewish Women, Jewish War Veterans, American Jewish Committee, American Jewish Congress, National Jewish Community Relations Council—and there are so few Jews! I sometimes think as I visit from organization to organization and as often as not see the same faces that we Jews invented interlocking directorate—how else would there be enough of us to go around?"[93]

Until the mid-twentieth century, these methods shaped Jewish institutions as they engaged in world-building, from establishing social work as a Jewish sphere to framing out Jewish electoral politics. Much of their influence was outside of public view, exerted formally in boardrooms or informally in social settings. But one instance illustrates their reach: In the mid-1950s, the boards used their control over institutional infrastructure to

90. Goldberg, *Jewish Power*, 105.

91. Goldberg, writing as an insider historian of the informal relationships shaping Jewish leadership, notes that after the ADL and AJC quit the NCRAC coordinating structure, NCRAC's director and persuasive "foxy grandfather" Isaiah Minkoff kept them in close participation. "He solicited their views on policy. He wheedled, cajoled, and bullied them into sending representatives to NCRAC strategy meetings...made sure that their members continued to participate in comm-relations committees.... When Anti-Defamation League and the American Jewish Committee formally rejoined NCRAC in 1965, it was a mere technicality." Goldberg, *Jewish Power*, 126.

92. Daniel Judah Elazar, *Community and Polity: The Organizational Dynamics of American Jewry* (Jewish Publication Society, 1995), 114.

93. Nathan Perlmutter and Ruth Ann Perlmutter, *The Real Anti-Semitism in America* (Arbor House, 1982), 69.

literally fence out the left. Under the banner of fighting communism, they purged employees, banned speakers, and cut ties with leftist Jewish groups. In doing so, they converted Jews who did not fit into nonmembers of institutions, and often nonmembers of Jewish community.[94]

The sociality that gave German Jewish institutions their political heft—the interleaving of relationships, spaces, and roles in settings of power—is often described by historians with terms like "elites" or "cliques" that gesture at its exclusivity. As a potent resource that is not defined by formal transactions and is not traceable by the venerable research method of "following the money," elite sociality calls for more theorization as a currency mediating exchanges of power. German Jewish leaders themselves perceived that upper-class social life, business relationships, and political circles intersected as the central address of power that was both personally theirs and also entwined with the nation. They and their peers, members of that sphere extending well beyond the boundaries of Jewish community, wielded the tools that managed and built the state. As business leaders and philanthropists, they deployed capital in infrastructure like railroads, oil, and manufacturing, or in citizen-making institutions like schools, social work, and hospitals. In this sense, their personal stature and the advancement of the settler state were intimately connected. On the strength of their roles in trade, development, and philanthropy, many were elected or appointed as political officials, or consulted as political advisers. As such, their visions, interests, and their feelings about what was rational, from settler colonialism to the *shtadlan* model of communal representation, guided the state's development. This rested crucially on their shared sociality as peers: members of the state-capital class.

Seeing the state-capital class begins with seeing the operations of government, business, and ideology as a co-constituted system. David Harvey calls the conjunction of governance and capital the *state-finance nexus*: "a distinctively capitalist form of state power." This formation arose in the age of European colonialism and industrialization, when state power was reorganized around the logic of expanding private wealth, moving away from older imperatives like guarding sovereign territory.[95] As Cedric Robinson eluci-

94. The anti-left purges of Jewish institutions during the Red Scare of the 1950s are discussed in chapter 2.

95. David Harvey, *The Enigma of Capital and the Crises of Capitalism* (Profile, 2010), 204–5.

dates, capitalism and *racism* are co-constituted. Foundational to capitalism is an exploitable labor class that is made available, dominated, and kept elastic through racism that excludes its members from citizenship. Similarly, the extraction of resources from new lands and constant expansion into new markets is worked through the racist rationales of colonialism as a civilizing, improving, productive force. In other words, racial capitalism is not only economic, but a system of ideological and epistemic structures that convinces people to play their parts.[96] Mapping these ideological structures in the post–World War II United States, Jodi Melamed points to the high value placed on individualism and the belief that wealth is available to those who choose to work hard. The promise of advancement through individual effort naturalizes the violence and dispossession of extraction and works to define racialized, unequal power arrangements as "fair."[97]

Expanding the concept of *state-finance nexus* to account for the combined political, economic, ideological, and social operations of capital, Melamed calls this conjunction the *state-capital formation*.[98] The notion of the state-capital formation provides the groundwork for understanding a *state-capital class*: the set of people who occupy, move between positions in, and have ongoing access to spheres of racialized, capital, political power—spheres in which social and institutional power are co-constituted. As German Jewish leaders recognized, that sociality is built on familial and peer connections, shared social spaces, histories, cultural references, and behavioral expectations, a degree of accountability to group norms, and, conversely, the opportunity and agency that each member of the class enjoys because they are members of this highly empowered sphere. What is added by recognizing the attachment of this sociality to the state-capital formation is that it describes the social spaces and processes through which state-capital logics are naturalized. Indeed, the state-capital class forms and occupies what sociologist Pierre Bourdieu calls a *habitus*: an ecosystem of shared relationships, expectations, and history that determines what individual and collective practices are possible, "an internal law" that "ensures the active presence of past experiences, which, deposited in each organism in the form of schemes of

---

96. See Cedric J. Robinson, *Black Marxism: The Making of the Black Radical Tradition* (University of North Carolina Press, 2021 [1983]).

97. Jodi Melamed, *Represent and Destroy: Rationalizing Violence in the New Racial Capitalism* (University of Minnesota Press, 2011), 8, 31.

98. Melamed, *Represent and Destroy*, x.

perception, thought and action, tend to guarantee the 'correctness' of practices and their constancy over time."[99]

When German Jewish philanthropists contemplated teaching American ways to European Jewish immigrants at the turn of the nineteenth century, they intended skills like cleanliness, etiquette, and civics. But within a few decades their institutions had taken on a new role: They became cultural and capital conduits for upwardly mobile Jews to enter the state-capital class. Eastern European Jewish immigrants rose relatively quickly from poverty to accumulation that moved them into the middle and upper classes. In part, they were inducted into that role through the German Jewish institutions that eventually allowed them membership. They were also helped by fair historical winds that favored the work patterns of Eastern European Jewish immigrants (in tailoring or trade rather than construction, for instance), to their own efforts at unionization, and to their ability to move as "white urban dwellers in the heady years of the 1920s, [who] had taken advantage of the prosperity" of that decade. Each subsequent generation was increasingly professional and white collar. Even antisemitism did not thwart their progress: Jews had more constrained routes to education and economic advancement because of anti-Jewish exclusions, but not necessarily less successful routes, as Diner writes. By 1940, Eastern European Jews had gathered enough wealth that, as a group, their economic distinction from German Jews had faded.[100]

As Jewish communities assimilated and entered a new class stratum, the Progressive Era institutions again served as sites for inducting Jews into new worlds, inviting them to become members of the charitable class rather than recipients of institutional aid. The institutions cultivated fundraising practices that offered status to donors and emphasized public performance and spectatorship, creating pressure on men in wealthy social circles to best each other's donations. As early as the 1930s, federations held lavish dinners and "parlor sessions" with wealthy invitees who knew each other or did business together, and they called publicly on each attendee to announce their pledge. This practice, known as "card calling," became a de facto demand to demonstrate personal wealth or experience public shame.[101] *Fortune* magazine described the approach: "Each guest rises as his name is called, and the chair-

---

99. Pierre Bourdieu, *The Logic of Practice* (Stanford University Press, 1990), 54.

100. Diner, *Jews of the United States*, 229–31.

101. Bram Goldsmith, "Parlor Meetings," in Raphael, *Understanding American Jewish Philanthropy*, 103. See also Lee O'Brien, *American Jewish Organizations and Israel* (Institute for Palestine Studies, 1986), 123.

man coolly asks, 'All right, Jack, what will you give?' Or perhaps, 'Well now, Morris, you gave $25,000 five years ago, what will you give this time?'"[102] For "the wealthiest and most prestigious people," Daniel Elazar writes, contributions were "in effect a necessary tax that had to be paid in order to remain in the good graces of one's fellows."[103]

Fundraising as an important class-making function—a means of constructing donors' identities through associations with wealth and largesse—expanded in each subsequent decade. In the 1940s and '50s, Jewish upward mobility helped catalyze the development of a donor class. Additionally, the advent of income taxation, and new laws that allowed taxpayers to lessen their tax burden by donating to charities, made charitable donations a financial strategy as well as a community-minded gesture. The expansion of federal income taxation in the first half of the 1940s meant that more than 42 million people were newly subject to taxes (about one-third of the US population in 1945). As lawmakers and attorneys advocated for charitable tax exemptions (led by attorneys supporting Jewish philanthropies), they fueled the development of the charitable sector. A host of new federations and private foundations raised increasing, record-breaking funds, even as the charitable needs of US Jewish communities waned.[104] The new laws also changed the social calculus of donating—especially donating in public. Supporters could contribute as much or more than before, while donations cost less because they could be written off of taxes. And the numbers kept growing: more businessmen with funds to donate and taxes to abate, and more institutional fundraising.

The alchemy of dinners, honors, and public performances of charity was especially powerful because it lifted fundraising out of the realm of Jewish particularism, aloof from whatever charitable cause was being funded, and instead invited donors to an elite party scene where wealth and its rituals were the subject of the event. It tapped the social anxieties of the newly wealthy seeking to secure their class status, and provided them an arena in

102. Robert Sheehan, "The Miracle of Jewish Giving," *Fortune Magazine*, January 1966. Cited in Jack Wertheimer, "Current Trends in American Jewish Philanthropy," *American Jewish Year Book* 97 (1997): 11.

103. Daniel Elazar, "The Jewish Political Tradition and the English-Speaking World," in Mittleman et al., *Jewish Polity and American Civil Society*, 7.

104. These concurrently shifting conditions in tax policy, charitable organizing, and Jewish communal needs are historicized in Berman, *American Jewish Philanthropic Complex*, 55–56, 62, 74.

which to build business and political relationships.[105] The ADL made diligent use of these levers. Learning from the federations, it picked up the practice of card-calling dinners, and from the 1960s onward continued to expand its servicing of the social needs of capital and its uses of peer pressure.[106] Lester Waldman, the ADL's director of planning from 1959 to 1973, recounted inventing empty, prestigious-sounding honorifics for donors, then using the occasion of honoring them to invite and pressure more donors. He said:

> [We would] ... issue a membership card in an amorphous organization to be known as the Society of Fellows. . . . Those who gave contributions $1000 and up received metal plaques making them members of the Society of Fellows. . . . It was discovered that ADL's leadership around the country ... were substantial people who were able to make individual contributions ... up to 5000 dollars in a given year. . . . [T]he Society of Fellows adopted [the dinner] methodology and gradually began to go into the larger communities, choose one community leader and run a dinner in his honor, with "card calling."[107]

ADL Society of Fellows dinners alone soon raised more cash for the ADL than the federations allocated them each year, and in doing so evaded the federations' efforts to direct Jewish communal funding to other work.[108]

Although these practices developed in tandem with the emerging Jewish upper class, the ADL's leaders also recognized that conspicuous contribution was not a specifically Jewish practice and could appeal to a larger set of wealthy and aspiring donors. Just like Jewish donors, non-Jewish donors were attracted to fundraising events by the social and business rewards of donations that pleased powerful friends and by tax breaks that heavily subsidized their donations and made them economical. Indeed, Nathan Perlmutter, on

105. On charitable giving as a performance of investment in American capitalism and social order, and of rejection of socialist alternatives in the first half of the twentieth century, see Alisa Zhulina, "Performing Philanthropy from Andrew Carnegie to Bill Gates," *Performance Research* 23, no. 6 (2018): 50–57.

106. Notably, these efforts were contemporaneous with the ADL's work on civil rights. The two projects did not exist in contradiction; instead, they underscore the purely legal, formal, and transactional conception of equality on which the ADL's civil rights work rested, and its commitment to preserving rather than reorganizing economic and political structures.

107. Lester J. Waldman, "Vol Vc: Waldman, Lester J., 1985–1987," Box 1, Folder 1, MS-365, pp. 108–9, B'nai B'rith Anti-Defamation League Oral Histories, American Jewish Archives, Cincinnati, Ohio.

108. Waldman, "Vol Vc," 108–9.

becoming the ADL's assistant national director in 1973, made ramping up dinners a priority because they allowed the agency to bring in many more donors, including "about 50 percent" of attendees "who couldn't care less about your cause."[109] Accordingly, programs for conspicuous contribution expanded along with their potential audiences. In the early 1970s, for instance, as upper-class women took up feminist calls to define themselves beyond their marriages, the federations began offering wealthy women a status symbol that implied their financial independence. The Lion of Judah program, launched in Miami in 1972, conferred a golden pin on women who donated. That talisman, encrusted with specific jewels reflecting the amount of their donation, became a national offering in 1980.[110] Such social fundraising practices became lucrative essential elements of agency budgets, ensuring their continued use across the sector.[111]

The exalted social function of awards dinners meant that they also served as celebrity-studded platforms for the ADL's political advocacy and for narrating ideas about democracy, rights, and the ADL itself. The ADL gave its first "America's Democratic Legacy" award in 1949 to President Truman, which

109. Perlmutter indicated that such dinners were "becoming the heart of many a Jewish fund raising operation." Other histories also reflect the move to claim a share of the communal wealth that was increasing in the post–World War II decades. For instance, Goldsmith describes the careful and deliberate cultivation of the social setting in LA in the late 1960s to elicit higher donations. It appeared successful: Between 1968 and 1969, as LA dinnergoers increased their major gifts by 60 percent. Nathan Perlmutter, "Vol Ib: Perlmutter, Nathan, 1985–1987," Box 1, Folder 1, MS-365, p. 57, B'nai B'rith Anti-Defamation League Oral Histories, American Jewish Archives, Cincinnati, Ohio; Goldsmith, "Parlor Meetings," in Raphael, *Understanding American Jewish Philanthropy*, 107.

110. Arielle Angel, editor-in-chief at *Jewish Currents*, brought the Lion of Judah to my attention. See United Jewish Federation of Greater Stamford, New Canaan and Darien, Inc., "Women's Philanthropy," https://web.archive.org/web/20210803020044/https://www.ujf.org/womens-philanthropy.

111. The dinner circuit remains a force in fundraising and networking. The ADL's 2024 annual Home Furnishings Industry Dinner raised $1.7 million, for instance. The UJA-Federation's Wall Street division raised $31 million, or nearly 15 percent of the UJA annual budget, at each of its 2018 and 2019 annual dinners. Bill McLoughlin, "ADL Home Furnishings Dinner Raises over $1.7M," *Furniture Today*, June 26, 2024; UJA-Federation of New York, "UJA-Federation of New York's Wall Street Dinner Raises More than $31 Million," December 12, 2019, https://www.prnewswire.com/news-releases/uja-federation-of-new-yorks-wall-street-dinner-raises-more-than-31-million-300974348.html; UJA-Federation of New York, "Record-Breaking $31 Million Raised at UJA-Federation of New York's Wall Street Dinner," December 13, 2018, https://www.prnewswire.com/news-releases/record-breaking-31-million-raised-at-uja-federation-of-new-yorks-wall-street-dinner-300765248.html.

Truman accepted along with a reciprocal request that the ADL support his proposed fair employment bills. The award provided the ADL with a White House ceremony and a presidential endorsement of its "vigorous educational program and practical efforts to foster an understanding of democratic rights and responsibilities," a credential that helped solidify the ADL's reputation as a political insider and a trusted source for educational materials on civil rights and citizenship.[112] In subsequent decades, the ADL continued the practice of giving awards to sitting presidents—Eisenhower, Kennedy, Johnson, Reagan, and George W. Bush—as well as other political and corporate figureheads. Over time, it added national and local awards in an array of communities and industries where it aimed to develop relationships as well as raise funds: legal practice, law enforcement, statesmanship, entertainment industry, film, home furnishings, technology, consumer technology, democracy, human rights, women's achievement, and men's achievement.[113]

The fundraising, awards, and celebrity circuit produced the institutions' leadership circles, building a sociality that circulated through directorate structures and extended outward into powerful corporate and political spheres. The threads of interconnection translated to material power, and indeed were the ADL's primary means of getting things done. This arrangement surprised ADL national chairman Maxwell E. Greenberg, an attorney who had assumed, before taking up the ADL position, that "rational argument was extremely important" in policymaking. At the ADL, though, he found that cultivating ties with those in power superseded all other kinds of advocacy. "Much of the rest is a form of window dressing," Greenberg explained. "We may need the full-page ad in the newspaper in order to say to our constituency and, indeed, to say to the non-Jewish of the United States that the ADL exists and this is our job . . . but not [for] the purpose of changing anyone's mind."[114]

Recounting another example of the material power of relationships, ADL director Benjamin Epstein explained how an ADL awards dinner led to the

112. Jewish Telegraphic Agency, "Truman Receives ADL Annual Award in White House Ceremony; Pledges Civil Rights Fight," April 7, 1949.

113. By the 1960s, the ADL was habitually running fundraising dinners that leveraged donors' social relationships "on a trade basis, e.g. functions are held within the liquor trade, laundry trade, etc." Kirman, "Major Programs of the B'nai B'rith Anti-Defamation League," 49.

114. Maxwell E. Greenberg, "Vol IIc: Greenberg, Maxwell E., 1985–1987," Box 1, Folder 1, MS-365, pp. 118–19, B'nai B'rith Anti-Defamation League Oral Histories, American Jewish Archives, Cincinnati, Ohio.

1977 law preventing US corporations from honoring "the Arab boycott"—a campaign by the Arab League since 1951 requiring that its business partners boycott Israeli firms and any firms doing business with Israel. The ADL had long opposed the Arab League boycott, but it had deemed it "an impotent affair" in the earlier part of the 1960s.[115] During the US oil crisis of 1973–74, though, access to Arab oil became critical, and the boycott gained leverage. The ADL resumed its campaigning for legislation to block it. "What happened was this," Epstein began. "I was sitting at an ADL dinner ... [honoring] the president of General Mills. I sat next to Irving Shapiro, who was then the General Counsel of DuPont."[116] Shapiro was a longtime friend of ADL chairman Burton Joseph. "He turned to me and said 'Ben, you know next year I'm going to be the Chief Executive Officer of DuPont and I also just might be elected Chairman of the Business Roundtable [a newly formed conclave of major corporations to exert political influence].'" Given this new opportunity, Shapiro exhorted Epstein to think like a power broker. By gathering a few highly placed guests at the dinner to "go over in the corner and talk for five minutes," he proposed they could leverage corporate and US state power to crush the boycott.[117] That informal conversation—which included Shapiro, the president of General Mills, the chairman of IBM, and ADL leadership—did indeed produce a strategic partnership that forced the Business Roundtable companies to agree with the ADL on terms for refusing the boycott. In turn, that alliance drew the secretary of state into direct conversations with the ADL and corporate leaders. Finally, it forced the Carter administration and Congress to hammer out and pass legislation that rendered the Arab boycott effectively illegal. The episode formed a lasting relationship between the ADL and the Business Roundtable, which Epstein rightly characterized as "the leadership of the power structure of America."[118]

The ADL's oral histories, as well as scholarly histories of Jewish communal organizations, are replete with similar stories that read like standard political and corporate memoir: acquaintances slotted into positions of authority,

115. Arnold Forster, "The Arab Boycott Misfires," *ADL Bulletin*, January 1964, 1–2.

116. These events seem to take place in November 1976. ADL gave its Americanism award to General Mills board chairman James P. McFarland. See *The American Israelite*, "To Head ADL's Awards Dinner," October 28, 1976.

117. Benjamin R. Epstein, "Vol Ia: Epstein, Benjamin R., 1985–1987," Box 1, Folder 1, MS-365, p. 151, B'nai B'rith Anti-Defamation League Oral Histories, American Jewish Archives, Cincinnati, Ohio.

118. Epstein, "Vol Ia," 151–59.

casual conversations that drove policy, private transactions that changed the balance of power. As Jewish communal institutions transitioned out of German Jewish leadership, their practices ensured that the bulk of their budgets, and their donors and leaders, continued to come from a sector deeply invested in the state-capital formation, opposed to redistributions of power, and insulated from the needs and interests of the larger community.[119] With remarkable consistency throughout their first hundred years, they enforced a conservative politics by which the broad state-capital class stood to gain, articulating it as Jewish communal politics. "I believe," Epstein explained in 1986, "whether we want to say it publicly or not, that the power structure of this country is still in the hands of big business and big business wants to work with the Jewish community . . . they see the Jewish community as a powerful lobby . . . having aims and desires that are not too far from theirs."[120]

The ADL's origin story hews closely to the origin story of the United States (far more closely than any parallels with Black history), beginning from a strong ideological and affective foundation in settler colonialism. While initially aiming to discipline immigrants, the ADL became a mechanism for absorption: a kind of conveyor belt to middle- and upper-class whiteness. As the state-capital class developed in the United States, the ADL developed along with it, reaping the benefits of growing Jewish incomes, and, more significantly, the benefits of a powerful informal sociality among corporate and political actors. Rather than a platform for challenging the state, that position made the ADL its close partner and defender.

119. Goldsmith notes that in the 1950s and '60s, millions of dollars were raised in parlor sessions for the federations. In 1979, the same fundraising model produced the vast bulk of funds from a few donors: 7 percent had given 76 percent of all funds—and just 3 percent had given 63 percent. Goldsmith, "Parlor Meetings," in Raphael, *Understanding American Jewish Philanthropy*, 103.

120. Epstein, "Vol Ia," 159.

TWO

———

Red Jews, Anticolonial Arabs, Black Leftists, and Colorblind Anticommunism

THE '50S AND '60S

IN 2016, THE CALIFORNIA LEGISLATURE mandated that the state's Department of Education create a model curriculum for teaching ethnic studies. The law had been fifty years in the making. In 1968, California students had demanded that public education be a platform for interrogating, resisting, and transforming systems of repressive racial and economic power rather than reinforcing them. They had organized, protested, and put forward a new vision for education under the banner of the Third World Liberation Front.[1] Ethnic studies developed from those origins: the field attends to Black, Indigenous, Latinx/Chicanx, and Asian/Pacific Islander experiences of colonization and decolonization. The 2016 ethnic studies law codified the commitment to teach it and assembled a panel of ethnic studies experts to develop the model. But when they published their first draft in May 2019, the Anti-Defamation League, the California Legislative Jewish Caucus, and a handful of Zionist organizations roared into action to shut it down. By 2021 the opposition groups had gutted the work of ethnic studies educators. They called instead for teaching about diversity in a contributionist mode: cataloguing various groups' contributions to the nation and celebrating the state itself rather than studying those groups' analyses of colonization and resistance. Citing ethnic studies' attention to Palestinian experiences of colonization and resistance in particular, they denounced the entire field as "antisemitic" and "radical." Another powerful national campaign against antiracist education was emerging at the same time—the

———

1. See organizers' articulation of "self-determination" in Karen Umemoto, "'On Strike!' San Francisco State College Strike, 1968–69: The Role of Asian American Students," *Amerasia Journal* 15, no. 1 (1989): 3–41, 16.

63

white/multiracial nationalist and Christian Right "anti–Critical Race Theory" (anti-CRT) movement—and the opponents of ethnic studies soon adopted its language.[2]

Although the inclusion of Palestinian voices was the spark that set off attacks on ethnic studies by Zionist groups, the attacks soon widened. More conservative groups joined in. The study of settler colonialism, capitalism, racism, and political resistance movements writ large was denounced as "neo-Marxism" and "Soviet communist propaganda."[3] Scholars were denounced as extremists. ADL regional director Seth Brysk described the ethnic studies model curriculum as "nothing more than an attempt by fringe activists to highjack the model ethnic studies curriculum . . . in the service of radical political goals."[4] Where the anti-CRT movement had propagated the claim that learning about racism harmed white children and sowed discontent, the anti-ethnic studies movement adapted it. Its proponents claimed that Jewish children were harmed by bringing Palestinian voices into the classroom, or indeed any Indigenous and antiracist voices in sympathy with Palestinian anticolonial struggle. Unlike the anti-CRT movement, though, anti-ethnic studies forces described themselves as caring deeply about both racism and ethnic studies. Asserting that protecting civil rights required dismantling ethnic studies, conservative groups derailed policy that had been hard-won by communities of color and immigrants and asserted control over educators, school districts, and antiracist education.[5]

How could the language of racism and inclusion become so inverted, and so weaponized? Saree Makdisi calls this process *affirmation as denial*, as he writes about civil rights talk as a primary means of denying the Nakba, anti-Palestinian dispossession, and genocide.[6] In this procedure, tightly choreo-

2. Emmaia Gelman, "The World Upside-Down: Zionist Institutions, Civil Rights Talk, and the New Cold War on Ethnic Studies," *Critical Ethnic Studies* 8, no. 2 (2023). On the claims of the anti-CRT movement, see Kevin Lawrence Henry et al., "Conjuring the Devil: Historicizing Attacks on Critical Race Theory," *Thresholds* 46, no. 1 (2023).

3. Gelman, "The World Upside-Down"; Maya Phillips, "I Grew Up with Soviet Communism; Now as a Trustee I See It Embedded in California's Ethnic Studies," *California Globe*, September 14, 2024.

4. Jackson Richman and Sean Savage, "Proposed Anti-Israel Ethnic-Studies Curriculum in California Has Jewish Community on Alert," Jewish News Syndicate, August 2, 2019.

5. Gelman, "The World Upside-Down."

6. Saree Makdisi, *Tolerance Is a Wasteland: Palestine and the Culture of Denial* (University of California Press, 2022), 45. *Nakba* is the common term for the expulsion of Palestinians and the destruction of Palestinian land, life, and history during and after the founding of the

graphed performances of care about people and their experiences of marginalization are used to signal that the performers (who may be people, institutions, or policies themselves) are moral actors who closely attend to injustice. When they refuse to recognize the *foundational* injustice, their position as moral, caring advocates works to deny the very reality of that injustice, obscure the people who experience it, and deny the denial itself.[7] The conditions for these affirmations and disavowals arose in the mid-twentieth century, as the United States entered the Cold War. In that period, the ADL turned from its focus on fighting antisemitic defamation as a Jewish institution, and became a national agency "fighting prejudice"—an affirmation of rights, interwoven with anticommunism, that became a platform for authorizing US imperial expansion. In the same period, the ADL and major Jewish organizations pursued anticommunist measures to change the meaning of Jewish identity, which in turn dramatically changed the meaning of "care" for Jewish rights. This chapter details the development of the ADL's work to produce anti-prejudice, anticommunism, and race-liberal citizenship together, and to try to reconstitute the meaning of Jewishness as their embodiment.

The close of World War II and the advent of the Cold War brought a deep shift in the politics of race in the United States—a "racial break," as Howard Winant has termed it.[8] The violence of European colonial regimes in Asia and Africa and the Nazi genocide in Europe underwrote a popular understanding of racial supremacism as a moral wrong and a counterforce to democracy. European fascism, which had produced a decade of war and

---

Israeli state in 1948. Rabea Eghbariah describes *Nakba* as an ongoing process overlapping with and including episodes of genocide and apartheid: "Meaning 'Catastrophe' in Arabic, the term 'al-Nakba' (النكبة) is often used to refer to the ruinous process of establishing the State of Israel in Palestine. But the Nakba has undergone a metamorphosis; it has evolved from a historical calamity into a brutally sophisticated structure of oppression." Rabea Eghbariah, "Toward Nakba as a Legal Concept," *Columbia Law Review* 124, no. 4 (2024): 887–992. Mitra Rastegar traces how such affirmations of care for rights are applied to individual "good" Muslims through "humanizing" narratives that reinforce the demand to surveil all Muslims as a potential population-level threat, so that "bad" ones may be policed. As Rastegar shows, affirmation/denial not only performs care for injustice, and hides the foundational injustice, but also demands further repression in the name of defending the inclusivity of the liberal nation. See Rastegar, *Tolerance and Risk: How US Liberalism Racializes Muslims* (University of Minnesota Press, 2021), 10–12 and chap. 1.

7. Mitra Rastegar, *Tolerance and Risk: How US Liberalism Racializes Muslims* (University of Minnesota Press, 2021), 10–12.

8. Howard Winant, *The World Is a Ghetto: Race and Democracy Since World War II* (Basic Books, 2001), 142–43.

anguish, was understood as a product of racist nationalism and the drive for territorial expansion. Opposing racism and resisting fascism became popular imperatives, twinned and woven into US political and cultural life. Biological notions of difference had served to naturalize slavery, Jim Crow, race-based labor and anti-immigrant laws, and discrimination against Jews and Catholics. Now, such ideas were discredited and reconceived as dangerous to democracy. Civic leaders set out to uproot such ideas and consign them to the past.

White supremacy, colonialism, and capitalism had long been the subject of critique from below. From the beginning of the twentieth century, Black sociologists had been producing research literature on the racist dynamics of systems including labor, urban geography, and policing, informed by political organizing against race and class subjugation. A rich public conversation on race and racism had run through the Black press, the labor movement, and major political organizations including the NAACP, National Negro Congress, and the Council on African Affairs. Among them, leftists and liberals alike comprehended racism as a tool of capital and colonialism—an organizing logic of systems of power, not simply the prejudice of individuals.[9] In European colonies and in the US, they made clear, racism was a tactic for dominating workers. Race was comprehended not just as an identity that ought to be overlooked in the interest of "tolerance," but rather as a set of historical and present conditions. Whiteness, too, had meaning that could not be overlooked for the sake of unity. Built on exploitation and overconfident expectations of dominance, it was attached to what Robin D. G. Kelley calls the "profligate character" of the white ruling class.[10] As the war drew to a close, Black organizers saw the United States taking on an increased role in reinforcing racialized power, rather than dismantling it. Instead of ending racist colonial regimes, in international treaty negotiations the United States was moving to replace such regimes with its own imperialism.[11] Opposing racism meant challenging a broad array of repressive systems.

But the national postwar fervor for breaking with racism did not follow the lines of Black critique. Instead, efforts by the Jewish defense organizations, other white-led religious and civic institutions, funders, and political

9. See Penny M. Von Eschen, *Race Against Empire: Black Americans and Anticolonialism, 1937–1957* (Cornell University Press, 1997), 14–21, and Robin D. G. Kelley, *Race Rebels: Culture, Politics, and the Black Working Class* (Free Press, 1996), chap. 5.

10. Kelley, *Race Rebels*, 110.

11. Von Eschen, *Race Against Empire*, 11–13.

actors advanced what Jodi Melamed theorizes as post-break *racial liberalism.* As German Jewish institutions had done for decades already, racial liberalism focused on legal approaches within existing systems, using the language of egalitarianism and civil rights, and psychological approaches to breeding tolerance and opposing hate, as the solution to the "race problem." Its proponents invoked both law and morality to assert that US citizens (although not noncitizens) should be understood and treated no differently on the basis of membership in a racial or ethnic group. "White liberal Americans . . . were to become moral heroes by ridding themselves of racial prejudice and skewed beliefs . . . [and] antiracism was absorbed into American nationalism," Melamed writes. Indeed, performing this enlightenment became a marker of good, deserving white citizenship.[12] In 1946, a Truman executive order establishing the Presidential Committee on Civil Rights set out its legal terms: "The preservation of civil rights guaranteed by the Constitution is essential to domestic tranquility, national security, the general welfare, and the continued existence of our free institutions. . . . The action of individuals who take the law into their own hands and inflict summary punishment and wreak personal vengeance . . . gravely threatens our form of government."[13] In defining justice in terms of the rights already outlined in US law, and in directing the state to police individuals who violated them rather than seeking to change the state itself, Truman helped cement this narrow approach.

It was the advent of the Cold War that pushed US officials and NGOs to offer the liberal state as a solution to racism. During World War II, the United States had positioned itself as an opponent of fascism and defender of democracy. The stark racism that pervaded US law and social structures, especially Jim Crow laws, belied that claim and hampered the effort to cultivate global allies against the Soviet Union. The federal government adopted domestic civil rights efforts and racial egalitarianism as a tool of anti-Soviet, anticommunist diplomacy, as Mary Dudziak documents. Through a range of efforts—from supporting the overturning of segregation laws to disseminating stories about egalitarian life in writing and by facilitating the travel of Black "celebrities and political figures . . . who would say the right thing"—they aimed to show US society on a constant trajectory of racial progress, buoyed by

12. Jodi Melamed, *Represent and Destroy: Rationalizing Violence in the New Racial Capitalism* (University of Minnesota Press, 2011), 21–22.

13. Harry Truman, "Executive Order 9808 of December 5, 1957, Establishing the President's Committee on Civil Rights," Code of Federal Regulations, 11 FR 14153.

capitalism's economic opportunity and the celebration of individualism.[14] Beginning with its 1952 amicus brief urging the US Supreme Court to rule against school segregation in *Brown v. Board of Education*, the "Truman administration [discussed] the negative impact on US foreign relations that a prosegregation decision might have" and outlined that a constitutional ruling against segregation would "show that the principle of racial equality was already there in the governing document of American democracy."[15] As the US political apparatus adopted support for this brand of "antiracism," many civil rights advocates made it their platform, whether in the hope of seizing the opportunity to leverage change or—as in the case of the ADL—because it aligned with their own ideological commitments.[16]

Unquestionably, postwar organizing made significant changes in conditions of racism, even where movements to redistribute power ran up against liberal efforts to preserve it. Black organizers, in collaboration with communists, were so successful in making civil rights a presidential campaign issue in 1948 that Truman was forced to abandon the Southern segregationist vote and voice strong support for civil rights demands just days before his election. That about-face won him the presidency, with Black voters providing the margin of victory. "For the first time since Reconstruction, civil rights occupied a central place on the political stage. Never before had so many written and said so much about the Negro's right to equality," writes historian Harvard Sitkoff.[17] On the other hand, these measures reinforced a definition of racial equality as disregarding race, and a reconception of equality in terms of individuals' right to buy from, vote in support of, soldier for, or otherwise participate in existing structures under the constant reassurance of "regardless of race or creed." As Melamed theorizes, these moves further entrenched white supremacy as the organizing logic of state and capital. They masked the ongoing violence of those systems and limited the conceptions of "difference" that could be recognized under the banner of inclusion: race, ethnicity, eventually gender and sexuality; not class, history, or myriad other

14. Mary Dudziak, *Cold War Civil Rights: Race and the Image of American Democracy* (Princeton University Press, 2000), 61.

15. Dudziak, *Cold War Civil Rights*, 90.

16. On the NAACP's Cold War turn away from anti-imperialism and toward anticommunism, see Gerald Horne's summary in Horne, "Who Lost the Cold War? Africans and African Americans," *Diplomatic History* 20, no. 4 (1996): 613–26.

17. Harvard Sitkoff, "Harry Truman and the Election of 1948: The Coming of Age of Civil Rights in American Politics," *Journal of Southern History* 37, no. 4 (1971): 598, 614.

aspects of being. As the US sought to assert its global reach during the Cold War, these claims facilitated the movement of US capital into decolonizing global spaces.[18]

The field on which the Jewish defense organizations took up *opposing racism* was intergroup relations, also called community relations. Intergroup relations and its action arm, intergroup education, drew together converging threads of history. It drew on efforts in the 1930s to gather religious leaders in dialogue, and it now emphasized solutions addressed to the masses.[19] It drew on wartime projects to connect the US population to efforts to build and defend the state, which included surveys to measure public opinion and, in the other direction, advertising campaigns urging national unity. It drew also on the rise of sciences, including psychology and sociology, and a modernist public regard for scientific expertise and measurement as the foundation of modern government. The idea of intergroup relations was a technocratic one: Intergroup conflict had been identified as a problem for democracy, and the institutions of democracy would work methodically to eradicate it. Much of the method they conceived was education. If racial and religious difference was irrelevant, conflict over difference was irrational and could be resolved through explanation and exposure to correct information. Willard Johnson, divinity school president and an official of the National Conference of Christians and Jews, wrote in 1947: "Until a few years ago, intergroup education was non-existent, or at least lost in the maze of general education. This is an amazing fact in light of the many widespread epidemics of hatred and conflict which have blighted our American democracy. The Knownothings, the Nativists, the A.P.A., and K.K.K., are major examples of persecution and discrimination. . . . But, thanks to the Nazis, Fascists and our own demagogues, many Americans now accept the fact that intergroup conflict injures everyone in a free society, and are working at solutions."[20]

Since education was the movement's key strategy, its proponents sought to propagate it as a coordinated national undertaking—just as the war effort had been national, economic problems that spurred intergroup resentment were national, and the circulation of opinion, too, had become the province

18. Melamed, *Represent and Destroy*, 41–42, 54.

19. Ariana Horn, "Paved with Good Intentions: The Rise and Fall of the 'Human Relations' Movement in Milwaukee, 1934–1980" (PhD diss., University of Wisconsin-Madison, 2015), 9–10.

20. Willard Johnson, "A National Strategy for Intergroup Education," *Social Science* 22, no. 1 (1947): 35–39.

of national news and advertising companies. Johnson wrote: "[A] group of unrelated local units cannot solve a national problem.... *The basic ideas of intergroup harmony must become a part of all the educational institutions of the land.*"[21] The year 1944 launched a decade of infrastructure-building for "tolerance" as a matter of civic engagement and governance. Community relations councils formed all over the United States, some by law or executive order, others by civic-minded volunteers.[22] By the late 1940s they were producing a frenzy of programming, with "hundreds of private and governmental agencies employing thousands of persons and spending millions of dollars in a sincere effort to do something about" racial and religious tensions.[23] The ADL and American Jewish Committee, CIO unions, the American Civil Liberties Union, the National Urban League, and the NAACP were joined by national religious organizations as well as civic and government agencies.[24] Sociologist Robin M. Williams identified seventy-five organizations addressing race through intergroup relations work via community organi-

21. Emphasis in original. Johnson, "A National Strategy for Intergroup Education," 37–38.

22. More and more community relations groups formed as the movement gathered force. The ADL's 1957 *Directory of Community Relations Agencies* includes ninety-five agencies with full listings, and forty-two more that did not respond to the ADL's survey with information to include. See Anti-Defamation League of B'nai B'rith, *Public Human Relations Agencies; 1957 Directory.*

23. Robin M. Williams, *The Reduction of Intergroup Tensions: A Survey of Research on Problems of Ethnic, Racial, and Religious Group Relations* (Social Science Research Network, 1947), 3. Although Stuart Svonkin cites the NAACP as a partner in intergroup relations, it was not consistently so. In at least some local instances over the two decades in which intergroup relations dominated approaches to racism, the NAACP opposed it as too slow and too optional for white people and institutions resistant to change. Ariana Horn documents the NAACP's role in opposition to intergroup relations and in favor of "direct action" and legislative work in Milwaukee, for instance. Svonkin, *Jews Against Prejudice: American Jews and the Fight for Civil Liberties* (Columbia University Press, 1997), 17; Horn, "Paved with Good Intentions," 33.

24. Along with the defense organizations, many other Jewish groups also turned to intergroup relations work after World War II. They included Hadassah, the Jewish Labor Council, Jewish War Veterans, the National Council of Jewish Women, the Union of American Hebrew Congregations, the Union of Orthodox Jewish Congregations, the National Women's League for Conservative Judaism, and the Women's American ORT. They also included over one hundred community relations councils, "which are usually branches of the American Jewish Committee, ADL, or American Jewish Congress, or affiliated to one of the hundreds of local federations." Lee O'Brien, *American Jewish Organizations and Israel* (Institute for Palestine Studies, 1986), 49.

zing, education, culture work, and legal advocacy.[25] By 1947 the field had a center of gravity in the University of Chicago's Committee on Education, Training, and Research on Race Relations (CETRRR). Housing a scientific approach to the race relations problem, it gathered academics, published a field-defining journal, and received funding from the Carnegie Corporation and Rockefeller Foundation. Tracing the history, Leah Gordon notes that the CETRRR served as an anchor that kept race relations research focused on individuals, even as some researchers urged attention to the structures and "the general situation." The appeal of an individual focus was that personal attitudes could be readily measured, satisfying the hunger of policymakers and funders for a scientific problem-solving approach. Just as important, academic researchers who gathered under its umbrella often presumed that economic and social structures were natural and immutable; the notion that liberal capitalism was just the order of things sharply limited their imagined possibilities for change.[26]

Initially, the Jewish defense agencies played a particularist role, measuring and intervening in antisemitism and identifying connections between anti-semitism's prevalence and broader threats to US democracy. In 1944 the ADL published a book by Sigmund Livingston titled *Must Men Hate*, which emphasized these themes. "Most of the lies published by anti-Semites in this country are inspired by Nazis trying to sabotage American unity and to break the spirit of our democracy," wrote Livingston. "It is not mere coincidence that almost every hate-monger is also . . . against our war strategy. . . . Tolerance of intolerance is the greatest weakness of American democracy."[27] As the intergroup relations movement progressed, though, the defense organizations—the ADL in particular—recast themselves as universalists advocating for everyone's rights, making democracy the object of protection. In its role as clearinghouse for the work of other groups and as a prodigious producer of its own materials, the ADL rose to a much more prominent position in intergroup relations. It was in this capacity that the ADL was transformed from a Jewish communal organization to a quasi-state agency, as the next chapter elaborates.

Intergroup relations was a deeply ideological project: The ADL described its school programming, Education for Democracy, as "a second front" in the

25. Williams, *Reduction of Intergroup Tensions.*
26. Leah N. Gordon, *From Power to Prejudice: The Rise of Racial Individualism in Midcentury America* (University of Chicago Press, 2016), 79–80.
27. Sigmund Livingston, *Must Men Hate* (Harper and Brothers, 1944), 124.

Cold War.[28] In one sense, it aimed to remodel people to better fit US values, much as Progressive Era reforms had intended. American Jewish Committee president John Slawson likened intergroup relations agencies to health departments and used the language of "hygiene" to describe anti-prejudice work.[29] In another sense, intergroup relations aimed to undermine US political groups that questioned the organization of the state or sought to change it. Like other intergroup relations agencies, the ADL attacked Soviet communism and anyone perceived to be in league with communism, labeling them totalitarian. It called on "enlightened citizens, rather than conforming drones" to reject communist organizations' assessments of social ills.[30] In more oblique terms, intergroup relations venerated US pluralism, democratic values, and orderly progress as the basis of antiracism and antifascism, and they rendered "undemocratic" a much broader set of civil rights and antiracist groups: those advocating anticolonialism, Afrocentrism, redistribution of wealth, or other devolutions of power.[31] In these stark terms, intergroup relations enacted what Charisse Burden-Stelly theorizes as the co-constructed Red Scare/Black Scare. It leveraged anticommunism to recruit Black as well as white leaders against antiracism, and leveraged racism to recruit the white underclass to support the interests of a white upper class.[32]

The document that served as intellectual infrastructure for intergroup relations was economist Gunnar Myrdal's report, *An America Dilemma: The Negro Problem and Modern Democracy*, published in 1944. This sweeping assessment was commissioned by the Carnegie Corporation, which selected Myrdal in part because, as a Swede, he was presumed free of "background or traditions of imperialism which might lessen the confidence of the Negroes

28. Anti-Defamation League, *Not the Work of a Day: The Story of the Anti-Defamation League of B'nai B'rith* (1965), 57.

29. Svonkin, *Jews Against Prejudice*, 25.

30. Ryland W. Crary and Gerald L. Steibel, *How You Can Teach About Communism* (Anti-Defamation League of B'nai B'rith, 1951), 29. This source can be found online: https://archive.org/details/How_You_Can_Teach_About_Communism_Democracy_Talks_Back.

31. See Williams, *Reduction of Intergroup Tensions*, 28, and Horn, "Paved with Good Intentions," 18–20, 27. The characterization of capitalism's "integrity and the dignity of the individual" posed against the characterization of communism and fascism as "the complete subordination of the individual to the state" is a common theme in the ADL's materials. See, for instance, Anti-Defamation League, *Primer on Communism* (1951), 75, http://hdl.handle.net/2027/uc1.b4029662, and Arnold Forster and Benjamin R. Epstein, *The Trouble-Makers: An Anti-Defamation League Report* (1952), 77.

32. Charisse Burden-Stelly, *Black Scare/Red Scare: Theorizing Capitalist Racism in the United States* (University of Chicago Press, 2023), 156–58.

in the United States as to the complete impartiality of the study."[33] Indeed, *An American Dilemma* intently documented and criticized individual and structural racism, called for sweeping societal change through social engineering, and was highly sympathetic to Black targets of racism. At the same time, it reflected Myrdal's racial and political views, including a white-centered, liberal capitalist approach to antiracism. It presumed that resolving racism largely meant that white people would be trained out of their prejudices while Black people would adopt white norms, and that capitalist economic opportunity was the route to erasing difference (encompassing education, housing, employment, and other aspects of life). Myrdal assumed anticommunism as the framework for these possibilities. Projecting the possible political outcomes of full Black citizenship, Myrdal reassured readers—and the Carnegie Corporation—that Black voters were unlikely to become fascists or communists, even though communists "are the only American group which has in practice offered Negroes full 'social equality,' ... [and] the present investigator has been surprised to find how it has spread also to Negro professionals and, occasionally, even to the Negro press."[34]

Myrdal's report moved civic groups and scholars into an energetic machinery. A school of prominent academics took shape whose research and writing on prejudice was funded and published by the institutions of intergroup relations, including the ADL. For its part, the ADL published experts including Arnold M. Rose, who had assisted Myrdal and coauthored *An American Dilemma*, and paradoxically was one of the few CETRRR scholars who did call for investigations of structural racism.[35] In 1950, Rose published a much-condensed version of *An American Dilemma* with the ADL, retitled *The Negro in Post-War America*, within the ADL's Freedom Pamphlets educational series. The ADL also published Gordon Allport, Charles Glock, Oscar Handlin, and others whose research from the mid-1940s through the mid-1970s defined an anti-prejudice canon, often under the ADL's own imprint.

Even as the ADL took up prejudice and democracy as universal issues, its Jewish identification remained enormously important. Cold War opposition to racism and fascism was a national ideological structure organized around global symbols. Nazis were a proxy for racial supremacism, and Soviet communism a proxy for totalitarianism. Together they represented, for liberals,

---

33. Gunnar Myrdal, *An American Dilemma* (Harper and Brothers, 1944), vi.
34. Myrdal, *An American Dilemma*, 508, 510.
35. Gordon, *From Power to Prejudice*, 80.

the antithesis of "Americanism." Indeed, racial liberalism and its enactment through civil rights advocacy became so deeply integrated as a framework of the state that historian Taylor Branch describes Martin Luther King Jr., who became its embodied representation nearly two decades later, as a new founding father.[36] In this crucible of morality, ideology, and existential fear for the nation, the US state-sponsored brand of racial egalitarianism was forged already intertwined with anti-antisemitism and anticommunism.

The ADL, and the American Jewish Committee alongside it, was uniquely positioned to knit them together as World War II ended. Already well-known intermediaries on civil rights, the defense organizations conceived Jewish communal interests and US national interests as one and the same. The ADL had documented antisemitic Christian nationalist groups that had opposed the war effort, and the league worked with media to diminish their influence.[37] Summing up the ADL's qualifications in 1943, B'nai B'rith public relations director Bernard Postal wrote:

> In the years of persecution and propaganda that began in 1933 . . . B'nai B'rith [brought] . . . the full weight of its prestige and manpower to bear against the dogmas of communism, nazism and fascism. When war engulfed the nation in 1941, the A. D. L. again was ready with proved techniques and a national program for strengthening the attachment of the people to the ideals and practices of democracy. On the alert against the divisive tactics of Axis propagandists, the A. D. L. is now dedicating its energies to the end that the people may understand that anti-Semitism is not primarily a weapon against Jews but rather a dagger aimed at the heart of all who love freedom.[38]

Perhaps unspoken were two further qualifications: First, these were civil rights organizations led by members of the state-capital class itself, not "from below." Second, as anticommunists they were well positioned to discipline a threat from their own communities: Jewish leftist and communist organizing. In short, the ADL and American Jewish Committee were poised as

36. Taylor Branch, *Parting the Waters: America in the King Years, 1954–63* (Simon and Schuster, 1989), 887.

37. In one such instance, *Life* magazine's thirteen-page feature on "Voices of Defeat," produced with the support of the ADL, pilloried white Christian nationalist, anti-Jewish, anti-Chinese, anticommunist, and isolationist organizations opposing US participation in World War II. *Life*, "Voices of Defeat," vol. 12, no. 15 (1942).

38. Bernard Postal, "B'nai B'rith: A Century of Service," *American Jewish Year Book* 45 (1943): 112.

convincing communal leaders—and safe, necessary allies of the Cold War US state.

Just as the intergroup relations movement had its roots in the national war effort, the ADL's expansion into it was an extension of its wartime activities. Throughout the war, the Jewish defense organizations had tackled antisemitism in the same fashion as they had since the 1910s, with messaging and public relations campaigns that emphasized non-discrimination as an American value. In the 1930s the ADL had begun publishing educational pamphlets. Its Fireside Discussion Group, which targeted Jewish audiences, "especially those individuals who are detached from Jewish life," published thirty-two pamphlets between 1937 and 1944 that set out information and posed questions for discussion. These were animated by the need to counter the circulation by antisemitic demagogues, including Henry Ford and Hitler, of Jewish "world conspiracies" to "despoil existing governments and destroy present civilization."[39] To that end, their titles included *Facts About Fictions Concerning the Jew* (authored by Sigmund Livingston), *Hitler's Communism Unmasked*, and *How Far Zionism?* as well as more anodyne subjects like *The Vocational Adjustment of Jewish Youth*. During the war years, the American Jewish Committee and the ADL worked together, running programs in partnership with war-oriented agencies, including the US Office of War Information and Veterans of Foreign Wars. They also funded an extensive list of other civic organizations doing similar work.[40] Their message that "prejudice endangered the war effort" was meant quite directly to strengthen the United States, in addition to inoculating the population against antisemitism as Nazi ideas gained traction among US nativists.[41] But by 1941, they judged that Nazism had lost its domestic sway, and noted instead "almost a tidal wave

39. Anti-Defamation League of B'nai B'rith, *Fireside Discussion Group of the Anti-Defamation League B'nai B'rith* (Anti-Defamation League, 1939).

40. Historian Richard Steele summarizes: "A partial list of the beneficiaries of Jewish largesse suggests its importance to the overall democracy/tolerance propaganda effort. In the period 1939 to 1942, for example, the American Jewish Committee provided subsidies totalling over $400,000 to various organizations including the Institute for Propaganda Analysis, Friends of Democracy, Council for Democracy, Mother's Day Declaration, League for Fair Play, 'Boaz studies and promotion,' Citizenship Educational Service, National Conference of Christians and Jews, National Council of Women, the American Council Against Nazi Propaganda, and the Common Council for American Unity." Steele, "The War on Intolerance: The Reformulation of American Nationalism, 1939–1941," *Journal of American Ethnic History* 9, no. 1 (1989): 29.

41. Svonkin, *Jews Against Prejudice*, 45; Naomi W. Cohen, *Not Free to Desist: The American Jewish Committee, 1906–1966* (Jewish Publication Society of America, 1972), 205–7.

of pro-democracy feeling sweeping the nation."[42] With the advent of the Cold War—and as the field of intergroup relations took shape—the ADL and American Jewish Commitee converted their efforts to those twin projects.

For the ADL, the intergroup relations movement was the pathway to its transformation to a quasi-state agency administering education and other aspects of civic life. In 1947, the ADL installed a new director, Benjamin Epstein, who had worked since the mid-1930s in anti-Nazi organizing. In taking the lead at the ADL, Epstein rebranded the ADL as a community relations agency, setting out "to combine education with community action and law." That meant, in part, focusing on public relations as a mode of "education for democracy." In 1948 "the AJC's comprehensive media program cost approximately $240,000 and employed 18 staff members and numerous outside writers and artists. The ADL spent a comparable amount on mass media activities in the same year," writes Stuart Svonkin, who astutely chronicles Jewish defense organizations in this era.[43] The turn to intergroup relations also meant that the ADL began to separate its work on antisemitism from more universal work. The ADL's 1948 publications mark the shift. That year, the ADL launched its Freedom Pamphlets series on prejudice and democracy. The pamphlets sought to add scientific authority to ideas that the ADL had long espoused: that racism was an aberration from the true nature of the US state and society, and that only in the context of capitalism and individualism—not communism—could racism be redressed. Creating ideologically directed public education materials was not unusual or specific to the ADL; its positions and the propagandistic nature of its anticommunism were standard at the time. Rather, the ideologies and methods reflected in the Freedom Pamphlets are important to note because they reflect the racial framings and political commitments that the ADL carried forward.

The first Freedom Pamphlets were prestige-affirming publications for the ADL, authored by Harvard professors. *Danger in Discord: The Origins of Anti-Semitism in the United States*, by historian Oscar Handlin and political scientist Mary Handlin, posited that antisemitism was a form of blame for social ills that periodically emerged, along with other forms of "intolerance," but that had gained particular force in the United States from the 1920s onward through the spread of white Christian nationalism and then Hitlerism. The book attached its study to the national questions of race and

42. Steele, "War on Intolerance," 28.
43. Svonkin, *Jews Against Prejudice*, 49.

democracy of the moment, but it focused on antisemitism. The second was a general treatise on prejudice by psychologist Gordon Allport titled *The ABC's of Scapegoating*. This title was a direct heir to the war effort. Allport and a colleague had published an earlier version in 1943, "for the use of morale-building agencies, both private and governmental, and . . . [others] in the field of national unity."[44] That version had devoted particular attention to Nazis. The revised Freedom Pamphlet edition broadened its attention to US domestic tensions, which included antisemitism but more strongly emphasized anti-Black discrimination. In a stark indicator of intergroup relations' refusal to reckon with the racial state, the Handlins asserted that racism had been invented by Southern planters as a response to abolitionism, only becoming a "full-fledged" aspect of US life around 1920. "Whether they agreed with the Southerners or not," they wrote, "people became accustomed to thinking in terms of race. Soon it was clear that the arguments developed against the Negroes could easily be applied to other groups."[45] Like the Handlins, Allport identified prejudice as the psychological product of frustration with other conditions, "the amount of aggression and blame being either partly or wholly unwarranted."[46] Six years later, Allport expanded the text into the field-shaping book *The Nature of Prejudice*. A third 1948 pamphlet, *The Responsibility Is Ours*, was also a psychological work: a self-help treatise, written by pop psychologist Bonaro Overstreet, guiding citizens to see themselves as important individual actors in democratic society. These publications together lent the ADL a founding authority on intergroup relations, grounded in but far beyond its authority in Jewish matters. From that point forward, the ADL presented itself as an expert agency on the subject.

The ADL's aversion to acknowledging race continued into the Cold War. Tolerance materials produced by the ADL and its partners mentioned race only as something to be considered immaterial, and Jewishness was represented as religious affiliation. In fact, the ADL was so accommodating to prevailing racial norms that it chose to stay out of sight in order to portray its messages as *not* Jewish. One strategy was to fund non-Jewish allied organizations to do parallel work, so that appeals to the US public could be made in their voices: the Bureau of Intercultural Education, the National Council of

44. Gordon W. Allport, *ABC's of Scapegoating* (Anti-Defamation League of B'nai B'rith, 1948), 2.

45. Oscar Handlin and Mary Flug Handlin, *Danger in Discord: Origins of Anti-Semitism in the United States* (Anti-Defamation League of B'nai B'rith, 1948), 2, 14, 24.

46. Allport, *ABC's of Scapegoating*, 9.

Women, the League for Fair Play, and a host of other recipients of Jewish defense funding.[47] Another was to simply create and run programming that appeared to be Christian-led. In 1944 the ADL set up the Institute for American Democracy (IAD) to serve as the ostensible source of its campaigns.[48] Although IAD was an ADL subsidiary, it deliberately gave the impression of being a completely different organization directed by Episcopal priest (and anticommunist demagogue) William C. Kernan.[49] The move succeeded: In catalogues of educational materials it was listed simply as "a nonprofit, nonsectarian educational corporation" of intergroup relations.[50] It produced "posters, blotters, book covers, and bookmarks proclaiming the principles and advantages of American democracy" and occupied a unique place among tolerance organizations as producer of advertisements.[51] The ads, which have endured as iconic images of the period, reinforced "Americanness" as everyone's primary identity, using a visual lexicon of soldiers, nurses, children, liberty torches, and Superman. The visual materials clearly represented Jews as white. Picturing groups of apparently white people, often under the banner "Protestant, Catholic, Jew," both wartime and postwar tolerance campaigns emphasized the impossibility of distinguishing between white people of different religions. Rather than shedding race and religion as a categories that defined national belonging, they recentered whiteness and biblical faith as the fields on which difference was measured. Historian Leigh E. Schmidt characterized the IAD's version of American inclusion as "a pluralism of expanding whiteness" that framed even religious tolerance "in a way that erased African Americans from the nation's religious landscape."[52]

47. Steele, "War on Intolerance," 29.

48. Svonkin, *Jews Against Prejudice*, 51.

49. Svonkin writes that the ADL set up IAD as a "front group." ADL director of programs Nathan Belth identifies IAD as a funded and "subsidiary" project of the ADL. However, the public impression was that IAD was Christian-led and made up of "all kinds." See, for example, Al Segal, "Al Segal Speaks on in Place of Speeches," *Jewish Post*, August 15, 1947; Svonkin, *Jews Against Prejudice*, 51; Joseph M. Kirman, "Major Programs of the B'nai B'rith Anti-Defamation League: 1945–1965" (PhD diss., New York University, 1967), 209, http://search.proquest.com/docview/302257477/citation/A43B927120DA47BFPQ/9.

50. See, for instance, *ALA Bulletin*, "Unity Bookmark," vol. 43, no. 4 (1949): 144.

51. June Blythe, "Can Public Relations Help Reduce Prejudice?," *Public Opinion Quarterly* 11, no. 3 (1947): 347n11; *English Journal*, "Report and Summary: NCTE High School Section Election," vol. 43, no. 3 (1954): 156.

52. Leigh E. Schmidt, "Pluralism, Secularism, and Religion in Modern American History," *Modern American History* 1, no. 1 (2018): 11.

This was both ideology and strategy. In making the IAD campaigns appear universal rather than Jewish, the ADL meant to reinforce a notion of national unity, avoiding particularism. Murray Friedman, who directed the ADL's Virginia/North Carolina office during the intergroup relations period, suggested that the Jewish defense agencies had been successful precisely because they had not made particularly challenging antiracist demands, but "operated within or anticipated the broader social and political consensus in the country."[53] Additionally, the ADL's leaders clearly understood that not identifying their messaging as Jewish meant that audiences would presume that it was white and Christian, the "neutral" identity that pertained unless another identity was noted. Reflecting later on the period, ADL director Nathan Perlmutter affirmed that the ADL's anti-prejudice and democracy messages had been powerful because they had successfully appealed to the dominant class, WASPs. Without their backing, Perlmutter pointed out, the ADL would have been dismissed as a special interest group.[54] The ADL's strategy was to leverage white Christian authority or even merge with it, not to interrupt it.

Another driver of the ADL's rise was its embrace of scientific method. For its first several decades, ADL work on antisemitism, Christian demagoguery, and communism had focused on countering their claims. Its publications had generally been issued under the name of the ADL as an organization, or under the authorship of Sigmund Livingston as its leading figure. But wartime brought a new devotion to science in the service of democracy. The war effort demanded strategic measurement of needs, marshaling of resources, and social discipline in support of the nation's goals. In 1947, Epstein put the ADL on the path of social science research, publishing its first methodical survey of antisemitism in the United States, segmented into regions, states, and cities. It was authored by Epstein and the ADL's Civil Rights Committee, which was made up of members of the ADL board. Two more research monographs quickly followed in 1949, political scientist Ruth Weintraub's *How Secure These Rights?* and Arnold M. Forster's *A Measure of Freedom.* As the ADL became a publisher of work by academic political scientists, sociologists, historians, and psychologists—and a resource for other civic

53. Murray Friedman, "A New Direction for American Jews," *Commentary* 72, no. 6 (1981): 37–44.
54. Nathan Perlmutter, "Vol Ib: Perlmutter, Nathan, 1985–1987," Box 1, Folder 1, MS-365, p. 22, B'nai B'rith Anti-Defamation League Oral Histories, American Jewish Archives, Cincinnati, Ohio.

institutions trying to do their part in postwar "prejudice reduction" efforts—it claimed national authority as an expert agency on racial and religious prejudice and democracy, and separate authority as the representative of Jewish communal thinking in that field. Despite the emphasis on academic expertise, however, the ADL (and other intergroup relations organizations) were largely winging their interventions. The Social Science Research Council complained in 1947 about the frenzied but ungrounded work of intergroup relations agencies, saying "much of their work has involved a minimum of examination of basic assumptions and of testing the effects of the methods and techniques they employ."[55] When new psychological studies on prejudice in individuals were published in the 1950s, the ADL, like other intergroup relations agencies, set out to put the authority of new science behind its work, particularly in turning new attention to schools and parenting. Even so, the contention that major ADL programs were built on unevaluated methods, or methods that did not produce change, persisted through later decades and expansions of education programming.[56]

The move to scientization greatly energized psychological approaches to prejudice. The field of psychology, developing since the 1920s, had gained wartime importance because of the state's interest in managing the ideas and allegiances of populations at home and abroad.[57] By the mid-1940s, Allport's work had made psychological research central to discussions about managing racial and religious hostilities. After the war's end, the arrival of the psychologists of the Frankfurt School, now Jewish refugees from the Nazi regime, catalyzed an explosion of research under the auspices of the American Jewish Committee.[58] A cluster of studies on the psychology of prejudice published in 1950 and 1954 responded to fears about the popular appeal of fascist ideology, which had been on terrifying display at Nazi rallies and, in more dispersed form, the conversion of citizens and neighbors to Nazi enforcers. *The Authoritarian Personality*, authored by Theodor Adorno and three psychologists in 1950, calibrated human

---

55. Williams, *Reduction of Intergroup Tensions*, 3.

56. For later examples, see the ADL's own publication, Earl Raab and Seymour Martin Lipset, *Prejudice and Society* (Anti-Defamation League of B'nai B'rith, 1959), 45; Lauren MacKenzie Whetstone, "An Evaluation of Prejudice Reduction Program for Children" (PhD diss., Claremont Graduate University, 1991), https://www.proquest.com/pqdt/docview/303928025/abstract/F81B8A26037944C7PQ/1.

57. Leah Gordon's history of the intersection of wartime social science, psychology, and intergroup relations provides essential grounding for understanding the ADL's entry into education as a national defense project. Gordon, *From Power to Prejudice*, 14.

58. Svonkin, *Jews Against Prejudice*, 37–40.

susceptibility to fascist ideology based on psychodynamic factors and identified prejudice as a social pathology arising in response to individuals' experiences of authoritarian control.[59] It anchored a new literature alongside Bruno Bettelheim and Morris Janowitz's *Dynamics of Prejudice* and Nathan W. Ackerman and Marie Jahoda's *Anti-Semitism and Emotional Disorder*, also published in 1950, and Allport's 1954 monograph *The Nature of Prejudice*.

For the field of intergroup relations, these studies served to confirm that psychology was the rightful locus of anti-prejudice work, and that individual, social intervention was an appropriate solution. Individual interventions were by no means the only need that researchers raised: From Myrdal onward, researchers assessing American problems pointed to unequal schools, housing, economic conditions, and histories of marginalization as critical factors producing racialization, as a structural inequality, and racial hostility as a set of attitudes. But for reasons of expediency and politics, the institutions of intergroup relations did not take them up. Myrdal's mapping of US problems and approaches to solving them was so vast that institutions could pick out the aspects that appealed to them, as Leah Gordon writes. The project of moving white Americans to live up to their egalitarian values was "more actionable than his expansive blueprint for social engineering."[60] Fixing people's attitudes was deemed a manageable project, while efforts to intervene in big systems were uncertain and risked demoralizing people if they failed.[61] Further, intergroup relations agencies viewed their role as defending capitalism and state order. Redressing racist economic systems was simply not on their agenda. "None of the Jewish agencies paid sufficient heed" to specific warnings from psychologist Bettelheim and sociologist Janowitz that ignoring socioeconomic factors would make intergroup relations programs flop, writes Svonkin. "Like their non-Jewish allies in the intergroup relations movement, [they] . . . tended to ignore questions of class." Indeed, in partnering with the American Jewish Committee, Adorno and other sociologists of the Frankfurt School had to "curb their criticism of liberalism and capitalism."[62] In this context, the ADL

59. Arie W. Kruglanski and Wolfgang Stroebe, *Handbook of the History of Social Psychology* (Taylor and Francis Group, 2011), 410–11.

60. Gordon, *From Power to Prejudice*, 39.

61. Williams, *Reduction of Intergroup Tensions*, 9.

62. Critiques of liberalism, capitalism, and state authority were not just ignored but suppressed by intergroup relations agencies. Adorno and sociologist Max Horkheimer had previously defined the opposite of "authoritarian personality" as "revolutionary." In their collaboration with the American Jewish Committee, it now became the "democratic personality" or "genuine liberal." Svonkin, *Jews Against Prejudice*, 36–37.

moved to expand the psychosocial approach as a bulwark against other modes of antiracism, and to expand its own scientific pedigree and footprint in national problem-solving.

The psychological studies identified early childhood as the critical period of intervention in racial prejudice. In response, both the ADL and American Jewish Committee turned to targeted educational programming, including teacher guides, trainings, and materials for classroom use. But here the two defense organizations diverged. The AJC set out to curate and disseminate materials that had been produced by researchers and scholars, some of whom it had been jointly funding with the ADL since the 1940s.[63] By contrast, the ADL set up shop as an expert authority. It dramatically expanded its work and footprint in the field of intergroup relations. Without apparently adding staff with expertise on the subjects, it began providing teacher training and curriculum development—undertaking the work of writing anti-prejudice materials and compiling and distributing catalogues to schools and civic organizations. The AJC supported the provision and analysis of anti-prejudice education, particularly through the Bureau of Intercultural Education (BIE), but its staff "explicitly criticized the ADL.... They believed that the league lacked the necessary expertise" for technical and training work. Rather, that work was the purview of professionals like those at BIE. Undeterred, the ADL by 1955 was devoting half of its time to education work, and Epstein aimed to make the organization "a leader in the field."[64]

From its platform in education, the ADL pursued two goals. The first was to counter communist messaging that capitalism brought inequality and racism, and that communism was the correct framework for racial justice. ADL materials proposed that communists were leveraging Americans' concerns about racism to lure them toward totalitarianism. Communists were in fact doing multiracial grassroots organizing and boisterously protesting racism. The Freedom Pamphlets decried those activities as a ruse. A pamphlet for teachers, *How You Can Teach About Communism* (1951), laid out the ADL's

63. The two groups initially outsourced educational programming to the Bureau for Intercultural Education. By 1954, though, the ADL and American Jewish Committee were covering so much intergroup education programming themselves (ADL as a direct provider, and American Jewish Committee as a clearinghouse) that they stopped funding the bureau and it shut down. Svonkin, *Jews Against Prejudice*, 64–67.

64. By the early '60s, some ADL lay leaders and professional staff worried additionally that ramped-up intergroup relations undertakings were crowding out Jewish self-defense work. Svonkin, *Jews Against Prejudice*, 64–65, 70.

own approach to persuasive education. Authored by Columbia historian Ryland W. Crary and US Army psychological warfare officer (and high school social studies teacher) Gerald L. Steibel, the pamphlet set out to arm teachers with nuggets of expertise in Russian history, Marxism, and US liberalism, to lend them authority as they refuted communist claims. In the tradition of propaganda, the pamphlet offered factual historical text in conjunction with broad ideological conclusions and aggrandizing moral rhetoric about anticommunists. "If public education is to serve the democracy which produced it . . . the public school teacher needs to know the facts which illustrate why Communists are antithetic to the democratic way of life. . . . He must be helped to appreciate and understand the democratic tradition, to know what is meant by free intelligence, free inquiry, free dissent, free choice—all of which are rooted out under Communism."[65] More than a curriculum guide, the pamphlet reads as a military-style psychological operations manual: a primer for undermining communists' arguments for race and labor equity, teaching "methods of taking the offensive" against them.[66] In keeping with the ADL's work to engineer prodemocracy thinking toward support for the state, the pamphlet also works in the other direction, naturalizing claims that history, sociology, and political science collectively confirmed that American capitalism was intrinsically antiracist and moral.

The ADL's campaigns were not pushing against a tide of contrary opinion. Mainstream politics, media, and schools were sites of attack on race consciousness and critiques of capitalism. One way that such ideas were dismissed was by calling them Soviet manipulations. Another, in the context of social science researchers' investments in liberal capitalism, was to dismiss them as "unscientific" and unobjective. Oliver Cox's 1948 *Caste, Class, & Race*, for instance, critiqued *An American Dilemma* for "avoiding a political-class interpretation" of racism, and in response sketched the beginnings of a racial theory of capitalism.[67] Cox understood this as a challenge to the scholarship that was forming around intergroup relations.[68] Deriding Cox's work, Oscar Handlin wrote a snide essay in *Commentary* magazine, published by the

---

65. Crary and Steibel, *How You Can Teach About Communism*, 9.

66. Crary and Steibel, *How You Can Teach About Communism*, 31.

67. Oliver C. Cox, *Caste, Class, & Race: A Study in Social Dynamics* (Monthly Review Press, 1959), 509, 531–38; Thomas J. Mann, "Oliver C. Cox and the Political Economy of Racial Capitalism," *Dialectical Anthropology* 46, no. 1 (2022): 85–102.

68. Susan E. Klarlund, "The Origins of Racism: The Critical Theory of Oliver C. Cox," *Mid-American Review of Sociology* 18, no. 1/2 (1994): 85–92.

American Jewish Committee, that invited readers to understand Cox as irrational, disloyal, and communist. Handlin included a litany of quotations that he thought ridiculous. "These sentences illustrate Cox's peculiar use of language; words are divorced from their usual meanings and endowed with esoteric identities known only to the author," Handlin began his complaint, before listing Cox's points: "There is only one political party in the United States 'with two factions: Republicans and Democrats.' Mercantilism is state capitalism. A ruling class is always intolerant. 'Businessmen constitute our ruling class.' . . . 'The bourgeoisie is unalterably opposed to democracy.' Russia is the only foe of fascism; most respectable Americans are fascists; southern poor whites are not hostile to the Negro; the late Senator Bilbo was a spokesman of capitalism. And no previous scholars revealed these truths because their 'bread and butter' depended upon 'avoiding the study of contemporary class conflict.'"[69] Cox's analysis, if unconventional at the time, now affirms his place as a groundbreaking theoretician of racial capitalism. However, Handlin was a weighty figure in US academia on the study of racial and ethnic conditions, and in Jewish life as a narrator of communal history.[70] His dismissal of Cox summed up the sense of leaders in both spheres that they spoke as authoritatively scientific, objective, and moral voices on race and democracy, while those who spoke from less central positions—at the time meaning leftist and Black scholars—did not. Their conception of ending racism did not include ceding that authority. Indeed, writing of all three Jewish defense groups (the ADL, American Jewish Committee, and the less elitist American Jewish Congress), Svonkin laments that they never addressed the idea that, to produce equality, "some Americans would have to pay a price, in the form of diminished political and economic power."[71]

By 1947, the ADL's involvement in intergroup relations was so clearly outside the frame of Jewish particularist politics that staff members suggested renaming the organization. But director Benjamin Epstein instead seized on the change to bridge the old and new authorities of the ADL, articulating a claim that "ancient Jewish ethical precepts" mapped precisely onto the American creed. The notion of a Jewish religious tradition of liberalism

69. Oscar Handlin, "The Study of Man: Prejudice and Capitalist Exploitation," *Commentary Magazine*, July 1, 1948.

70. On Handlin's significance, see Hasia Diner, "Oscar Handlin: A Jewish Historian," *Journal of American Ethnic History* 32, no. 3 (2013): 56.

71. Svonkin, *Jews Against Prejudice*, 5.

(much less progressivism) was arguably ahistorical, and it buckled in later decades as Jewish political allegiances moved to the right of the US spectrum.[72] But for the ADL and the defense agencies at the time, asserting an inherent Jewish alignment with the moral framework of the liberal state did important work. Svonkin argues that "Epstein's political judgement was impeccable. . . . He was acutely aware that these renovated, if mythic, 'Jewish precepts,' dehistoricized and largely secularized, closely corresponded with the basic tenets of postwar American liberalism."[73] This framing also transformed all of US Jewry into a de facto constituency for the defense agencies, softening their histories as elite *shtadlan* organizations and suggesting a representational approach better suited to a Jewish population that was increasingly middle class. (This shift did not change the structure of the organizations: Although each had a donor base in Jewish communities, only the American Jewish Congress had members.) Conversely, it positioned the defense organizations to become the locus of an assimilated Jewish identity that was increasingly separated from immigrant cultural and religious practice. Writing in 1964, sociologist Harold Weisberg noted the turn: "To be a Jew is to belong to an organization. To manifest Jewish culture is to carry out, individually or collectively, the program of an organization."[74] This alchemy of morality, nationalism, and Jewish identity was the beginning of the ADL's broad authority in political culture. It also allowed the ADL to narrate Jewish politics according to its own ideals, and to marginalize Jewish political dissenters as apostates.

In the years following the ADL's founding, the charge that Jews had driven the Russian Revolution circulated as a claim that Jews were inclined to communism, therefore inherently disloyal to governments and an obstacle to national economic and political health. The ADL confronted two problems: First, that the association of Jews with communism was used to fuel antisemitism. Second, that a great many Jews in the United States, as in Europe, were indeed leftists. Initially, ADL leaders set out to counter the narrative. As the United States entered World War I, wrote ADL secretary Leon Lewis,

72. See, for instance, Friedman, "A New Direction for American Jews."
73. Svonkin, *Jews Against Prejudice*, 20.
74. Excerpted in Jacob Neusner, *American Judaism, Adventure in Modernity: An Anthological Essay* (Ktav Publishing House Inc., 1978), 16.

"the great work then before us was the refutation of the ever-recurring charges that the Jew was unpatriotic, a slacker and a coward.... The piling up of insidious falsehoods anent Jewish participation in Russian Bolshevism had prepared the ground for fear of American Jews as spreaders of radicalism in this country." By 1918, the final year of World War I, its activities to combat such accusations in the United States included "numerous cases taken up with the Federal Government, the Fosdick Commission [the US agency charged with training soldiers in ethics and hygiene], the YMCA and other welfare organizations."[75] Their concerns only deepened at the end of World War I. In Germany, the rising Nazi movement blamed Jews and communists for Germany's defeat, and increasingly blamed Jews for communism itself. European Jews were the targets of antisemitic campaigns that used "Jewish bolshevism" as their rationale. Lewis wrote in his 1920 annual report to the ADL's executive committee, "Ukrainian pogroms, the reactionary White Terror in Hungary, the intensified oppression in Roumania, the economic boycott of Jews in Poland, the systematic solicitation of funds by reactionaries in Germany to drive the Jews from that country—all these were accompanied by organized propaganda work in Europe designed to justify the offenders in their course.... The majority of [these stories] charged the Jews with being responsible for terroristic conditions in Russia ... that the Jews constituted the warp and woof of Communism."[76]

In the United States the charges that troubled the German Jewish elites—that Jews were inherently leftists—converged with another emergent crisis for the state-capital class. Leftist movements were rising, including anticolonial and labor movements, spurred by immigrant, communist, and Black organizing. In the first Red Scare, between 1919 and 1920, these movements were attacked as "bolshevism," connecting them to the Russian Revolution and fueling the idea that Jews were behind them. But the charges were not just political; they were racial. Radicalism, bolshevism, and labor agitation were cast as un-American, un-white attacks on a presumptively white nation. While related attacks were taking place both in Europe and the United States, they were different: Anti-leftism and antisemitism responded to the specific contexts and histories of the places where they were undertaken.

75. Anti-Defamation League, *Report of Anti-Defamation League B'nai B'rith* (1920), 21–23.

76. Anti-Defamation League, *Report of Anti-Defamation League B'nai B'rith* (1920), 22–23.

Racialized anticommunism was a tactic deployed by business leaders seeking to counter the power of labor organizing, as Julie Powell writes, particularly as it called to immigrant workers. It placed calls for workers' rights in the sphere of treason, and invited them to "abjure all forms of collectivism as 'non-white'" and to adopt anticommunist, anticollectivist politics instead.[77] The German Jewish leadership of the defense agencies had a foot in both camps. They were members of the business class, portraying radical worker organizing as foreign, and they were Jewish institutional leaders trying to distance Jews from that racializing notion. In the struggle against bolshevism, they were constantly at pains to navigate a path between their own efforts to discipline the left and fending off the attacks of forces further to the right. Those included nativist efforts at policy like banning foreign-language press, the anti-leftist raids, mass arrests, and mass deportation efforts by Attorney General Mitchell A. Palmer, and in 1920, Henry Ford's publication of the antisemitic conspiracy tract *Protocols of the Elders of Zion*, which named some of those leaders themselves in its fabricated map of bolshevism.

Many Jews certainly were communists, and they organized *as* communists against antisemitism and state violence in the United States and Europe. "Communist" was a broad label; their relationship to Soviet communism varied widely as they spanned party members, workers organized by communist-aligned unions, and simply "fellow travelers" to whom class solidarity and collective resistance made sense. Anticommunism, though, proposed all as conspiratorial Soviet agents. As they were subjected to antisemitic attack, the Jewish defense agencies refused to come to their aid.[78] To the contrary, the ADL mounted campaigns of what it termed "counter-propaganda" that denounced communism and communists, and declared them anathema to Jewishness.

In its first salvo in 1920, the ADL blanketed US newsrooms with an article, "Russian Jews Against Bolshevik Rule," presenting evidence from a journalist in Russia about Jewish opposition to the revolution.[79] Whether or not

77. Julie M. Powell, "Making 'The Case Against the "Reds"': Racializing Communism, 1919–1920," in *Historicizing Fear*, ed. Travis D. Boyce and Winsome M. Chunnu (University Press of Colorado, 2019), 104.

78. On German Jewish dissidence in this period, including communism, see John M. Cox, *Circles of Resistance: Jewish, Leftist, and Youth Dissidence in Nazi Germany* (Peter Lang, 2009).

79. Anti-Defamation League, *Report of Anti-Defamation League B'nai B'rith* (1920), 46.

the papers actually published the article as the ADL requested, the message reached five hundred editors, whose newspapers in turn reached a third of the US population. In 1937, when the ADL began publishing its own mass audience materials as the Fireside Discussion Group pamphlets, it used them to oppose antisemitic claims specific to the United States and Germany while also denouncing communist Jews in both places. Its 1938 pamphlet, *Hitler's Communism Unmasked*, declared, "It's a lie in every language and every country! Communism never was Jewish! ... Communism can never be Jewish!"[80] Aiming to refute Hitler's charges as they related to Jews in Germany and the United States, it somewhat frantically enumerated Jewish contributions to US settlement and German heroism in World War I. Distancing Jews from communism, it listed prominent communists who were not Jewish, and prominent Jews who were "violently opposed to communism"; it noted that Engels was "an 'Aryan'" and that non-Jewish German voting districts leaned more toward communist candidates than Jewish districts. It pointed to German nationalist sources (whether in sympathy with German nationalism or desperation to convince German nationalists of their arguments), which argued that communist revolutionism was a product of Russian culture rather than Jewish culture. It also devoted a page to the battle in organized labor between communist organizers (whom the pamphlet obliquely framed as non-Jewish by naming only CIO leader John Lewis) and anticommunist Jewish labor leaders David Dubinsky and Sidney Hillman, whose "right-wing socialist" factions would become key allies in dismantling Jewish organizations to their left.[81] A second 1938 pamphlet reprinted a speech that Sigmund Livingston had delivered to B'nai B'rith members. Livingston declared communist Jews "apostates" and attached Jewishness to the secular religion of the US state. "Our American ideal must be maintained, unsullied by any foreign 'isms,'" Livingston implored his gathered listeners. "Communism, Fascism and Naziism are the mortal enemies of democracy. America is the holy ground of liberty and freedom—may no one defile by sacrilege this—The Cathedral of Humanity."[82]

After World War II the ADL transformed its anticommunism into a Cold War effort, conjoined with intergroup relations. Postwar anticom-

80. See the frontispiece of Anti-Defamation League of B'nai B'rith, *Hitler's Communism Unmasked* (Fireside Discussion Group of the Anti-Defamation League, 1938).
81. Anti-Defamation League, *Hitler's Communism Unmasked*, 12–13.
82. Sigmund Livingston, *Facts About Fictions Concerning the Jew* (Anti-Defamation League of B'nai B'rith, 1938), 27.

munism was grounded in a specific claim that the Soviet-centered Communist Party was a conspiratorial organ that puppeteered its supporters around the world, and was thereby infiltrating US organizations. With much less specificity, the ADL's 1951 Freedom Pamphlet *Primer on Communism* warned of fellow travelers and communist front groups that staked claim to "liberal causes" and "moral purity" but were, it revealed, in pursuit of revolution.[83] In portraying communism as a broad threat of attack on "Americanism," without real coherence, Larry Ceplair writes that the ADL made anticommunism available as a platform for fears, and opportunistic fear-mongering, on a wide range of issues.[84]

At the same time that it attacked the left, the ADL had also long been concerned about how the white right made anticommunism its cause. Christian nationalists like Gerald L. K. Smith were antisemitic and disinterested in liberal democracy, embracing racism and anticommunism as parts of the same nationalist vision.[85] Cold War anticommunist fervor brought those politics into the mainstream, personified by Senator Joe McCarthy. McCarthy began investigating suspected communists in 1950, and his power was amplified in 1953 when he became chair of the Senate Permanent Subcommittee on Investigations. As McCarthy hunted enemies in every corner of US life, his tactics included blacklists, closed-door investigations, and opaque edicts issued to government agencies and media organizations to fire (and in some cases hire) particular people. The ADL was quiet about McCarthyism as it developed, leading to speculation about whether its leaders supported or opposed his methods. Eventually, in 1953, under new national chairman Henry Schultz, it classed McCarthyists as "the extreme wing of the 'againsts,' the inciters to prejudice and even violence."[86] As such, McCarthy fell into the category of disreputable demagogues whom the ADL

83. On fellow travelers and front groups, see Anti-Defamation League, *Primer on Communism*, 25, 39.

84. The primer was also marked by a turn to polemical arguments. Its headings oscillated between inviting study and inviting panic: "What Is Communism?" and "What Is the Theory of Surplus Value?" were followed by "Does the Size of a Communist Party Indicate the Danger It Represents?" and "How Do Communists Try to Tear Down the Democratic World?" See Anti-Defamation League, *Primer on Communism*; Larry Ceplair, *Anti-Communism in Twentieth-Century America: A Critical History* (Praeger, 2011), 100.

85. See Arnold Forster and Benjamin R. Epstein, *Cross-Currents* (Doubleday, 1956).

86. Milton Friedman, "McCarthyism Viewed as Peril to Democratic Institutions by ADL," *American Jewish World*, December 11, 1953.

habitually disciplined. But the ADL's intent to play both sides would produce contradictions.

The effort to navigate a conservative line between left and right placed the ADL squarely in the domain of the *vital center*, an emerging postwar ideological movement. Vital centrism, also articulated as *centrist-extremist theory*, would come to dominate US politics in the postwar decades. It produced a durable bipartisan conservatism using the imperative to "protect civil rights and democracy" as a means of disciplining and marginalizing popular movements—resting largely on the terms set by intergroup relations. Drawing on Arthur Schlesinger Jr.'s 1949 book *The Vital Center: The Politics of Freedom*, the movement advanced a politics of moderation and investment in the state, organized around liberal capitalism. It framed a return to American ideals as the antidote to fascism and war, and rejected leftist challenges to the state and right-wing racism and religious rigidity as forms of extremism.[87] This idea gathered leaders in politics, media, religion, and academia, and the ADL—in part through its success in burying the Jewish left—situated itself as its natural steward in civic life.

In 1953, ADL leaders secured a major public relations coup that helped cement the connection between Jewish values and American values: They got the president of the United States to come to dinner—on television. Bringing the project of Jewish defense together with anticommunism, mainstream liberal politics, and new formations of mass media, the event stitched together a disparate set of interests and catapulted the ADL into their center. At the time of the dinner, in November 1953, Dwight D. Eisenhower had been president for a year, and he had not followed Truman's lead in making civil rights a national project. Nonetheless, in considering which celebrity might grace its fortieth anniversary celebration, the ADL invited Eisenhower to receive its America's Democratic Legacy Medallion. The award served multiple purposes, in addition to lending star power to the ADL's reputation. One aim was to induce Eisenhower to pay more attention to civil rights.[88] Another purpose, of concern to both Eisenhower and the ADL, was to edge Senator Joe McCarthy out of the anticommunist spotlight. In the same vein, a third purpose was to shore up a centrist anticommunism—a modern, respectable version personified by the likes of Eisenhower and Eleanor Roosevelt—and

87. Arthur M. Schlesinger, *The Vital Center: The Politics of Freedom* (The Riverside Press, 1949).

88. Erik Barnouw, *The Image Empire: A History of Broadcasting in the United States*, Vol. 3, *From 1953* (Oxford University Press, 1970), 13–14.

make clear that the ADL was its trusted representative. In an unexpected turn, Eisenhower's speech gave the last aim more force than anyone expected.

The event capitalized on the television industry that was just taking shape. The year 1953 had also been a period of mass expansion. Nearly half of all US households—23 million—now had TV sets, having jumped from 14 percent in 1950.[89] New stations had just extended the reach of networks to major cities. The expansion of television had created new stars, including Lucille Ball and Desi Arnaz.[90] Commercial advertisers were finding television to be an enormous multiplier: One lipstick company grew its annual sales from $50,000 to $4.5 million between 1950 and 1952 through television advertising.[91] Anticommunism, service to the national project, and engagement with the Jewish defense organizations were stitched into the roots of this burgeoning media ecology. Anticommunist adventures were regular subjects for film and television that did brisk business.[92] David Sarnoff, the head of broadcasting companies Radio Corporation of America (RCA) and National Broadcasting Company (NBC), was a brigadier general in the US Army who had played a key role in World War II communications. He was also a war-service friend of Eisenhower. Columbia Broadcasting System (CBS) head William S. Paley had been an early adopter of anticommunist blacklists. Sarnoff and Paley also collaborated with the Jewish defense agencies on their work "to popularize an American Jewish ideology" against communism: Even as the ADL was planning its 1953 dinner, Paley and Sarnoff were also on a multi-organization planning committee, led by the American Jewish Committee, to celebrate the tercentenary of Jewish life in the United States. That event in 1954 also featured Eisenhower, and expounded the same themes.[93]

In November, television networks suspended their programming for a historic hour of special anticommunist entertainment featuring the ADL and

89. US Census Bureau, "Historical Households Tables," 2020. Retrieved from https://www2.Census.Gov/Programs-Surveys/Demo/Tables/Families/Time-Series/Households/Hh1.Xls; Stephen J. Whitfield, *The Culture of the Cold War* (John Hopkins University Press, 1996), 153.

90. Barnouw, *Image Empire*, 25.

91. Barnouw, *Image Empire*, 5–6.

92. Ceplair, *Anti-Communism in Twentieth-Century America*, 83; Fred J. MacDonald, "The Cold War as Entertainment in 'Fifties Television," *Journal of Popular Film and Television* 7, no. 1 (1978): 3–31.

93. Arthur A. Goren, "A 'Golden Decade' for American Jews: 1945–1955," in *Central European Jews in America, 1840–1880: Migration and Advancement*, ed. Jeffrey S. Gurock (Routledge, 1998), 12.

the president. Media historian Erik Barnouw calls it "one of the strangest telecasts of the year, a program which in sixty minutes compressed a panorama of its time."[94] On the live broadcast, Eisenhower walked to his seat through a dinner crowd that included five US Supreme Court justices, FBI chief J. Edgar Hoover, the executives of RCA, ABC, and CBS radio and television companies, and the luminaries of the Anti-Defamation League. Senator Hubert Humphrey and former first lady Eleanor Roosevelt, who had recently founded Americans for Democratic Action to advance the principles of the vital center, were also guests. News anchor Walter Cronkite narrated the event. The hour-long program presented a lineup of superstars including Ball and Arnaz, Ethel Merman, Thelma Ritter, Rex Harrison, Helen Hayes, and Rodgers and Hammerstein—stars, as Cronkite pronounced, who had come "because they, like you, are dedicated to the proposition that all men are created equal—and to the conviction that, opinions from behind the Iron Curtain to the contrary, there is a lot that's right about America." First, though, a spunky Statue of Liberty confessed and absolved the sins of the United States. "Enlightening the world is a very weary job, citizens," she warned, though she soon perked up: "Oh, hi stranger, come right in! . . . Maybe I'd better stick around for a while. Take a stand for civil rights, and against uncivil lefts, welcome strangers and reassure old acquaintances. Oh, I've made a lot of mistakes in the past, but I've been the first to admit them! Look at all those amendments you've got! And I still stand, sometimes with egg on my sweet brave face, but brother, I stand! . . . And we're getting better and better and better!"[95] The evening's narrative continued in this vein, listing "debits and credits" of the United States, laying blame for institutional discrimination at the feet of local officials, lauding federal interventions to correct it, and promising progress only available, the speakers purported, under capitalism. At the peak of the evening's claims, composer Richard Rodgers asserted outright that the American theater was free of intolerance: "In other words, our house is in order."

As the star entertainers established that anticommunism, racial progress, collective humility, and humor were the shared fabric of American life, the proceedings wove in Jewish identity as a moral grounding for it.[96] At the

94. Barnouw, *Image Empire*, 13.

95. CBS, "Dinner with the President," posted November 16, 2019, by Free The Kinescopes!, YouTube, 1:03:56, originally aired in 1953, https://www.youtube.com/watch?v=-8_d2_yDxEU.

96. The event was an emblem of intergroup relations programming. It gestured to a racist history ameliorated by racial progress, but the production suggested it was largely

podium, ADL president and real estate magnate Philip Klutznick proclaimed Jews' commitments to "the sacred spirit of democracy and freedom . . . in the holiest tradition of our Hebrew faith"; and that "we believe, with the great philosopher Spinoza" that the state's purpose is the development of the liberty of the individual.[97] The speech was short but breathtaking in its public break with earlier assimilationist efforts to minimize Jewish difference. Periodically, the camera cut away to honor important attendees in business and politics, centering them as "great men" of democracy: Senator Hubert Humphrey, FBI director J. Edgar Hoover, the Jewish corporate and political leaders, and ADL leaders among them.[98] As the last stroke of the evening—in an off-script speech—Eisenhower denounced McCarthyism for the first time in public. The ADL's event had become a historic turning point in the domestic prosecution of the Cold War.

"Dinner with the President" was transformational for the ADL. In later interviews, public relations director Nathan Belth estimated that it had "close to forty million viewers and an equivalent proportion of the radio listeners"—nearly half of the US population at the time.[99] Viewers could not join the ADL, which had no membership, but B'nai B'rith gained twenty

---

a conversation that white people, including European Jews, were having with each other. Lucille Ball and Desi Arnaz presented a vaudeville sketch, a form derived from minstrel shows. Ethel Merman performed a number derived from African rhythms, "Alexander's Ragtime Band," by an Eastern European Jewish composer, Irving Berlin. Slavery and abolition were discussed through a Harriet Beecher Stowe monologue about President Abraham Lincoln, performed by Helen Hayes, which also lauded the US Army's burial of an Indigenous (Ho Chunk) Korean War veteran at Arlington National Cemetery. Jackie Robinson, who had become an important figure in postwar civil rights in 1947 as the first Black player in Major League baseball, was on stage for less than one minute. The sole Black performer was William Warfield, a rising opera star, who sang a French aria based on German legend, from Gounod's 1859 *Faust*. On the Arlington burial, see Thomas A. Britten and Larry W. Burt. "The Sergeant John R. Rice Incident and the Paradox of Indian Civil Rights," *Annals of Iowa* 63, no. 3 (July 2004): 279–310.

97. CBS, "Dinner with the President."

98. Deborah D. Moore identifies a shift in the ADL's *shtadlan* approach to politics in the Truman era. Rather than the private, backroom approach that de-emphasized Jewish identity, now it publicly identified Jewish community grievances and posed demands for rights. Still, it revolved around political and corporate elites, with whom the growing upper class now had denser relationships. Moore, *B'nai B'rith and the Challenge of Ethnic Leadership* (State University of New York Press, 1981), 124–25.

99. Nathan C. Belth, "Vol Va: Belth, Nathan C., 1985–1987," 113, B'nai B'rith Anti-Defamation League Oral Histories, American Jewish Archives, Cincinnati, Ohio.

thousand new members in the event's wake.[100] It recast Jewish identity as a special, even super-democratic, support for US society.[101] Eisenhower's surprise attack on McCarthyism, ADL director Ben Epstein noted, "brought the ADL into the limelight," generating intensive news coverage that expanded the event's reach even further.[102] It positioned the ADL as a *correct* force for anticommunism, in opposition to both the "red" left and the intemperate anticommunist right. Blessed by the president, media moguls, and patriotic celebrities, the ADL was confirmed as a trusted facilitator of the state's aims.

Following the televised hour, the ADL's national and global authority continued to grow. Its work on human relations and major legal issues contributed: Under Truman, the ADL had launched state-level campaigns to support anti-discrimination legislation covering housing, employment, education, and public accommodation.[103] Well beyond its civil rights projects, though, the ADL measured its expansion by its thickening relationships with state and knowledge-producing institutions. Following the televised event, in 1954, the ADL was enlisted by the West German government to assess German progress on antisemitism, and it used its reporting authority to advocate for continuing US oversight of democracy programming "even if West Germany should become a sovereign state," which, for the ADL, more than its work on Israel, marked its entry into the new transnational politics of the post–World War II United States.[104] In an indication that the ADL had moved from a class-making to a politics-making institution, its 1958 "Dinner with Congress" (presenting an award for the 1957 Civil Rights Act) was "one of the largest bipartisan gatherings of Congressmen ever held outside of the Capitol itself."[105]

These shifts capped a larger strategy to move the ADL into the national role in media, making and disseminating political narrative. Nathan Belth,

100. *Memorandum Submitted to the American Public Relations Association*, n.d., quoted in Barnouw, *Image Empire*, 16n6.

101. Klutznick's speech, referenced previously, was delivered in his introduction of President Eisenhower at the 1953 event.

102. Epstein, "Vol Ia: Epstein, Benjamin R., 1985–1987," Box 1, Folder 1, MS-365, p. 104, B'nai B'rith Anti-Defamation League Oral Histories, American Jewish Archives, Cincinnati, Ohio.

103. Moore, *B'nai B'rith and the Challenge of Ethnic Leadership*, 124.

104. *New York Times*, "Germans Accused of Anti-Semitism; B'nai B'rith Mission Asks US to Continue Its Program of Democratic Education," July 20, 1954.

105. Anti-Defamation League, *Report of Anti-Defamation League B'nai B'rith* (1959).

the ADL's public relations director from 1946 to 1971, outlined the postwar plan. To situate itself as a news-making agency, it had established an internal art and production department and a process for making local news stories out of information sent from the central office of the ADL. These materials became the basis for a flow of content that the ADL pushed out to mass media. It also began publishing the *ADL Bulletin*, a free national monthly, mailed to organizations and funders as well as individual subscribers. Although initially aimed at Jewish readers, "[a]s a little extra dividend . . . the ADL Bulletin became a source for research, for newspapermen, for scholars and others who were seeking material on subject matter that ADL was concerned with. The Bulletin . . . began to publish short, pithy, but accurate articles on civil rights issues and anti-Semitism and so forth."[106] The ADL's scholarly materials did the same work, generating both publicity and scientific bona fides. The ADL's practice of recruiting high-level business leaders to its leadership, along with its awards circuit, built funding and access capacity with clusters of leaders in individual industries, including network media executives. "This was a new era. . . . I am convinced it was established in part through the series of Dinners with the Presidents. . . . It was established through the kind of public relations work of men like Shap Shapiro of *Look* magazine, which printed the history of the ADL under the leadership of [Hollywood producer and ADL national chairman] Dore Schary . . . that kind of public acceptance . . . put us on the way to where we are today."[107] In that elevated role, the ADL established new authority over the content of civil rights discourse, inflected with the authority of the US state, Jewish religiosity, and a hybrid position as both representative of minority interests and a white organization.

As the ADL's stature rose as a mainstream democracy organization, its claims to represent US Jewry gained importance, and its antipathy toward the Jewish left became more consequential. Jewish communal politics were increasingly tightly coordinated among the more conservative, wealthier groups. The National Community Relations Advisory Council, created in 1944, coordinated among the Jewish defense and community relations agencies. It was

106. Belth, "Vol Va: Belth, Nathan C., 1985–1987," 108.

107. Benjamin R. Epstein, "Vol Ia: Epstein, Benjamin R., 1985–1987," Box 1, Folder 1, MS-365, p. 131, B'nai B'rith Anti-Defamation League Oral Histories, American Jewish Archives, Cincinnati, Ohio.

understood as an effort to present a unified "program of postwar Jewish demands" and served as a de facto "promoter of Jewish thoughts and consciousness."[108] A decade later, in 1955, the Conference of Presidents of Major American Jewish Organizations put forward a unified Jewish voice on Israel, and it too staked a claim to representing US Jewish interests as a unity.[109] The member groups of these formations commanded the bulk of Jewish communal funding and were led by boards and directors who were members of the state-capital classes. They were buoyed by a membership that was itself rising through the middle class and separated by generations from immigrant origins, by the whittling down of the Yiddish-accented left. By contrast, Jewish organizations to their left, including the Jewish People's Fraternal Order and the Workmens' Circle, lacked their political and economic leverage and struggled for a voice in spaces where Jews were to be represented as a polity.[110]

In the context of the Red Scare, NCRAC organizations moved to cleanse themselves of any connection to communism and to purge the leftist Jews whose existence they had wishfully denied—including members of the Communist Party, believers in communist principles who had not joined the party, and "fellow travelers" who sympathized with their ideals. In the late 1940s and early 1950s, an American Jewish Committee intelligence-gathering committee tracked Jews' communist activities and shared the information with other groups. In 1950 the ADL's National Commission, acting on recommendations from its Civil Rights Committee, resolved "together with other community agencies, our national organization and regional office shall help to expel Communist groups from organized Jewish life." In a collective push, Jewish institutions did just that. In public statements, they joined in the rhetoric and attacks of the Red Scare and denounced leftist Jews who decried the antisemitism deployed by anticommunists. The purges of Jewish organizations paralleled the purges of communists from their unions, as well as the excision of entire communist-led unions from labor coalitions, that would also decimate the infrastructure of Jewish life.

108. The American Jewish Congress's *Congress Weekly*, from June 1943, as quoted in Oscar Handlin, "Freedom or Authority in Group Life? Voluntary Agreements Work, Our Experience Teaches Us," *Commentary Magazine*, December 1, 1952.

109. Moore, *B'nai B'rith and the Challenge of Ethnic Leadership*, 218; Daniel Judah Elazar, *Community and Polity: The Organizational Dynamics of American Jewry* (Jewish Publication Society, 1995), 306.

110. Arthur Liebman, "The Ties That Bind: The Jewish Support for the Left in the United States," *American Jewish Historical Quarterly* 66, no. 2 (1976): 316.

The national uproar around the case of Julius and Ethel Rosenberg provided the ADL with a chance to demonstrate its renunciation of Jews who were communists. The Rosenbergs, Ethel's brother David Greenglass, and their friend Morton Sobell were charged with passing US secrets to the Soviet Union. Their trial in 1951 was the subject of enormous publicity, in which the group was portrayed as a personification of the charge of "Jewish communism." While leftists scrambled to challenge the antisemitism and anti-leftism that were working together to vilify the accused, the ADL insisted that antisemitism did not play a role. The NCRAC institutions collectively denounced the very idea, issuing a statement: "Attempts are being made . . . to inject the false issue of anti-Semitism into the Rosenberg case. . . . We denounce the fraudulent effort to confuse and manipulate public opinion for ulterior purposes."[111] Ethel and Julius Rosenberg were sentenced to death and executed in 1952. The judge, Irving Kaufman, was a member of the ADL's national Civil Rights Committee at the time. (An inveterate anticommunist, when he had joined the committee two years earlier, he first checked with the FBI to make sure the ADL was not "infiltrated by communists"—a rumor spread by white nationalist groups like the John Birch Society.)[112] The NCRAC groups made a full and public sacrifice of the Rosenbergs, cheering their conviction and firmly refusing to call for clemency to forestall their execution.[113] When the Rosenbergs were executed, the American Jewish Committee's 1953 *Jewish Yearbook* mentioned it only as a footnote. Thirty-five years later, ADL lawyer Arnold Forster reflected that "Jewish defense agencies were motivated more by fear . . . than principle" and worried that the case had in fact been precipitated by antisemitism.[114]

The ADL's anticommunist fervor superseded any distaste for right-wing anticommunist crusaders, leading to its cooperation with McCarthy and his widely reviled lieutenant prosecutor Roy Cohn. In December 1951, a secret

111. S. Andhil Fineberg, *The Rosenberg Case: Fact and Fiction* (Oceana, 1953), 69.

112. A. Rosen to E.A. Tamm, Office Memorandum, US Government, Subject: Antidefamation League, May 18, 1948, File 1199215-000 --- 100-HQ-530 --- Section 7, p. 171, The FBI and the Anti-Defamation League, Israel Lobby Archive, Institute for Research: Middle East Policy, https://www.israellobby.org/adl/.

113. For a collection of letters and statements on major Jewish organizations' calculations around the Rosenberg trial, see Lauren Gilbert, "'A Very Ticklish Problem': The AJC Response to the Rosenberg Trial & Execution," *The Word: The CJH Blog*, April 27, 2023, https://blog.cjh.org/index.php/2023/04/25/a-very-ticklish-problem-the-ajc-response-to-the-rosenberg-trial-execution/.

114. Arnold Forster, *Square One: A Memoir* (D.I. Fine, 1989), 128–29.

meeting between McCarthy, ADL counsel Arnold Forster, and ADL national chair Judge Meier Steinbrink was reported in the Jewish press as a "bombshell" revelation.[115] The session had been quietly arranged by Hearst newspaper columnist George Sokolsky, who championed McCarthy's anticommunist career. The ADL addressed outrage over the meeting by announcing that it was "not involved in politics" and had only wanted to hear from McCarthy. However, McCarthy described the meeting otherwise. As *Jewish Life* reported: "McCarthy said that it was a 'good gab session' lasting four hours on 'a number of questions bothering some of the fellows.' According to the report, the meeting ended with a friendly gin rummy session. McCarthy described the talk as 'one of the most profitable sessions I have ever experienced.' Observers are disturbed at this extraordinary spectacle of appeasement of fascists."[116]

The meeting with McCarthy was not a onetime connection, but perhaps a beginning, as the ADL's relationship with McCarthy and the House Un-American Activities Committee (HUAC) continued to make the news. Indeed, Arnold Forster moved in overlapping circles with McCarthyists. Forster was a close friend and colleague of Walter Winchell. He was a central player in the production of Winchell's gossipy news column, which targeted Nazis, communists, and others in a show that captured nearly a third of the US population on a weekly basis. Through the ADL's surveillance of the right, Forster regularly provided Winchell with material for his column. Winchell, in his fervor to rout communism, also worked with McCarthy, and was close to Cohn. Although Forster and others in Winchell's circle reportedly disapproved of his embrace of McCarthy, all shared the same anticommunist passion; Forster's objection was to McCarthy's methods that "hurt many innocents and damaged Jewish reputation [*sic*] in the process."[117] This, too, was the context in which the ADL surveilled Martin Luther King Jr., who was a target of McCarthy's allegations of communism and a constant subject of FBI monitoring. That surveillance "was common knowledge and

115. *The Sentinel*, "Report McCarthy Slurs Jews; Calls Them 'Slick,'" February 21, 1952.

116. Louis Harap, "From the Four Corners," *Jewish Life*, February 1952, http://archive.org/details/sim_jewish-currents_1952-02_6_4.

117. Neal Gabler, *Winchell: Gossip, Power, and the Culture of Celebrity* (Knopf, 1995), 294–95, 454–58; Forster, *Square One*, 159.

casually accepted," former ADL national publications director Henry Schwarzschild later told the *San Franscisco Weekly*.[118]

A year after the secret meeting, more collaboration between the ADL and McCarthy came to light. The episode began in 1953, when HUAC subpoenaed *Jewish Life* editor Louis Harap to an investigative hearing. Harap took the opportunity to denounce the body as an undertaking to violate freedoms of speech, press, and academic work, and to produce "the same conditions under which 6 million Jews were murdered." In the exchange, HUAC interrogators asked whether Harap would "shrink with the same horror from the things that the Russian government is doing to the Jewish people," and Harap again used the platform to take a stand—first against the implication that HUAC was concerned about antisemitism, and then in defense of communism. "The fact of the matter is that in the Soviet Union the Jews have a higher degree of freedom and equality than they have, I think, in any other part of the world," Harap answered.[119] The ADL was outraged. Epstein called the committee's chairman, Congressman Harold Velde, to complain that HUAC had given Harap the stage. It should have publicly distinguished Harap from "the responsible Jewish organizations" but instead had "provided him with a million dollars worth of free publicity. . . . for his Commie propaganda line."[120]

The Harap incident led to a meeting between Velde, ADL staff, and leaders of the American Jewish Committee and the Jewish War Veterans in which the ADL directly asked to work with HUAC. In reporting an ADL memo leaked by *Jewish Life*, Harap reported the "treacherous proposals" with which "these Jewish professionals . . . scurry to the UnAmerican Committee."[121] The proposed plan aimed to suppress the Jewish left and sharpen the propaganda value of the hearings. To HUAC, Epstein offered the ADL's advice and support, conspicuously casting aside concern for democratic processes. He suggested that HUAC bar the public from its initial questioning of people under investigation, to "screen such witnesses first in

118. On Schwarzchild, see Thomas M. Hilbink, "Filling the Void: The Lawyers Constitutional Defense Committee and the 1964 Freedom Summer," *SSRN Electronic Journal* (1993). On surveillance of Martin Luther King Jr., see Robert I. Friedman, "The Jewish Thought Police," *Village Voice*, July 27, 1993.

119. *Jewish Life*, "The Harap Testimony," September 1953, 10–11.

120. *Jewish Life*, "Memorandum of the ADL," September 1953, 8.

121. Morris U. Schappes and Louis Harap, "Open Letter to the Jewish People of the United States," *Jewish Life*, September 1953.

executive session to explore what the witnesses might be up to." Then he offered up ADL and American Jewish Committee files to be "consulted for information about such witnesses." If "responsible Jewish organizations" had already attacked someone, that evidence could be added to HUAC's case and also serve to distance the witnesses from the agencies. The meeting had been intended as a secret, and *Jewish Life*'s exposé produced scandal in Jewish newspapers. But it helped rather than hurt the ADL. Based on that meeting, the ADL built a working relationship with the right-wing Hearst newspapers, which it parlayed into editorial support for a variety of aims, including US aid to Israel.[122] Shortly after the meeting, HUAC denounced as "subversives" the rabbis Judah Magnes and Stephen Wise, leaders of the American Jewish Congress, the third defense organization that rankled the ADL and American Jewish Committee. For the leadership of the "responsible" organizations, allying with autocrats was strategic.[123]

Finally, in the mid-1950s, the Jewish defense agencies and many other Jewish organizations officially purged their ranks of leftists. Members of the fifty-thousand-strong Jewish People's Fraternal Order, the Jewish section of the communist International Workers Order, were fired from their jobs in Jewish organizations. Jewish social welfare agency workers lost their eighty-two-thousand-member communist-led, racial justice–focused union to a CIO anticommunist purge. It was replaced with a union committed to anticommunism.[124] The National Jewish Welfare Board, the central body for Jewish community centers, instructed local organizations not to invite "controversial" speakers.[125] The left, despite being a substantial force in US politics, had been made vulnerable to such assaults by postwar changes: Eastern European Jews had begun to suburbanize and espouse a middle-class American nationalism; leftist organizations were riven by ideological division; and anticommunist fervor had surged among "right-wing socialist" organizations. For leaders who had chafed at communist-linked organizing

122. Epstein, "Vol Ia: Epstein, Benjamin R., 1985–1987," Box 1, Folder 1, MS-365, p. 148, B'nai B'rith Anti-Defamation League Oral Histories, American Jewish Archives, Cincinnati, Ohio.

123. *Jewish Herald*, "Confirm Deal Between Velde and Top 'Defense' Organizations," October 9, 1953.

124. Martha Biondi, *To Stand and Fight: The Struggle for Civil Rights in Postwar New York City* (Harvard University Press, 2006), 149.

125. Liebman, "The Ties That Bind," 316.

in their own ranks, the anti-red fervor was a chance to dispense with the problem.

Throughout the 1960s, the organizational Jewish left was diminished. It suffered internal splits as well as disappointments with Soviet positions on antisemitism and Zionism.[126] In practice, the purges removed leftists not only from Jewish institutional leadership, but from social work, teaching, community center jobs, and rabbinical posts in the much larger sector of organizations sponsored by Jewish institutions; leftist labor unions were replaced with centrist, capitalist unions.[127] Arguably, this shift also allowed the ADL to move concretely away from its outdated construction as a German Jewish institution (as it had begun already to do in the 1940s) to an institution inclusive of upwardly mobile, rightward-moving Eastern European Jews, embracing a more democratic vision of community without diminishing its hold on class and political respectability. The defense organizations' purge was largely successful at separating Jewishness from leftism, at least temporarily.[128] Looking backward in 1976, historian Arthur Liebman wrote, "After 1950, there were very few sources within the Jewish community that actively promoted and worked for left objectives and values. . . . The left in the Jewish community bereft of defenders and beset by attackers was in the 1950's de-legitimized in the eyes of American Jewry."[129] By 1960, when Jewish leftists flocked to Students for a Democratic Society and other New Left movements, most did not identify as *Jewish* leftists at all.[130]

While the ADL had long denounced communism, its investment in Cold War framings—the threat from the left—marked a shift. Through the 1940s, it had mainly identified nativists, Christian demagogues, the Ku Klux Klan,

126. On the splits and decline of communist-linked institutions of the Jewish left, see Gennady Estraikh, "Professing Leninist Yiddishkayt: The Decline of American Yiddish Communism," *American Jewish History* 96, no. 1 (2010): 33–60.

127. Svonkin, *Jews Against Prejudice*, 166–69.

128. On the rekindled, politically complicated organizing of the Jewish left of the late 1960s and early '70s, see Keith P. Feldman, *A Shadow over Palestine: The Imperial Life of Race in America* (University of Minnesota Press, 2015), 134–42; and Michael Staub, *Torn at the Roots: The Crisis of Jewish Liberalism in Postwar America* (Columbia University Press, 2004).

129. Liebman, "The Ties That Bind," 316.

130. Sol Stern, "My Jewish Problem—And Ours: Israel, the Left, and the Jewish Establishment," in *Jewish Radicalism: A Selected Anthology*, ed. Jack Nusan Porter and Peter Dreier (Grove, 1973).

and Nazis as the primary threats to US democracy. Its antipathy toward the left had mostly focused on the reputational risk to respectable, "responsible" Jewry, and the need to impose discipline on Jewish populations. But in the 1950s it recast leftist movements, Jewish and non-Jewish, as a threat to US democracy. That shift had everything to do with the new centrality of civil rights, racism, and egalitarianism to mainstream US politics—and the fact that the left had already been organizing on those issues for decades.

The move from right to left threat is perhaps most clearly visible in two books published by the ADL on either side of the shift. In 1950 the ADL published *A Measure of Freedom* under the direction of its civil rights director and counsel Arnold Forster. That book, leaning on the new science of research and polling, aimed to describe the sources and pathways of antisemitism and to call for the "militant unity" needed to support "democracy's principles."[131] It conceived the threats to democracy almost exclusively from the right, and it used the jaunty style of wartime adventure narratives. Titillating readers with an endorsement from Walter Winchell, the book jacket advertised: "8 pages of documented atomic energy on [antisemite] Upton Close . . . 20 pages of hydrogen bombs exposing Merwin K. Hart, and nearly 100 additional pages on 20 other targets of this column." It did not leave the left entirely unmentioned, but fretted about right-wing responses to it. One such instance was the Peekskill riots of 1949, which were white race riots intended to prevent a concert by Paul Robeson, the leftist, antiracist, and labor advocate. Robeson had just returned from the Soviet Union (where, he declared, he was viewed as a human being rather than a Black man) and the Civil Rights Congress (CRC), a Black-led communist-aligned group, had organized the concert. Initially, Forster wrote, "some believed" that the anticommunist protest was "a healthy sign of Americanism." As the rioting went on, though, it became more focused on anti-Jewish and anti-Black messages. Forster's concern was that such organizing led to Jewish and Black people being "lumped together with the controversial Communist issue."[132]

Soon the ADL adopted questions of race and rights as its own turf, identifying Jewish, Black, and Arab organizers as a threat to democracy. Initially

131. Arnold Forster, *A Measure of Freedom: An Anti-Defamation League Report* (Doubleday, 1950), 7.

132. Charles H. Martin, "Internationalizing 'The American Dilemma': The Civil Rights Congress and the 1951 Genocide Petition to the United Nations," *Journal of American Ethnic History* 16, no. 4 (1997): 35–61; Forster, *A Measure of Freedom*, 90–91.

it placed Jewish and Black organizers on the left, and Arab organizers on the right; however, within a few more years Arabs, too, and all antiracist, anticolonial movements, would be on its left-looking radar. Epstein and Forster's reasoning was the reasoning behind Cold War civil rights: To a "world [that] differs from us in color of skin or religious persuasion," treatments of race and rights in the United States conveyed the meanings of freedom and democracy that US leadership portended for the globe. This presumptively white perspective anchored the ADL's worry that communists were conspiring to usurp the politics of civil rights and recruit unwitting Americans by playing on their instincts for racial justice.

Epstein and Forster's 1952 book, *The Trouble-Makers*, described this tactic as "confusion from the left." It portrayed Black populations as desperate to attain civil rights and therefore "obviously and unhappily . . . a fertile field for troublemakers on the left."[133] Specifically, the ADL charged that Black defendants in Jim Crow cases were often gulled by leftists (usually Black leftists) into allowing their cases to be used to foment anti-state, anticapitalist sentiment. As ever, they turned to sensational headlines to make their case. Willie McGee was a young Black man who had been executed in 1951 after being accused by a white woman of rape in Mississippi under dubious circumstances. The Trenton Six had been coerced to confess to a murder in New Jersey; four were finally acquitted in 1951.[134] In both cases, the CRC had sought to defend against the racist contortions of justice. The ADL was outraged at the CRC's involvement because the CRC described the prosecutions as a function of liberal capitalism, which provided no justice to Black workers. Accordingly, the case garnered exactly the kind of international attention to US racism that Cold War civil rights work aimed to avoid. The CRC "disseminated widely their lurid evaluations of the case, charging that capitalist forces were at work in America to railroad the men to the electric chair," wrote Epstein and Forster. "Moscow newspapers had a field day. India and the Philippine Islands became interested and indignant. . . . The popular

133. See Forster and Epstein, *Trouble-Makers*, chap. 6 ("Confusion from the Left"), 218.
134. For a concise history of these cases, see Denise Lynn, "Losing Willie McGee," African American Intellectual History Society, July 6, 2020, https://www.aaihs.org /losing-willie-mcgee/; Lynn, "Before the Central Park Five, There Was the Trenton Six," African American Intellectual History Society, July 3, 2019, https://www.aaihs.org /before-the-central-park-five-there-was-the-trenton-six/.

Reynolds News of London—certainly no Communist publication—printed the story under a blaring headline: 'They Must Die for Being Black.'"[135]

In fact, the two cases had generated substantial international support for the defendants and outrage over Jim Crow laws.[136] To the ADL, though, this meant only that communists had exploited the cases to internationalize anti-US sentiment and "turn colored peoples in colonial lands against the United States." The defendants themselves got no more respect from the ADL. Epstein and Forster lamented that they were "utterly obscure"—meaning Black, poor, and gormless—and were ideological marks easily duped by communists and their offers of fundraising. The book grimly summarized their view: "By the time the state executioner wrote finis to Willie McGee's tragic and confused life, this Mississippi Negro had been closely identified with Communist propaganda; his wife had toured the country widely under Communist auspices; and the Party itself had so manipulated the cause to promote protest parades, mass meetings, and demonstrations throughout the world that millions had all but forgotten the basic question of his guilt or innocence. In American cities, thousands massed to shout support of Willie McGee and to attack American foreign policy."[137] In this tragic pattern, ADL leaders insisted, Black men became "pawns in a global propaganda struggle" when they failed to recognize that working with the left polluted their defenses and damned them.[138]

Much of the ADL's censure focused on the use of public protest, a tactic common to labor and leftist political organizing. In the long tradition of German Jewish elitism, it declared protests to be unruly, unseemly, and publicity for bad actors. Instead its leaders insisted on faith in American political

135. Forster and Epstein, *Trouble-Makers*, 221.

136. Alex Heard writes of the international protests against the execution of Willie McGee: "Cables came in from Mexico City (Diego Rivera, Frida Kahlo, and others wrote Truman, calling the sentence 'monstrous'), the Soviet Union (Dimitri Shostakovich, Anton Chekhov's widow, and others, who informed the supreme court of Mississippi that 'mankind shall not forgive those guilty of this terrible infamy'), Ireland, England, and France. In early April, the Daily People's World ran a photo of protesters in front of a London movie theater, holding up signs that said, WILLIE MCGEE MUST NOT DIE! Later that month, Mississippi lieutenant governor Sam Lumpkin complained about having to deal with pro-McGee letters and telegrams when Governor Wright was out of the state. 'They must have an effective underground to keep up with what's going on,' he said, mentioning one letter that came from '30 residents, 19 Cornwall Ardens, London.'" Alex Heard, *The Eyes of Willie McGee: A Tragedy of Race, Sex, and Secrets in the Jim Crow South* (Harper Collins, 2011), 327.

137. Forster and Epstein, *Trouble-Maker*, 219.

138. Describing the Trenton Six. Forster and Epstein, *Trouble-Makers*, 221.

systems and the capacity of elite Jewish leadership to deal in them. Just as it lamented the Black "dupes" who were seduced into communism, the ADL drew new attention to Jewish "dupes" in *The Trouble-Makers*. For instance, it denounced a 1947 protest *against* antisemitic demagogue Gerald L. K. Smith, a villain who appeared regularly in the ADL's reports. When Smith appeared in Boston for a speaking event, protests were organized by the largely Jewish Fur and Leather Workers' Union, the United Office and Professional Workers of America, and the International Workers Order. Since the organizers were aligned with the Communist Party, Forster and Epstein denounced their recruitment of Jewish protesters, as well as their work to gather clergy to sign a newspaper ad objecting to Smith's event. Communists, they claimed, were exploiting others' concerns about fascism as a means of recruiting them to the Communist Party. In the ADL's accounting, the Jews and others who protested Smith were coerced, and the "responsible" Jewish organizations were the only acceptable opponents of antisemitism. Jews overall, according to this logic, were rightly and only conservative.[139]

In the same turn, the ADL's 1952 *Trouble-Makers* launched attacks on Palestinian resistance and Arab anticolonialism. This attention was not completely new. In 1946 the ADL had begun reporting on "Arab propaganda," denouncing the efforts of Arab groups to narrate, for policymakers in Congress and the United Nations, the injustice of British and Jewish colonialism in Palestine. The Arab League had made various efforts to engage the US and UN policymaking that was roiling the region. In the United States, Arab American immigrants established the Institute for Arab American Affairs (IAAA), aiming to have a voice in affairs that concerned them, much as Jewish leaders had conceived the American Jewish Committee as a way to intervene in the Kishinev pogroms.[140] The ADL viewed both efforts as equally foreign and as intrusions into the political process rather than part of it. Rather than recognizing Arab Americans as a domestic constituency, the ADL suggested that IAAA acted on behalf of US oil companies that had a commercial stake in Arab affairs. As such, Forster and Epstein called the Arab organizers "professional agitators" seeking to "create hysteria in the British Foreign Office and in the American State Department" in order to block Zionist aspirations in Palestine. For their part, the Arab organizations

139. Forster and Epstein, *Trouble-Makers*, 226.
140. Hani J. Bawardi, *The Making of Arab Americans: From Syrian Nationalism to US Citizenship* (University of Texas Press, 2014), 240.

took pains to articulate their opposition to colonialism. "Zionism is neither a humanitarian nor a religious program. It is a political program," read an Arab Office advertisement in the *New York Times* in November 1945. "The 'Jewish problem' is a European problem. The refugee problem is also a European problem. . . . The Arabs of Palestine should not be held alone responsible for the solution. It does not lie in the artificial establishment of a Jewish state in Palestine, but in the assurance of true democracy and the guarantee of security throughout the world." The absence of antisemitism and the reference to democracy were read by the ADL as a clever feint: "Their propaganda, apparently plausible and reasonable, is the more effective and consequently the more dangerous," the ADL cautioned in its monthly investigative newsletter, *The Facts*.[141]

By 1948 the ADL had begun viewing advocacy for Palestine as a threat to US democracy. Using the lexicon of threat that it had developed over its three prior decades, it portrayed Arab organizations as part of the right; later it would place them on the left. Its reporting pointed to figures of intolerance and demagoguery who endorsed Arab opposition to Western colonialism, among them Benjamin H. Freedman, who produced the racist tabloid *Common Sense* and used Palestine advocacy as an avenue for antisemitic invective. Having sketched Arab advocacy as the domain of the racist right, the ADL broadly accused all anti-Zionists of fostering right-wing politics. The May 1948 issue of *The Facts* made this accusation against Barnard College dean Virginia Gildersleeve, Islamic Studies scholar Bayard Dodge, and Standard Oil executive Max Thornburg, academic and civic leaders who had no such connections to the right. Alfred M. Lilienthal, anti-Zionist Jewish activist and former US State Department official who often challenged the ADL, described this tactic in the same year as "guilt by juxtaposition." Lilienthal wrote: "The evaluation of these men and women whose motivation the Anti-Defamation League concedes might be sincere is intermixed with an analysis of Coughlin, Gerald L. K. Smith, and others patently insincere."[142] As Geoffery Levin notes, the Arab League's advocates were "'inundated with offers of co-operation from anti-Semitic organisations . . .' that sought to use its anti-Zionist material to advance their aims." Some of those offers were accepted before their motives were clear to the Arab League (or to the ADL); others were accepted more deliberately, particularly in the

141. Anti-Defamation League of B'nai B'rith, *The Facts*, June 1946.
142. Alfred M. Lilienthal, *What Price Israel* (Henry Regnery Company, 1953).

1940s. By the mid-1950s Arab advocates, including Fayez Sayegh and the Arab Information Center, formed in 1955, worked to block antisemites from associating with Arab work.[143]

The ADL's objections extended well beyond right-wing instrumentalization of Arab concerns. Its leaders now contended with the effects of Arab advocacy on their own ability to assert authority on race and rights. By 1948 ADL leaders were supportive of a Jewish state as a response to problems of their own, if still not fully invested in Zionism. In the United States, Nazi-inspired groups had gained traction, unemployment was high, and President Roosevelt had snidely been nicknamed "President Rosenfeld" by those who thought he had too many Jewish advisers and that the New Deal was a communist plot.[144] The matter of Jewish war refugees, which all Jewish groups approached as a grave humanitarian crisis, also pressed on their self-interest. Since 1933, when Nazis had seized control of Germany, and Jews en masse contemplated the need to escape, US Jewish leaders had feared and avoided bringing a new round of Jewish refugees to the United States. Their responses to the crisis danced around Jewish class tensions: In 1933, B'nai B'rith called on Congress to allow in more Jewish refugees, but it clarified that this meant admitting some "non-laborers and some exceptional persons" rather than expanding immigration quotas. When many more Jews fleeing Nazism did arrive, a 1937 editorial in *B'nai B'rith Magazine* bluntly complained that they were having trouble finding work, and "their increasing numbers may become a social irritation as they seek places in the life of a community already overcrowded." (Although their positions against immigration softened after the advent of war in 1939, the worries remained.)[145] If Palestine could be a place of rescue for Jews fleeing Nazis, it would relieve pressure on US Jewry, too.

By the early 1950s, major US Jewish organizations had additional interest in advancing colonization and marginalizing Palestinian voices of opposition. Although they had not yet collectively adopted Zionism as a politics, challenges to the Israeli project undercut the power of major Jewish organizations themselves. US Jewish organizing had become the lifeline of the Zionist settlement project, raising funds, galvanizing the support of the US state and

143. Geoffery P. Levin, "Before the New Antisemitism: Arab Critics of Zionism and American Jewish Politics, 1917–1974," *American Jewish History* 105, no. 1 (2021): 114, 131.

144. Hasia R. Diner, *The Jews of the United States, 1654 to 2000* (University of California Press, 2006), 213–17; Cohen, *Not Free to Desist*, 205–11.

145. David Brody, "American Jewry, the Refugees, and Immigration Restriction (1932–1942)," *Publications of the American Jewish Historical Society* 45, no. 4 (1956): 221, 224, 243.

the United Nations, and helping to dissuade the UN from facilitating the return of Palestinian refugees to their homes. As Forster and Epstein saw it, the objective of Arab advocacy was to change the political climate so that "the United Jewish Appeal and other forms of Israel aid would find it difficult to function; and, at the most, the United States Government would find it inexpedient to assist Israel financially, or stand by its side in international disputes at the United Nations." In other words, US major Jewish organizations' political credentials were now entwined with Israel's, and the ADL saw Arab organizing as an antisemitic bid for "the utter destruction of Jewish prestige in America."[146] Similarly, Arab advocacy threatened the ADL's main currency: its moral authority. In a discourse about violations of Palestinians' rights, US Jewish organizations were positioned as rights *deniers*. The ADL understood, too, that the process of Zionist colonization fed US antisemitic narratives, both because conspiracy theorists leapt on any political project of Jewish organizations, and because of the actual violence of colonization. And indeed, Arab advocates pulled the same political levers that the ADL regularly used—anticommunism and appeals to protect the biblical Holy Land—in portraying Zionist settlement as a communist-aligned project that targeted Christian holy sites. For the ADL, it was immaterial that Jewish colonization was brutalizing and dispossessing Palestinians, had created a new population of refugees, and used biblical Judaism as its rationale.[147] Its only job was defense.

The Trouble-Makers set out to discredit Arab challenges. Under the heading "Invasion," Forster and Epstein presented a sensational exposé on the Arab League's work before the United Nations and its plans for US advocacy for Palestine refugees. The text was Cold War entertainment, replete with racially and ideologically villainous foreigners, written in the rat-a-tat style of tabloid radio newsreaders. Also, it was spy drama: its minute detail on the Arab League's plans, movements, collaborations with US groups, and reports "marked 'top secret' and rushed off to Cairo"—no source cited—suggested that the ADL had gone undercover in Arab League operations.[148] It suggested that Arab diplomats, too, were undercover in the United States. Noting that they had traveled to New York on the occasion of UN meetings on Palestine, *The Trouble-Makers* purported to expose their arrival as an

146. Forster and Epstein, *Trouble-Makers*, 170; Forster and Epstein, *Cross-Currents*, 304.
147. Forster and Epstein, *Trouble-Makers*, 170–71.
148. Forster and Epstein, *Trouble-Makers*, 185–86.

infiltration. "Had the League decided to launch a secret propaganda drive in this country at any other time, it might have had difficulty explaining a sudden influx of Arab publicists into the United States," wrote Forster and Epstein suggestively.[149] In the same vein, it used cinematic Orientalist tropes in describing the diplomats of the Arab League as "propagandists": its characters were "shrewd, suave, personable, no amateur," "notorious," an "intriguer," "one of the smoothest international operators who ever came to sell a cause to the United Nations," and, for contrast, "shrill-voiced and frequently hysterical."

The ADL's takedowns of Arab advocacy did not end at racist characterizations of individuals, but covered the whole infrastructure of Arab political efforts. The Arab Information Office, as the ADL portrayed it, closely resembled the ADL itself: a diplomacy, lobbying, and political education effort to build an infrastructure of support for rights and democracy, attack communism, and oppose racist narrations that claimed otherwise. Without irony, the ADL described this work as conspiracy. "[Arab League political director] Azzam literally lived, ate, and slept anti-Semitism," wrote Forster and Epstein.

> He called a meeting of Arab UN delegates and suggested furnishing them with 'combat bulletins' for their private information . . . [Met] a well-known, anti-Zionist lecturer . . . [who] prepared to deliver a lecture at City College entitled 'How the State of Israel was Created Against the Will of the Palestinians' . . . [Consulted] an expert on Arab affairs who was frequently in touch with State Department circles . . . [Met] oil company officials . . . [who] discussed techniques of propaganda and promised to subscribe to a hundred tickets for each Arab fund-raising function.[150]

Often the ADL's own anti-Arab messaging mirrored claims that the ADL had called antisemitic. Azzam's reported claim that "Jewish capitalism throughout the world is precipitating World War III" was mirrored by Forster and Epstein's claim that oil companies' interests were the political force and financiers of the movement. The advocates' efforts to distinguish between Jews on the whole and "the Jews in Palestine," and between anti-Zionism and antisemitism, were denounced by Forster and Epstein as propaganda. They were followed with the ADL's identical claim in reverse: "The

---

149. Forster and Epstein, *Trouble-Makers*, 173.
150. Forster and Epstein, *Trouble-Makers*, 180–81.

authors of this book do not indict the Arabs . . . but we do indict those Arabs who use religious hatred and prejudice to achieve their ends."[151]

The enabling practice of this project—the cinematic staging of "Arab conversation"—affirmed the ADL's role as an expert reporter while obscuring facts and context through mischaracterization, omission, and racist presumption: a close parallel of *affirmation as denial*. These inaccuracies were publicly challenged in ways that certainly tarnished the ADL, even if they did not dissuade friends like Winchell, much of the Jewish press, and Hearst newspapers from treating it as an authoritative source. Alfred M. Lilienthal, the former US State Department official who often used his access to diplomatic information to challenge Zionist accounts, charged the ADL with inventing at least some of the stories in its 1952 book: *Trouble-Makers* "tells of a secret meeting between Azzam Pasha . . . and members of H.E.L.P. who conspired with Azzam Pasha in his anti-Jewish propaganda. No such meeting ever took place: at the time of the alleged meeting, H.E.L.P. had ceased to exist for more than three months."[152] Epstein and Forster's 1956 book *Cross-Currents* made even more extensive claims about Arab collaborations with nativist antisemites, which were also challenged. "I am the Deputy Director of the Arab States Delegation," Fayez Sayegh told a radio interviewer. "I have never met any of the [nativist] gentlemen referred to . . . never communicated with them . . . never known of anyone in my office . . . [who has] received the support of any of the persons mentioned. . . . Even the contentions which, in the form of conclusions, were heralded last week with all the hullabaloo and fanfare of a soap opera . . . were not in any way vindicated . . . by any of the alleged facts that are contained in the book."[153] Internally, Sayegh reported: "It is obvious . . . that the Anti-Defamation League bases its charges on reports from its own operatives and distorted handling of innocuous and meaningless documentation."[154] Sayegh continually challenged the ADL to produce the documents it claimed to report on and to show any instances of antisemitism in Arab Information Center materials.[155] Forster

---

151. Forster and Epstein, *Trouble-Makers*, 194–95.

152. Lilienthal, *What Price Israel*, 131.

153. WMCA, "Sayegh Challenges Authors of Cross-Currents," Radio Reports Inc., March 15–16, 1956, Box 60, Folder 1, p. 2, Fayez A. Sayegh Collection, University of Utah.

154. Memo from Fayez Sayegh, March 14, 1956, Box 60, Folder 1, Fayez A. Sayegh Collection, University of Utah.

155. Sayegh regularly wrote letters to news agencies, as well as columns, calling attention to the ADL's unsubstantiated accusations, affirming that the Arab Information Center was not making antisemitic arguments as the ADL claimed, and calling for full factual coverage.

claimed he welcomed the challenge but only, effectively, if Sayegh sued the ADL so that it would be done "in a proper legal forum."[156] These interventions generated conversation and political questions, but did not overcome the narratives of the ADL and other pro-colonization advocates.

In this turn to anti-Arab conspiracy, the ADL made a domestic enemy of global anticolonialism in the same move as it asserted authority over the domain of race and rights. Its reports on discrimination, which still monitored the Christian Right and civil rights violations, now regularly added sections that portrayed Arabs and Palestine advocacy as a menace to tolerance. Newspaper coverage of *Cross-Currents* carried the ADL's breathless warning that "Arab nations have loosed upon the United States the worst religious-racial divisive campaign since the pre-World War II Hitler Nazi-Bund days."[157] Borrowing from the tactics of anticommunism, Epstein and Forster found conspiracy in political organizing. Like communists, they argued, Arabs duplicitously spoke in terms of rights, particularly the right to be free of imperialism and the rights of refugees, while in fact the ADL claimed that no such rights had been violated and that Arab League nations "do not give a damn whether the refugees live or die." Arab Americans and Arab students in the US, anti-Zionist Jews like Lilienthal, and the myriad others who organized against US support for colonization could not be counted as legitimate political actors; instead, their efforts to participate were to be considered foreign and insurgent.[158] Borrowing from the tactics of intergroup relations, the text omitted history, racialization, capital, and other crucial contexts for the discussion of rights. As it conjured Arab advocacy for Palestine as a foreign conspiracy to interfere in US democracy and instill antisemitism, it performed what Eqbal Ahmed calls "a denial of causes," portraying these ostensible attacks not as political responses, but as evidence of a nefarious Arab nature.[159]

Cross-Currents marked a turn in the ADL's attacks on Arabness and Arab politics. It portrayed them in conjuncture with the white, Christian, and nativist right, but its core objection was to anticolonialism, which it conceived along with communism as nonwhite politics. These complaints would

156. WMCA, "Authors of 'Cross-Currents' Willing to Prove Their Truthfulness," Radio Reports Inc., April 13–14, 1956, Box 60, Folder 1, p. 1, Fayez A. Sayegh Collection, University of Utah.

157. *Herald Tribune*, "B'nai B'rith Says Arabs Help Foment Bias in US," March 11, 1956.

158. Forster and Epstein, *Cross-Currents*, 301, 303, 338–48.

159. Eqbal Ahmad, *Terrorism: Theirs & Ours* (Seven Stories Press, 1998), 15.

soon become material for the ADL's broad opposition to the antiracist left. Meanwhile, the ADL's stock soared as it turned the breathless tone of anti-communist investigative journalism toward a new national enemy. The announcement of *Cross-Currents'* publication was on the front page of at least three syndicated national newspapers, including the Hearst papers: "A declaration of war in the Middle East could scarcely have been given greater prominence," the anti-Zionist *Jewish Newsletter* noted with some annoy-ance.[160] But the public was titillated. "The fact is," Forster told a radio audi-ence on the eve of *Cross-Currents'* publication, "that the entire Arab propa-ganda machine is today anti-West. They attack Eisenhower, they attack the United States, and they're making love to the Soviet[s]." *Cross-Currents* sold over fifty thousand copies before its release.[161]

In labeling anticolonial advocacy for Palestine an "invasion" of the United States, the ADL began to stake out what Melani McAlister terms a moral geography. Its complaint at once constructed a presumptively white United States, in which Jews (excluding leftists or dissenters) were white and Arabs racially foreign. In the same move, it extended whiteness and US kinship to a Jewish version of Palestine.[162] In this construction, Jews were domestic and integrally connected to US political morality: tolerance, honesty, democracy, anticommunism. Their presence in Palestine was part of the same set of val-ues, which, as Epstein now argued, was intrinsic to Jewishness. Arabs and Arab Americans were portrayed as foreign and destabilizing to democracy, and a broad spectrum of Arab life was deemed threatening: cultural identity, resistance to colonization, advocacy for refugees, and participation in poli-tics. These constructions of state-inflected identity would persist many de-cades later, even as anticommunism faded from view as their rationale. They repeat in paradigm-setting moments, as Keith Feldman has traced, among them the United States' rejection of the 1975 UN resolution that "Zionism is racism," which established the United States, Israel, and a putative Jewry as emblems of (white) universalist nonracist democracy, posed against the (Marxist) racialized, intolerant anticolonialism of the Third Worldist move-

160. William Zukerman, *Jewish Newsletter*, March 26, 1956, Box 60, Folder 1, p. 1, Fayez A. Sayegh Collection, University of Utah.

161. WMCA, "Dr. Sayegh Mentioned in Interview with Authors of Cross-Currents," Radio Reports Inc., March 14, 1956, Box 60, Folder 1, pp. 2–3, Fayez A. Sayegh Collection, University of Utah.

162. Melani McAlister, *Epic Encounters: Culture, Media, and US Interests in the Middle East Since 1945* (University of California Press, 2005), 4–6.

ment—prefiguring the affective arrangements of the War on Terror."[163] In the later episodes of this history, they carry through the ADL's moves to oppose antiracist education and anticolonialism, and protests against genocide, by conceiving them as racialized, Marxist threats to a universalist democracy. Arising from the multilayered constructions of race, rights, and nation laid out in racial anticommunism, *affirmation as denial* was set to work.

163. Feldman, *A Shadow over Palestine*, 44, 56.

THREE

White Anxieties, "Black Antisemitism," and "New Antisemitism"

THE '60S AND '70S

"ISRAEL REGARDS ITS EXCELLENT BILATERAL relations with African countries as a great triumph," wrote Abe Foxman, the Anti-Defamation League's Middle East affairs director, in 1972. Since the late 1950s, Israel had courted newly independent African nations by proffering development assistance. Its aims were to develop regional allies, counter Arab overtures to Africa, and break the Third World solidarities that cost Israel votes at the United Nations. Israel's offer to African leaders was technical assistance on how to set up a country: irrigation, town planning, computerization, and the like. Ironically, its proposition to African leaders was that it had no colonial designs on their lands but offered simply "to serve, to teach, to leave." On the other hand, as colonial settlers in Palestine, Israelis had gained what Foxman called "experience in doing things in a hurry."[1] The outreach had been successful on some fronts: African leaders made state visits to Israel and brought teams of Israeli experts to run development projects in Africa.[2] In 1972, despite the fact that African nations voted against Israel at the United Nations, Foxman insisted that the ties were strong: "If some countries must vote against their friends in order to form a strong all-African bloc in the world forum, they accept the 'sacrifice' as necessary. Unofficially, they explain to Israel that resolutions are, after all, only words."[3] For the Anti-

1. Abraham Foxman, "Israel and Black Africa," *ADL Bulletin*, October 1972, 4–5; Moshe Decter, *"To Serve, to Teach, to Leave": The Story of Israel's Development Assistance Program in Black Africa* (American Jewish Congress, 1977).

2. Zach Levey, "Israel's Strategy in Africa, 1961–67," *International Journal of Middle East Studies* 36, no. 1 (2004): 71–87; Abel Jacob, "Israel's Military Aid to Africa, 1960–66," *Journal of Modern African Studies* 9, no. 2 (1971): 165–87.

3. Foxman, "Israel and Black Africa."

Defamation League, Israel's relations with Africa were a point of pride. Not only did they portray Israel as a well-run, charitable, contributing member among nations, they also positioned it as a supporter of decolonial racial liberation. The ADL had long understood its job as interpreting Israel for US audiences and using Israel as a vehicle for portraying Jews and their relationship to democracy. The racial self-determination narrative was essential to the project.[4]

Foxman's sanguine outlook on Africa-Israel relations did not hold. In July 1975, the World Conference on Women adopted a declaration that named Zionism as an object of anticolonial struggle, and in August the Organization of African Unity adopted opposition to Zionism as a Pan-African cause, identifying it as a racist regime like South African Apartheid.[5] Within a few months, African and Asian states had brought a parallel resolution to the United Nations General Assembly: UN Resolution 3379, which declared that Zionism was racism. UN bodies had already been outraged by Israel's intransigence in ignoring international law. It had expanded its occupation, refused the right of return to refugees, and pillaged antiquities. Now, the Palestine Liberation Organization's skilled research team, led by Fayez Sayegh, laid out the arguments for defining Zionism as racism using the logic of existing UN doctrine, the US civil rights movement, and Zionists' own descriptions of their intent to define a Jewish race and colonize an Arab one.[6] In opposition to Resolution 3379, US ambassador to the UN Daniel Patrick Moynihan argued that racism referred to biological difference while Zionism was a "strictly political movement" for national liberation. The ADL, for its part, declared the resolution "the most unbelievable nonsense," borrowing the phrase from Chaim Herzog, the ambassador for Israel to the United Nations. Herzog's outraged speech to the United Nations filled the

4. The ADL adopted a role "interpreting to the American public favorable facts concerning outstanding achievements within Israel" in the wake of the formation of the Israeli state on the basis that "part and parcel of our operations have always involved the favorable interpretation of Jews and Jewish activities to non-Jews." See the 1948 ADL committee minutes on Israel and public relations quoted and discussed in Joseph M. Kirman, "Major Programs of the B'nai B'rith Anti-Defamation League: 1945–1965" (PhD diss., New York University, 1967), 309.

5. Noura Erakat, "Unfinished Business," in *Race and the Question of Palestine*, ed. Lana Tatour and Ronit Lentin (Stanford University Press, 2025), 82–83.

6. Erakat, "Unfinished Business," 88–89. Thanks to John Harfouch and the "Engaging Sayegh's Archives" workgroup of the Institute for the Critical Study of Zionism for many illuminating conversations on Sayegh's antiracist thought and narrative strategies.

front page of the November 1975 edition of the *ADL Bulletin*. "How dare you talk of racism to us," Herzog thundered. "And from whom? From countries who are the archetypes of racism." Reiterating Israel's claim as an outpost of Western liberal democracy, Herzog rehearsed the arguments: The Israeli state was "a free democratic country, which can be visited by anybody, in which all citizens, Jewish and Arab, are free and equal . . . who suffered more than any other nation in the world from racist theories and practice." Echoing Theodor Herzl's characterization of Zionism as "civilization against barbarism," Herzog now invoked "decency and civilization" as the stakes of the vote.[7] Resoundingly, in November 1975 the UN General Assembly passed Resolution 3379: It declared Zionism a form of racism.

The rancor over Resolution 3379 reflected a long deterioration of Cold War race logics in antiracist and anti-discrimination discourse, and new strains of white backlash. The idea that colorblindness and integration were opposites of racism, once prevalent in postwar political culture, had been replaced with conversations on race and racism that were conscious of transnational, historically persistent structures of power and capital. Also, among Jewish organizations and in some spheres of Jewish life, the sense had faded that Black and Jewish communities were connected by experiences of marginalization. In its place, white grievance was rising: the complaint that white people were wronged by civil rights measures that directed resources and opportunities to racialized groups. It was matched by a sense that the United States itself was beleaguered by Black and brown nations that were animated by leftist ideas and had an axe to grind. These contentions between racial liberation and white resentment catalyzed the rise of a new political movement—neoconservatism—that was intently focused on liberal civil rights, Zionism, and Western global authority. In this landscape of grievance and authority, the ADL moved to curate seemingly contradictory discourses about race, reaffirming itself as a civil rights organization aligned with Black struggle while also narrating a "crisis of Black antisemitism."

In the late 1960s the field of intergroup relations collapsed. The postwar race-liberal consensus gave way to calls, reverberating from the speeches of Malcolm X, to reckon with the United States as a racial state ruled by white violence; calls for integration had turned to demands for Black Power. Student organizers, instead of adulating higher education institutions, were

7. Anti-Defamation League, "The Most Unbelievable Nonsense," *ADL Bulletin*, November 1975, 1–2.

protesting universities' role in reproducing racial repression. The rising movement against the Vietnam War denounced the United States as a destructive imperial force. For ADL leaders, such talk amounted to anti-American extremism. Through intergroup relations, it had envisioned a capitalist, race-unconscious, and integrated US democracy as a bulwark against Soviet communism. That vision had been the basis of mainstream Jewish institutions' alliance with Black civil rights organizations for the preceding two decades. In the 1940s Jewish organizations had opposed the "exclusionary principle," which addressed both anti-Jewish and anti-Black practices. In the 1950s they had taken up legal cases and legislative advocacy along the same lines, working on "major civil rights cases dealing with housing, employment, education, and public accommodations."[8] In the ferment of the 1960s, the ADL had joined in with "non-militant" and "white-collar" civil rights demands of Black organizations, as Joseph Kirman writes, but drew the line at the civil disobedience that was central to the movement. Quite belatedly it endorsed public protest against racist Jim Crow laws, and even then it approved only "orderly demonstrations." It refused to endorse the Freedom Rides that sent buses of Black and white passengers into Jim Crow states to defy segregation laws.[9] The ADL's commitment to law and order—what it termed "responsible" organizational practices—did not allow for allying itself with such tactics.

The work of Cold War civil rights alliances did not deliver racial equality; inequality *increased* after World War II. Postwar government programs intended to build a middle class had propelled only white populations into higher education and suburban life. Jews were now included in that category, while Black and brown people were left out. In the mid-sixties, grassroots Black-led civil rights groups rejected integration as the presumptive means of

8. Nostalgic takes on the Black-Jewish alliance often continue from Jewish organizations' efforts in the 1950s to an account of Jewish civil rights work in the US South in the 1960s. In *Bittersweet Alliance*, for instance, authors Weisbord and Stein note that, in 1964, "a significant percentage of the twelve hundred youths recruited by CORE, SNCC, SCLC, and the NAACP to work in the deep South were of Jewish background." As discussed in the previous chapter, Jewish *activists* and Jewish *institutions* did not share the same alliances. By the 1960s, mainstream Jewish institutions had purged leftists and excluded them from institutional Jewish life. If Jewish activists who went South helped forge a Black-Jewish alliance, it was not one that Jewish institutions could claim. Robert G. Weisbord and Arthur Stein, *Bittersweet Encounter: The Afro-American and the American Jew* (Negro Universities Press, 1970), 134–35, 139. On the gulf between Jews of the New Left and "the Jewish community," see Sachar, *A History of the Jews in America*, 806–7.

9. Kirman, "Major Programs of the B'nai B'rith Anti-Defamation League," 363–68, 375.

achieving rights. They withdrew from alliances with white-led organizations, including Jewish ones, seeking to develop liberatory strategies without centering white groups' interests. While plenty of individual Jewish activists stayed involved in antiracist organizing, Jewish institutions' claims of connection to Black institutions had been a key part of the narrative of a civil rights "Black-Jewish alliance." Now those connections were threadbare.[10]

Other changes also contributed to the distance between Jewish and Black politics and, indeed, Jewish and antiracist politics. By the late 1960s decolonizing nations had organized to push back on Western governments' moves to reassert global control. As US organizers developed a Third Worldist politics that critiqued racist and capitalist power, they began to see their own struggles as linked with Arab, African, Asian, and Latin American struggles.[11] In June 1967, Arab League states attacked Israel's colonial borders and were swiftly and unexpectedly defeated by the Israeli military. The Six-Day War elicited sharply different responses in the United States. Many Jews were newly drawn to Zionism, both through concerns about Israeli Jews under attack and excitement about Israel's display of strength. Conversely, many Black observers who had admired Zionism were now shaken away from it. In July 1967, the Student Nonviolent Coordinating Committee (SNCC), a major force in civil rights organizing, rocked the US public by denouncing Zionism. In September, two thousand organizers assembled at the New Politics Conference adopted an explosive resolution from the Black caucus that named and condemned "imperialistic Zionist war." Reflecting on the turn in 1972, *MERIP Report* editor Joe Stork characterized it as an ideological break: "The shift in New Left opinion regarding Israel, while difficult to document, has occurred not out of close study of the history of Zionism, but as a consequence of the emergence of a genuine anti-imperialist commitment which has evolved from simple opposition to American troops in Viet Nam. With regard to the Middle East, confusion is giving way to hunches and hunches are leading to new insight. The result has been the slow but steady disintegration of Zionist ideological hegemony of the left in the United

10. Marc Dollinger, *Black Power, Jewish Politics: Reinventing the Alliance in the 1960s* (Brandeis University Press, 2018), 87–89; Cheryl L. Greenberg, *Troubling the Waters: Black-Jewish Relations in the American Century* (Princeton University Press, 2010).

11. On the transit of ideas about liberation from Africa, Asia, and Latin America to the United States, see Robin D. G. Kelley, *Freedom Dreams: The Black Radical Imagination* (Beacon Press, 2003), 63–64.

States."[12] If the intergroup relations movement had been a means of shoring up the US as a moral force organizing the Cold War world, now both ideas were seriously challenged by antiracist movements from below.

The anticolonial turn in civil rights thinking posed a strategic problem for the ADL, and it was compounded by the demands of Zionist advocacy. From 1967 through the mid-1970s, the Israel lobby was gaining steam. Largely through the work of US Zionist organizations, by 1976 Israel was the largest recipient of US aid, of which 85 percent was military. Given Israel's emergence as a military power, the American Israel Public Affairs Committee (AIPAC) and other members of the lobby had shifted tactics. Rather than asserting a moral imperative to protect Israel, they were making the case that Israel was an essential geopolitical ally of the United States. As former AIPAC director Morris Amitay noted in 1983, "Moral authority has very little influence in politics. Few would attempt to convince a congressman to vote for an aid bill for Israel with an appeal on behalf of Israel's 'moral authority.' Rather, I would make an appeal based on its value."[13] The Kennedy administration accepted the geopolitical view in the early 1960s, as Soviet aid increased to Egypt, Syria, and Iraq. By the 1970s US policy was fully oriented toward Israel.[14] Even as the United States made these investments, it found that Israel was a difficult ally, as John Mearsheimer and Stephen Walt write. Aid was extremely costly and created expensive trouble in US relations with Arab states. Making matters worse, Israel was not a reliable friend: Although it served as an important point of access to intelligence on the Soviet Union and deterrence for Soviet action in the Arab world, it also provided misleading intelligence in a likely effort to manipulate a US response, and passed along US technology to enemies of the United States.[15] The job of the Israel lobby was to keep aid flowing anyway. While other organizations presented geopolitical arguments, the ADL's role was to situate Israel as a moral imperative: It was a refuge for survivors of the Nazi Holocaust, a platform for opposing ostensibly bigoted Arabs, and a bulwark against Soviet influence. As anticolonialism shaped US discourses

12. Joe Stork, "The American New Left and Palestine," *Journal of Palestine Studies* 2, no. 1 (1972): 64–69.

13. Morris Amitay quoted in Helena Cobban, "The US-Israeli Relationship in the Reagan Era," *Conflict Quarterly* (Spring 1989): 15.

14. John J. Mearsheimer and Stephen M. Walt, *The Israel Lobby and US Foreign Policy* (Farrar, Straus and Giroux, 2008), 26, 43, 50, 52.

15. Mearsheimer and Walt, *Israel Lobby and US Foreign Policy*, 26, 38, 52, 76, 119, 368n95.

on race, keeping those moral arguments viable required tourniqueting Israel's loss of credibility as a project aligned with antiracist movements. Conversely, the ADL now encountered antiracist organizing as an enemy.

From this period, the ADL's domestic law-and-order agenda was entwined with its advocacy for the imperial engagements of the United States and Israel. As before, it curated ideas about race, racism, and rights in support of projects of state. The terms were now rearranged, though. Rather than seeking to portray Jews as white, it borrowed the lexicon of racial justice to reimagine Jews as racially marginalized, pitched especially against Black- and Arab-led calls for racial justice. This chapter traces the ADL's rewriting of the meanings of key ideas animating *civil rights*, including race, antisemitism, marginalization, and justice.

The anticolonial turn of US social movements in the late 1960s has often been read as a shift that pushed US Jewry to the right, away from leftist immigrant politics, away from the broad civil rights movement, and toward concerns with guarding class privilege and opposing antisemitism.[16] As the story is narrated, Jewish public opinion shifted whiteward and rightward through the post–World War II decades of suburbanization and upward mobility. Spurred by the 1944 federal G.I. Bill, which extended a host of economic and social uplift measures to veterans, a generation of working-class Jews accessed college, professional careers, and suburban homeownership, propelling them into the middle class. The same federal programs actively denied those pathways to Black veterans.[17] As Jews entered the white, suburban middle class and shed their parents' immigrant struggles, they no longer felt common cause with Black communities confined to deteriorating urban landscapes and excluded from housing, jobs, education, and social life.[18] "The present posture of American Jewry is not one of enthusiastic involvement in and with the larger community.... We are ... in the midst of a massive Jewish withdrawal syndrome with a concomitant fallout

16. Murray Friedman, *What Went Wrong? The Creation & Collapse of the Black-Jewish Alliance* (Simon and Schuster, 1994), 263.

17. Matthew Delmont, *Half American* (Penguin Random House, 2022), 263–70.

18. On Jewish moves to whiteness through suburbanization and upward class mobility, see Karen Brodkin, *How Jews Became White Folks and What That Says About Race in America* (Rutgers University Press, 1998). For an account of the impact of Jewish "whitening" on the break with the civil rights movement, see Greenberg, *Troubling the Waters*, 206.

of social conservatism," a Reform movement official lamented at a 1972 NCRAC discussion on Jewish civil rights work.[19] This distance was compounded by Jews' resentment that Black populations viewed them as landlords or merchants whose pockets they could not escape from lining, or through their roles as social workers and teachers in racist institutions.[20]

Perhaps more than a political turn, though, this story reflects a persistent denial of the racial state, grounded in race liberalism. While mainstream Jewish organizations doubled down on colorblindness, Black communities and antiracist movements identified whiteness as membership in an owning class from which racialized groups were excluded, and in which Jews were included. Jews who presumed the existence of a Black-Jewish alliance were forcefully confronted with these structural, relational meanings of race in 1967, with the publication of James Baldwin's essay "Negroes Are Anti-Semitic Because They're Anti-White." Baldwin wrote in the *New York Times Magazine*: "When we were growing up in Harlem our demoralizing series of landlords were Jewish, and we hated them. We hated them because they were terrible landlords, and did not take care of the building. . . . We knew that the landlord treated us this way only because we were colored, and he knew that we could not move out. . . . He has absolutely no relevance in this context as a Jew. His only relevance is that he is white and values his color and uses it."[21] Baldwin's frank gaze on the operations of race was followed by more discussion of the same. A 1968 letter from Martin Luther King Jr. printed in *Jewish Currents* offered a similar analysis of Black-Jewish relations as a Northern ghetto phenomenon, distinct from Jewish participation in civil right struggles that spanned wider geographies. "A great number of Negro ghettos were formerly Jewish neighborhoods; some storekeepers and landlords remained as population changes occurred," King wrote. "They operate with the ethics of marginal business entrepreneurs, not Jewish ethics, but the distinction is lost on some Negroes who are maltreated by them."[22] Similarly, in 1969, *Time* magazine described with clarity the extent to which Black

<hr>

19. Quoted in Joshua Michael Zeitz, "'If I Am Not for Myself . . .' : The American Jewish Establishment in the Aftermath of the Six Day War," *American Jewish History* 88, no. 2 (2000): 283.

20. Zeitz, "If I Am Not for Myself," 273.

21. James Baldwin, "Negroes Are Anti-Semitic Because They're Anti-White," *New York Times Magazine*, April 9, 1967.

22. Martin Luther King Jr., "Negroes, Jews, Israel, and Anti-Semitism," *Jewish Currents* 22, no. 1 (238) (1968): 7–9.

communities' view of Jews located both the observer and the observed in the racial structure of capitalism: "So strongly is the Jew identified with the merchant image that Negroes frequently use anti-Semitic epithets in referring to ghetto businessmen who are unmistakably not Jewish. A Negro will frequently refer to his 'Jew landlord' even though the man's name may be O'Reilly, Karwolski or Santangelo. In black areas of Detroit, white storekeepers are often called 'Goldberg,' even though many shops are owned by Iraqis and Syrians. And a Cadillac, even if it is owned by a wealthy Negro, is still known as a 'Jew canoe.'"[23]

Ironically, when Jews had been more marginalized—and when Jewish defense was still an elite German Jewish undertaking—the ADL had addressed accusations of Jewish anti-Black racism with real concern. In the 1930s and 1940s the ADL had heard complaints from Black communities about mistreatment by Jewish merchants and found them reasonable even if sometimes framed in antisemitic terms. Local ADL officials had at times tried to intervene: In Washington, DC, they counseled Jewish department store owners against anti-Black discrimination. Other Jewish organizations had done the same, meeting with Jewish employers, real estate agents, and businesses.[24] In the 1960s, though, ADL officials (and many other Jewish commentators) responded to antiracist demands by describing themselves as friends who had been cruelly cast off. "Despite all the support Jews had given to blacks from Harlem to Watts," former ADL regional director Murray Friedman summarized the complaint, "[Jews] had been rewarded only with hatred."[25]

This story of a broad Jewish turn to the right is unsatisfying for a second reason: It conflates a Jewish polity—spanning political ideologies, class strata, and even racial identities—with major Jewish organizations that were never on the left or marginalized in the way that much of US Jewry had been. Class rifts had arisen as some Jews suburbanized and others did not; Friedman, a sympathetic historian of the neoconservative movement, noted that working-class Jews shared neither the same politics nor the same experiences of racialization as wealthier Jews.[26] Elite institutions had banished the Jewish left, but the Jewish left did not disappear. In fact, so much of the New Left was Jewish that NCRAC, the coordinating body of major Jewish orga-

---

23. *Time*, "The Black and the Jew: A Falling Out of Allies," January 31, 1969.
24. Greenberg, *Troubling the Waters*, 104–5.
25. Friedman, *What Went Wrong?*, 264.
26. Friedman, *What Went Wrong?*, 265.

nizations, designed its anti-left strategies specifically to account for Jewish opposition.[27] Jewish leftist organizations, too, persisted outside the infrastructure of mainstream institutions, as Michael Staub has shown. They took on racism, capitalism, housing justice, sexuality, gender, Israel, and Vietnam, and mounted "an intra-Jewish civil war" over the mainstream groups' conservatism.[28] The Jewish left was conscious that any notion of a Black-Jewish alliance was troubled by the erasure of power dynamics and positionalities from the picture. Writing in 1969, Reform Jewish leader Albert Vorspan called on Jews to reconsider their gauzy recollections of "black-Jewish relations [that] used to be good." Calling for a clear-eyed history of Jewish organizations' role, he wrote: "We were the leaders, we called the shots, we set the timetable, we evolved the strategy, we produced the money. It was kind and benevolent but it was also colonial."[29]

If not really a "turn to the right," in the late 1960s there was an undeniable shift. It was announced by the ADL's sudden and surprising claim in 1969 that a new "Black antisemitism" was at "crisis levels." Five years later, it was given concrete and enduring form with the publication of *The New Anti-Semitism*.

In July 1967, Black and Puerto Rican parents and educators in Brooklyn won control over their local schools in an experimental district, Ocean Hill-Brownsville. The experiment was precipitated by emergency. A decade of failed school integration efforts had made schools in Black and brown neighborhoods in major US cities places of abandonment. Rather than educating, the schools were "mainly custodial, a place where [students] could be kept off the streets for six hours a day," as organizer Grace Lee Boggs recounted from her time as a teacher in Detroit. "White teachers openly talked about black kids as less than human.... The black teachers weren't much better."[30] Curriculum was part of the problem. White history, white social norms, and capitalist advancement were presented as the presumed standard, at the

27. NCRAC 1968 plenary session background memorandum cited in Zeitz, "If I Am Not for Myself," 268.

28. See Michael Staub, *Torn at the Roots: The Crisis of Jewish Liberalism in Postwar America* (Columbia University Press, 2004).

29. Albert Vorspan, "Blacks and Jews," in *Black Anti-Semitism and Jewish Racism*, ed. Wilson Record and Nat Hentoff (Richard W. Baron, 1969), 208.

30. Grace Lee Boggs, *Living for Change* (University of Minnesota Press, 2016), 120.

expense of students' own histories, identities, and contentions with racist barriers.[31] "You can't become white. We are black," said educator and Afro-American Teachers Association leader Al Vann. "They have been preparing us for something we can never be."[32] Outraged at the refusal of the city officials to address the community's urgent needs, Brooklyn parents had taken over a Board of Education hearing and occupied the building. The Ford Foundation, a regular partner of city officials in projects to quell racial unrest, developed a plan to delegate control of the schools to a local independent board.

The Ocean Hill-Brownsville district joined a national upsurgence of experiments in building alternative institutions that "offered a method of discrediting the structures of white elite power while gradually subverting their control over black life," Russell Rickford writes.[33] Once in place, the board set out to turn its eight schools around. It hired new teachers, mainly Black, white, and Jewish, whom the board believed were committed to the experiment. Teachers launched curriculum on African history, anticolonial thought, and Black culture. A reporter from England noted that some classes were "taught by a self-professed Black nationalist teacher [educator and organizer Jitu Weusi] . . . mildly nationalistic, but hardly the stuff that revolutions are made of."[34] As community control was unfolding in Ocean Hill-Brownsville, students in California were organizing a strike with deep resonances to Brooklyn. Their movement, the Third World Liberation Front, rejected integrationism as a project designed to keep them compliant with white supremacy. They linked their resistance to liberation movements from Africa to Palestine. "Initially, following the myth of the American Dream, we worked to attend predominantly white colleges," a statement from the students of Philippine-American Collegiate Endeavor (PACE) read, "but we have learned through direct analysis that it is impossible for our people, so-called minorities, to function as human beings, in a racist society in which

31. Jerald E. Podair, *The Strike That Changed New York: Blacks, Whites, and the Ocean Hill-Brownsville Crisis* (Yale University Press, 2004), 76.

32. Alex Poinsett, "Battle to Control Black Schools: National Drive Mounts for Ghetto Self-Determination in Education," *Ebony* 24, no. 7 (1969): 44. Referenced in Russell John Rickford, *We Are an African People: Independent Education, Black Power, and the Radical Imagination* (Oxford University Press, 2016).

33. Podair, *Strike That Changed New York*, 98; ThamesTv, "1960s New York | Crisis in the City | Teachers Strikes | Racial Tension | John Lindsay | 1968," originally aired July 11, 1968, posted April 3, 2022, YouTube, https://www.youtube.com/watch?v=RRTQsFpH7P8.

34. Rickford, *We Are an African People*, 15.

white always comes first. . . . So we have decided to fuse ourselves with the masses of Third World people . . . to create, through struggle, a new humanity . . . and within that context collectively control our own destinies."[35] And indeed, the Ocean Hill-Brownsville pilot project reflected the view of racism as a transnational structure entwined with capitalism—and of whiteness as a position of dominance within it. Opposing racism meant exiting those structures.

As the Ocean Hill-Brownsville experiment proceeded, it produced anxious pronouncements from some school and city officials that it represented a dangerous turn away from race liberalism. Rather than stoke these fears, ADL officials initially tamped down fears about Black nationalist "intolerance"—perhaps in the interest of trying to minimize Black radicalism and stem racial discord. The ADL had been closely attentive to the way that schools were fields for negotiating ideas about racial fairness. School conflicts over integration often became battles between low-income Black parents fighting for access to quality education and white Jewish parents who had left poverty behind and saw "good" schools—white schools in white neighborhoods, untroubled by the disruptions of integration efforts—as their due. Additionally, the ADL was attentive to Black nationalism and "militancy" that called for rejecting integration. Marc Dollinger notes that at least by 1964, the ADL had been monitoring the rise of Black militancy through its regional offices.[36] As the Ocean Hill-Brownsville project opened, though, the ADL did not raise any alarms.

In October 1967 the ADL published the results of a study, *Protest and Prejudice: A Study of Belief in the Black Community*, by sociologist Gary T. Marx, that proposed to calm concerns. The report concluded that Black populations were the least antisemitic of Christian groups; that Black nationalism should be understood simply as "an affirmation of Negro experience and Negro values" and Black Power as an additional "emphasis on the development of Negro institutions and programs of self-help."[37] A survey of Black militancy asked respondents, "Which person . . . has done the most to help Negroes?" The choice of Malcolm X represented the height of militancy,

35. Philippine-American Collegiate Endeavor (PACE) 1968 statement, quoted in Karen Umemoto, "'On Strike!' San Francisco State College Strike, 1968–69: The Role of Asian American Students," *Amerasia Journal* 15, no. 1 (1989): 15.

36. Dollinger, *Black Power, Jewish Politics*, 87.

37. Historian Lerone Bennett, quoted in Gary T. Marx, *Protest and Prejudice: A Study of Belief in the Black Community* (Greenwood Press, 1967), 107.

while NAACP chair Roy Wilkins represented the most accommodating integrationism. Ninety percent of respondents came in at a comforting in-between level, choosing Martin Luther King Jr.[38] Following the report's publication, ADL leaders, journalists, and others regularly cited it to allay concerns about community control.

A key feature of the study was its introduction by civil rights movement leader Bayard Rustin. Rustin's preface was validation, naming the data as a true picture of Black politics and the ADL as a true civil rights agency. It also previewed the ADL's turn to neoconservatism. Like the ADL, Rustin was animated by strong commitments to liberalism, anticommunism, and integrationism.[39] He was a globally recognized figure, central to key events, including the 1956 Montgomery bus boycott, 1963 March on Washington, and 1964 mass boycott of segregated New York City schools.[40] He was also a staunch opponent of Black radicalism—and increasingly so as organizers articulated the call for Black Power in 1966 and after.[41] In prolific public speaking and writing, he declared the rejection of accommodationism to be immature, racist, and "positively harmful," pushing instead for Black organizers to leverage the resources of the liberal state to build labor power: to end racism by removing the economic drivers of hostility.[42] In Jewish institutional spaces, he spoke to leaders as civil rights allies, urging their patience and continued work on economic reforms, even when chiding

38. Marx, *Protest and Prejudice*, 26.

39. On the precedence of Rustin's anticommunism in A. Philip Randolph's disillusionment with the Communist Party as a vehicle for Black political power, and on Rustin's complicated political legacy, see Manning Marable, "A. Philip Randolph and the Foundations of Black American Socialism," in *Workers' Struggles, Past and Present*, ed. James Green (Temple University Press, 1983).

40. Daniel Hiram Perlstein, *Justice, Justice: School Politics and the Eclipse of Liberalism* (Peter Lang, 2004), 90.

41. In August 1964 Rustin seriously alienated Black organizers by advising the Mississippi Freedom Democratic Party to accept a token two seats at the Democratic Convention, rather than the full delegation that was their right. The following February, he repeated the message in the essay "From Protest to Politics" in *Commentary* magazine. This break deepened as Rustin continued to denounce Black radicalism. Bayard Rustin, "From Protest to Politics: The Future of the Civil Rights Movement," *Commentary*, February 1965; Bay Area Veterans of the Civil Rights Movement, "MFDP Challenge to the Democratic Convention," Civil Rights Movement Archive, 9, https://www.crmvet.org/info/mfdp_atlantic.pdf, accessed December 3, 2024.

42. Rustin as quoted in Paula Pfeffer, "The Evolution of A. Philip Randolph and Bayard Rustin from Radicalism to Conservatism," in *Black Conservatism: Essays in Intellectual and Political History* (Garland Pub., 1999), 214.

them for retreating into whiteness when civil rights demands were too challenging. ("If you are going to remain Jews only so long as Negroes remain nice, give it up," Rustin told the American Jewish Congress in 1966.)[43] He was already a fixture in Jewish newspapers and meetings when he spoke for the first time to an ADL audience. At the ADL's National Commission meeting in May 1968, he denounced Black radicalism and internationalism and reaffirmed the place of Jewish institutions alongside moderate Black institutions in the civil rights movement.

> If the nation is not viable, and no program is needed, then all those people who have worked over the years for civil rights and are still working for integration into this society become the enemy. Not the Ku Klux Klan, not the John Birch Society, but those closest to you. This is what Jews need to understand: That in the list of whom you attack, those you love come first. . . . The point is that if Jews are under attack by the extreme left in the Negro community, they are in the same basket with Negro leaders and even the most progressive political leadership.[44]

The ADL's *Protest and Prejudice*, blessed by Rustin, wove together all of these threads: It reaffirmed that Black antiracism was still liberal, not radical; that the ADL was still a venerable civil rights voice; and that the Black public's impatience with Jewish organizations was only circumstantial.

At nearly the same moment, the Ocean Hill-Brownsville experiment erupted in controversy, a conflagration over education and labor set against the backdrop of Black Power—and that situated much of US Jewry as a white force opposing it. As battle lines were drawn through civil rights organizing, labor, schools, and Black internationalism, the new connection between Rustin's political circle and the ADL became quietly consequential. The events began three days after Rustin's speech, on May 9, 1968. As Ocean Hill-Brownsville superintendent Rhody McCoy implemented community control, he ordered the transfer of a number of white, mostly Jewish, teachers who were "out of sympathy with the experiment." The United Federation of Teachers (UFT) rebelled against the changes, saying that the transfer amounted to firing the teachers and violated union rules. When McCoy refused to bend, UFT head Albert Shanker called a citywide strike and denounced the whole

---

43. Dollinger, *Black Power, Jewish Politics*, 85.

44. Rustin's speech to the ADL National Commission was published and distributed as *The Anatomy of Frustration*. Bayard Rustin, *The Anatomy of Frustration* (Anti-Defamation League of B'nai B'rith, 1968), 6.

project as an anti-Jewish attack by intolerant Black radicals.[45] In response, many voices refuted the notion that the governing board was anti-Jewish or even antiwhite. (Indeed, when the governing board announced that it was hiring teachers to replace strikers, half of the 350 new hires were Jewish.)[46] New York Civil Liberties Union director Ira Glasser, the Jewish parent of a Brownsville student, declared that the UFT had concocted the allegations because the decentralization plan diminished the union's power.[47] Noting the UFT's use of dog-whistle terms—including *Nazi, mob rule, vigilantes, extremists, criminals, black militants,* and *black racists*—Glasser wrote that the intent was to construct a scenario in which attacking an antiracist project could be cast as opposing racism and fascism "by incessant use of such words; by the fraudulent leaflets, and by the whole tone and tenor of the campaign, the UFT did what no one else has ever before been able to do in this city. It legitimized liberal racism."[48]

The ADL did not immediately endorse the UFT's claim that community control advocates were antisemitic. Its approaches to race and class conflict over integration had varied in the preceding years, during which all of the Jewish defense agencies had been involved in New York City's desegregation planning.[49] Where Jewish parents expressed anti-Black prejudice, the ADL, along with the other defense agencies, called on them to stop. Even so, the ADL was positioned to the right of other white liberal advocates. It had catered to the anti-integration positions of white Jewish parents, opposing busing and other "non-voluntary measures" for desegregation. It had interpreted some conflicts over racist schools as anti-Jewish and often viewed civil rights leaders' pushback against such obstacles as "extreme."[50] But schools were so clearly sites of inequity and racial marginalization, and the white

45. Podair, *The Strike That Changed New York*, 100–116.

46. Jane Anna Gordon, *Why They Couldn't Wait: A Critique of the Black-Jewish Conflict over Community Control in Ocean Hill-Brownsville, 1967–1971* (Psychology Press, 2001), 66.

47. NYCLU director Ira Glasser's recollections in John Kifner, "Echoes of a New York Waterloo," *New York Times*, December 22, 1996. On NYCLU data refuting the charge that Ocean Hill-Brownsville was historically antisemitic, see Wendell E. Pritchett, *Brownsville, Brooklyn: Blacks, Jews, and the Changing Face of the Ghetto* (University of Chicago Press, 2003), 234.

48. "Memorandum from NYCLU to Special Committee on Religious and Racial Prejudice," quoted in Weisbord and Stein, *Bittersweet Encounter*, 172.

49. David Rogers, *110 Livingston: Politics and Bureaucracy in the New York City Schools* (Random House, 1968), 137.

50. Rogers, *110 Livingston*, 81, 26, 153.

educators and officials in those schools so often Jewish, that the lens of anti-semitism simply could not be applied to every such conflict. "The 'Jewish principal' stands for [racial] oppression and failure in Harlem, Brownsville, and other ghetto communities, if only because so many principals there are Jewish and so many schools are inferior," sociologist David Rogers observed in 1968.[51] Initially, in response to charges that community control was anti-semitic—and, in particular, that it was a program of Black antisemitism—ADL officials repeatedly and publicly pointed to the 1967 Marx study. What was sometimes called "Black militancy," the report concluded, was simply impatience with the speed of social change. "The militant Negro is one who actively opposes discrimination and segregation," the study explained. "He demands his rights *now* and is likely to agree with Martin Luther King that 'the oft-repeated clichés,' 'the time is not ripe,' 'Negroes are not culturally ready,' are a stench in the nostrils of God."[52]

It was a surprise, then, when the ADL suddenly reversed itself and declared that Black antisemitism was not only pervasive but at "crisis levels." In January 1969, it published a twenty-five-page "preliminary report" on the Ocean Hill-Brownsville conflict declaring the existence of a special, pernicious form of Black antisemitism. It named "a black separatist 'philosophy' that charges both 'mental genocide' of ghetto children by Jewish teachers and supervisory personnel and the 'willful exclusion' of black teachers and principals by a 'Jewish establishment.'"[53] Its special nature, as the ADL's executive vice president Rabbi Jay Kaufman described it, was that it merged old antisemitism, which cast Jews as malicious interlopers, with new Black anticolonial internationalism. The new threat was a "'Third World' ideology which is essentially a pitting of the black against the white world. . . . They have gone further and successfully depicted the white Arab people as blacks and the Israelis as oppressive whites."[54] If the UFT's claims of antisemitism had before been seen as tactical, the ADL's report lent them validation. Within a month, the ADL's accusations had produced a furor—an antisemitism scare—that

51. Rogers, *110 Livingston*, 161.

52. Marx, *Protest and Prejudice*, 42.

53. Anti-Defamation League of B'nai B'rith, "Anti-Semitism in the New York City Schools Controversy," January 1969, Dore Schary Papers, Box 153, Folder 14, p. 2, Wisconsin Historical Society.

54. Rabbi Jay Kaufman, "You Shall Surely Rebuke Thy Neighbor," in *Black Anti-Semitism and Jewish Racism*, ed. Record and Hentoff, 51.

turned attention away from educational racism and the community's effort at solutions. Instead, attention was focused on a Black ideological threat, replete with comparisons to Nazism.[55] Walter Karp and H. R. Shapiro wrote in their journal of politics, *The Public Life*, "Calls now go out almost daily to find and denounce the black culprits; to denounce, dismiss, and impeach any official deemed derelict in his duty to suppress these black attacks upon Jews. . . . 'We put black racists on notice,' warns the American Jewish Committee, 'that we are determined to use every legal means to let no one get away with any efforts to inflict pain or suffering on any Jewish person.'"[56]

The ADL report prompted a fresh wave of Jewish resistance to the ADL and the UFT, from liberals as much as the left. The American Jewish Committee, which had been involved in integration struggles in Brownsville since the 1950s, broke character by positioning itself against the conservatism of the ADL. The committee's work in Brownsville had been led by Annie Stein, an NAACP member, communist organizer, and member of the radical Teachers' Union, which had been destroyed in the fervid events that had lifted Albert Shanker's UFT to power.[57] A caucus of UFT members organized as Teachers for Community Control (with a robust subgroup, Jewish Teachers for Community Control) and placed a *New York Times* ad in November 1968 titled "Anti-Semitism?—A Statement by the Teachers of Ocean Hill," in which they detailed Shanker's process of fabricating the anti-semitism claim.[58] Many other teachers also rejected the UFT's narrative. One mayoral aide who was tasked with mediating the tensions later described Shanker as "one of the worst villains of the era, a race baiter without regard to the consequences."[59]

55. Walter Karp and H.R. Shapiro, "Exploding the Myth of Black Anti-Semitism," reprinted from *The Public Life* in *Black Anti-Semitism and Jewish Racism*, ed. Record and Hentoff, 134, 140.

56. Karp and Shapiro, "Exploding the Myth of Black Anti-Semitism," 130.

57. For an account of 1950s Brownsville school organizing and its intersections with Jewish and Black institutional history, as well as anticommunist purges, see Adina Back, "Blacks, Jews and the Struggle to Integrate Brooklyn's Junior High School 258: A Cold War Story," *Journal of American Ethnic History* 20, no. 2 (2001).

58. *New York Times*, "Anti-Semitism?—A Statement by the Teachers of Ocean Hill," November 11, 1968, reprinted in Clayborne Carson, *The Eyes on the Prize: Civil Rights Reader: Documents, Speeches, and Firsthand Accounts from the Black Freedom Struggle, 1954–1990* (Penguin Books, 1991).

59. Sid Davidoff, former aide to New York City mayor John Lindsay. As historians have reaffirmed, the UFT was motivated by a range of concerns, including ideological

Jewish commentators sought to diagnose the ADL's frustrating turn and the outrageous claims of the UFT. The ADL's antipathy toward Black liberationism was familiar, although grotesquely amplified in the new report. Why, though, was the ADL suddenly so committed to the UFT? Critics from Jewish institutions attended most closely to the reversal of positions. Albert Vorspan, the social action director of the Union of Associated Hebrew Congregations, wrote:

> What is the "crisis" that so dramatically reversed the thinking of that agency? ... [A] stitching together of twenty plus anti-Semitic incidents.... There wasn't a revelation in the carload.... A handful of anti-Semites from a black community of 2,100,000 people? What is the crisis? Did not the reproduction of reams of anti-Semitic propaganda by the [UFT] play any part in the "crisis"? Does not the screaming of "[n*****]-lover" and "black bastard" by some striking Jewish teachers belong in the picture at all? Does one ignore the fear-mongering of the Yiddish press? The anti-black thunderbolts hurled from some synagogue pulpits? The manipulation of the Jewish community by those who sought to line it up on one side (to fight the "black Nazis") in an economic dispute? And what of the failure of responsible Jewish leaders to condemn Jewish extremists at the same time as we beat black leaders over the head for not condemning their extremists?[60]

Asking the same questions about the UFT, some observers looked under the hood of the union's emerging politics. Writing in 1969, schoolteacher and organizer Maurice R. Berube pointed to the particular strain of socialism

---

commitments to integrationism and labor commitments to the bureaucratic rules that led its members to the middle class—both of which were structures that had marginalized Black and brown communities. Notably, the retrospective histories offered by both Shanker and the ADL also downplay antisemitism, even though they made it the central issue at the time. The ADL's 1992 report, *The Anti-Semitism of Black Demagogues and Extremists*, claims that "some Black extremists attempted to turn the controversy into an ethnic conflict." Shanker, in a 1988 interview for the PBS series "Eyes on the Prize," also claimed that antisemitism was not a primary issue in the conflict. See Stephen Brier, "The Ideological and Organizational Origins of the United Federation of Teachers' Opposition to the Community Control Movement in the New York City Public Schools, 1960–1968," *Labour/ Le Travail*, no. 73 (Spring 2014): 179–93. Anti-Defamation League, *The Anti-Semitism of Black Demagogues and Extremists*, 1992; Albert Shanker, "Interview with Albert Shanker, Conducted by Blackside, Inc. on November 15, 1988, for Eyes on the Prize II: America at the Racial Crossroads, 1965 to 1985," Washington University Libraries, Film and Media Archive, Henry Hampton Collection," n.d., accessed August 7, 2019.

60. Vorspan, "Blacks and Jews," 203.

from which most of the UFT's recently installed leadership was drawn. "By 'socialist,' of course, I do not mean that large invisible army of radicals nurtured for many generations in the humanism of Marx, Engels and Debs."[61] Rather, Berube explained, he meant Social Democrats, whose organizing perpetuated the anticommunist "right-wing socialism" of the 1930s and '40s. At the time of the Ocean Hill-Brownsville experiment, Social Democrats were attacking the anti–Vietnam War movement and denouncing Black radicalism, both for their implicit links to communism and their rejection of US liberal values.[62] The leadership of the UFT itself was also drawn from Social Democratic circles. Among them, Sandra Feldman, Shanker's deputy, and Yetta Barsh, Shanker's aide, were simultaneously movement leaders. So was Bayard Rustin. Unnoticed by leftist critics, the ADL had also just hired key Social Democratic figures to its own leadership: longtime intellectual and political leader Irwin Suall, and a new leader of the youth wing, Carl Gershman. These intersecting relationships were in fact new political alliances. As neoconservatism took shape in the late 1960s, Rustin, the UFT, Social Democrats, and the ADL entered it together. Their concern was fused with new US interests in Israel, producing a new white ethnic politics. It stitched together their shared ideological commitments to US liberal capitalism, and their shared enemies: communists, radicals, and internationalists. Still working in the lexicon of civil rights, they pressed domestic concerns that Black and brown communities' demands for liberation, along with global anticolonial movements, stood in the way of democracy.

The ADL's 1969 "Black antisemitism" panic expanded on another racial anxiety beyond white fears of Black Power. It was the anxiety that Jews, having ascended to whiteness—a position not only of inclusion but of dominance over other groups—had lost the leverage that came with demanding remedies

61. Maurice R. Berube, "'Democratic Socialists' and the Schools," *New Politics* (Summer 1969): 57.

62. Brier, "Ideological and Organizational Origins of the United Federation of Teachers' Opposition," 188. Berube wrote in the movement journal *New Politics*: "The list of 'democratic socialists' opposed to black communities' desire for lay control of public schools reads like a letterhead from the Socialist Party: Michael Harrington (Village Voice); Maurice Goldbloom (Commentary); Tom Brooke (Dissent); Tom Kahn of the League for Industrial Democracy, who wrote ads supporting the UFT in the Ocean Hill-Brownsville confrontation; Paul Feldman, editor of New America, who published pieces against the black communities." Berube, "'Democratic Socialists' and the Schools," 58.

for their exclusion. At that time, the mode of antisemitism that Nathan Perlmutter called "the old discrimination that hurt Jews in their pocketbook or in their pride," was coming to a close.[63] This was exactly the outcome that Jewish defense agencies had been created to achieve: first, to erase the racialization and radicalism that had developed with the arrival of Eastern European immigrants; second, to place Jewish communities on the political and economic ladders of liberal capitalism in the United States. Nathan Belth, ADL public relations director from 1946 to 1971, described the completeness of the accomplishment: "Jews had truly merged into the majority; we were in thought, aspirations, commitment and status part of the majority. . . . And what was equally important, the recognized American majority looked upon us no longer as a minority, subject to special treatment, good and bad, but as a part of themselves."[64]

As it achieved its aims, the ADL started to worry about success. One concern was that Jews and non-Jews alike would become complacent about Jewish inclusion. Another was that the end of antisemitism, and the sense of Jewish whiteness, would make others indifferent to antisemitism if it did reemerge. Underlying the first fear was the idea, canonical at the ADL since 1960, that antisemitism always lurked latent in US society. It drew on the swastika epidemic of 1960, in which a single graffiti incident in Germany had seemed to unleash a massive international wave of swastika daubings, signaling that Nazism lay in wait everywhere.[65] Questioning that conclusion, observers noted that intensive reporting on the swastikas had carried the phenomenon from place to place. The ADL's own study, *Swastika 1960: The*

63. Nathan Perlmutter, "Vol Ib: Perlmutter, Nathan, 1985–1987," Box 1, Folder 1, MS-365, p. 85, B'nai B'rith Anti-Defamation League Oral Histories, American Jewish Archives, Cincinnati, Ohio.

64. Nathan Belth, "Vol Va: Belth, Nathan C., 1985–1987," n.d., p. 120, B'nai B'rith Anti-Defamation League Oral Histories, American Jewish Archives, Cincinnati, Ohio.

65. A wave of swastika graffiti in 1960 prompted the ADL to focus on ways that antisemitism might remain latent in the United States. The "swastika epidemic" was launched by Nazi vandalism in Cologne, Germany, on Christmas 1959: a paint attack that covered a synagogue with swastikas and the text "Germans Demand 'Out With the Jews'" and defaced a nearby anti-Nazi memorial. On the heels of international publicity about Cologne, a two-month "mass phenomenon" of copycat graffiti swept through Europe, Australia, and the United States. The ADL's worries about the appeal of Nazism had been primed by anti-Catholic rhetoric targeting John F. Kennedy's presidential campaign and by violence against civil rights sit-ins in the South. Howard J. Ehrlich, "The Swastika Epidemic of 1959–1960: Anti-Semitism and Community Characteristics," *Social Problems* 9, no. 3 (1962): 264–72.

Epidemic of Anti-Semitic Vandalism in America, concluded that the US wave had mostly been the work of teenage boys seeking thrills rather than prosecuting an anti-Jewish ideology, and that fewer than half of the incidents had targeted Jews at all. Still, as Benjamin Epstein summarized, it showed that "anti-Semitism is a more serious problem in the United States than is generally thought to be the case," and it raised concerns that the new generation, which had not witnessed Nazi atrocities, was more susceptible to be drawn in by Nazi groups that were certainly still active.[66]

The second fear rested on another event, also the subject of a 1966 ADL study. In 1962, Nazi war criminal Adolf Eichmann was tried in Jerusalem for the crimes of his role in the genocide of Jews.[67] The trial had been carefully composed by prosecutors and the Israeli state as a public-facing event on human evil, and the national ADL had issued directives to local groups to tread carefully in discussing it, given that it might affect the US public's sense of Jews as "a fairminded and merciful people."[68] Instead, it produced so little public response that Jewish institutions grew concerned about apathy.[69] The ADL report found that as the trial had taken place it had been received sympathetically by the US public, but was now "as good as forgotten by most," having "[failed] to overcome public, complacence, while virtually assuring the failure of its ultimate educational objectives." Even if antisemitism no longer loomed as a threat, the report noted that an "apathetic majority" could be puppeteered by a "prejudiced elite." If antisemitism was always latent, then Jews could only rest easy when society was on high alert.[70]

These worries arose from the merger of Jews into "the majority," where they no longer needed special defense. The report hinted at an uneasiness that whiteness itself might come under attack and that Jewish whiteness was

66. David Caplovitz and Candace Rogers, *Swastika 1960: The Epidemic of Anti-Semitic Vandalism in America* (Anti-Defamation League of B'nai B'rith, 1961), 8, 33–35.

67. Michael J. Bazyler and Julia Y. Scheppach, "The Strange and Curious History of the Law Used to Prosecute Adolf Eichmann," *Loyola of Los Angeles International and Comparative Law Review* 34, no. 3 (2012).

68. Peter Novick, *The Holocaust in American Life* (Houghton Mifflin Harcourt, 2000), 131.

69. ADL officials were also concerned with the impact of publications that they viewed as minimizing the monstrosity of Nazis and indicting Jewish leaders or Jewish victims of Nazis as "passive." On the ADL's response to Hannah Arendt's essays on the trial, published as *Eichmann in Jerusalem: A Report on the Banality of Evil*, and works by Bruno Bettelheim and Raul Hilberg, see Novick, *Holocaust in American Life*, 136–41.

70. Caplovitz and Rogers, *Swastika 1960*, 167, 170, 179.

now a liability.[71] The study had set out to measure the extent to which people were "critical" of the Eichmann trial, as a measure of sympathy for the trial's ideological aims. Yet their sample failed: The UC Berkeley researchers had conducted surveys in Oakland, California, where most respondents had not known about the trial at all. As a result, the interviews yielded very little data, and the data they had managed to get from poor Black respondents in particular had not been favorable. "Among Negroes," the authors wrote, "it was the least sophisticated and the most deprived who were the most critical." The authors struggled to draw meaning from their survey. In place of conclusions they offered tenuous suggestions about what might have happened, a menu of possible worries. The authors, white academics who described themselves as being a world apart from respondents, hopelessly guessed at the reasons. "It was surmised that in being critical the more deprived Negro was giving expression to his general alienation from the norms of society and the justice of white society," they wrote. "There is the possibility that, if the alienation of the deprived Negro is aggravated, his rejection of the prevailing norms will serve to increase his anti-Semitism." In the last sentences of their 1966 work on apathy, the researchers pointed to apathy's opposite— race-consciousness—and its potential to generate backlash against white liberalism.[72]

Based on these anxieties, the ADL moved in the 1960s to amplify public concern about antisemitism against Jews who had "made it," and in the 1970s to reassert Jewish difference. Certainly, discrimination and ideological hostility persisted in plenty of instances, if not in the same pervasive ways as before. But the thrust of the ADL's new messaging was the tortuous claim that, having moved collectively into economic and social positions of power, Jews were still marginalized, sometimes by the very fact of having arrived. Turning its attention from the old sites of discrimination, housing and employment, to the new milieus of country clubs and boardrooms, the ADL issued clarifications about what did *not* constitute a resolution of antisemitism. To begin with, Epstein and Forster declared, "success is not the

71. Matthew Frye Jacobson historicizes the rise of white anxiety, in response to the civil rights movement and the rise of anticolonial thought, about the possibility of being accused of white privilege. See Jacobson, *Roots Too: White Ethnic Revival in Post-Civil Rights America* (Harvard University Press, 2006), chap. 1.

72. Charles Y. Glock, Gertrude Jaeger Selznick, and Joe L. Spaeth, *The Apathetic Majority: A Study Based on Public Responses to the Eichmann Trial* (Harper & Row, 1966), 180.

test."[73] Following a 1962 report finding that 67 percent of upper-class social clubs practiced religious discrimination against Jews, ADL Civil Rights Committee chair Bernard Nath called such discrimination "far harsher and more severe . . . [and] in the long run, just as damaging" as discrimination in education and employment.[74] The American Jewish Committee took a similar approach, campaigning to pressure major corporations that had not advanced Jewish executives; in 1966, the ADL joined that effort.[75] In reupping antisemitism as a major national problem, the ADL continued its familiar reporting on racist measures like exclusionary housing covenants, now adding the new message: "For the nonwhites, virtually any kind of housing is a tremendous problem; they simply cannot find adequate homes in sufficient numbers to meet their living needs and are forced to live in slum areas. American Jews are not underprivileged on this score. Whatever their financial bracket, they are able to find homes in every part of the country that meet their *material* circumstances. But American Jews have only limited access to homes in some of the neighborhoods that conform to their *social* aspirations."[76] In beginning to characterize antisemitism as different from other forms of racism, ADL materials moved to detach it from the measures of class and political advancement that had been at the heart of postwar egalitarianism. Now, it was a matter of justice for members of a dominant class.

The ADL itself was upwardly mobile. Throughout the 1960s it had greatly expanded its role as a legal and political institution, becoming enmeshed with the apparatus of the US state. By 1961 it was working on curriculum or training with all but two of the state education departments in the United States and 250 local school systems.[77] Through court action and in legislative campaigns, it pursued and won fair employment, housing, and public accommo-

73. Benjamin R. Epstein and Arnold Forster, *Some of My Best Friends . . .* (Farrar, Straus and Cudahy, 1962), 34.

74. A small percentage of the clubs were Jewish-only clubs, which the ADL report pointed out were created in response to Jews' lack of access to Christian-only clubs. The ADL denounced both as discriminatory, *Jewish Telegraphic Agency*, "Anti-Defamation League Reports Discrimination in 781 Clubs in US," January 15, 1962.

75. American Jewish Committee, "American Jewish Committee: Press Release," January 17, 1962, https://web.archive.org/web/20200715223130/http://www.ajcarchives.org/AJC_DATA/Files/619.PDF.

76. Emphasis in original. Epstein and Forster, *Some of My Best Friends . . .*, 86.

77. Henry Edward Schultz and Benjamin R. Epstein, *Report of the Anti-Defamation League* (1962).

dation laws across multiple states.[78] When the Civil Rights Act passed in 1964, the ADL launched its first collaborations with police departments, holding a national training conference orienting them to the new law.[79] The ADL also expanded its publications and public relations beyond antisemitism and intergroup relations, becoming a major knowledge producer on moral issues of state: the civil rights movement, religion, law enforcement, foreign policy. Its research project on antisemitism with UC Berkeley, which had been launched in 1960, produced throughout the decade a series of book-length studies whose findings were widely cited in the press and boosted the ADL's claims to scientific authority. In its long-running insider publication, *Facts*, the ADL continued to track the "mushrooming" of the radical right in backlash against the civil rights movement. The ADL had begun the decade as such a ubiquitous presence, its 1960 chairman's report noted, that its name had become "a commonly accepted term of description" for defense, as in "someone should organize an anti-defamation league for mothers-in-law."[80]

One measure of the ADL's reach into political culture was the *ADL Bulletin*, a glossy, often chatty magazine of news features and insider tidbits on domestic and international civil rights issues. The *Bulletin* started the decade with a paid circulation of 150,000—already a major publication, matching about 11 percent of the concurrent circulation of the *New York Times*. By 1967 it had grown to nearly 169,000 subscribers.[81] With a civil rights and democracy bent, the *Bulletin* reported on domestic and international politics, provided intergroup relations guidance, presented ADL research, and posted reader letters and ADL responses. Its cachet was magnified by guest articles from political figures (including President John F. Kennedy, who also published a book, *A Nation of Immigrants*, with the ADL

78. While anti-discrimination laws are generally lauded, at the time leftist Jewish critics of the ADL charged that its legislative work was calibrated to avoid the need for mass mobilization, and its reporting on campaigns against antisemites and fascists habitually left out the impact of community organizing, effectively erasing it from public knowledge. See Louis Harap, "ADL Reports on Anti-Semitism," *Jewish Life*, June 1950.

79. Schultz and Epstein, *Report of the Anti-Defamation League* (1962); Dore Schary and Benjamin R. Epstein, *Report of the Anti-Defamation League* (1964).

80. Henry Edward Schultz, "Chairman's Report to ADL National Commission," 1960, Records, Box 2, Folder 1, p. 19, Amistad Research Center, Anti-Defamation League of B'nai B'rith Race Relations Work.

81. Circulation data: Schultz and Epstein, *Report of the Anti-Defamation League* (1962); Anti-Defamation League of B'nai B'rith v. American Italian Anti-Defamation League, Inc., 83 N.Y.S.2d 828, 54 Misc.2d 830 (N.Y. Sup. Ct. 1967), https://case-law.vlex.com/vid /anti-defamation-league-of-886991762.

in 1964), eminent scholars, and major religious figures drawn from its efforts at interreligious cooperation. The benefit worked in the other direction, too. In 1953, when FBI director J. Edgar Hoover opened federal investigations into white supremacist groups, several governors protested that the FBI was encroaching on state law enforcement. The *Bulletin* came to Hoover's defense. A short essay by ADL national chairman Henry Schultz lauded the FBI and succinctly shamed the governors for holding themselves above the law. Just below Schultz's piece, Hoover himself laid out the FBI's legal mandate for the investigations. In the same pages, the ADL's announcement of its "Dinner with the President" gala added the weight of Eisenhower's endorsement.[82] In subsequent years, as the ADL tried persistently to build closer ties to Hoover and "be of assistance" to the FBI—and FBI officials weighed the wisdom of inviting them in—this episode prompted FBI officials to view the ADL as a useful partner.[83]

In 1967, the ADL's anxieties about too-high Jewish class stature in the United States were exponentially magnified when the Israeli state suddenly and unexpectedly established itself as a military power. For its first two decades Israel had been discussed in the United States as a state that was morally strong but physically diminutive, dependent on the support of US Jewry and populated by refugees in a heroic process of overcoming hardship. It was elevated to mass audiences and embedded as affect in US political culture, as Amy Kaplan writes, through the 1958 novel (and 1960 film) *Exodus*. Identifying Israel as a refuge, stitched to American frontier narratives, enabled the claim that it was owed US support. It portrayed Israeli militarism as defense and retribution against Nazi and Arab antisemitism, rather than colonial expansionism.[84] Additionally, the classification of Israel as refuge provided an essential element of claim that the Arab states calling for Palestinian refugees to return to *their* homes were simply antisemitic. In a

82. *ADL Bulletin*, Advertisements. September 1953, 4, 8.

83. L.B. Nichols, Office Memorandum, US Government, from Mr. L.B. Nichols to M.A. Jones, "Subject: Herman Edelsberg; Henry E. Schulz; Arnold Forster; Judge David A. Rose Anti-Defamation League of B'nai B'rith meeting with director 10:30 A.M., 6-21-54." June 22, 1954, in Anti Defamation League -- HQ 100-530, p. 70, https://archive.org/details/AntiDefamationLeagueHQ100530/page/n69, accessed June 5, 2025.

84. Amy Kaplan, *Our American Israel: The Story of an Entangled Alliance* (Harvard University Press, 2018), 58–59, 76–77.

June 1964 article titled "The Truth About Arabs," Forster exemplified the simple turn. A Jordanian mural at the World's Fair had narrated Palestinian dispossession, reading: "The strangers, once thought terror's victims, became terror's fierce practitioners." Forster named the mural as an act of hatred, "cast[ing] aspersions on all Americans of the Jewish faith" in a manner "as vicious as Nazi Germany's."[85] The defense agencies had already come to view Israel as a strategic geopolitical ally of the West rather than as a vulnerable protectorate during the 1956 Suez Canal crisis.[86] In making the public case for Israel, though, the ADL stuck closely to moral arguments, juxtaposing Jewish strivers against the hostile armies of the Arab League.[87]

In May, ongoing provocations between Israeli forces and Palestinian, Syrian, Egyptian, and Jordanian forces exploded when Israel launched a preemptive attack by air. In a short but bloody six days, the attack hobbled the allied forces of Egypt, Syria, and Jordan, and Israeli forces occupied land belonging to each of them: the Sinai, the Golan, and the West Bank. Inside the United States, the war produced different turns in different spheres. For much of US Jewry and the larger public, post-Holocaust existential fearfulness gave way to a new sense of Israel's military prowess, its projection of muscular Jews, and the confirmation of the United States as Israel's geopolitical ally and Arab states as aggressors against that order.[88] For US Jewish organizations, the Six-Day War was a clear instruction that the catalysts of *Israel* and *danger* could organize, unify, and elicit funds from Jewish communities in unprecedented ways.[89] For SNCC, parts of the New Left, and civil rights organizers tuning in to neocolonialism, it clarified that Zionism was an imperial project

85. Arnold Forster, "The Truth About Arabs," *ADL Bulletin*, June 1964.

86. Matthew Berkman, "Coercive Consensus: Jewish Federations, Ethnic Representation, and the Roots of American Pro-Israel Politics" (PhD diss., University of Pennsylvania, 2018), https://repository.upenn.edu/edissertations/3093.

87. Issues of the *ADL Bulletin* from 1957 to 1967 reflect this discussion. After a burst of coverage around the Suez crisis, Israel was not regularly covered as a subject of concern. The coverage that did appear mostly took the form of human interest stories about Jewish refugees, often in the first person. Other coverage focused on attitudes of the press and Christian churches toward Israel, and their sympathy toward Arab states, and not much on Israel itself.

88. On the resonance of Israeli military dominance in US popular political narrative, see Kaplan, *Our American Israel*, 96–110. On the confirmation of Israel as a US proxy and ally, see Mearsheimer and Walt, *Israel Lobby and US Foreign Policy*, 51–52.

89. Sachar's history captures the self-organizing ferment of Jewish communities concerned about Israel's fate before and during the 1967 war. Its intensity was such that Jewish institutions struggled to catch up to it. Howard Morley Sachar, *A History of the Jews in America* (Vintage Books, 1993), 736, 946.

and Israel a US-backed aggressor.[90] When Jewish organizations collectively denounced SNCC in reply, it also showed that those institutions that claimed a place in civil rights movements—and that had recently resented Black organizations' moves to distance white organizers—would turn on Black organizers in pursuit of their own interests.

The 1967 war created another layer of tension for the ADL as it confronted the problem of power. Israel's show of strength overturned the idea of Israeli and Jewish vulnerability. US Jewish institutions were also aware of a future risk that the occupation of Arab lands and populations threatened to shift the racial calculus of Jewish identity. In the lands that Israeli forces now occupied, the refugees were not outside the borders: Israel was now an explicitly Jewish power exerting militarized domination over a Palestinian Arab population, their homes, and their land. The Zionist project did not allow for absorbing refugees as citizens or for giving the land back.[91] These were live issues particularly in Israeli Jewish politics, but US Jewish leaders avoided them; they ran in stark opposition to the egalitarian and democratic principles that they emphasized in discussion of Israel. NCRAC dealt with them only internally in 1967. As Matthew Berkman documents, "No official NCRAC document or forum—internal or external—would revisit these vexing political questions or the diversity of Jewish-Israeli orientations toward Palestinian refugees until the late 1970s, and only then in response to irrepressible controversy."[92] The racial project of Zionism could not be reconciled with the centrist race liberalism espoused by the major Jewish organizations.

Responding to the war, the ADL launched a new project of presenting Israel to the US public, and to Jewish communities themselves. This was a major pivot. The ADL's public relations work had frequently covered "the Arabs," casting Arab states as Soviet conspirators and extremists, and jeering as propaganda Arab American efforts to narrate Israel's dispossession of Palestinians. In the *ADL Bulletin*, these narratives appeared under sensational headings like "Cairo's Radio Talks Red," "Arab Students: Conspiracy in the US," "The Hate Parade of Khan Younis," and "The Soviet-Arab Axis," beginning in the 1950s and spanning subsequent decades. Each portrayed Arabs as Soviet conspirators and racial supremacists. In juxtaposition, they

90. Stork, "American New Left and Palestine."
91. Tom Segev, *1967: Israel, the War, and the Year That Transformed the Middle East* (Macmillan, 2007), 473.
92. Berkman, "Coercive Consensus," 314.

narrated the US and European Jews who confronted them in Israel and abroad as patient, principled defenders of justice.[93] The ADL's discussions of Israel itself, though, were infrequent and limited. Neither its books nor the *Bulletin* had covered Israel in the familiar, local way that they reported on civil rights advocacy, education, or democracy efforts in the United States. After the 1967 war, the shift was marked. The ADL launched an extensive outward public relations effort, established an information office to provide other institutions with materials on Israel, and began treating Israeli society as an extension of US life. It took some months to organize the ADL's new role as interpreter of Israel. The brief war took place in June 1967, and the *ADL Bulletin* did not muster any articles on Israel until September. But Epstein and Forster had traveled to Israel. There, in addition to gathering impressions of the war and Israeli strategy, Forster sought out human interest stories for US viewers. The trip and their reporting heralded a new project of blanketing US media with articles about Israelis as salt-of-the-earth Westerners, mixing human interest with political argument, and flatly denying Palestinian dispossession. In September, the first of these odes appeared in the *Bulletin* under the heading "The Miracle." Epstein wrote:

> I write this from Jerusalem, called *Yerushaliem*, Foundation of Peace. . . . It is impossible to convey the spirit of excitement and warmth that greets all visitors to Israel this summer. The people are deeply appreciative of the financial aid and unified support that came from . . . all over the world, and are proud, so very proud of their own accomplishments. They are proud of men like the taxi driver who took us from Tel Aviv to Jerusalem. Over 50, and recently returned from the fighting, he explained why he had gone: "Everybody did. I took my taxi and went right to the front." . . . We are impressed by the peaceful intermingling of Arab and Israeli in the Old City of Jerusalem and the freedom of movement everywhere. . . . Israelis and Arabs who haven't seen each other in 19 years meet like old, lost friends.[94]

The trip launched what would become a long-running radio and film project for Arnold Forster, extending into the 1980s, to make the case for

<hr>

93. Anti-Defamation League of B'nai B'rith, "Cairo's Radio Talks Red," *ADL Bulletin* 13, no. 3 (March 1956); Anti-Defamation League of B'nai B'rith, "Arab Students: Conspiracy in the US," *ADL Bulletin* 23, no. 10 (December 1966); Anti-Defamation League of B'nai B'rith, "The Hate Parade of Khan Younis," *ADL Bulletin* 24, no. 10 (October 1967); Anti-Defamation League of B'nai B'rith, "The Soviet-Arab Axis," *ADL Bulletin* 25, no. 10 (October 1968).

94. Benjamin R. Epstein, "The Miracle," *ADL Bulletin*, September 1967, 2.

Israel as an enlightened force and portray its challengers as petty or nonsensical. Five years earlier, Forster had attended the Eichmann trial and sent home taped segments, finding that radio stations were interested in his reporting.[95] Now he picked up the form again. His interviews with Israeli officials, cultural figures, and "average citizens" were mixed with observational commentary, bringing a curated picture of Israeli life into US living rooms as a familiar presence.[96] The new series, eventually formalized as *Dateline Israel*, was distributed at no cost to thousands of radio stations and reportedly aired on five hundred stations. The episodes presented Israel as bustling, hopeful, modern, and, above all, as Forster wrote, "a living democracy, Western-style."[97] Dozens of fifteen-minute radio segments highlighted Jewish ingenuity, character, and desire for peace. They highlighted an ostensible pluralism alongside grateful and supportive Arabs who welcomed colonization, contrary to "Arab propaganda" that detailed the dispossession and violence of Israeli settlement. The radio series was followed by a series of twenty-eight-minute films in the same reportage style, calibrated to fit into television programming slots and distributed for free to television stations. These, too, were presented as journalism, despite their unvarnished tilt. As the series stretched into the 1970s, Forster presented episodes on Black Jews, Israeli women, Soviet refugees, and myriad other topics that catered to US liberal interests in racial integration, feminism, and democracy—as well as episodes on the primary threat to liberal colonization: Arab resistance, always portrayed as terror.[98] One such episode, "The Jerusalem Dig," from 1975, hit back against UNESCO's finding that Israel had illegally occupied Jerusalem, failed to comply with UN resolutions, and was now abusing the notion of archaeological exploration to undermine al-Aqsa Mosque.[99] "Are you violating any religious rights by digging here?" Forster asks of the archaeologist overseeing Israel's dig, adopting the stance of a reporter. "Of course not," the

95. Arnold Forster, *Square One: A Memoir* (D. I. Fine, 1988), 197.

96. Arnold Forster, *Report from Israel* (Anti-Defamation League, 1968), https://www.adl.org/sites/default/files/adl-report-from-israel-arnold-forster-1969.pdf.

97. Forster, *Report from Israel*, 237; Jewish Telegraphic Agency, "ADL Announces New Radio Series on Israel," July 22, 1976.

98. Jewish Telegraphic Agency, "ADL Announces New Radio Series on Israel"; Arnold Forster, "Roots of Terrorism," *Dateline Israel*, directed by Gideon Hausner, September 9, 1979, https://archives.libraries.emory.edu/repositories/7/archival_objects/62969.

99. UNESCO, *Records of the General Conference, Eighteenth Session Paris, 17 October to 23* (1974), 59–60, https://en.unesco.org/inclusivepolicylab/system/files/teams/discussion/2022/2/UNESCO%20Records%201974.pdf.

archaeologist answers obligingly. "This problem never arise [*sic*]. It doesn't exist."[100]

The emergence of a muscular US Israel lobby posed an additional problem that defined the 1970s and early '80s. Following the 1967 war—as resistance by Palestinians, and at the United Nations, continued to present crises for Zionist organizations in the United States—NCRAC and the Conference of Presidents of Major American Jewish Organizations built their Israel advocacy into a machinery that could respond to Israel's needs and harness the power of Jewish public concern for Israel. NCRAC's efforts included high-traffic channels of communication with public officials and media outlets, sending a flow of background materials and current issue briefs, and readying networks of community members who could write letters, show up at protests, and make phone calls carrying Israel's messages to local officials. The Conference of Presidents developed its capacities to push out details about Israeli life, economy, and culture; a cultural offensive that would prepare audiences to sympathize with Israel when called upon.[101]

The lobby was further catalyzed by events in the early and mid-1970s. In 1973, Egyptian forces mounted the surprise attack that launched the Yom Kippur War. When US Jews responded as they had in 1967, with an outpouring of support and mobilization for Israel's defense, Jewish institutions were now prepared to direct it. The emergency drove a rush of funds into Israel advocacy organizations that laid groundwork for the scaling up of a permanent Israel advocacy infrastructure, what Berkman calls "a quantitative turning point."[102] The lobby was expanded again when the 1974 federal campaign finance law authorizing political action committees (PACs) as vehicles for ramping up political fundraising. In the later 1970s and throughout the 1980s, PACs produced an exponential rise in the power of pro-Israel groups to aggregate funds to elect and reward legislators, or punish and prevent their election, in a moment when pro-Israel donors themselves were experiencing vast increases in wealth.[103] These changes also produced a leap in US funding

100. Arnold Forster, "The Jerusalem Dig," *Dateline Israel*, produced by Zev Furst and Igal Efrati, Israel Film Service, 1975, https://jfc.org.il/en/news_journal/108804-2/.

101. Berkman, "Coercive Consensus," 288–93.

102. As one measure of the shift to a more permanent expanded Zionist advocacy structure, Berkman notes that AIPAC's budget jumped from $260,000 to $400,000 in 1973, after which it continued to "consistently and dramatically" increase. Berkman, "Coercive Consensus," 294, 345.

103. Michael Thomas, *American Policy Toward Israel: The Power and Limits of Beliefs* (Routledge, 2007), 49–50; Lee O'Brien, *American Jewish Organizations and Israel* (Institute

for Israel: from $50 million in economic aid in 1972, to $785 million in economic aid *and* $500 million in military aid in 1978; characterized by additional spikes and a "ratcheting effect: voting for less aid than the previous year was not seriously considered."[104]

As the idea of Israel as a vulnerable site of marginalized people became increasingly untenable in the early 1970s, the ADL adjusted course by dramatically rewriting the definition of antisemitism itself. Since its beginnings, the ADL had framed its advocacy in terms of liberal individualism, insisting on the right of Jewish citizens to be "accepted on their merits as Americans."[105] Now it turned to group rights and the idea of Jewish interests, closely identified with American interests. Newly, it insisted that Zionism was both.[106]

The New Anti-Semitism, a 1974 Epstein and Forster book, signaled the ADL's changing course. Whereas their earlier books had reported on ADL research, this book argued for a new way of thinking about the very meaning of marginalization. It sketched Jewishness, Israel, whiteness, and US liberal capitalism as a shared moral universe attacked by an intolerant left. In earlier works they had described evolving dangers to freedom and democracy.[107] On the right were white Christian supremacists propounding nativist narratives of racial siege, including the fantasy that Jews were a leftist cabal aiming to "mongrelize the American race." On the left were communists.[108] *The New Anti-Semitism* offered a revision that dramatically expanded the category of antisemites. It contended that, given the merger of US Jewry into "the Establishment," the broad-based social justice movements critiquing "the Establishment" were actually attacking Jews. The concerns of the state-

---

for Palestine Studies, 1986), 183–87. On the expansion and restructuring of the donor base of major Jewish organizations in the 1970s–1980s, see Lila Corwin Berman, *The American Jewish Philanthropic Complex: The History of a Multibillion-Dollar Institution* (Princeton University Press, 2020).

104. Thomas, *American Policy Toward Israel*, 51.

105. Arnold Forster and Benjamin R. Epstein, *The Trouble-Makers: An Anti-Defamation League Report* (1952), 275.

106. Arnold Forster and Benjamin R. Epstein, *The New Anti-Semitism* (McGraw-Hill, 1974), 10–11.

107. Forster and Epstein, *New Anti-Semitism*, 7.

108. Gerald Smith's racist diatribe quoted in Arnold Forster, *A Measure of Freedom: An Anti-Defamation League Report* (Doubleday, 1950), 87. Despite identifying the key role played by corporations in funding and propagating Christian nationalism, the ADL did not portray corporate interests on the whole as an aspect of the political right.

capital class, which were also Jewish communal concerns, were now *"legitimate* objects of criticism, scorn and calumny." And since political criticism was considered perfectly acceptable, "the respectable community" did not perceive it as discrimination. That was a failure, Forster and Epstein argued, that threatened Jews and the US liberal order in tandem: "[T]he Radical Left sees the Jewish community and its institutions as part of the 'Establishment': an affluent, smug, 'liberal' obstacle to the growth of revolutionary consciousness. . . . To the Radical Left . . . liberalism is the great enemy, the force which sows and perpetuates illusions that progress can be achieved steadily and peacefully through normal democratic processes."[109] ADL leaders understood this as a paradigm shift, since antisemitism was generally understood as a feature of the political right. In a 1972 issue of *Facts*, they had made the call explicit: "Movements of the Left, especially those aimed at combatting tyranny and autocracy, or at achieving social reform and betterment, have often seemed solicitous of minority rights and protective of Jewish security." Now, though, the left's support for "the revolutionary 'national liberation' movements of the 'Third World'" meant opposing "the operation of US foreign policy [and] . . . the natural concerns of the American Jewish community."[110]

What Forster and Epstein meant by "Jewish interests" encompassed Israel itself and the Zionism that had developed among US Jews since 1967, as well as Cold War race liberalism.[111] They reiterated the ADL's running denunciations of Arab anticolonialism, Third Worldism, and communism, and described Black liberation as a period of "violence, civil disorder, confusion, and . . . turning inward."[112] Additionally, they called for a renewal of efforts to discipline Jewish dissent, which was vibrant. Despite the purges of the 1950s that had excised leftists, Jewish organizers still challenged the major Jewish organizations and denounced Israeli colonialism "as a client of American empire." (Michael Tabor, organizer of Jews for Urban Justice, based in Washington, DC, decried "the acceptance by Jewish establishment leadership and their following of the worst principles of the Pharaohs—racism, their domination, cutthroat competition, exploitation as their own.")[113] Naming

109. Forster and Epstein, *New Anti-Semitism*, 9.

110. Anti-Defamation League of B'nai B'rith, "Danger on the Left," *Facts*, November 1972. Reprinted in Congressional Record, Extension of Remarks, February 8, 1973, pp. 4126, 4132.

111. Forster and Epstein, *New Anti-Semitism*, 7.

112. Forster and Epstein, *New Anti-Semitism*, 9, 179.

113. Staub, *Torn at the Roots*, 15, 232.

Jewish leftist organizing as an antisemitic threat, Forster and Epstein pointed ominously to Tufts University Hillel's Non-Zionist Caucus, which had joined the previous year with the MIT Arab Club and others to host a panel on "Israeli Zionist Terrorism in the Middle East" in 1973, and to the Jews and Yiddish publications of the Soviet Union as puppets, "occasionally parade[d] . . . to disprove charges of anti-Semitism." To disqualify Jewish leftists from conversations about racial justice and antisemitism, Epstein and Forster borrowed the language of Black resistance, dismissing them as "house Jews," or simply as ghouls: "Among some Jews in the Radical Left, here and abroad, there is an interesting psychological phenomenon at work . . . they are in fact celebrating death over life . . . they are asking for new Jewish martyrs; they are joining that element of the non-Jewish world which in its heart of hearts believes that the best kind of Jew is a dead Jew."[114] *The New Anti-Semitism* stitched together the conservative politics of "the Establishment" as a like-race identity in the lexicon of civil rights, defended by prohibitions on antisemitism. With this move, the ADL reclaimed its authority on racism and civil rights and returned Israel to its privileged position as a US moral interest.

Finally, *The New Anti-Semitism* marked as Jewish interest an accumulating investment in whiteness, as it laid claim to membership in "the Establishment" as a right that must be protected.[115] For several years the ADL had resisted and ridiculed the efforts of Black liberation and antiwar organizers to interrogate whiteness. Epstein and Forster now reiterated the central argument: that the articulation of whiteness and capitalism with colonialism was a Black nationalist delusion, fueled by frustration over the slow progress of equality, and encouraged by foreign revolutionists from Fanon to Mao.[116] Additionally, they feared that civil rights remedies— economic and social policies that redistributed resources and privileges— meant that white people would be required to cede opportunity or even property. The ADL had been feeling its way through these conflicts in the context of school desegregation. It now objected to what it viewed as excessive moves toward racial justice.

Indeed, while Forster and Epstein prepared their manuscript for publication, ADL attorneys were building the agency's arguments in the *DeFunis v. Odegaard* case, opposing the affirmative action university admissions policies

114. Forster and Epstein, *New Anti-Semitism*, 137, 152.
115. On this concept, see George Lipsitz, *The Possessive Investment in Whiteness* (Temple University Press, 1998).
116. Forster and Epstein, *New Anti-Semitism*, 179.

that were designed to overcome deep histories of exclusion of Black and brown law school applicants. Their 1974 amicus brief, filed with the US Supreme Court as *The New Anti-Semitism* arrived in bookstores, argued that affirmative action constituted antiwhite discrimination against a Jewish applicant. The ADL's argument mixed concern for past antisemitic discrimination with disregard for past anti-Black discrimination: It held that Jews, having once been excluded, should not be resubjected to exclusion now that they were members of the majority—but also that present-day white populations should not be asked to give up privileges to redress "past racial inequities."[117] The central claim was that whiteness was an identity now subjected to something like anti-Black discrimination. "Yesteryear it was blacks; it was Jews; Catholics," explained Nathan Perlmutter, who was shortly to succeed Epstein as director. "Today those being arbitrarily bumped by quotas are white."[118] Four years later the ADL would again oppose affirmative action in *University of California Regents v. Bakke.*[119]

As the ADL confronted the New Left in the late 1960s, its problem was not only its upward mobility, but also that the presumed Black-Jewish alliance had melted into air. This presented multiple crises. It tarnished the ADL's credentials as a US civil rights agency. It implied that the ADL and the Jewish leadership class were an oppressive force rather than a democratic one, which rankled them. It also hurt their credibility in speaking to Black publics. In the Cold War battle to keep people of color from Third Worldism, and the Zionist battle to keep them from sympathizing with Palestinians, such credibility was crucial. It was not enough for the ADL to attack its Black and left critics. To fill the gap, it projected a Black-Jewish alliance and generated messaging in collaboration through a few key figures, presenting race liberalism and Zionism as Black interests.

Bayard Rustin's treatise against Black revolt, *The Anatomy of Frustration,* was originally delivered as a speech to the ADL National Commission

117. ADL brief quoted and discussed by Larry Lavinsky, chairman of the ADL's National Law Committee in Forster, *A Measure of Freedom,* 87; Larry M. Lavinsky, "Defunis v. Odegaard: The 'Non-Decision' with a Message," *Columbia Law Review* 75, no. 3 (1975): 520.

118. Bureau of National Affairs, "Affirmative Action Today: A Legal and Political Analysis," 1985.

119. For a history of major Jewish organizations' opposition to affirmative action, see Greenberg, *Troubling the Waters,* 236.

meeting in May 1968, one month after the assassination of Martin Luther King Jr. and in the fraught context of Ocean Hill-Brownsville conflicts. The ADL's decision to publish it marked a campaign to speak to two distinct audiences. Among white liberals, the ADL needed to reassert its authority to speak on race and rights. It also aimed to inoculate the Black public against invitations to radicalism, Black internationalism, and anti-Zionism. Rustin had established himself as a friend of mainstream, integrationist Jewish institutions in the mid-sixties. He spoke regularly at meetings of Jewish institutional bodies. In 1965 and 1966 alone, he headlined the National Conference of Jewish Communal Service, the National Community Relations Advisory Council annual meeting, the American Jewish Congress convention, the Jewish Labor Committee convention, and several forums on Black-Jewish relations.[120] His speeches covered civil rights, intergroup relations, critiques of the Soviet Union, and his economic policy proposal, the Freedom Budget—all subjects that Rustin discussed wherever he spoke.

In speeches to Jewish organizations, Rustin regularly added another rhetorical line: He confirmed the existence of Black antisemitism as the major Jewish organizations conceived it, and then he tried to assuage fears about it, explaining that frustrations led to "adopt[ing] a slogan of 'to hell with everybody, regardless of their color, race, or creed.'"[121] At the same time he denounced the separatism that was sidelining white civil rights groups.[122] Rustin's affirmations were triumphantly received by the institutional leaders and commentators of the mainstream Jewish world. He was "the wisest of current negro leaders" and an authoritative figure "who called the Jewish community one of the finest elements in the broad coalition of civil rights forces"; furthermore he disentangled Black resentments from Jewish institu-

120. Rustin was also a familiar figure in Jewish communal news media. Among many appearances in news reports, see, for instance: *Indiana Jewish Post and Opinion*, "Negroes Seem Likely to Jump on Jews Next," April 16, 1965; *American Jewish World*, "Ashamed of Negro Bias, Rustin Says," December 30, 1966; *American Jewish World*, "'The Negro and Anti-Semitism' Will Be Discussed by Negro and Jewish Leaders on the WNBC-TV 'Open Mind' Program Sunday," photo caption, June 3, 1966.

121. *Detroit Jewish News*, "Conclave Experts Disagree on Roots of Anti-Semitism," May 8, 1964.

122. On Rustin's opposition to separatism and conjunction with major Jewish organizations, see Jervis Anderson, *Bayard Rustin: Troubles I've Seen* (HarperCollins, 1997), 313–21, 326–28.

tions' virtues with "the patience of a brilliant, patient sociologist."[123] Additionally, Rustin's call to shift politics from the streets into the conference rooms of labor unions and government agencies resonated with their discomfort with mass movements. "Rustin's program must be considered carefully by all who truly want to avoid violence and the unending tramp-tramp-tramp of civil rights demonstrators."[124] These many speeches formed the backdrop, in 1967, for Rustin's denunciation of SNCC's positions against Zionism. (Rustin was joined by his mentor A. Philip Randolph, Whitney Young of the National Urban League, and other centrist voices.)[125] In 1968, Rustin joined the ADL and the UFT in denouncing Ocean Hill-Brownsville parents as antisemitic and illiberal.

In keeping with Rustin's usual oratory, *The Anatomy of Frustration* offered a Social Democratic program for the next moves of the civil rights movement and lamented Black radicalism as a form of degradation. Rustin urged embracing the state to advocate for mass-scale economic programs for full employment and guaranteed income. He stretched a validating arm around mainstream Jewish institutions suffering rejection by the New Left: "You attack those who have in fact carried the banner. . . . Next in the list of enemies of the frustrated come Roy Wilkins, Whitney Young, A. Philip Randolph." Finally, he reaffirmed that shared experiences of marginalization connected Jewishness to Blackness, and he asked that Jews view Black antisemitism with some empathy—effectively, to be the proverbial adult in the room.[126] These were things that ADL leaders wanted the world to hear, too.

In 1969 the ADL extended its efforts to undercut Black radicalism by creating an "urban" (Black) affairs department to coordinate work "relevant to the urban crisis and race relations." National Urban League staffer Kenyon Burke was hired to lead it.[127] Burke was the ADL's first Black director, and he immediately set about organizing the support of "opinion molders" for the

123. *The Sentinel*, "Is Negro Condemning Jew for Becoming 'White Christian'?," September 28, 1967; *American Jewish World*, "NCRAC Formulates Guidelines for US Jewry," July 2, 1965.

124. *B'nai B'rith Messenger*, "As We Were Saying," July 2, 1965.

125. Whitney Young and his successor at the National Urban League, Vernon Jordan, were regular ADL allies. Kathleen Teltsch, "SNCC Criticized for Israel Stand; Rights Leaders Score Attack on Jews as 'Anti-Semitism,'" *New York Times*, August 16, 1967.

126. Rustin, *Anatomy of Frustration*.

127. Jewish Telegraphic Agency, "ADL Names First Negro Executive as Urban Affairs Unit Director," August 23, 1968.

ADL's mission with an Israel junket for Black journalists from prominent outlets: *Jet, Amsterdam News, Chicago Daily Defender, Michigan Chronicle,* the *Afro-American, Miami Times,* and *St. Louis Sentinel.* The trip was billed as a way to draw lessons from Israel that might advance racial equality in the United States, and to that end included schools, kibbutz visits, and presentations on Israel's aid work in Africa. On behalf of the delegation, Burke reported the finding that Israel was a model of antiracism from which Black organizers could take inspiration. "There is a determined national commitment to . . . provide equal and quality services to all citizens—including Arab Israelis," Burke wrote. He wished aloud that the United States could be more like Israel: "A commitment as strong in our country could make democratic principles of equality a reality here."[128] That Burke was able to make such a report affirms that the trip was highly curated. It would have required not encountering Palestinians who could speak freely, despite Burke's proud report that the group met with a former Jordanian official "with no Israelis present."[129] It would have meant not seeing Palestinian or indeed Arab Jewish villages (to which the Israeli state had largely denied the municipal status needed to access water and basic services); refugee camps (crammed with three hundred thousand Palestinians refugees since the 1967 war); or the West Bank and Gaza, now under Israeli military rule.[130] Whether other junket participants saw through the propaganda is hard to gauge; their newspapers seem to have published no articles related to the trip.

The ADL engaged somewhat obliquely in one more major effort, in 1975, to imbue Zionism with the moral authority of Black civil rights leadership. Rustin's objections to Black Power included its antagonism toward Israel, and he had been especially exercised by the anti-Zionist resolution at the 1972 New Politics Conference. He marshaled a series of arguments aimed at Black audiences, including framing Arabs as past and present anti-Black oppressors, blaming the Palestinian refugee crisis on Arab states, and lauding Israel as a friend of African development. Shortly after the conference, his article "Black Links to Israel" placed that reasoning in twenty-six Black newspapers and a dozen union newspapers, as Michael Fischbach documents. "Blacks must know that democracy, wherever it is, must be supported, because all

128. *The Carolinian,* "Black Editors, Publishers, Plan 10-Day-Stay in Israel," November 22, 1969; Kenyon C. Burke, "A Trip to Israel," *Negro History Bulletin* 33, no. 4 (1970): 95–96.
129. Burke, "A Trip to Israel," 94.
130. Adnan Abed Elrazik, Riyad Amin, and Uri Davis, "Problems of Palestinians in Israel: Land, Work, Education," *Journal of Palestine Studies* 7, no. 3 (Spring 1978): 31–54.

minorities … need democracy in order to attain economic, political and social justice," Rustin wrote. "Thus, rather than calling for the dismantling of Israel, black people all over the world should take an active interest in securing Israel's survival."[131] In the same spirit, Rustin turned to a set of comrades to generate more ideas, including ADL fact-finding director Irwin Suall and Jewish Labor Committee director Emanuel Muravchik.[132] As much as a meeting between Rustin and Jewish institutional leaders, it was a meeting of a Social Democratic network that linked the UFT, the ADL, and Rustin's own organization, the A. Philip Randolph Institute.

Together the group conceived BASIC, the Black Americans to Support Israel Committee, a project that loosely gathered dozens of Black leaders to support Israel. In parallel with the ADL's efforts, its role would be to present Zionism as a mode of civil rights politics in the domestic arena, and anticolonial politics in the global arena. At BASIC's launch in April 1975—featuring Rustin, A. Philip Randolph, and the head of the Israeli national oil company, Paz—Rustin articulated the imperative to oppose Palestinian organizing. In the language of Holocaust remembrance and a civil rights–derived nationalism, he attacked Palestinians for seeking "the destruction of another people" and referred to the boycott of Israeli state-supporting firms as "imported Arab discrimination."[133] By the time BASIC formally rolled out with a list of high-profile signatories on September 11, 1975, it was primed to make real interventions in support of the aims of the ADL. On October 2 its members wrote open letters to the UN African delegations opposing a move to suspend Israel from the General Assembly. On October 16, BASIC filed an amicus brief in an ADL lawsuit seeking to prevent the US Department of Commerce from "aiding and abetting" the Arab boycott.[134]

131. Michael R. Fischbach, *Black Power and Palestine: Transnational Countries of Color* (Stanford University Press, 2023), 171, 244n5; Bayard Rustin, "Black Links to Israel," *Wichita Times*, April 20, 1972.

132. While the meeting was clearly a gathering of Jewish institutional leaders—the meeting is recorded in the American Jewish Congress archives—it is less clear in what capacity Suall was acting. He was close to Rustin and Muravchik through their work in Social Democrats USA, as well as through their respective institutions, as chapter 4 details. Fischbach, *Black Power and Palestine*, 173.

133. Jewish Telegraphic Agency, "Randolph Initiates Committee of Black Americans to Support Israel," April 28, 1975; *Milwaukee Star Times*, "Black for Israel Forms New Committee," September 18, 1975.

134. *Milwaukee Star Times*, "Black Americans Committee Condemns Boycott," October 16, 1975.

Borrowing the ADL's methods, BASIC also planned Israel junkets. For its first trip in the summer of 1975, BASIC organizers recruited twenty DJs from Black radio stations because, Rustin explained, "our folks listen to him 24 hours a day."[135] BASIC did not capture Black public opinion, and it lost steam after 1977 as Israel was tainted by its ties with South African Apartheid and its election of avowedly right-wing leadership, as Fischbach writes.[136]

It was the demands of Israel advocacy, then, that reanimated the ADL's work on race, even as it moved against antiracist organizing and mainstream civil rights policy. The project was to thread the needle, conveying that policing Black radicalism was actually an act of antiracist care. In March 1969, shortly after sounding the cannons about the "Black antisemitism" crisis, Epstein reasserted the ADL's role as a loving paternal hand guiding Black communities toward freedom: "In most important aspects Negroes are less anti-Semitic than whites . . . [but] separatist philosophy, built on a base of hatred, is a cruel hoax on the black community," he warned.

> Equality has been deferred so long that while the Negro average family income is up, it is not likely to catch up with that of whites for decades. . . . That is what the black man in the ghetto, tired of being analyzed and graphed, sees. He wants and needs action, but not the extremists' way as long as other ways remain viable. The [ADL] shall continue our efforts because it is a work that will benefit society as a whole—and may be the only way to keep our society whole. We have worked too long . . . to see the American Dream dwindle to a struggle between the two groups that have been most subject to discrimination.[137]

Israel, too, ran in increasingly stark opposition to its own claims as a racial liberation project and an egalitarian democracy. The ADL had framed Israel as a civilization project, a home for Jewish refugees, an anticommunist bulwark, and a civil rights project in parallel to US Black organizing. After 1967, though, it produced and immiserated more Palestinian refugees. In 1977 Israeli voters elected Menachem Begin—a territorial expansionist who had

135. Jewish Telegraphic Agency, "Randolph Initiates Committee of Black Americans to Support Israel."

136. Fischbach, *Black Power and Palestine*, 175–77.

137. Benjamin R. Epstein, "Negro Anti-Semitism: National Director, Anti-Defamation League," *American Israelite*, March 27, 1969.

overseen the massacre of Palestinians. Rather than pushing back, US Jewish leaders followed along.[138]

It is notable, then, that as Israel advocacy topped the ADL's internal agenda, civil rights and community relations remained its most public-facing work. Rather than thinking of them as separate from Israel advocacy, the defense agencies understood them as necessarily entwined. In 1973, contemplating the ADL and American Jewish Committee, Gary S. Schiff noted that Israel advocacy was conducted in every department, rather than operating as a single project. Domestic civil rights work was its natural home. "[Are] community relations and Israel-overseas spheres becoming more and more synonymous ...? Has the fund raising sector ... [recognized] community relations as an effective and long term means of achieving pro-Israel aims?"[139] His conversations with agency staff suggested that the two had merged. The effects of the civil rights narration were concrete—if Black popular opinion was not particularly swayed, *white* ethnic popular opinion was. White polities that identified racially, ethnically, or morally with Jews adopted the framing of Israel as a homeland/liberation project. Schiff writes that the American Jewish Committee, which conducted heritage industry work "to foster ethnic self-awareness and appreciation," elicited support for Israel from Polish, Ukrainian, Lithuanian, Italian, Greek, and Japanese ethnic populations on the basis of "empathy for a beleaguered national homeland fighting for existence against Soviet-based aggression."[140]

The ADL had entered the 1960s uncertain how to navigate between Jewish whiteness and the ongoing calls to dislodge white dominance. Faced with the demands of Black liberation against race liberalism—from unequal schools to neocolonial regimes—it retooled. As "Arab antisemitism" had served to dismiss Palestinian calls for rights, now "Black antisemitism" and "new" anti-establishment antisemitism obviated challenges to power. Crucially, the ADL's break with antiracist movements did not reflect a break with its earlier commitments. The ADL's political arc, rather than moving from left to right, is better understood as an always-conservative politics that expanded from the United States territorially outward. It began with the local, domestic anxieties of settler colonialism, then expanded to foreign

<hr>

138. Thomas, *American Policy Toward Israel*, 35, 231–62.

139. Gary S. Schiff, "American Jews and Israel: A Study in Political and Organizational Priorities," in *Understanding American Jewish Philanthropy*, ed. Marc Lee Raphael (Ktav Publishing, 1979), 165–95.

140. Schiff, "American Jews and Israel," 184.

policy through World War II, the establishment of the Israeli state, and the Cold War. Later, it grew to encompass a global "clash of civilizations" anxiety, featuring Israel and the United States as models of order and discipline in a nefarious world. Following the 1967 war, these ideas and anxieties took form as the neoconservative movement, with the ADL as a natural participant.

FOUR

Israel and Neoconservative Internationalism

THE '70S AND '80S

IN 1972, THE UNITED STATES was afire with protests over the brutal war in Vietnam. President Richard Nixon insisted that the war was necessary to prevent communism from taking root, a thin rationale that faded as the costs of war mounted. A majority of the US public favored the immediate withdrawal of US troops. But in December of that year, one group of socialists passed a resolution in support of *continuing* the war. Once simply the Socialist Party, it had gone through several reformulations and was now the Social Democrats USA (SDUSA). It was small, but it was a fixture of the left. The Socialist Party had been a serious force in electoral politics before World War II, and SDUSA was still part of the ecosystem that included student, antiwar, and counterculture movements. Its energetic leaders had built ties to labor which, they strategized, could become an engine for a worker-led, racially egalitarian democracy. Like other movement groups, its members hotly debated questions of policy. Pushing it increasingly away from other groups, though, its leaders were staunch anticommunists. Anticommunism was the reason for their position on the Vietnam War.[1] "Real peace requires resistance to the attempts by the armed Communist minority to impose its rule on the country," they explained.[2]

At the 1972 convention, SDUSA cochair Bayard Rustin opened the meeting. Tom Kahn, a former SNCC organizer who now worked as an adviser to the top brass of the AFL-CIO, proposed a resolution opposing the

---

1. See Jack Ross's intimate history of the Socialist Party in this period. Jack Ross, *The Socialist Party of America: A Complete History* (Potomac Books, 2015), 468–519.

2. This 1970 statement explained the party leaders' position on the same issue. It was revisited and adopted as SDUSA position in 1972. James Burnett et al., "Statement on Vietnam," *Hammer and Tongs*, no. 1 (October 1970).

155

withdrawal of US troops from Vietnam. While it opposed "any efforts to bomb Hanoi into submission," it equally called for "firmness against Communist aggression" as a necessary measure for democracy. The resolution sharply divided SDUSA members but, guided by longtime party leader Irwin Suall, the resolution was rammed through.[3] Then the group splintered: antiwar members quit. The SDUSA, which now endorsed anticommunist war—led by Rustin, Kahn, Suall, and their cadre—now grounded in anticommunist organized labor rather than the left, formed an arm of the emerging neoconservative movement.[4] Suall was a director at the Anti-Defamation League at the time, where he was building what would soon become the ADL's famed intelligence operation for monitoring white nationalists—and more quietly, for infiltrating the left. SDUSA's Vietnam vote made national news, but no newspaper mentioned Suall's day job.

SDUSA's neoconservative turn had been in development for more than forty years. A generation earlier, another cadre of former Marxists had taken a similar left-to-right path. This group had gathered at City College in the 1930s. Many were second-generation Jewish immigrants who had grown up working class, within view of the labor movement if not in leftist families. They had initially been excited by Marxism and the mass movements that rose up around it. But as they watched the development of Stalinist repression in the Soviet Union, and then Stalin's 1939 nonaggression pact with Nazi Germany, they fell away. The rise of Stalinism was not just a branch of history, they concluded, but the inevitable outcome of Marxist ideas. They were reborn as anticommunists. After college, as sociologists and writers, they had stayed interested in race, class, democracy: Nathan Glazer, Seymour Martin Lipset, Daniel Bell, and others of their cadre became leading scholars on those subjects. Through the lenses of race liberalism and anticommunism, they tracked the development of white suburbs and Black and brown ghettos, increasing inequality, racial conflict, and the rise of leftist cultural and political movements. Their concern for inequality was intermingled with a moralistic view of poverty and racist suppositions—for example, that Jewish cultural traits like "the propensity for hard work" and "intellectual pre-eminence" drove success, while groups that remained poor were impeded by cultural

3. *New York Times*, "'Firmness' Urged on Communists," January 1, 1973. For a firsthand account from the proponents of the resolution, see Social Democrats USA, *For the Record* (1973), http://archive.org/details/ForTheRecord1973.

4. See Bill King, "The Origins of Neoconservative Support for Democracy Promotion, 1960–1991" (MA thesis, University of Calgary, 2007), 68–108.

traits, not structural barriers.[5] This generation, too, had gathered under the banner of Social Democratic thought. By the late 1960s, many of this older group were college faculty, presiding over campuses that were exploding in student protest, and serving as mentors to the younger Social Democrats.

A third branch of neoconservatism took shape in the early 1970s among Democrats opposing the New Left. It was marked by a 1972 *New York Times* ad under the banner headline "Come home, Democrats!" It announced the formation of a new organization, the Coalition for a Democratic Majority (CDM) in the wake of the Democratic Party's failure to win the presidential election: Their candidate George McGovern had been defeated by Richard Nixon in a landslide. CDM's message was that Democrats had bent to the demands of the New Left rather than what they believed voters wanted: for the United States to proudly claim global power, focus on law-and-order policing at home, reject affirmative action, and roll back the excessive attention to social ills like racism and sexism that was demanded by leftist movements. The impetus for CDM had come from the office of Senator Henry "Scoop" Jackson, where young Social Democrat Penn Kemble was a strategist. Its list of eighty-one signatories brought together the City College ex-Marxist crowd, Democratic party figures, organized labor, and civil rights movements leaders A. Philip Randolph and Bayard Rustin. Soon afterward, it would add one of its most prominent voices: presidential adviser, soon-to-be United Nations ambassador, and future US senator Daniel Patrick Moynihan. CDM's foreign affairs and defense task force, and the later groups that formed from it, gathered the SDUSA members who would move into key positions in think tanks, legislative offices, federal agencies, and the hierarchy of organized labor throughout the 1970s and 1980s.[6]

These political streams produced a neoconservatism that was more a gathering of interests and organizations than a singular movement. Indeed, efforts to assess and describe the neoconservative movement grapple with the fact that it had no formal organization and was often denied by its key

5. On the origins and history of the neoconservative movement, see Peter Steinfels, *The Neoconservatives: The Origins of a Movement* (Simon and Schuster, 2013). For examples of later neoconservative academic work, see Seymour Martin Lipset and Everett Carll Ladd Jr., "Jewish Academics in the United States: Their Achievements, Culture, and Politics," *American Jewish Year Book*, 1971, 97, 103; Daniel P. Moynihan, "The Professors and the Poor," *Commentary*, August 1968.

6. Justin Vaïsse, *Neoconservatism: The Biography of a Movement* (Harvard University Press, 2010), 87–93.

figures.[7] Nonetheless, its players were unified by Cold War liberalism and collectively pitched against the leftward turn of US popular movements, articulating their own position as "the vital center."[8] As they moved into foreign policy projects in the 1980s and '90s, the same antipathies to the left animated them. They viewed the shifts that popular uprising had achieved as immoderate and antidemocratic; they were proponents of ideas like "meritocracy" and "colorblindness" that antiracist movements were rejecting as formal civil rights failed to end actual racial subjugation.[9] Historian John Ehrman explains that as "the left . . . articulated a case against the vital center, its assumptions about America's virtues, and the legitimacy of its global interests," those who stayed loyal to the vital center became neoconservatives.[10] Beyond the concern that civil rights measures were antiwhite, they also objected to the left's calls to rethink the cultural norms of liberal capitalism, from gender roles to the drive to climb the ladder of capitalist success. Indeed, the focus of much of their advocacy was "the kind of character and discipline that neoconservatives judged necessary to make liberal political institutions work," writes Peter Steinfels.[11] Democracy, they held, rested on Western cultural norms of family, labor, and capitalist incentives. In that view, programs like welfare and affirmative action were damaging to democracy, disrupting competition and meritocracy and enabling a "culture of poverty."[12]

As advocates for Zionism, neoconservatives applied the same rationales. Israel was a model of the modern Western state-building at the center of their vision of democracy. By contrast, they portrayed Arab nations as culturally and politically retrograde, Soviet-friendly, and antisemitic, and the Palestinian liberation movement as emblematic of those characteristics.

---

7. Steinfels, *Neoconservatives*, x. See also Mark Gerson, *The Neoconservative Vision: From the Cold War to the Culture Wars* (Madison Books, 1996), 8.

8. As Chip Berlet and Matt Lyons have written, this framework marked dissent against the state as a "slippery slope" to "extremism," and viewed even mild leftist dissent as a harbinger of communist-driven "totalitarianism." See Arthur Schlesinger Jr., "Not Left, Not Right, but a Vital Center," *New York Times Magazine*, April 4, 1948; Chip Berlet and Matthew N. Lyons, "Repression and Ideology: The Legacy of Discredited Centrist/Extremist Theory," *Police Misconduct and Civil Rights Law Report* 5, nos. 13–14 (1998). The article is now republished at Political Research Associates: https://politicalresearch.org/1998/04/15/repression-and-ideology-legacy-discredited-centristextremist-theory.

9. Vaïsse, *Neoconservatism*, 76.

10. John Ehrman, *The Rise of Neoconservatism: Intellectuals and Foreign Affairs, 1945–1994* (Yale University Press, 1995), 17.

11. Steinfels, *Neoconservatives*, xix.

12. Vaïsse, *Neoconservatism*, 70–73.

Where Black liberation organizing made common cause with Palestine, neo-conservatives read that as "extremism." As neoconservative figure Carl Gershman argued, in calling for Palestinian rights "some black leaders [were trying] . . . to move a significant segment of the black leadership toward an ideological and political alignment with Third World radicalism," and they were targeting Israel because it was a Western force pushing against Soviet-aligned movements.[13] The ADL had been making the same claims since the start of the Cold War.

Situating the Anti-Defamation League as part of the neoconservative movement is in some respects a project of pointing out the obvious: Many mainstream Jewish institutions endorsed neoconservative ideas and alliances in the 1970s and '80s. However, it also calls for tracing the dense field of relationships between the ADL and the people and organizations who made up the movement. The ADL forged relationships with figures in academia and politics who are now recognized as neoconservatives—its advisers and authors included Moshe Decter, Earl Raab, Max Kampelman, Harvey Klehr, Seymour Martin Lipset, Murray Friedman, and Bayard Rustin, and its network of commission members, colleagues, and collaborators extended much further into neoconservative circles.[14] ADL national director Nathan Perlmutter, appointed in 1979, was also a neoconservative. However, its vascular connection was through Irwin Suall, who spent three decades at the ADL. His close connections spanned SDUSA and the wider network of relationships that formed the Social Democratic sphere. Members of Suall's party cadre took up high-level positions in federal agencies, political offices, and organized labor beginning in the late 1960s, at the same time that Suall joined the ADL. Their organizations read as a map of the neoconservative sphere: the American Enterprise Institute, the Jewish Institute for National Security Affairs, the National Endowment for Democracy, the Free Trade Union Institute, the Committee for Democracy in Central America (PRODEMCA), and others. As they moved into powerful positions, they applied neoconservative ideas about capitalism, culture, and democracy to Cold War foreign

13. Gershman quoted in Ehrman, *Rise of Neoconservatism*, 127.

14. A sample of some of these publications: Moshe Decter, *The Profile of Communism: A Fact-by-Fact Primer* (New York, 1961), http://hdl.handle.net/2027/uc1.b4098850; Earl Raab and Seymour Martin Lipset, *Prejudice and Society* (Anti-Defamation League of B'nai B'rith, 1959); Harvey Klehr, *Far Left of Center: The American Radical Left Today* (Transaction, 1988); Seymour Martin Lipset, *"The Socialism of Fools": The Left, the Jews & Israel* (Anti-Defamation League of B'nai B'rith, 1969).

policy projects. Following Suall from his roots in Social Democratic politics through his time at the ADL, this chapter begins to historicize how the ADL joined or overlapped with neoconservative projects.

The first oblique acknowledgment of the ADL's link to the neoconservative movement came in 1974, in Forster and Epstein's book *The New Anti-Semitism*. ADL books usually began with a preface explaining the urgency of the work in countering imminent threats to democracy, and calls to the reader to stand up to protect it. This book did just that—but in a turn that must have surprised readers, Epstein and Forster endorsed socialists as allies in the effort. It rang strangely. The ADL had never endorsed any alternative views on economy or state. Stranger still, the text delved into internecine left politics, distinguishing good leftists from bad. "[T]he totalitarian Radical Left—whose major groups include the Communist Party . . . the Socialist Workers Party and . . . Students for a Democratic Society . . . —fails to eschew anti-Semitism and actively uses hostility against Jews as a weapon in its political struggle," wrote Forster and Epstein. By contrast, "the Western-oriented social-democratic movement . . . has supported Israel's right to exist . . . [and] been a friend of the Jewish community.[15] . . . Today the organized democratic left in America consists of the Social Democrats, USA . . . and its youth section, the Young People's Socialist League."[16] This uncharacteristic nod to socialism did not, in fact, reflect a major shift. Instead, it signaled the ADL's induction into the new political ecology that spanned Social Democrats, anticommunist labor, and even the CIA, and was quietly prosecuting the Cold War.[17]

Suall joined the ADL in 1967 as the director of a new fact-finding department under the Civil Rights Division. Suall was an experienced researcher and a keen political writer. Most immediately, he went to work investigating leftist challenges to Israel. A long-form article appeared in November 1972 in

15. While the Socialist International at times offered support to Israel, and Prime Minister Golda Meir's attendance at the 1972 Vienna convention was widely noted, that connection did not animate US Jewish institutions' interest in socialism. The ADL's engagement, as discussed in the following section, came through other connections. Paul Hoffman, "Socialists at Parley Hail Their Golda," *New York Times*, June 28, 1972.

16. The full passage includes a litany of other organizations. Arnold Forster and Benjamin R. Epstein, *The New Anti-Semitism* (McGraw-Hill, 1974), 8.

17. Ross, *Socialist Party of America*, 507.

the ADL's newsletter *The Facts*, titled "Danger on the Left," just a few weeks before the SDUSA decision on Vietnam. Likely written by Suall in his role as fact-finding chief, it reflected intimate knowledge of the left's swelling opposition to Zionism. It crystallized the ADL's antipathy toward the New Left.[18] Where the ADL had first found leftist movements responsible for "Black antisemitism," it now found that they constituted a pervasive "extremism" in which Jewish leftists were a particularly frustrating problem. Painting a picture of energetic anti-Zionist organizing and connection with Palestinian political groups, the article listed a litany of enemies, including the Socialist Workers Party, Communist Party USA, National Peace Action Coalition, Committee for a Just Peace in the Middle East, and the Middle East Research and Information Project (MERIP).[19] The groups that Suall had contended with in his role at SDUSA were targets of the ADL as well. Suall continued to pursue them throughout his tenure as fact-finding director.

Suall's anti-left antipathies did not gain much public notice, though; instead, he rose to prominence as an opponent of the white nationalist right. Under his stewardship, the ADL's investigations of white nationalist groups became more sophisticated. In 1977 Suall published the ADL's first warning that the Ku Klux Klan was reorganizing and growing, and he suddenly became known not only for that work, but his prior work on the same subject: "Irwin Suall . . . is the foremost authority on Klan activity, having monitored the group for more than 30 years," read a 1979 article in *Ebony* magazine.[20] The ADL's earlier books and reports on the right had emphasized case studies, narratives, and exhortations to the public to be vigilant against demagoguery. Professionalizing the output, Suall produced intelligence and threat analysis based on infiltration and surveillance. He also provided US readers with a more sociological sense of the problem: the appeal of white nationalism to new recruits, the internal details of its culture and codes. If in the past the FBI had wondered whether the ADL was a serviceable partner,

---

18. Lara Deeb and Jessica Winegar note an earlier beginning of this argument among the Jewish defense organizations, in a 1969 American Jewish Committee confidential memo alleging an Arab propaganda campaign on US university campuses. Lara Deeb and Jessica Winegar, *Anthropology's Politics: Disciplining the Middle East* (Stanford University Press, 2015), 90.

19. Anti-Defamation League of B'nai B'rith, "Danger on the Left," *Facts*, November 1972. Reprinted in Cong. Rec., Extension of Remarks, February 8, 1973, p. 4130.

20. *Ebony*, "The Ku Klux Klan," October 1979, 168. Until Suall's arrival, Arnold Forster had overseen a fact-finding committee rather than a division.

under Suall's leadership it was firmly established as an expert resource for policymakers, law enforcement, and media.

This limited public profile left outside the frame Suall's work with a powerful set of organizational leaders that reached into the US foreign policy and national security apparatus. Between the 1960s and the 1990s, members of Suall's Social Democratic circle created a dizzying roster of organizations and held significant leadership roles in long-established organizations. They were highly placed at the AFL-CIO, the League for Industrial Democracy, the A. Philip Randolph Institute, the Coalition for a Democratic Majority, the American Enterprise Institute, the Jewish Institute for National Security Affairs, Freedom House, the National Endowment for Democracy, and others.[21] Spread across institutions, they formed a loose collaborative, working collectively but diffusely in what strategist Penn Kemble called "a blizzard of letterheads."[22] Their work was "democracy promotion," a central plank of neoconservative foreign policy. Suall's history, and the ADL's, were closely entwined with it.

He began on the left. The Socialist Party was the structuring experience of Suall's life, and within it Suall was renowned for his intellect and skill in leading its work. He joined as a teenager around 1943, and a decade later he became a leading intellectual and strategist of the party. In that role, in 1957, he helped shore up the flagging party by negotiating a merger with another group, the Independent Socialist League led by former Trotsky surrogate Max Shachtman.[23] Serving as elected national secretary of the party from 1957 to 1962, Suall came briefly to national notice for economic proposals and reports on the right. His seven-point plan to end economic recession, published in 1958, included shortening work hours to create more jobs, expand-

21. The extensive overlaps among Social Democratic/neoconservative leaders and organizations are hard to map because they are so dense and multidirectional. Many are documented in a 1989 snapshot pulled together from dozens of primary sources by the Militarist Monitor watchdog website of the International Relations Center/Interhemispheric Resource Center. See Militarist Monitor, "A. Philip Randolph Institute," January 7, 1989, https:// militarist-monitor.org/a_philip_randolph_institute. Other efforts to sketch the relationships are offered in Sims, *Workers of the World Undermined*, 46–50, and Scipes, *AFL-CIO's Secret War Against Developing Country Workers*, 231n58.

22. Ben Wattenberg, "A Man Whose Ideas Helped Change the World," *Baltimore Sun*, April 22, 1992.

23. At the same time, the Socialist Party also merged with the Social Democratic Federation and the Jewish Labor Bund and was renamed the Socialist Party-Social Democratic Federation (SP-SDF). Ross, *Socialist Party of America*, 468.

ing unemployment insurance, providing free health care for the jobless, and establishing state-owned industries to compete with the private sector. In 1961, Suall and socialist politician Norman Thomas unveiled research on ultra-right recruitment in the ranks of the US military that caused a national stir; in 1962 he published more extensive research in the report *The American Ultras: The Extreme Right and the Military-Industrial Complex*.[24] Later, Suall worked as an educator and organizer at the International Ladies Garment Workers Union and then at the Jewish Labor Committee, before landing at the ADL.

The reminiscences of Suall's friend and colleague Carl Gershman shed some light on Suall's role as a thought leader in the movement that would become a branch of neoconservatism. Their lifelong friendship was distinctly political, a neoconservative comradeship undergirded by a continuous history of shared work and political principles. It began at the ADL, where Gershman briefly worked for Suall in the research department in 1968. Gershman described his job as "covering the left"—in other words, producing research in the vein of "Danger on the Left." As the spying scandal later revealed, for the ADL's "fact-finders" it also meant surveilling organizations from the liberal American Civil Liberties Union to revolutionary groups.[25] Suall had hired Gershman to his ADL department but soon recognized his capacity for party work. Suall introduced Gershman to the party (then the

24. Suall's report, *The American Ultras: The Extreme Right and the Military-Industrial Complex*, grappled with the US military officials' propagation of white nationalist and Christian anticommunism, supported by corporate leaders and business elites—which Suall perceived to be a way of opposing any programs for social change. (He termed this "devil-theory politics.") Intended as a leftist text, it was partly a call for the preservation of liberal freedoms and against the use of the military to espouse political views. It resisted, too, the construction of a communist bogeyman that empowered right-wing opposition. Suall's anticommunism at the time was softer than that of the national ADL leadership, and the report would not have sat particularly well with them. Still, it confronted a problem shared among liberal anticommunists: how to manage the racism and violence of anticommunists to their right without supporting the targets of anticommunism to their left. Suall placed his economic proposal in local papers, including in California, Oregon, Kansas, Oklahoma, and West Virginia, mostly in letters to the editor, eliciting national discussion. As noted later in this chapter, Suall was moving ideologically rightward in this period. Irwin Suall, *The American Ultras: The Extreme Right and the Military-Industrial Complex* (New America, 1962), 6; *Holdrege Daily Citizen* (Nebraska), "Editorial: 'What the Socialists Would Do,'" April 18, 1958; *Washington Post*, "Pentagon Studying Indoctrination Charges: Likened to Walker Criticized Locally," November 23, 1961.

25. Carl Gershman, "Irwin Suall Memorial," National Endowment for Democracy, September 24, 1998.

SP-SDF) the same year. There, Gershman quickly rose to leadership as the vice chairman of the youth wing, the Young People's Socialist League.[26] For his part, Gershman encountered Suall not as a diminutive researcher, but as a firebrand and "brilliant polemicist," a powerful political thinker whose reasoning set the terms of debate.[27] Gershman's entry to the party brought him into the tight-knit family of political intellectuals who made up its leadership: Suall and his sister-in-law Joan Suall, Bayard Rustin, Tom Kahn, Rachelle Horowitz, Paul and Sandra Feldman, Joshua Muravchik, and Penn Kemble. In future decades, even where the members of this group diverged on tactics, they remained close as collaborators and friends: a cadre.

The seeds of neoconservatism may be traceable to the Socialist Party's embrace of the same Americanism that animated the ADL's founding. It was an egalitarianism threaded through with colorblindness, individualism, and an embrace of the settler state. The catalyst, though, was the 1957 merger with Shachtman's Social Democratic Federation (SDF). Shachtman, a charismatic leader and long-range political strategist, called for setting aside international revolution in favor of international democracy-building, beginning at home and using US influence to work abroad. His plan was to "realign" the Democratic Party, elevating the AFL-CIO—a powerful, recently unified body representing fully one-third of US nonagricultural workers—as a "predominant and hegemonic" force. From the platform of the AFL-CIO, Shachtmanites planned to push through reforms to achieve full employment through public works and intensive public spending in the United States. They would also adopt, in their terms, a democratic foreign policy that would advance the same policies in other nations: an imperialism of rights. These measures, they contended, would eliminate the causes of racial conflict.[28] Beginning in 1957, Suall, Shachtman, and a tight set of colleagues began to build Shachtman's program.

The merger cemented into Suall's orbit a new set of organizers who were either rising to prominence in the civil rights and labor movements or already central to them. It would also begin their march toward right-wing politics. Suall himself became an instrument of the shift: Swayed by Shachtman's force, he organized Socialist Party members into the plan. Suall's comrade in party leadership, David McReynolds, recounts that the Shachtman merger

26. Ross, *Socialist Party of America*, 507.
27. Gershman, "Irwin Suall Memorial."
28. Peter Drucker, *Max Shachtman and His Left: A Socialist's Odyssey Through the "American Century"* (Globe Pequot Press, 1993), 293.

forced Suall himself to change. Suall found to his bewilderment that he could not do his job—organizing the party to adopt positions and take actions—if he disagreed with Shachtman. Some party members broke with Shachtman, McReynolds wrote, but Suall did not. Instead, he wrote, "I watched Shachtman 'break' Irwin." Nonetheless, the change was gradual. Suall had considered himself a leftist and radical beforehand; for some time after, he still did. In 1960 Suall wrote disparagingly of "warmed-over" liberalism and called for radicalism. "In coping with revolutionary events, radical responses are the only realistic ones," he wrote, quoting socialist leader William Davidson.[29]

For the party, too, the leftward- and rightward-moving strands of its work developed together. "From roughly 1959 to 1964, the Shachtmanite-infused Socialist Party actually led the kind of popular activist movement of the left to which [Shachtman's organization] had aspired," writes Jack Ross, chronicler of the Socialist Party. "The major catalyst for its rise, of course, was the civil rights movement, to which the [Socialist Party] was intimately tied through Bayard Rustin, as well as A. Philip Randolph."[30] Indeed, the party's relationships to organizers were all-important. A. Philip Randolph was a longtime socialist and labor leader and would soon co-organize the 1963 March on Washington. His protégé Rustin would mastermind the 1963 March on Washington and then set up shop at the AFL-CIO in 1965 as director of the A. Philip Randolph Institute.[31] Comrades of those older leaders also now developed relationships with the SP-SDF, including political theorist Sidney Hook and sociologist Seymour Martin Lipset, both members of the City College crowd. Among the younger generation, Penn Kemble, also close to Shachtman, had helped organize the 1963 march before becoming part of the intellectual cadre of *Commentary* magazine as it, too, moved away from the left and became a forum for neoconservative

29. David McReynolds, "The Evitability of War, Revolution, Socialism," September 2009, 3, https://www.onthewilderside.com/2009/09/11/david-mcreynolds-comments-on-war-revolution-and-socialism/; Irwin Suall, "Letter from Irwin Suall to Members of the Socialist Party-Social Democratic Federation," February 2, 1960, Thomas Barton Papers (MS 539), Box 2, Folder "YPSL: Fund Raising (Efforts and Publicity for Raising Funds)," University of Massachusetts Amherst.

30. Ross, *Socialist Party of America*, 474.

31. Daniel Perlstein, "The Dead End of Despair: Bayard Rustin, the 1968 New York School Crisis, and the Struggle for Racial Justice," *Afro-Americans in New York Life and History* 31, no. 2 (July 2007): 20.

thought.[32] Rustin's assistants Tom Kahn and Rachelle Horowitz, already Young People's Socialist League members, would go on to direct several organizations in the sphere of the AFL-CIO and democracy promotion.[33] This intricate roster of people and organizations intersected constantly across decades, forming the dense network, often overlaid by family connections, that would characterize the Social Democratic wing of the neoconservative movement.[34]

Democracy promotion was a natural bridge between party organizers, labor, and the CIA: supporting "democratic forces" in foreign states, meaning insurgents contesting Marxist governments or state regimes repressing popular movements. As conceived by the SP-SDF in a 1951 policy blueprint, it called for propagating civic organizations that would organize locally along the right political lines and for providing concrete infrastructure, such as trucks, buildings, or books. While the blueprint called for public interest to be prioritized over profit, that was a fungible aim. "At the heart of the document was a ringing defense not of 'socialism' per se, but of democracy," writes Bill King, who documents the socialists' turn.[35] It also called for US state intervention as the vehicle, pitched as a "sharing" imperative for US socialists: "We believe in democracy for ourselves and for others," they affirmed.[36] They saw the global disciplinary power of the US state as a tool for attaining it. Indeed, political scientist Jeremy Menchik identifies democracy promotion as an extension of the missionary impulse driving Western colonization: a moral obligation to reshape the world according to ostensibly universal moral codes; a reshaping that also claims and reorganizes territory.[37]

Unsurprisingly, then, democracy promotion in its implementation was arguably closer to military intervention than to civic uplift. By the time

32. Jake C. Miller, "Black Viewpoints on the Mid-East Conflict," *Journal of Palestine Studies* 10, no. 2 (1981): 37–49; King, "Origins of Neoconservative Support for Democracy Promotion." On *Commentary*'s development of neoconservatism, see Benjamin Balint, *Running Commentary: The Contentious Magazine That Transformed the Jewish Left into the Neoconservative Right* (PublicAffairs, 2010).

33. Ross, *Socialist Party of America*, 464.

34. Another was Joan Suall, who would later marry Bert Suall, Irwin's brother. Joan Suall's history in the Socialist Party and her work with Irwin Suall is written using her married name. Ross, *Socialist Party of America*, 465.

35. King, "Origins of Neoconservative Support for Democracy Promotion," 35.

36. King, "Origins of Neoconservative Support for Democracy Promotion," 36. From the minutes of the 1957 SP-SDF Convention.

37. Jeremy Menchik, *The Missionary Impulse in World Politics: Democracy Promotion at the End of American Liberal Imperialism*, forthcoming.

Social Democrats connected with the AFL-CIO, the labor movement was already partnered with the US foreign policy apparatus, including the CIA, to undertake anticommunist foreign projects in capitalist economic and ideological development.[38] Since the start of World War II, the American Federation of Labor (AFL) had carried out operations in Europe, Africa, and Asia in coordination with US intelligence forces, "wedded to a militant anticommunism which aligned them neatly with the long-term political objectives of Washington."[39] Other labor organizations, including the American Federation of Teachers and a host of AFL-CIO training institutes, established CIA links from the 1960s onward. As Beth Sims describes the dense overlay of labor and US government intervention, labor groups financed "organizing and propaganda activities, selected candidates to lead foreign unions, financed their campaigns, paid off supporters, and helped build pro-western union infrastructures."[40] That was not all: As labor activists' research revealed, the AFL-CIO and Social Democrats' organizations channeled resources to right-wing military operations, enabled coups and death squads, and undermined local efforts to counteract violence.[41]

The networks of friends and colleagues moving between democracy promotion agencies sketch a sociality comparable both to the organizing culture of the left and the business elites who gathered at ADL dinners. "[F]or the Social Democrat, 'democracy is not merely a political concept but a moral one. It is democracy as a way of life,'" Gershman explained.[42] Historians of neoconservatism describe these relationships as "the family," a web of friendship and kinships, marriages, and generations of neoconservative offspring.[43] Historians who have addressed the ADL, mostly in the context of Jewish communal history before the 1970s, observe a different set of familial relations interwoven in Jewish institutional politics, but they have not documented Social

38. Jeff Schuhrke, *Blue-Collar Empire: The Untold Story of US Labor's Global Anticommunist Crusade* (Verso, 2024), 120–21.

39. Beth Sims, *Workers of the World Undermined: American Labor's Role in US Foreign Policy* (South End Press, 1992), 38.

40. Sims, *Workers of the World Undermined*, 38–39.

41. See Tom Barry and Deb Preusch, *AIFLD in Central America: Agents as Organizers* (Resource Center, 1990).

42. Carl Gershman, "Eulogy for Penn Kemble," National Endowment for Democracy, December 2, 2005. Quoting Social Democratic first-generation neoconservative Sidney Hook.

43. See Balint, *Running Commentary*.

Democratic threads.[44] These frameworks of left-to-right, labor, and neoconservative sociality add essential context for the ADL's operations.

Suall arrived at the ADL in 1967, when the ADL was encountering some trouble in its three main areas of work: anticommunism, race politics, and the Middle East. The disruptions piled up: the Ocean Hill-Brownsville conflict, SNCC's full-throated rejection of Zionism as a liberation movement, and mass protests against US mores, wars, and anti-left interventions abroad. As Alex Lubin writes, the Six-Day War and the occupation of the West Bank and Gaza catalyzed international organizing by the Palestine Liberation Organization (PLO) that resulted in strong new ties with the US Black Panthers, in addition to launching a Palestinian armed resistance movement in the region.[45] In 1971, a tangentially related antiracist movement emerged in Israel, the Israeli Black Panthers, Moroccan and Iraqi Jewish youths who demanded the basic rights that were denied them in the Eurocentric Israeli state. They complicated the Zionist binary of "civilized" Jews dominating "barbarous" Arabs that the 1967 war had projected.[46] Instead, they protested white (Ashkenazi) Jewish Israelis as colonial invaders: "Go back to Russia!" one protester aimed a barb at Prime Minister Golda Meir.[47] From within, they disrupted what Ella Shohat calls Israel's "façade of egalitarianism," met with the PLO, and called for "the destruction of the [Israeli] regime and the legitimate rights of all the oppressed without regard for religion, origin, or nationality."[48] Such disruptions, spanning Palestine and the United States, posed problems for the ADL. Moral, race-liberal arguments were still the main strategy for willing US support for Israel. While the 1967 war had set the stage for ramping up defense establishment interest in Israel, the United

44. See, for instance, Cheryl Lynn Greenberg, *Troubling the Waters: Black-Jewish Relations in the American Century* (Princeton University Press, 2010); Stuart Svonkin, *Jews Against Prejudice: American Jews and the Fight for Civil Liberties* (Columbia University Press, 1997); Deborah D. Moore, *B'nai B'rith and the Challenge of Ethnic Leadership* (State University of New York Press, 1981).

45. Alex Lubin, *Geographies of Liberation: The Making of an Afro-Arab Political Imaginary* (University of North Carolina Press, 2014), 115.

46. Lubin, *Geographies of Liberation*, 134.

47. Amos Elon, "The Black Panthers of Israel," *New York Times*, September 12, 1971.

48. Ella Shohat, *On the Arab-Jew, Palestine, and Other Displacements: Selected Writings of Ella Shohat* (Pluto Press, 2017), 63, 70, 73.

States had not yet adopted Israel as a proxy and strategic ally.[49] If the late 1960s were uncertain times in US political culture, the ADL was a political organization on uncertain ground.

Whether Suall was hired with the intention of connecting the ADL to SDUSA is unclear, but his role was certainly to confront the threats that ADL leaders perceived from the left—and as those threats mounted, Suall became increasingly important.[50] The ADL had collaborated with the elder sociologists of the SDUSA: Seymour Martin Lipset had cowritten the ADL's 1959 study *Prejudice and Society* (which undergirded the ADL's program of psychologizing racism), and went on to write *The Socialism of Fools* (on the New Left's rejection of Israeli colonialism, in 1969), *The Wallace Whitewash* (1969), and *The Politics of Unreason* (1970). After Suall arrived, the collaborations continued. Bayard Rustin's speech "The Anatomy of Frustration," which laid out his economic proposals and exhortations against Black radicalism, was published by the ADL in 1968. SDUSA member Harvey Klehr wrote his 1988 *Far Left of Center*, a blistering round-up of the "American radical left," under the ADL's imprint; Klehr and Suall sat together on the board of another Social Democratic group, the League for Industrial Democracy.[51] Social Democratic elder Max Kampelman was a long-standing collaborator with the ADL. He had led the ADL's partnership with the Business Roundtable in the 1970s, opposing the Arab boycott, and supported its advocacy on Soviet Jewry and Israeli military interests until at least 1991.[52]

49. Jack Wertheimer, "Jewish Organizational Life in the United States Since 1945," *American Jewish Year Book* 95 (1995): 48–56; Yaacov Bar-Siman-Tov, "The United States and Israel Since 1948: A 'Special Relationship'?," *Diplomatic History* 22, no. 2 (1998): 246.

50. Ross suggests that Suall may have been hired because the ADL was concerned about New Left opposition to Israel and wanted a staffer who was well acquainted with the landscape. Suall did not become personally interested in Israel until he visited in 1967 as an ADL staffer, just after the 1967 war. Ross, *Socialist Party of America*, 507; *Forward*, "Irwin Suall [Obituary]," August 21, 1998.

51. "Examination of Irwin Suall," deposition in Larouche v. National Broadcasting Co., Inc., United States Court of Appeals, Fourth Circuit (n.d., circa 1984), 50, 279, 33, 45–64, Laird Wilcox Collection, https://archives.lib.ku.edu/repositories/3/archival_objects/379179. On the 1989 board, see Militarist Monitor, "League for Industrial Democracy," https://militarist-monitor.org/league_for_industrial_democracy/.

52. Kampelman's personal papers sketch his ongoing involvement with the ADL through 1991, including issue-advocacy speeches and awards. See Ernest Ditcher and American Friends of the Hebrew University, "Max M. Kampelman: An Inventory of His Papers at the Minnesota Historical Society," text, Balkan Peninsula—Politics and government—20th, http://www2.mnhs.org/library/findaids/00772.xml, accessed February 1, 2021.

The organization also hired from the cadre: Though Gershman's job there was short-lived, David Lowe, another Social Democrat, was Suall's right hand in fact-finding from the 1980s to the early 2000s, after which he joined the leadership of Gershman's National Endowment for Democracy.[53]

With Suall in charge, the ADL finally won the attention of the FBI—then in the throes of COINTELPRO disruptions of Black, student, and antiwar movements—and Suall placed "the full range of New Left organizations" on his surveillance agenda.[54] Its newsletter *The Facts* frequently mixed reporting on white nationalism with reporting on Palestinian political and armed resistance, Arab League organizing, leftist/anticapitalist organizing, and Black nationalism and transnationalism as insurgent crises. To the ADL they were the same, simply classed as intolerance or extremism. The ADL's 1967 fact-finding report, *How Racists, Black and White, Used Arab Propaganda Sources*, charged that SNCC and Nazis had both used PLO materials as the basis for their own anti-Israel writings.[55] It was followed in 1969 with a *Facts* article "Al Fatah and Black Extremists in the USA," charging a litany of Black and leftist organizations with having been recruited as extremists by Palestinian militants. Another report in 1970, *The Black Panthers*, detailed Black anti-Zionism and the Panthers' "all-out support of Fatah."[56] This mixture of disciplinary coverage of antiracism, anticolonialism, and the left became a core project. By 1993, when the ADL's fact-finding work came under momentary media scrutiny, investigative journalist Robert I. Friedman

53. Ross suggests that Suall sent Gershman to lead YPSL, which may be why his work at the ADL was cut short. Lowe's participation is less well documented. Ross, *The Socialist Party of America: A Complete History*, 507.

54. FBI, Memo from FBI Director to SAC Atlanta et al: Liaison with the Anti-Defamation League of B'nai B'rith, January 17, 1968, File 1199215-000 --- 100-IP-16164 --- Section 1, p. 5, The FBI and the Anti-Defamation League, Israel Lobby Archive, Institute for Research: Middle Eastern Policy, https://www.israellobby.org/adl/; *Jewish Advocate*, "ADL Board to Meet March 17," March 11, 1971, 17.

55. Anti-Defamation League of B'nai B'rith, "How Racists, Black and White, Used Arab Propaganda Sources," *Facts* 17, no. 5 (1967). See also Michael R. Fischbach, *The Movement and the Middle East: How the Arab-Israeli Conflict Divided the American Left* (Stanford University Press, 2019), 39–40.

56. *The Black Panthers* excerpted in remarks from "Assistant to the Director William C. Sullivan, Federal Bureau of Investigation, on October 12, 1970, at the United Press International Conference, Williamsburg, Virginia," in US House Committee on Internal Security, *Black Panther Party: Hearings Before the Committee on Internal Security, Ninety-First Congress, Second Session* (US Government Printing Office, 1970), 5061.

reported that "[u]nder Suall's stewardship, [the] Fact-Finding Department had become the ADL's heart and soul."[57]

By the mid-1980s, the ADL's anti-left antagonism faded from public view, not because it had changed its positions but because there was less of the left to fight. The radical movements of the New Left were dismantled in the late 1970s, replaced in the 1980s with identity politics that moved toward a liberal center.[58] Zionism had become the presumptive tissue of US Jewish communal life, and Israel had been fully adopted by the US state as a strategic ally and proxy. Although Suall was still an active Social Democrat, his public persona was detached from any reference to his past on the left, or to opposing the left. Instead he was known as an expert on white nationalism. As the Ku Klux Klan underwent a revival in the wake of the Vietnam War, it was Suall's 1977 report that brought it to national attention. Suall became a regular source in the press for updates, opinions, and forecasting on the subject. Although the ADL did not retreat from its familiar bugbears, from Black leftists to the PLO—and although that, too, was Suall's work—it did not propel him into the public eye. The ADL's 1975 report, *Target USA: The Arab Propaganda Offensive*, a 120-page warning that the Palestinian cause was gaining support from college campuses, unions, churches, and the media, was unsigned, although it was likely produced under Suall's supervision. Another 118-page ADL blacklist of "pro-Arab propagandists" generated public outrage in 1983. Suall's department had likely produced that, too, but much of the outcry focused on the Boston-based Leonard Zakim, the ADL regional director who had circulated a version of it marked "confidential" among campus groups on behalf of the ADL's campus Hasbara Network.[59]

Just as Suall's personal reputation was oddly detached from the ADL's anti-left efforts, the ADL itself was becoming less legible as a conservative organization by the 1980s. This was partly a function of neoconservatism, which confusingly deployed the language of civil rights and racial justice. It

57. Robert I. Friedman, "How the Anti-Defamation League Turned the Notion of Human Rights on Its Head, Spying on Progressives and Funneling Information to Law Enforcement," *Village Voice*, May 11, 1993.

58. Lisa Duggan, *The Twilight of Equality? Neoliberalism, Cultural Politics, and the Attack on Democracy* (Beacon Press, 2003), 9.

59. Anti-Defamation League, *Target USA: The Arab Propaganda Offensive*, 1975; Anti-Defamation League of B'nai B'rith, *Pro-Arab Propaganda in America: Vehicles and Voices. A Handbook*, January 1983; Leonard Zakim, Letter to Campus Jewish Leaders, November 1983, Israel Lobby Archive, Institute for Research: Middle Eastern Policy, http://www.israellobby.org/ADL-CA/111983_ADL_pro-Arab_Sympathizers.pdf.

was also a function of shifting political circumstances of the United States as a whole. In light of the broad shifts in political culture, the ADL's opposition to Black nationalism and Arab anticolonialism no longer appeared particularly conservative. Its antagonism to the Soviet Union and communism, now redefined as advocacy for the freedom of Soviet Jewry, also appeared less stridently right-wing. To the contrary: The ADL was the primary organization contending with expanding white nationalist organizing, which, in the simplified binary of US politics, positioned it in presumptive opposition to the right.

A headline in spring 1993 delivered a sharp jolt to this depoliticized view of the ADL. In San Francisco on April 8, police raided the Anti-Defamation League's offices. The raid was coordinated with the FBI, which had been investigating a leak of classified FBI materials for months. At the ADL's office they found stolen police surveillance dossiers and files on the ADL's own monitoring of leftist groups. The fact that the ADL's surveillance overwhelmingly targeted the left came as a surprise to observers, including many groups that learned they had been surveilled. The *New York Times* primly reported that it had "caused confusion for some liberals."[60] The confusion was particularly acute for those outside of the spheres to whom the ADL directed its prodigious bulletins on the Black and Arab left. Jewish communities, public officials, and journalists might have been familiar with the ADL's anti-left antagonisms, but the larger public had not absorbed them.

Shortly after the spying scandal broke, investigative journalists Chip Berlet and Dennis King offered a rueful analysis that did note the ADL's neoconservative turn. Although the spying was unexpected, they said, it could be understood as a product of the ADL's "lunge to the right . . . in the Reagan-Bush years [when it] became a neo-conservative citadel." They recalled that in the 1980s they had interviewed Suall and were shocked then to find him targeting the left: "Irwin Suall told us in conversations in the early and mid-1980's that the chief domestic danger to American Jews was the American left—especially black leftists—backed by the Soviet Union. He argued that right-wing extremists, even those with high-level connections, were insignificant by comparison; to focus on them, he said, would be a dangerous diversion from the struggle against Communism at home and abroad."[61] In fact,

60. *New York Times*, "A Dealer in Art and, Some Say, a Dealer in Secret Police Data," April 25, 1993.

61. Dennis King and Chip Berlet, "The ADL Under Fire; Its Shift to the Right Has Led to Scandal," *New York Times*, May 28, 1993.

Suall's Fact-Finding Department had been spying on Berlet and his colleagues themselves. *Village Voice* reporter Robert I. Friedman, who chronicled the ADL spying scandal, shared another story from Berlet and journalist Russ Bellant, who also met with Suall in the 1980s.

> "Our view then of Irwin Suall was that he was this really terrific investigator," says Berlet. "So we introduce ourselves ... and Suall leans back in his chair and basically runs down a dossier on each of us: about what our political activities are, who we work with, what organizations we belong to.... And then he leans forward and says, 'The right-wing isn't the problem. The left-wing is the problem. The Soviet Union is the biggest problem in the world for Jews. It's the American left that is the biggest threat to American Jews. You're on the wrong track. You're part of the problem.' We were stunned.... We basically stumbled out of there in a daze."[62]

Even though Suall's position surprised them, they had not thought of the ADL as hostile or right-wing. Even later, when the ADL's alliances with the right were again a subject of popular political discussion, Berlet found it dissonant to view the ADL as anything except progressive. From his own perspective as a researcher of the white right, and as a colleague of ADL staffers lower in the ranks, it seemed that Suall's anti-left views must have been an aberration: "Several senior ADL staff ... later privately apologized to me and distanced themselves from the increasingly anti-Left histrionics of ... Suall. ... [Another] told me that it seemed the New York National Office was more interested in helping Mossad track leftists than pursuing the ADL's original mandate."[63] The spying scandal did reveal some shifts, however. The ADL was engaging in intelligence work with the US and Israeli governments; its surveillance had expanded to international movements, and the scope of its international surveillance far exceeded concerns about Israel. Instead, it reflected the concerns of democracy promotion on three continents.

Making sense of the ADL's surveillance requires returning to its relationships with Social Democrats and looking at its turn to global engagements in

---

62. Friedman, "How the Anti-Defamation League Turned the Notion of Human Rights on Its Head."

63. King and Berlet, "The ADL Under Fire." In a 2019 account, Berlet repeats the story and detaches it from the ADL's longer history, recounting that "several senior ADL staff ... later privately apologized to me and distanced themselves from the increasingly anti-Left histrionics of ... Suall. ... [Another] told me that it seemed the New York National Office was more interested in helping Mossad track leftists than pursuing the ADL's original mandate." Chip Berlet, *Trumping Democracy: From Reagan to the Alt-Right* (Routledge, 2019), 208.

South Africa, Central America, and South America in the mid-1970s and 1980s. The ADL established a Latin American affairs department in 1966.[64] As in the United States, this office navigated its commitments to elitism and state order in tension with its interest in opposing antisemitism. Central American and South American states, led by European descendants and familiar with anti-Indigenous conquest, had been supportive of Israel's formation, although the rise of resistance movements and the arrival of Palestinian refugees was changing the balance.[65] The ADL was generally concerned with the welfare of European Jews who had arrived in Central America and South America earlier in the century, and were primarily interested in the state-capital class rather than the (smaller) Jewish working class and the left. In pan-continental tensions between right-wing regimes and leftist insurgencies, upper-class Jews faced familiar threats. Nazism and anti-semitic conspiracy theories found fertile ground, class antagonism targeted upper-class Jews as "the establishment," and Jewish leaders feared alliances between local leftist movements, the Soviet Union, and Arab anti-Zionist organizing.[66] In the early 1970s, the ADL saw Soviet-Arab threats to Jews in Chile, Bolivia, Peru, and Uruguay. Argentina, though, posed a right-wing threat. The ADL focused its first efforts there.[67]

64. Jewish Telegraphic Agency, "Anti-Defamation League Appoints Director for Latin American Dept," June 22, 1966, https://www.jta.org/archive/anti-defamation-league-appoints-director-for-latin-american-dept.

65. See, for instance, the ADL's warning in 1970 that "Palestinian and Jordanian Arabs illegally enter Latin American countries by the thousands, turn to peddling for their income and dispense hatred of Jews and Israel along with their wares." ADL report quoted in Jewish Telegraphic Agency, "Arabs in Latin America Reported Whipping Up Anti-Semitic, Anti-Israel Hatred," March 20, 2015.

66. Early in the tenure of ADL Latin American affairs director Morton M. Rosenthal, as right-wing Jews emigrated from Chile under socialist leader Salvador Allende, Rosenthal described their situation. Major factors in their decision to leave were class-based: worries that the new regime would prohibit the emigration of skilled professionals, or that economic and class disparities would be dismantled, costing them their elevated and comfortable status. A third factor, wrote Rosenthal, was "the fear that Chile might . . . come under the influence and control of the Soviet Union." Although Rosenthal affirmed that "Jewish students, intellectuals, and processionals from the lower middle class, who actively supported Allende's candidacy" would likely have no reason to leave—and although Allende himself was supportive of the Israeli state—Rosenthal saw mounting anti-Zionism as an imminent threat to upper-class Jews in particular. Given that Palestinian resistance was already active in the region, "a combined Soviet-Arab effort might make their position untenable." Morton M. Rosenthal, "Jews in Marxist Chile, on the Way Out," *Sh'ma, A Journal of Jewish Responsibility*, January 22, 1971, 43–44.

67. Rosenthal, "Jews in Marxist Chile," 45.

In Argentina, antisemitism was thriving under right-wing rule. A series of attacks on Jewish institutions in 1970 had been orchestrated from within the Argentinian military. In the years that followed, further acts of overt Nazi violence escalated to terrifying levels. The Delegación de Asociaciones Israelitas Argentinas (DAIA), a parallel to the US Conference of Presidents of Major American Jewish Organizations, was a conservative group of elites who were both concerned about antisemitism and deeply invested in preserving their relationship to the regime. Rather than acknowledge state racism and repression, they initially pointed a finger leftward, blaming antisemitic violence on Arab agitation of the Argentinian working class against Zionism. ADL Latin American affairs director Rabbi Morton M. Rosenthal presented DAIA's claims as fact to US audiences.[68] But as conditions deteriorated and the Argentinian junta began disappearing people—Jews, Zionists, leftists, and others—that claim became untenable. For the ADL's leaders, DAIA's continued refusal to respond to state violence was confounding. In a 1979 memo, Epstein expressed horror at DAIA's complicity with state violence. "My meeting with the DAIA was in many ways a frightening experience," Epstein wrote. "The fear of being overheard, the care with which they choose their words, and their request that I take no notes was the climate of our luncheon. . . . The most shocking thing to me was to hear intelligent Jews condone the disappearance or arrest of people if they were communist."[69] The irony that the ADL had taken a similar position in the United States, supporting McCarthyism as it targeted Jewish communists, was not mentioned.

Building on Epstein's indignation, the ADL briefly declared some independence from the right, if only in its advocacy for Argentinian prisoners. This was especially notable in the case of journalist Jacobo Timerman, a major figure in Jewish Argentinian life and a bold resister of the regime's anti-Jewish attacks. He had been arrested in 1977, tortured, and then banished in 1979. In 1981, in Israel, Timerman published a memoir of his captivity, the regime, and the complicity of Argentinian Jewish leadership, titled *Prisoner Without a Name, Cell Without a Number*, then followed it with an

68. Morton M. Rosenthal, "The Threatened Jews of Argentina: Extremist Nationalist Groups and Arab Propagandists Are Natural Allies in an Organized Anti-Semitic Campaign," *ADL Bulletin*, March 1971. Reprinted in US Congress, Proceedings and Debates of the 92nd Cong., 1st Session, Congressional Record 117, pp. 8259–9468.

69. ADL internal memo authored by Benjamin Epstein, February 16, 1979, quoted in Marguerite Feitlowitz, *A Lexicon of Terror: Argentina and the Legacies of Torture* (Oxford University Press, 1998), 102.

anguished critique of Israel's 1982 invasion of Lebanon, *The Longest War: Israel in Lebanon*. Additionally, the Reagan administration had adopted a Cold War doctrine of supporting anticommunist regimes as allies against left or potentially pro-Soviet regimes; this meant refusing to respond to the crimes of the Argentinian regime, which Timerman publicly criticized.[70] In national media, neoconservatives set out to discredit Timerman as an unstable witness, a self-aggrandizing "Solzhentitsyn-of-the-left."[71] At the ADL these events prompted a frantic strategy debate. Timerman was an important voice against antisemitism and a devoted Zionist, but criticizing Israeli "defense" incursions against Arab neighbors was intolerable. In a brief digression from its history, the ADL did not take the neoconservative or anti-left line; instead it resolved that it would support Timerman against anti-Jewish violence while distancing the organization from his views.[72]

The ADL abandoned any such nuance as Central America and South America became a center of gravity for Israel in the 1980s, through the arms trade. The region had already been of concern to Israel as a site of revolutionary solidarity with the PLO.[73] Since the 1967 war, arms exports had become a pillar of the Israeli economy, far out of proportion to its overall level of industrialization.[74] Arms dealing was essential to the Israeli project in multiple ways: By 1980 arms production employed around 10 percent of Israeli

70. Reagan's UN Ambassador, the neoconservative figure Jeanne Kirkpatrick, explained the doctrine in a 1979 *Commentary* article titled "Dictatorships and Double Standards." Kristol reiterated it in a *Wall Street Journal* article denouncing Timerman. Jeane J. Kirkpatrick, "Dictatorships & Double Standards," *Commentary Magazine*, November 1, 1979; Irving Kristol, "The Timerman Affair," *Wall Street Journal*, May 29, 1981.

71. Kristol, "Timerman Affair"; William F. Buckley, "Jacobo Timerman, Hero and— Perhaps—Dupe," *New York Daily News*, May 31, 1981; Ralph de Toledano, "Media Uses Anti-Semitism to Downgrade Argentina," *The News World*, May 30, 1981.

72. By 1989 the ADL had taken a firmer position that antisemitism was rampant in Argentina, but without linking it to other countries in the region. Dan Mariaschin to Nathan Perlmutter, "Memorandum from Dan Mariaschin to Nathan Perlmutter: Administrative Staff Meeting— June 5, 1981," June 16, 1981, Nathan Perlmutter (1923–87) Papers, Box 11, Folder 7, American Jewish Historical Society; Stephen Kinzer, "Argentina's Jews: Days of Uncertainty," *Boston Globe*, November 29, 1981.

73. Milton Jamail and Margo Gutierrez, "Israel in Central America: Nicaragua, Honduras, El Salvador, Costa Rica," *MERIP Middle East Report*, no. 140 (1986): 26–47.

74. As one observer noted, "The real significance of Israel's arms industry lies not in its size, but rather in the disparity between the general sophistication of the defense companies compared with the relative backwardness of much of the rest of the economy." Seth Carus, cited in Sheila Ryan, "US Military Contractors in Israel," *MERIP Middle East Report*, no. 144 (January 1987): 17.

workers, comprised between one-fourth and one-third of Israeli industrial exports, and created economies of scale that reduced the cost of Israel's own massive military apparatus to control its colonized territory, as Bishara Bahbah has meticulously documented.[75] The arms trade was also key to Israel's effort to position itself as a strategic partner of the United States. In 1977, the Carter administration restricted arms sales to human rights violators, cutting off Central and South American regimes that were repressing Marxist insurgencies. Despite the new policy, the US interest in arms trade with those regimes did not disappear. Israel stepped in. The US fueled the industry by licensing technology to Israel, providing funding, and buying back Israeli-made armaments. Israel supplied weapons to the dictatorships. Central and South American right-wing regimes were Israel's biggest customers; warplanes and heavy equipment were sold to military dictatorships in Guatemala, Honduras, Nicaragua, and El Salvador.[76] By 1984 "at least eighteen Latin American countries had purchased military equipment—all, indeed, but Guyana, Suriname, French Guyana, and Uruguay." The sales came with Israeli military advice, too, on the brutal management of insurgent Indigenous populations.[77]

The development of Israeli interests changed the context for the ADL's work in Latin America. So, too, did the advent of the Reagan administration in 1981, which brought neoconservatives to the center of US anticommunist foreign policy. One effect was that the ADL's work on antisemitism shifted. Before, it had been a matter of concern for the *targets* of antisemitism. Even if the ADL had deliberately misconstrued anticapitalist and anti-Zionist sentiment as anti-Jewish to construct ideological arguments, it had been concerned with the upper-class Jews whom it viewed as the objects of harm. Now, the ADL became more concerned about measuring antisemitism as a way to mark leftist regimes as retrograde and rightist regimes as not-so-terrible. Nicaragua, where the Marxist Sandinista revolution toppled the Somoza dictatorship in 1979, provided a clear view. In May 1983, Morton Rosenthal raised an alarm about antisemitism in Nicaragua, claiming in the *ADL Bulletin* that the Sandinistas, who had a mutual support relationship with the PLO, had "succeeded in driving the entire small Jewish community

75. Bishara Bahbah, *Israel and Latin America: The Military Connection*, 1986, 16–25.

76. Bahbah, *Israel and Latin America*, 147.

77. Bahbah, *Israel and Latin America*, 71, 91. See also Itai Segre, "Israel and the Contras: A Buried History" (Master's thesis, University of Chicago, 2023), https://knowledge.uchicago.edu/record/7213.

numbering about 50—into exile." He charged that Sandinistas had expropriated Jewish property, including a community center, and that the Sandinistas' anticolonial opposition to Zionism had made them "[unwilling] to distinguish between the Nicaraguan Jewish community and the State of Israel."[78] The ADL blasted the charges across US media. It punctuated the story by organizing a US speaking tour for the two exiles whose testimony was included in the report, both supporters of the US-backed, anti-Marxist Somoza dictatorship.

The project was transparently political: It used the charge of antisemitism to attack the Sandinista government. It worked well. The *Washington Post* reported, "Some influential Americans considered friends by the Sandinistas have harshly criticized them on the basis of the league's report and the Reagan administration has added anti-Semitism to its accusations against the Nicaraguans."[79] No amount of evidence to the contrary seemed to unstick the charges. In August, the Nicaraguan ambassador Antonio Jarquin sent a nine-page investigation report to Rosenthal, which the ADL did not publicize. The report gave names and background on Jews who were still living and doing business in Nicaragua, and provided details on the two men. Their property had indeed been confiscated—because of their role in the Somoza regime and business fraud, not because they were Jewish. "[A]ll Nicaraguan Jews presently living abroad—except those who actively collaborated with the Somoza dictatorship—are welcome to return to Nicaragua at any time," wrote Jarquin. The American Jewish Committee's Latin American division also tried to intervene, explaining that "the situation is more complicated and less simplistic than some Jewish groups have made it out to be by screaming headlines that reduces everything to anti-Semitism"; the American Jewish Committee called instead for attention to the Sandinistas' opposition to Israel.[80] Nonetheless, the charges of "Sandinista antisemitism" continued to circulate. In 1984 a delegation from New Jewish Agenda (NJA) traveled to Nicaragua and reported again that the charges did not stand up.[81] They did

78. Morton M. Rosenthal, *Nicaragua Without Jews* (Anti-Defamation League of B'nai B'rith, May 1983), 2.

79. Edward Cody et al., "Managua's Jews Reject Anti-Semitism Charge," *Washington Post*, August 29, 1983.

80. Marc H. Tanenbaum, "Is Nicaragua Anti-Semitic?," American Jewish Committee, press release, October 14, 1983.

81. Ezra Berkley Nepon, *Justice, Justice Shall You Pursue* (Thread Makes Blanket Press, 2012).

find, though, that Nicaraguan people understood Israel as a source of violence in their own lives. "They know only one Hebrew word—*galil*—written on all the weapons in the hands of the Contras."[82]

The ADL's work on antisemitism in Central America and South America had become a foreign policy project. In March 1985, as Congress prepared to vote on sending $14 million in aid to the anti-Sandinista Contra rebels, several "conservative Nicaraguan Jews" in the United States reinvigorated the charges, and the ADL reaffirmed them.[83] "In essence, the Sandinistas' anti-Semitism is a manifestation of their solidarity with the Arab world," Rosenthal wrote in a letter to the *Los Angeles Times*.[84] Notably, these events repeated exactly a year later in March 1986, this time with a cast drawn from the Social Democratic cadre. Reagan had proposed a $100 million aid package to the Contras. A new report on Nicaraguan Jews was released, now with "more extensive" interviews claiming to confirm the right-wing account. It was paired with a claim that the New Jewish Agenda's investigative interviews in Nicaragua, which had refuted the antisemitism charges, were inadequate. This new report had been overseen by Joshua Muravchik, now working at the Washington Institute for Near East Policy. It was sponsored by PRODEMCA, Penn Kemble's pro-Contra organization.[85] The release and publicity were produced by the ADL.[86]

The limits on the ADL's work in the region are also noteworthy. For instance, it did not undertake any projects with the Jews who did live in Nicaragua, despite openings to make a useful difference. For instance, while New Jewish Agenda had not found "Sandinista antisemitism," its members in Nicaragua reported that they *had* encountered the standard antisemitic myths that "Jews killed Christ" or "Jews run the world," which the ADL

82. Nadine Joseph, "3 Dispute Charges of Anti-Semitism by Nicaragua," *Northern California News Bulletin*, December 14, 1984.

83. Laurie Becklund, "Sandinistas Are Anti-Semitic, Group Says," *Los Angeles Times*, March 14, 1985.

84. William A. Alvarez, Morton M. Rosenthal, and Richard Silverstein, "Letters to the Times: Sandinistas and Anti-Semitism," *Los Angeles Times*, April 8, 1985.

85. Jewish Telegraphic Agency, "New Report Charges Anti-Semitic Campaign by Sandinistas," June 25, 1986.

86. NJA Rabbi Balfour Brickner dismissed the report: "I'm not impressed by any white paper by the Anti-Defamation League which presumes to set the record straight. All it actually does is to confirm their own previously held position, which happens to be in line with the view of the President." See Alexander Reid, "Bias in Nicaragua Reported by Jews," *New York Times*, March 20, 1986.

might have been well positioned to address.[87] Even in the many states where the ADL presumably suspected antisemitism because the PLO was active there, it conducted almost no communal work. In Chile, Paraguay, Guatemala, Costa Rica, and Honduras, where repressive regimes had strong state ties with Israel, resistance movements drew support from Palestinian movements throughout the 1980s.[88] The ADL's treatment of those places was sporadic and mostly concerned with Nazi war criminals or Palestinian resistance figures.

Instead the ADL took up Latin American work under the auspices of the Reagan administration—and under the leadership of Suall's cadre, fanned out across organizations. In 1983, ADL representatives joined the Reagan administration's new Outreach Working Group on Central America. The working group was a project of the White House's Office of Public Diplomacy, a bid to win over public opinion for Reagan's policy of backing right-wing dictatorships. Its strategy was to reach the public through conservative civic and religious organizations and to counteract critical views presented in the press, including reporting on the leftist Central American solidarity movement.[89] For participating organizations it was something of an orgy of access to high-level politics. The group "coordinated the efforts of the NSC [National Security Council] and CIA with those of more than fifty private organizations," including religious and military right-wing groups, and organizations created and led by Social Democrats.[90] They included the Institute on Religion and Democracy, led by Penn Kemble, and the AFL-CIO's Institute for Free Labor Development, led by Penn's sister Eugenia Kemble.[91] The Jewish Institute for National Security Affairs participated,

<hr>

87. Joseph, "3 Dispute Charges of Anti-Semitism by Nicaragua."

88. Bruce Hoffman, "The PLO and Israel in Central America: The Geopolitical Dimension," *Terrorism and Political Violence* 1, no. 4 (1989): 482–515.

89. Charles T. Strauss, "Quest for the Holy Grail: Central American War, Catholic Internationalism, and United States Public Diplomacy in Reagan's America," *US Catholic Historian* 33, no. 1 (2015): 185.

90. The ADL appears not to have publicized its connection with the workgroup despite its nominal "outreach" aim. Sara Diamond's 1995 book on the US political right, *Roads to Dominion*, unearthed the ADL's participation in the Hoover Institution archives. More recently digitized documents in the National Security Archive at George Washington University add new detail to Diamond's research. Greg Grandin, *Empire's Workshop* (Metropolitan Books, 2006), 452; Sara Diamond, *Roads to Dominion: Right-Wing Movements and Political Power in the United States* (Guilford Press, 1995).

91. Gerda Ray, "Legitimating the Right: The Neoconservatives Build a Base," *Crime and Social Justice*, no. 19 (1983): 75–86.

led by JINSA cofounder and chair Max Kampelman, who was also a Social Democrat and ADL lay leader.[92] Joining on behalf of the Reagan administration was Elliott Abrams, assistant secretary of state for inter-American affairs at the time. Abrams had joined the cadre as a college student, then worked with Penn Kemble, Muravchik, and others on staff for US senators Henry "Scoop" Jackson and Daniel P. Moynihan.[93]

The Outreach Working Group was a site of consequential encounters. At its monthly meetings, participating organizations were able to present reports to high-level officials, and White House officials briefed them in return. At one meeting in June 1983, the ADL's Morton Rosenthal spoke on "the persecution of the Jewish people in Central America," accompanied by one of the touring Somoza functionaries, and President Reagan dropped in for a fifteen-minute talk. In another instance, ADL director Nathan Perlmutter advised the group's convenor, the head of the Office of Public Diplomacy, on a monthly issue of the White House bulletin on Central America. The *Digest* disseminated "short factual papers"; Perlmutter's contribution covered the Sandinistas, their relationship with the PLO, and supposed Sandinista antisemitism. A CIA official regularly briefed the group, as did US Marine Corps Major Oliver North, who was working at the time to provide materials and weapons to the Nicaraguan Contras fighting the Sandinista government.[94] To the Reagan administration, the group provided connections to wealthy individuals who funded Contra activities.[95] Possibly it provided similar connections to North, who in 1987 admitted to establishing a network to direct funds to the Contras without the official approval of the White House.

The ADL's participation in the Outreach Working Group underlines its adoption of foreign policy as a sphere of its ideological and practical work. Its battles against the left, defense of the state-capital class, support for Western order and opposition to Soviet influence, and need to thwart Palestinian alliances, all demanded foreign engagement. Not only did Marxism have to be fought in Central America; *domestic* public outcry against Central

92. Jewish Institute for National Security of America, "CAFTA," July 19, 2005, https://jinsa.org/jreport/cafta/, accessed May 6, 2021; Jewish Institute for National Security of America, "Ambassador Max Kampelman Passes Away," n.d., http://archive.constantcontact.com/fs160/1101496577013/archive/1112284636455.html, accessed May 6, 2021.

93. Ross, *Socialist Party of America*, 527–28.

94. Strauss, "Quest for the Holy Grail," 186, 190, 188.

95. Strauss, "Quest for the Holy Grail," 189; Keith Schneider, "North's Record: A Wide Role in a Host of Sensitive Projects," *New York Times*, January 3, 1987.

American right-wing regimes, and US complicity with them, also empowered the left. Indeed, the left's criticisms had become mainstream. This turn to international work, particularly characterized by attention to Central America, connected the ADL even more closely with Social Democratic efforts. These collaborations make sense of the ADL spying scandal.

When the ADL spying scandal broke in 1993, the ADL was already known as a surveillance operation. White nationalists were its putative target. In the Jim Crow South, ADL staffers had done daring work to infiltrate segregationist White Citizens' Councils and report on their operations; later they had closely tracked the Ku Klux Klan. Forster and Epstein's books had hinted at informants, or even undercover work, as the source of their information. But the spying scandal revealed an intensity of surveillance of civil rights and popular movement groups that sharply contrasted with the public's understanding of the ADL's surveillance. In part, the shock was that its spying looked far beyond white nationalist groups, the ADL's presumptive target; additionally, the ADL's methods seemed incommensurable with its respectable, responsible public image. Not only had it compiled dossiers using data from such untoward places as trash bins and the Department of Motor Vehicles, and amassed "contraband"-like rap sheets, it had infiltrated organizations directly.[96] An ADL agent, Roy Bullock, had been embedded in the American-Arab Anti-Discrimination Committee (ADC) as a regular volunteer—often working security—at the time that ADC offices were bombed and its director, Alex Odeh, murdered. That information raised harrowing questions about whether the ADL had been involved in Odeh's assassination, and what dangers it might now pose. Additionally, Bullock told FBI interviewers that he had been spying for the ADL for nearly thirty years, raising more questions about what else the ADL had done outside the public view. One thing became clear: Since the 1960s, the ADL had not solely feared the Black liberationist expansions of the civil rights movement, the anti-

96. Jim McGee, "Jewish Group's Tactics Investigated," *Washington Post*, October 18, 1993; "Exhibit C: SFPD Interview of Roy Bullock," January 25, 1993, https://www.israellobby .org/ADL-CA/Ex_c_sfpd_interviews_bullock.pdf; Friedman, "How the Anti-Defamation League Turned the Notion of Human Rights on Its Head"; Richard C. Paddock, "New Details of Extensive ADL Spy Operation Emerge: Inquiry: Transcripts Reveal Nearly 40 Years of Espionage by a Man Who Infiltrated Political Groups," *Los Angeles Times*, April 13, 1993, http://articles.latimes.com/1993-04-13/news/mn-22383_1_spy-operation.

Vietnam War movement, the Palestine solidarity movement, the student movement, and anticapitalist counterculture, and it hád not only hoped to be useful to the FBI. Rather, it had expanded its own role as disciplinarian beyond Jewish communities, and beyond efforts to "foster democracy." The apparatus that had surveilled white nationalists had been trained on a wider set of enemies.[97]

On the other hand, the spying scandal suggested that something was still not transparent. The list of organizations surveilled were filed under "PINKO," "ARAB," and "ANC" (South Africa–related) as well as "RIGHT." These categories and their contents were both wider and narrower than the ADL's stated interests; they did not quite make sense.[98] Certainly, the ADL's targets reflected its interest in Israeli militarism and narrative, and its embrace of repression in Israel's service. US Arab groups were targeted, including cultural and business associations.[99] The ADL monitored efforts to build community and educate the public about Palestinian issues. It also provided the Israeli government with intelligence on US activists to an extent that was not fully explored in the investigation. (Epstein had previously confirmed that the ADL surveilled Arab groups and shared information with US and Israeli intelligence; the FBI investigation raised, but never answered, questions about whether this surveillance material had also been sold or shared. In the 1993 arrest and subsequent prosecution of Muhammad Salah, a Palestinian American from Chicago who traveled to Palestine to deliver charitable aid, more evidence emerged of coordination between the ADL and Israeli intelligence.)[100] Its surveillance of anti-Apartheid groups was also motivated by its worries about "public opinion regarding relations between

97. For a more detailed account of the ADL's spying activities, including a full list of the organizations on whom the ADL's files held surveillance data, see Abdeen Jabara, "The Anti-Defamation League: Civil Rights and Wrongs," *Covert Action*, no. 45 (Summer 1993), 28–37.

98. FBI, "Exhibit I: Organizations Listed in Gerard and Bullock Computers," n.d., archived at Institute for Research: Middle East Policy, Criminal investigation and successful civil lawsuits against the ADL over privacy right violations - 1992–1993, https://www.israellobby.org/ADL-CA/Exhibit%20I_orgs_in_Gerard_Bullock_computersb.pdf.

99. The Independent Grocers' Association (IGA), initially formed among the predominantly Arab community of Bay Area shop owners before becoming a national organization, was among the groups surveilled.

100. Jabara, "The Anti-Defamation League: Civil Rights and Wrongs," 36; Michael E. Deutsch and Erica Thompson, "Secrets and Lies: The Persecution of Muhammad Salah (Part II)," *Journal of Palestine Studies* 38, no. 1 (Autumn 2008): 25–53, 38.

Israel and South Africa."[101] Some of those dossiers were sold by the ADL's agent to the South African government, possibly simply for profit, and likely contributed to the 1993 assassination of African National Congress leader Chris Hani in South Africa.[102] A third set of organizations in solidarity with the Sandinistas might also have been surveilled as an effort to stay on top of anti-Israel activities, given their relationship with the PLO.

But these interests did not quite match the list of surveilled groups. First, surveillance had disproportionately targeted leftist political organizations that were active in the 1980s. The ADL had *not* kept tabs on US groups connected to key Central American and South American sites of support for Palestinian liberation. For instance, it did not have files on Chilean organizing, despite the fact the anti-Pinochet resistance was allied with Palestinians and had vibrant support organizations in the Bay Area.[103] It had not followed solidarity groups working in Paraguay, Guatemala, Costa Rica, and Honduras, where ruling regimes were allies of Israel, and resistance movements were linked with the PLO.[104] When interrogated by the San Francisco police, Bullock provided plenty of information, but he hedged the question of how "pinko" groups were chosen for surveillance. Implausibly, Bullock claimed that no one at the ADL directed him, and that he barely knew Suall despite having worked on fact-finding for three decades. Instead, Bullock claimed that he simply read leftist papers and opened files on whatever groups were mentioned. That process would not have led him to focus on groups working on such a specific set of issues or to miss so many Bay Area organizations.[105]

A closer match for ADL surveillance was the set of groups and issues of concern to Social Democrats, particularly the work of the National Endowment for Democracy (NED) and the AFL-CIO. Suall's close Social Democratic colleagues led those organizations' interventions in Central America, the Philippines, South Africa, and at home. Their project was to

101. McGee, "Jewish Group's Tactics Investigated"; Rachelle Marshall, "It's Now the ADL Spy Case," *Washington Report on Middle East Affairs*, June 1993, 17; FBI, Memo from SAC San Fran. to FBI Director (subj. redacted), Mar. 15, 1993, File 1199215-0-65X-LA-153918-Section1, pp. 27–30, FBI Investigates the ADL for Espionage, Israel Lobby Archive, Institute for Research: Middle Eastern Policy, https://www.israellobby.org/ADL-FBI.

102. Marshall, "It's Now the ADL Spy Case."

103. Meaghan Kachadoorian, "¡Junta No! Chilean Solidarity in the Bay," Found SF, 2015, https://www.foundsf.org/index.php?title=%C2%A1Junta_No!_Chilean_Solidarity_in_the_Bay.

104. Hoffman, "PLO and Israel in Central America."

105. "Exhibit C: SFPD Interview of Roy Bullock."

hamper labor organizations that opposed US-supported, right-wing regimes in those places, and provide training and resources for projects that offered resistance to leftist movements and anticolonial, internationalist ideas.[106] (Other friends and their organizations were also engaged in the same work: Elliott Abrams as assistant secretary of state; PRODEMCA, led by Penn Kemble; Freedom House, with Rustin, Shanker, and Kampelman; and League for Industrial Democracy, with Puddington, Kahn, Rustin, and Shanker.) Approximately 290 organizations in the ADL spy's files were categorized as "pinko." Apart from the regular targets of the ADL's domestic discipline—Black liberationists, white nationalists, and critics of Israel— thirty-seven were labor organizations that supported Third Worldist struggles, mostly union locals, organizing drives, and social justice committees. At least fifty were solidarity groups supporting resistance movements in Central America and the Philippines, and active since the late 1970s or early 1980s. Nicaragua featured heavily; El Salvador and Cuba were a second focus.

Gershman's NED overlapped significantly with the ADL and its Social Democratic crew. It had been created in 1983 by the US Congress and the AFL-CIO during the Reagan administration. The effort was led by AFL-CIO president Lane Kirkland with Eugenia Kemble, sister of Penn Kemble and Al Shanker's former deputy at the American Federation of Teachers.[107] Suall's former fact-finding deputy at the ADL, David Lowe, had gone directly from his assistantship at the ADL to serve as NED vice president; Suall had proposed him to Gershman as a good candidate for the job.[108] NED pursued Reagan's program of "public diplomacy" in support of national security objectives; in other words, democracy promotion. As sociologist William Robinson writes, this entailed "political operations and psychological warfare" in "countries designated as hostile and under Soviet influence," those whose political shifts might allow "stable 'democratic' governments inside the US orbit."[109] NED conducted its work through subgroups, two of which were run from within Suall's circle: the National Democratic Institute for International Affairs,

106. On SDUSA leaders and their role in Latin American and African ideological projects bridging labor and US state efforts, see Schuhrke, *Blue-Collar Empire*, 160–62, 225–29.

107. Robert Pee, *Democracy Promotion, National Security and Strategy: Foreign Policy Under the Reagan Administration* (Taylor and Francis Group, 2015), 130.

108. National Endowment for Democracy, "Staff Bios," February 7, 2008, https://web .archive.org/web/20080207060620/https://www.ned.org/about/bios.html; "Examination of Irwin Suall," 359–60; Gershman, "Irwin Suall Memorial."

109. National Security Decision Directive 77, unclassified version, cited in Robinson, *A Faustian Bargain*, 16–17.

where Rachelle Horowitz was secretary and Penn Kemble was a board member, and the AFL-CIO's Free Trade Union Institute (FTUI) run by Eugenia Kemble.[110] Tom Kahn also sat on the FTUI board and participated as assistant, then director, at the AFL-CIO's International Affairs office.[111] Together, NED and the AFL-CIO/FTUI throughout the 1980s seeded public discourse and supported the development of "opposition unions" and civic institutions that supported US aims. Through these soft power mechanisms they opposed leftist movements, supported political and military forces bolstered by the Reagan administration, and generated enthusiasm for US intervention.[112]

The projects implemented by Social Democrats are stunning for their puppeteering of political processes and their violence, and dissonant in their claims of moving toward peace and democracy. In Nicaragua in the 1980s, the AFL-CIO had been conducting anti-left "solidarity" work for several decades and had several affiliated unions.[113] In one example of tactics, it had organized workers to press demands that the Sandinista government could not meet, then arranged for the opposition to nominally back those demands. Finally in 1990, the opposition ousted Sandinista president Daniel Ortega. In El Salvador, NED and the AFL-CIO funded and organized a coalition of labor and peasant unions to leverage the 1984 election of US-backed candidate José Napoleón Duarte. Although Duarte ran death squads, they continued to prefer him to the possibility of a leftist government.[114] In the Philippines, NED and the AFL-CIO worked together to throttle a vibrant leftist movement in aid of the US move to replace dictator Ferdinand Marcos

110. The AFL-CIO conducted its NED-funded operations through a series of institutes. The Free Trade Union Institute (FTUI) received NED funds, then passed them along to its subordinate programs. In Central America and South America, it operated the American Institute for Free Labor Development (AIFLD); in the Philippines, the Asian American Free Labor Institute (AAFLI); in Africa, the African American Labor Institute (AALI). For an explanation of the NED's formation through the US National Security Council, its supervision by "high-ranking CIA propaganda specialist" Walter Raymond Jr., and its operations, see National Democratic Institute for International Affairs, *NDI Reports* (Spring 1988), https://www.ndi.org/sites/default/files/1267_NDI_Rep_Intl_Affairs_Spring_1988_1.pdf; Robinson, *A Faustian Bargain*, 15–20.

111. Barry and Preusch, *AIFLD in Central America*; Anthony Carew, "The American Labor Movement in Fizzland: The Free Trade Union Committee and the CIA," *Labor History* 39, no. 1 (1998): 25.

112. See Tim Shorrock, "Labor's Cold War," *The Nation*, May 1, 2003.

113. Anti-Sandinista work included labor groups beyond the Nicaraguan border, including Venezuela, Costa Rica, and Mexico. Robinson, *A Faustian Bargain*, 68–70.

114. Adam Bernstein, "Donald S. Slaiman, 81, Dies," *Washington Post*, October 25, 2000.

with Corazon Aquino. According to the AFL-CIO officer in charge, had there been no intervention, "the success of the political left in the [Filipino] trade unions would have been phenomenal. Nationally and internationally it would have been a Waterloo." In 1983, NED and the AFL-CIO ramped up support to the pro-business Trade Union Congress of the Philippines (TUCP) to oppose the growing influence of more radical labor and to secure its support for antiworker and pro-US military policy.[115] Aquino was elected in 1986, and the NED/AFL-CIO project continued through 1988.[116]

The ADL was not conducting these soft power incursions abroad; rather, its role was, as before, to contain and discipline the US left. Throughout the 1980s, US activists were carrying out work that pushed in the opposite direction, and they were particularly strong in the Bay Area. As movement historian Emily Hobson writes, activists traveling often between the US and Nicaragua created bonds of material support between the two communities. US visitors aided in the harvests, construction, and services that helped shore up the revolutionary government. In the US, Nicaraguan comrades fueled feminist and queer imaginings of life that agitated against capitalist norms.[117] This was where the ADL's work lay. Bay Area groups, including the Committee in Solidarity with the People of El Salvador, worked closely with the Salvadoran resistance movement against Duarte and US intervention; those groups were on the ADL's list. Of the Filipino organizations in California in the ADL's "PINKO" files, many have faded in the historical record but at least two were clearly troubling the NED/AFL-CIO. The Alliance for Philippine Concerns was founded in 1986 and within a year had launched campaigns for "ending US aid to the Philippine Military (including education about CIA subversion of Philippine labor, church and other sectors); the withdrawal of US bases (seeking mutual withdrawal of Soviet and US bases to pave the way for demilitarization of the Asian Pacific region); emergency economic relief; cultural tours, and coordination of North American activities on significant dates in Philippine history."[118] *Ang Katipunan*, another of the Filipino targets

---

115. Bud Philipps, AAFLI administrator, cited in Holly Sklar and Chip Berlet, "NED, CIA, and the Orwellian Democracy Project," *Covert Action*, no. 39 (Winter 1991–92).

116. Kim Scipes, *AFL-CIO's Secret War Against Developing Country Workers: Solidarity or Sabotage?* (Lexington Books, 2011), 52.

117. Emily K. Hobson, *Lavender and Red: Liberation and Solidarity in the Gay and Lesbian Left* (University of California Press, 2016), 124, 127.

118. *Resist Newsletter*, "Grants: Alliance for Philippine Concerns," no. 201 (December 1987): 9.

of surveillance, was the newspaper of the antiracist, anti-imperialist Katipunan ng mga Demokratikong Pilipino movement.[119] Both worked in direct opposition to NED/AFL-CIO projects.

The ADL's surveillance of anti-Apartheid and labor organizations also gestured to Social Democratic interests. Israel had maintained diplomatic and arms trade relations with the South African Apartheid regime between 1975 and 1987, a poorly kept secret that provided Black radicals with powerful material for denouncing Israel.[120] Social Democrats brought their own South African engagements as well. Bayard Rustin ran AFL-CIO democracy promotion work in South Africa in the mid-1980s, funded by NED and, in secret, by the Reagan administration.[121] The project called for combating the influence of communists in the anti-Apartheid movement, countering calls for divestment, and discouraging armed struggle. To do that, the AFL-CIO aimed to prop up right-wing unions and deradicalize Black unions.[122] In South Africa, the Congress of South African Trade Unions and the Council of Unions of South Africa rejected the AFL-CIO's overtures as labor imperialism.[123] In the United States, the activist union AFSCME (the American Federation of State, County and Municipal Employees) and its anti-Apartheid committee denounced the interventions. Suall's surveillance included two AFSCME locals and the anti-Apartheid committee.[124]

These convergences, and the absence of other explanations for the political turf it covered, suggest that Suall's Fact-Finding Department was conducting surveillance in consideration of, and perhaps directly in support of, Social Democrats' brutal interventions. Whether the ADL's archives bear this out is a question for future researchers. In the words of civil rights attorney and

119. Helen C. Toribio, "We Are Revolution: A Reflective History of the Union of Democratic Filipinos (KDP)," *Amerasia Journal* 24, no. 2 (1998): 155.

120. Lubin, *Geographies of Liberation*, 125.

121. *Labor Notes*, "South African Unionists Tell AFL-CIO 'No Trade Union Imperialism!,'" February 1985; *Labor Notes*, "Reagan Funds AFL-CIO's South Africa Activities," August 1986. I encountered most of the *Labor Notes* articles cited here in Scipes, *AFL-CIO's Secret War Against Developing Country Workers*.

122. Sandy Boyer, "Here's Who the AFL-CIO Is Funding in South Africa," *Labor Notes*, December 1986; Yevette Richards, "The AFL-CIO and South Africa," in *Conversations with Maida Springer: A Personal History of Labor, Race, and International Relations* (University of Pittsburgh Press, 2004), 283–305.

123. *Labor Notes*, "South African Unionists Tell AFL-CIO 'No Trade Union Imperialism!,'" February 1985, and *Labor Notes*, "Reagan Funds AFL-CIO's South Africa Activities," August 1986.

124. FBI, "Exhibit I."

Arab community organizer Abdeen Jabara, who sued the ADL over its spying program, "it was all Cold War shenanigans."[125]

The purpose of this account is not to relitigate the ADL spying scandal, but to illustrate the significance of reading the overlap between the assemblage of the neoconservative movement, coercive state forces, and the ADL itself. Suall died in 1997, Kahn in 1992, Feldman and Penn Kemble in 2005, and Eugenia Kemble in 2018. From 1972 until the end of their lives, each person placed their institutions in the service of their shared ideals, jointly pursuing projects that combined discourse and on-the-ground implementation. Their dispersion across organizations was itself a way of getting work done. It allowed multiple platforms, funding, division of labor, and the perception of a collection of civic institutions simply agreeing that this was a legitimate pursuit of democracy. Gershman's eulogy for Suall emphasized this commitment, which superseded other ideology and allowed them to leave socialism behind: "During the faction fight and after the split, the issue that aroused Irwin's strongest political feelings was not the struggle for socialism but rather the defense of freedom against totalitarianism. The defense of freedom was much more important to Irwin than proclaiming allegiance to an ideology that had ceased to offer a compelling response to the core challenges that faced America and the world. . . . He was prepared to follow his core values regardless of where they might lead him."[126] The construction of *freedom* as the liberalism of the settler state and the violence to defend it, and

125. Author interview with Abdeen Jabara, July 8, 2021. Meanwhile, these connections are refracted in an adjacent history. David Jessup was another SDUSA leader, and cofounder of the Institute for Religion and Democracy (IRD), a democracy promotion/anti-left organization formed in 1981 to target church funding for leftist and anticapitalist groups, particularly those supporting Latin American movements. He also worked as the AFL-CIO's Latin America director of human and trade union rights. There, his work was both neoconservative democracy promotion and surveillance of the left. He was "point man for the quite substantial efforts by organized labor . . . to resist Communism in Central America," as Joshua Muravchik described him. He also worked "to identify for the unions radical groups that would undermine the cause of labor and democratic values," according to IRD author Riley C. Case. Jessup's files, too, substantially paralleled the ADL's targets; his archive is filled with folders bearing the names of leftist activists and solidarity groups with Central American, Filipino, Palestinian, and African resistance movements. Case, *Evangelical and Methodist: A Popular History* (Abingdon Press, 2004), 109–16; Ken Silverstein and Alexander Cockburn, "Big Labor's Goon Squads," *Counterpunch* 2, no. 18 (October 15, 1995); Joshua Muravchik, "Comrades," *Commentary*, January 2006, 52–58; David Jessup, "David Jessup Papers, circa 1970–1996 (Finding Aid)," Emory University Stuart A. Rose Manuscript, Archives, and Rare Book Library.

126. Gershman, "Irwin Suall Memorial."

totalitarianism as the left and its moves to imagine and produce other ways of being, is a substantially different notion from the presumed work of the ADL in anti-discrimination, civil rights, and anti-antisemitism.

The ADL's projects of empire—not its flying of the civil rights banner, but its other work—have often seemed to sit just outside the frame of view. As its "turns to the right" have at times "produced confusion in some liberals," as the *New York Times* commented, that other work has sometimes briefly appeared before being forgotten again. The 1993 spying scandal produced such a glimpse. What seems an incommensurably odd and contradictory episode—a thirty-year surveillance effort far wider in scope than antisemitism, race, even Zionism—is no contradiction at all. Instead, it gestures to a larger set of projects that are also just out of view: labor's Cold War collaborations with the CIA, Social Democrats' seeding of neoconservative foreign policy, and the ADL's own role as a node in a neoconservative movement defined by a political sociality. These soft power projects, pulled into the frame, illuminate the operations of empire itself.

FIVE

Schoolbooks and Rulers

THE '80s

AS THE 1980S OPENED, the United States was having another tough national conversation about racism. News reports resounded with racial conflicts: violence by white nationalists, turf wars in segregated cities, individual assaults. Boston had become a national symbol of these tensions in 1974, when efforts to redress segregation by "busing" Black children into white schools were met with school boycotts and violence by white protesters.[1] Through the end of the decade, racist attacks, race riots, and attacks on antiracist events persisted. Responding to a pervasive sense of emergency, in December 1980 the *Boston Globe* published a thirty-five-page special section with street interviews and commentary, airing racial grievances and pleas for action.[2] The *Globe* editors wrote: "There have been many cases in recent years in which people have been prevented by threats or actual violence from peaceably exercising such basic rights as living where they choose, from using public transportation, from going to school, . . . from access to all parts of the city."[3] Television consultant Jerry Wishnow later put it in blunter terms: The problem was "busing, race-based beatings, 'You know where I stand' politics . . . [that] made Boston look more like a town in South Africa than the 'city on a hill.'"[4]

1. These events are often referred to as a conflict over busing Black students, but in fact reflect a three-decade struggle by Black parents against an ongoing denial of education, as parent organizers and historians documenting the struggle articulate. See Matthew Delmont and Jeanne Theoharis, "Introduction: Rethinking the Boston 'Busing Crisis,'" *Journal of Urban History* 43, no. 2 (2017): 191–203.

2. *Boston Globe*, "Voices from Our City: Racism in Boston," December 14, 1980.

3. *Boston Globe*, "Massachusetts' Own Civil Rights Law," November 7, 1979.

4. Jerry Wishnow, "Letter: Coppersmith Also Gutsy, Generous," *Marblehead Reporter*, September 14, 2010.

When Wishnow approached the local Anti-Defamation League office about making a series of TV spots about racial tolerance—with the hopeful title "A World of Difference"—he tapped powerful converging currents in education, television, and marketing. In the preceding years, education experts concerned about growing racism had looked to educational messaging as a solution. Desegregation in schools had been a constitutional mandate since the US Supreme Court's 1954 *Brown v. Board of Education* ruling, and overt expressions of racism in schools had become more taboo. But even as white communities might avoid using overtly racist language, their adherence to white supremacist ideas and efforts to preserve segregation persisted in "more subtle forms."[5] To address this ongoing problem, researchers in the 1970s and '80s again turned to the possibility of using early educational messaging to shift racial attitudes, mirroring the psychological studies that had underwritten intergroup relations work three decades earlier. Research found that no intervention worked consistently. Rather, researchers pointed out that even if education shifted students' attitudes in their early years, the students lived in a world thoroughly structured by racism, which had the effect of continually reinforcing racist ideas.[6] Still, they remained hopeful about teaching against it. Since the 1970s, public health advocates and marketing researchers had been testing "social marketing," using advertising in

5. Vernay Mitchell, "Curriculum and Instruction to Reduce Racial Conflict," *ERIC/CUE Digest*, no. 64 (n.d.); Donald R. Kinder, "The Continuing American Dilemma: White Resistance to Racial Change 40 Years After Myrdal," *Journal of Social Issues* 42, no. 2 (1986): 151–71, 152.

6. A study of research on programs to reduce racial prejudice, between 1966 and 1994, identified nine separate approaches tested on students in the wake of concern about the racial tensions of urban riots and busing. Nearly all focused on white students in overwhelmingly white schools. Among them, audiovisual programming was relatively successful when it showed people having experiences that changed their attitudes, but less so when it included direct messaging that opposed prejudice. Human relations training was inconsistent. Research found it "promoting lip service" in its moralizing push for participants to do "the right thing" and found that participants who sensed they were being manipulated finished the training with an oppositional recommitment to their prejudices. By contrast, a 1969 experiment had shown the success of incorporating positive images of multiracial actors into regular curriculum (using stories with "multi-ethnic characters portrayed as middle class people who worked hard, dressed nicely, and were clean," and in which teachers "did not initiate any discussions of a racial nature") rather than treating it as a separate curriculum. More broadly, researchers commented that effective interventions required more consideration of the causes of prejudice. Glenn S. Pate, *Prejudice Reduction and the Findings of Research*, 1995, ERIC Database, Institute of Education Sciences within the US Department of Education, https://files.eric.ed.gov/fulltext/ED383803.pdf, 2, 13, 21.

conjunction with other social programs as a means of familiarizing the public with concepts like family planning, and encouraging behaviors like using contraception. In the arena of race relations, too, researchers were seeking ways to seed information that would counter racist presumptions and naturalize tolerance as common sense.[7] Lastly, television producers were increasingly thinking of their medium as a platform for conveying social messages. (*Roots*, an epic miniseries following a family's story from Africa to enslavement and through the civil war, had been an unexpected blockbuster in 1977, revealing a public appetite for television that reflected complex and challenging issues.) The idea that television could provide social benefits while drawing a viewership that boosted profits—and that it could be aimed at children in particular—called for innovation and experimentation.[8]

Wishnow's project was propelled by these currents and was further boosted when he secured as a partner Leonard Zakim, the ADL's New England regional director. Zakim had worked at the ADL for just a few years, but he was already a force in local Democratic Party politics, close to the governor, cochair of the Greater Boston Civil Rights Coalition, and "a very important and significant force between the Jewish community and the black churches and the business community . . . an extraordinary figure and a force," as Senator Edward (Ted) Kennedy later remembered him.[9] Taking up Wishnow's project, Zakim recruited WCVB-TV, which had its own history of producing such programming in Boston; it had also worked in a national group of local stations to produce documentaries on social issues, including changing gender roles and neighborhood fears about crime.[10] Wishnow, the ADL, and WCVB-TV together now planned "A World of

7. Karen F. A. Fox and Philip Kotler, "The Marketing of Social Causes: The First 10 Years," *Journal of Marketing* 44, no. 4 (1980): 24–33.

8. Lynda Sharp Paine et al., "Children as Consumers: An Ethical Evaluation of Children's Television Advertising [with Commentaries]," *Business & Professional Ethics Journal* 3, no. 3/4 (1984): 119–69; Les Brown, "Hype in a Good Cause," *Channels*, August 1987.

9. Harlan Loeb, "Resources: Civil Rights Human Rights Hero: Lenny Zakim," Section of Individual Rights & Responsibilities of the American Bar Association, n.d., https://web.archive.org/web/20060217155145/http://www.abanet.org/irr/hr/spring01/loeb.html, accessed September 20, 2024; Interview with Edward M. Kennedy, May 31, 2007, by James Sterling Young, Edward M. Kennedy Oral History Project, Miller Center, University of Virginia.

10. "What Does Your Mom Do?" (1980) and "Fed Up with Fear" (1981) were prominent examples of these segments. See *Broadcasting*, "Do-It-Yourself Movement: Stations into Syndication," June 30, 1980; Tony Schwartz, "Some Say This Is America's Best TV Station," *New York Times*, February 15, 1981.

Difference" (AWOD) as a series of short programs in response to Boston's particular problems.[11] The collaboration was launched in 1985 with the backing of Boston's new mayor, Ray Flynn, and Zakim's former boss, Massachusetts governor Michael Dukakis.[12] By the time it reached Boston schools in 1986, AWOD featured twenty-six hours of television mini-programs and public service announcements, paired with a 350-page curriculum for high schools and a parallel set of twenty lessons for grades K-8.[13]

If AWOD made use of cutting-edge ideas in television and marketing, the conceptions of racism it propagated were far more dated and conservative. The social movements of the 1960s and '70s had succeeded in bringing attention to racism as a historical, logistical structure of state, and US policymakers were was responding with experiments like affirmative action, intended to shift those structures. Those ideas, the policies themselves, and even the conflicts over the policies were central to public discourse on race. AWOD simply omitted them from the curriculum. Instead, the lessons drew overwhelmingly on the ADL's own canon: the literature of intergroup relations and individual, psychologically driven prejudice, beginning with Gordon Allport's 1948 and 1954 texts *ABC's of Scapegoating* and *The Nature of Prejudice* and continuing with ADL publications through the 1980s.[14] The guidebook's introduction carefully laid out the major concepts organizing the curriculum: individual prejudice, stereotyping, discrimination, scapegoating, and racist beliefs.[15] These were the old tenets of intergroup relations.

11. Brown, "Hype in a Good Cause."

12. Jack Thomas, "Year-Long TV Project Combating Prejudice Set," *Boston Globe*, January 24, 1985.

13. Judith Foy, a WCVB programming developer during this period, records on her personal website that "[t]he programming and the name were donated to the Anti-Defamation League, national, which laid the foundation for the ADL's 'World of Difference Institute,'" ostensibly by the other partners in the AWOD project. Terry Ann Knopf, *The Golden Age of Boston Television* (University Press of New England, 2017); Judith Foy, *Awards | Foy Communications, LLC*, n.d., https://web.archive.org/web/20170629130324/foycommunications.com/awards; K-8 lesson plans cited in the Anti-Defamation League B'nai B'rith's "A World of Difference, a Prejudice Reduction Program of the Anti-Defamation League of B'nai B'rith: Teacher/Student Resource Guide," 1986.

14. ADL intergroup relations guides included, among others, *The Prejudice Book* (1979), *Individual Differences: A Program for Elementary School* (1981) and *Being Fair and Being Free: A Human Relations Program for the Secondary School* (1986). See Anti-Defamation League of B'nai B'rith, "A World of Difference," 1986, 253–55.

15. Anti-Defamation League of B'nai B'rith, "A World of Difference," v.

More than just a program to shape racial attitudes, AWOD was a concerted bid by the ADL to oppose the antiracist education programming of organizations more closely connected to bottom-up social movements. In 1981, the National Education Association, a union of 1.7 million education workers at the time, had partnered with the Council on Interracial Books and the National Anti-Klan Network (later renamed the Center for Democratic Renewal) to develop their own curriculum on white nationalist violence. Titled "Violence, the Ku Klux Klan, and the Struggle for Equality," the seventy-two-page curriculum was to be shared through all three organizations with teachers across the United States.[16] It offered a historically grounded pedagogy, beginning with the development of the Klan and its role in suppressing Black citizenship for the first decade after slavery was outlawed, until "the white elite no longer needed the Klan, for suppression of blacks could be accomplished by official, 'legal' means." Rather than portraying the Klan as an anomaly in the United States, the curriculum traced its convergences with formal party politics and law enforcement, as well as the role of "the press and the pulpit" in naturalizing its violence.[17]

To the ADL, this historical, systemic approach to understanding racism directly contravened its insistence that US liberal capitalism was inherently egalitarian and democratic. Worse, it lent support to the left's critiques of the US state. Before the anti-Klan curriculum had a chance to roll out, the ADL denounced it for "indicting American society as innately racist." The NAACP hit back, declaring that the Klan was not "an aberration, as the ADL claims" and rejecting "psychological games" in avoiding confrontations with racism. NAACP education director Dr. Beverly Cole wrote: "For the ADL to be 'diametrically opposed' to the notion that America is institutionally racist is to be either incredibly insensitive or incredibly naïve. . . . It serves no useful purpose for Americans to adopt self-righteous and defensive views about its problems."[18]

To counter the NEA-sponsored curriculum, the ADL pledged to create its own school programming on "extremist groups left and right" that would

16. I am grateful to the late NEA activist and veteran antiracist organizer Boyd Bosma for bringing this historical episode to my attention.

17. Connecticut Education Association, "Violence, the Ku Klux Klan, and the Struggle for Equality: An Informational and Instructional Kit," 1981, 19, 23.

18. ADL director Nathan Perlmutter, quoted in Steve Askin, "Unteaching Racism," *Black Enterprise*, March 1982; National Association for the Advancement of Colored People (NAACP), "NAACP Education Chief Says Klan Is Not an Aberration," press release, October 28, 1981, Box 106, Folder 6, Series II, Field Files: Civil Rights Organizations: ADL, 1984–90, National Gay and Lesbian Task Force records, #7301, Cornell University.

"highlight modern progress toward racial justice" rather than gesturing to unpleasant histories of state racism.[19] The following year, it published *Extremist Groups in the United States: A Curriculum Guide*, with 315 pages of lesson plans, readings, and audiovisual materials. Although *Extremist Groups* covered the Klan and neo-Nazis, its central message was that the US political *left* was to be viewed as just as racist, hateful, and extremist as the right—in fact, it asserted, the left was a global and therefore greater threat. In particular, the left's animus toward Israel and imperialism was to be understood not as opposition to the domination of Palestinian people and land, but as a product of "totalitarian, anti-democratic" positions. In the ADL's portrayal, it was bent on destroying democracy through "violence and terror," and coordinated by the Soviet Union and China.[20] Readings in the *Extremist Groups* guide were excerpted from neoconservative writer Midge Decter and other anticommunist campaigners, and warned students not to believe that leftists were driven by concern for racial or economic justice. To the contrary, the text claimed that leftist dogma permitted "trickery, deceit, law-breaking, withholding and concealing the truth, violence . . . as long as they serve the cause."[21] Constructing the left as a hate movement akin to white nationalism, the curriculum claimed that leftists were hostile to Jews both because they viewed Israel and Jews as representatives of Western democracy and because they harbored "hatred of Jews, as Jews."[22] Like ADL narratives of earlier decades, the curriculum simply disappeared Jewish leftists, omitting them as targets of Nazism, leftists, and critics of Zionism.[23] "In

19. Askin, "Unteaching Racism."

20. Anti-Defamation League of B'nai B'rith, *Extremist Groups in the United States: A Curriculum Guide*, 1982, 1.

21. The ADL curriculum attributed this quotation to V. I. Lenin, but it appears to be invented. Often cited in anticommunist texts, it is taken from Max Eastman's 1955 *Reflections on the Failure of Socialism*, where it is uncited. Another quotation in the section of the ADL curriculum intended to reveal "the philosophy of Marxism-Leninism" is similarly apocryphal. "The dictatorship of the Communist Party is maintained by recourse to every form of violence" is cited as a quote from Trotsky's *Terrorism and Communism*, 1924, 71. However, no such text appears in *Terrorism and Communism*, nor was any version published in 1924. The bogus citation, which also appears repeatedly in anticommunist materials with the same page number and publication date, seems to originate in a 1967 book of quotations, George Seldes, *The Great Quotations* (Pocket Books, 1967).

22. Anti-Defamation League of B'nai B'rith, *Extremist Groups in the United States*, 239, 260.

23. Anti-Defamation League of B'nai B'rith, *Extremist Groups in the United States*, 52, 268.

the discussion of the reading," the guide instructed teachers, "include the following … [the] three targets of international [leftist] terrorism are Western democracy, Israel, and Jews."[24] It was a Cold War document in its focus on communism as an existential threat to the West, but amplified—indeed, electrified—by its assertion that communism's engine was an apolitical, antisemitic *hate*.

The curriculum guide for "A World of Difference" published four years later did not make the same assertions. Although it cited and included excerpts from some of the same texts, the excerpts were shortened and left out the authors' exhortations to beware of the left and defend Israel. Texts from well-known neoconservative figures were absent. Indeed, AWOD so thoroughly excised the fervid Cold War anti-left tone of *Extremist Groups* that it suggests a strategic decision, likely in consideration of local politics and partners. What remained was more anodyne: the insistent portrayal of the United States as intrinsically moral, and prejudice as individual. It was a successful formula that did what the ADL had intended *Extremist Groups* to do: Capturing the national political will to educate against racism, it displaced and replaced curriculum that located racism in the state itself.

By some measures, "A World of Difference" was a wild success. Initially announced as a one-year experiment, it was immediately extended for another six months.[25] By the end of its pilot period, AWOD had reportedly "reached 71 percent of Massachusetts' public schools, providing educational materials, seminars and workshops for almost 6,000 teachers."[26] It was propelled by accolades and far-reaching media access: "It won a bundle of local and national awards, including a Peabody … a Presidential Commendation and a national Emmy," Wishnow later recalled. "More importantly, its on-air components helped change the tone and volume of the public discourse.'"[27] Expanding from its Boston origins, AWOD would become a national program that would persist for four decades, until 2025, when the ADL closed it down in favor of addressing only antisemitism.[28] The program also faced critiques, but they did not command much attention. Early on, the *Boston Globe* panned WCVB's television programming as "weak" and complained

24. Anti-Defamation League of B'nai B'rith, *Extremist Groups in the United States*, 229.
25. Thomas, "Year-Long TV Project Combating Prejudice Set."
26. *Bankers Monthly*, "Periscope—Public Service Pays Off," vol. 106, no. 3 (1989): 82.
27. Wishnow, "Letter."
28. Alex Kane, "ADL Shutters Flagship Anti-Bias Program," *Jewish Currents*, March 27, 2025.

that it failed to illuminate prejudice.[29] The lesson plans gamely tried to move children to see difference as a positive asset, build empathy through storytelling about characters who experienced bias, and develop insights into how they see and categorize others. Such exercises were fine for building kindness and self-awareness, but not as a means of intervening in racism. As Bay Area organizers later pointed out (discussed in this chapter), these were features of a curriculum developed by white educators, from a white perspective, and presumed whiteness as the norm from which "racial difference" diverged.

The criticisms were not picked up for discussion by school officials, press, or the ADL itself. Neither were the program's effects measured at the time. Looking backward in 2017, TV historian Terry Ann Knopf summed up the gap, "'Significant,' yes, but how 'impactful'? Tough question. For other than testimonials, the outcomes of the laudable campaign by independent researchers were never measured in a scientific way."[30] Until "A World of Difference" curriculum was implemented elsewhere, no one appears to have asked whether the Anti-Defamation League itself was an appropriate vehicle for curriculum on racism, even though Zakim was the ADL official who, just a year earlier, had distributed the blacklist of "pro-Arab sympathizers" that decried the "Arab anti-Semitic threat" on college campuses and denounced Jewish anti-Zionists. The political positioning of the ADL made its curriculum not just hard to oppose, but nearly inevitable. Zakim's anti-Arab blacklist had been national news, but locally Zakim and the ADL were credentialed as supporters of civil rights efforts in housing, schools, and corporate responsibility. The New England ADL was not just part of a powerful civil rights coalition; it was integral to Boston racial politics.

The momentum that made the ADL curriculum inevitable in Boston continued to propel it into public school systems around the United States. Within a few years, the ADL was a ubiquitous partner in US school districts—effectively, a quasi-state educational institution. By late 1986, AWOD had been pulled into Allentown, Pennsylvania, by the city's human relations commission; Miami and its suburbs; Detroit, with a local newspaper, two TV stations, the city's civil rights agency, and a school district together contributing "millions of dollars," securing the governor's support; and Houston, with a local TV station, the *Houston Chronicle* newspaper, and

29. Jack Thomas, "'World of Difference' Extended," *Boston Globe*, January 27, 1986.
30. Knopf, *Golden Age of Boston Television*, 75.

the energy corporation Enron.[31] Each city proudly noted that they were early adopters of programming forthcoming in thirty other cities; indeed, the ADL's pitch to new cities included endorsements from those that had come before.[32] Hallie Rosen, who directed the Philadelphia AWOD program, described disseminating the program in the first year. "The materials . . . were definitely put together by ADL staff, white people, and it was all going to be available for free in the schools. And everybody took it."[33]

Nationalizing a local program meant further problems, though. As it spread, it continued to displace research-based pedagogy on racism, as well as efforts by marginalized communities to represent their own stories and analyses in education. The defining aspects of AWOD's success in Boston were its local character, including extensive case studies on local conflicts that were familiar and pressing, and its connection to the Greater Boston Civil Rights Coalition. Its stewardship by WCVB also mattered: The station's staff who developed the AWOD television approach were personally enthusiastic about challenging racism. Those features were specific to Boston's social fabric and the ADL's history there, and did not follow AWOD into new markets. The Boston programming and the name "A World of Difference," now associated with a 1986 Peabody award for impactful television, were donated to the national Anti-Defamation League.[34] The national ADL office set about sending it to other markets, still operating without the benefit of research or evaluation.[35] "Nobody seemed to be concerned about it," Rosen recounted. "The materials just appeared, and that was the material you used. . . . That was very much the way ADL worked . . . 'We'll train you to do it the way we want to do it . . . we're not going to work collaboratively.'"[36]

31. David M. Erdman, "Groups Announce Effort to Fight Prejudice in L.V.," *Morning Call*, November 19, 1986.

32. Donald T. Butler to Robert Mullin and Concord city councilmembers, December 4, 1986, Box 33, Folder 11, Community United Against Violence (CUAV) records, GLBT Historical Society.

33. Author interview with Hallie Rosen, March 4, 2021.

34. Peabody Awards, "PeabodyAwards.Com: A World of Difference," n.d., https:// peabodyawards.com/award-profile/a-world-of-difference/, accessed March 22, 2018; Foy, "Awards."

35. Only when Philadelphia announced its participation in late 1987 did any adopting city appear to insist that curriculum be developed on the basis of research: Philadelphia's AWOD programming used curriculum that was developed by Temple University. Murray Dubin, "1-Year Program Celebrates Cultural Diversity in Phila.," *Philadelphia Inquirer*, November 13, 1987.

36. Author interview with Hallie Rosen.

Although reporting on AWOD's adoption in each school district was minimal, some local groups were clearly concerned about the imposition from afar of curriculum that was limited in the topics it covered and not tailored to the conflicts troubling the communities where it was taught. When school officials in Allentown announced that AWOD would be used in classrooms there, a local Lenni Lenape group and a gay group reached out to ask the ADL to include Indigenous and lesbian and gay matters in the curriculum. Both had experienced discrimination as a pressing local problem.[37] Allentown's concerns presaged the ADL's struggle with better-resourced groups in the San Francisco/Bay Area over AWOD's exclusions, and likely reflect parallel concerns among the dozens of other regions where AWOD was adopted. At the same time, the political boundaries of this public program were clearly set by the ADL's ideological commitments. Rosen recalled that the Quaker group American Friends Service Committee (AFSC), which conducted domestic social justice work and supported Palestinian rights, wanted to be among the community groups involved. The Philadelphia ADL director flatly refused them.[38]

AWOD quickly developed enormous reach as it was adopted by one school district after another, driven by the urgency of addressing racial conflict. By 1988, AWOD was rolling out in classrooms and teacher trainings in Los Angeles and New York City. In New York City, *Newsday* reported in March 1989 that the ADL had trained one thousand teachers in a two-week period, and aimed to train a total of ten thousand—about one-sixth of the city's teaching staff—by June of that year. The ADL announced that more than $20 million in airtime had already been devoted to its segments and PSAs.[39] A newspaper reporter's 1989 interview with a white teacher, David Bellel, captured the sense of urgency and the commitment to forging the American melting pot, that drove its adoption.

> The elementary school's mostly Caribbean student body hails from a variety of different islands. This has caused a considerable amount of tension and intergroup hostility, as nationalist pride has turned bitter. Haitians now

37. I could not locate any ADL response to the Lenni Lenape group. The ADL affirmed that sex and sexuality could be covered. It seems unlikely that this promise was fulfilled, though, since the ADL refused to include gay topics in 1988 and had no available content. Erdman, "Groups Announce Effort to Fight Prejudice in L.V."

38. Author interview with Hallie Rosen.

39. The Wishnow Group, "A World of Difference (Overview)," posted April 15, 2015, by Jeffrey Wishnow, YouTube, 13:44, https://www.youtube.com/watch?v=W4hfPTt5-c4.

occupy the bottom of the cultural hierarchy because they have fewer skills than other students, Bellel said. . . . Right now, in the minds of students, the differences among groups are obscuring the vast amount they have in common. . . . "Because times are hard, people take it out on whoever is beneath them on the totem pole—because you see them as possibly passing you by."[40]

Teachers like Bellel felt compelled to support students by educating against these conflicts. Even those who were attentive to the root causes of racism were attracted to "teaching tolerance" as a critical near-term intervention in a fractured society; if it fell short of intervening in racism, it was not particularly objectionable as one tool in a larger toolbox. Perhaps for that reason, the ADL's attack on curriculum with a more systemic, historical approach to racism, like its broader conservative politics, did not impede its progress. Where school officials themselves were conservative, it likely helped.

The ADL's bid to spread AWOD widely was ambitious and resonant of social engineering. A 1989 promotional video pitched it as a "fight for a better America." Echoing postwar intergroup relations, it looked at schools as a vast public ideological infrastructure. The strategy it proposed was to work through "our most impressionable Americans," children and teenagers, and to harness "the power of television."[41] The television strategy was wide-ranging, including "carefully crafted public service announcements, documentaries, news stories, and high quality prime-time specials." In a 1989 promotional video for AWOD, Black, Latinx, Japanese, Jewish, and Polish commenters opened up to the camera about fears that racism was so deep and constant that it might not be remediable, and recounted stories of internalized and external prejudice. Video clips of television talk shows, teacher trainings, student workshops, and documentary news clips showed public conversation as buoying, hopeful, and interracial. In that year, the ADL claimed, AWOD had "brought our agenda" to more than 30 percent of American households (presumably referring to television market share).[42] The popularity of the programming extended the ADL's reach far beyond television and

40. Nick Chiles, "In the Schools: Learning to Combat Inter-, Intra and Just Plain Racism," *Newsday*, March 6, 1989.

41. In a 1989 interview, A World of Difference Institute director Caren Keller Niss affirmed: "We identified who to target: children; where they spend their time: in school and in front of a TV set. It is not an original program, but it seems to work." Keller Niss quoted in Tim Kingston, "Together We Can Make a Difference," *Coming Up!* 10, no. 4 (January 1989), Box 33, Folder 11, CUAV records, GLBT Historical Society; Wishnow Group, "A World of Difference (Overview)."

42. Wishnow Group, "A World of Difference (Overview)."

school audiences. It developed spin-off programs that invited colleges, corporations, and public and private agencies into the national effort to address racism. "A World of Difference" was followed by "A Workplace of Difference," "A Campus of Difference," and "A Community of Difference," and anti-bias trainings for law enforcement and others.[43] They elevated the ADL to a presumptive role as education expert, authority on civil rights issues across racial, ethnic, and identity groups, and vetted vendor for public procurements. The effect was cyclical: The ADL established a slew of new relationships with major media, public school systems, and local governments. As it did so, its standing as a partner for such institutions appeared to increase.

A striking feature of AWOD in this early stage—suddenly and massively scaled up with a vast new set of state partners—was its inconsistency, or at least porous boundaries. In some cases AWOD staff tried to make the program's intervention more substantive.[44] Rosen recalled a national AWOD staff conference in Chicago in 1988 or 1989 in which Black ADL staff members, realizing that they would never advance to leadership in a white, Jewish-led organization working on racism, opened a serious discussion of white privilege. "The people who were doing the workshops for [the staff] weren't ready . . . to really talk about institutional racism and systemic racism," she recalled. But where those staff members were implementing the program, they brought their own understandings of racism. "I would often say . . . 'I'm pretty sure the national office . . . doesn't really know what the A World of Difference staff is doing.'"[45] Even official ADL productions conveyed varied approaches to the subject. Alongside candid, confessional clips about painful individual experiences of racism, the ADL's videos presented invitations to consider structural matters: A Black father and son in a car being racially profiled by police in a suburban neighborhood, for example, seemed by design to demand an accounting for racialized space, class, housing, and policing. However, the same series presented speakers who steadfastly described racism in race-liberal terms as interpersonal bias. Over Waylon Jennings's country

43. Rosen credits the expansion of AWOD to workplaces and beyond, beginning within the first several years of the program, to New York ADL director Caryl Stern.

44. In 1988, the AFT's newly elected president was Suall's SDUSA comrade Sandra Feldman. By 1989, Feldman had sent nine thousand AFT members to AWOD trainings. Even if AWOD was not part of a specific cadre project, Feldman's relationship with Suall likely influenced the AFT's embrace of the program. Felicia R. Lee, "Intolerance Will Be Topic for Students," *New York Times*, September 18, 1989.

45. Author interview with Hallie Rosen.

song "America," a closing clip renewed the call to intergroup relations: "After more than two hundred years, our strength is our diversity. Together we can make a world of difference."[46] These inconsistencies lent AWOD legitimacy as a facilitator of fairly expansive and inclusive conversations on race. As a result of the promise conveyed by these moments of openness, AWOD itself became contested space in which communities of color and queers struggled against the ADL for control over definitions of rights, race, and antiracism.

The implementation of "A World of Difference" in the San Francisco Bay Area is unusually well documented. In 1988, local groups in the Bay Area were strong enough to undertake a sustained battle with the Central Pacific regional ADL to challenge the program. Unlike Zakim's Boston ADL, the Central Pacific ADL office did not have a strong foothold in local racial justice organizing. To the contrary, Arab community organizations and anti-Zionism played a central role in local politics. In fact, one-third of Zakim's blacklist of pro-Arab sympathizers had consisted of Northern California groups operating on and off campus. In the preceding years, the public projects of the Central Pacific ADL focused on Israel: supporting the migration of Soviet Jews, opposing the Arab Boycott, and establishing cultural relations between Israel and the US.

Bay Area politics in the late 1980s were closely attuned to Third World popular movements and efforts to repress them, whether by local forces or US interventions. A 1983 referendum in San Francisco had called for an end to federal aid to El Salvador; a 1987 referendum had adopted a boycott of Apartheid South Africa. In 1987, as the Palestinian uprisings of the First Intifada garnered global attention and further exposed Israeli military repression, San Francisco and Berkeley erupted in conflict over referenda supporting Palestinian rights. The San Francisco resolution called for recognition of a Palestinian right to self-determination. In Berkeley, voters were deciding whether to make Gaza's Jabaliya refugee camp a sister city, as they had partnered with cities in El Salvador, Nicaragua, and South Africa. The resolutions threatened to define Israel as a racial, colonial project in the image of the South African Apartheid regime, and to challenge US funding. Organizing to pass the resolutions in both cities was undertaken by groups spanning Arab, Jewish/left, Mexican, queer, and Black communities, along

46. Wishnow Group, "A World of Difference (Overview)."

with religious and interfaith leadership groups, and with support from national Arab organizations. In Berkeley, the Jewish left led the "Yes" organizing. The opposition was mounted by mainstream Jewish organizations, including the Central Pacific ADL, also with support from national groups including the ADL and AIPAC. In San Francisco, "almost every public official in the area including San Francisco Mayor Art Agnos and California senators Pete Wilson and Alan Cranston" aligned with the "No" campaign. In national politics, however, these events produced ten state Democratic Party resolutions in support of Palestinian rights, and a debate at the party's national convention in July 1988.[47] In short, anti-Zionist organizing posed a substantive challenge to the Bay Area's strong, and strongly Zionist, major Jewish organizations.[48]

The ADL was organizing to quash two threads of opposition. One was Jewish dissent, which was taking shape in response to Israel's 1982 invasion of Lebanon and the massacre of Palestinians at the Sabra and Shatila refugee camps. The shocking brutality of the massacre had created a climate of possibility for the first organized Jewish criticism of Israel, Ezra Berkley Nepon writes. A new set of US Jews had come to understand Palestinian resistance as political, and to reject the Zionist claim that it was antisemitic.[49] While there had always been Jews on the left who opposed Zionism, this new critique—which included staff and members of mainstream Jewish groups and reached a substantial scale, with five thousand members and forty-five chapters—threatened the purported "Jewish consensus." Even more threatening, it galvanized Jewish objections to settlements, which were a core element of Israeli colonial strategy and needed US financial backing.[50] The ADL, along with other major Jewish organizations, mounted a strong campaign to reshape media coverage of the war and suppress New Jewish Agenda, the organization leading this work.[51]

47. Andrea Barron, "Referenda on the Palestinian Question in Four US Cities," *Journal of Palestine Studies* 18, no. 4 (1989): 71–83.

48. For an account of the historical political entrenchment of Zionist-motivated institutions, actors, and funders in the Bay Area, see Tallie Ben-Daniel, "Branding Israel: Queer Markets and Politics in San Francisco and Tel Aviv" (PhD diss., University of California, Davis, 2014).

49. Ezra Berkley Nepon, *Justice, Justice Shall You Pursue* (Thread Makes Blanket Press, 2012), 28.

50. Nepon, *Justice, Justice Shall You Pursue*, 9, 13–14, 36.

51. The ADL's media campaign crystallized in its 1982 report *Television Network Coverage of the War in Lebanon*, which charged news networks with overemphasizing Israeli

At the same time, the ADL was alarmed by the development of a legible, vocal Arab American political constituency. Arab organizing had been galvanized by the Six-Day War and, in the early 1970s, by the FBI's Operation Boulder, the first War on Terror–style program of surveillance, interrogation, and deportation of Arabs and Iranians in the US (1972–74). By the mid-1980s, several national Arab political organizations were working to carve out an Arab representational politics: Among others, the national Arab American Institute was conducting electoral work, and the American-Arab Anti-Discrimination Committee was conducting defense work along much the same lines as the ADL.[52] The ADL labeled these groups "PLO fronts" or artificial groups funded by Arab oil interests, with the aim of preventing elected officials and candidates from engaging with them. It had circulated blacklists of the leadership of most, if not all, Arab representational organizations in 1975 and again in 1983.[53] Northern California was a central site of Arab community organizing—so consequential that the ADL's blacklist devoted an entire section to denouncing its members.[54]

In addition to its concerns about Jewish and Arab organizing, the ADL had directed sustained hostile attention to the left in the Bay Area, as the 1993 spying scandal later revealed. It surveilled, infiltrated, and worried especially about organizations of people of color in support of anticolonial movements—Palestinian resistance in particular. The Bay Area was a site where Cold War Americanism was failing to hold. Viewing the left as a bilious scourge, and education as a crucial way to stop it, the ADL had plenty of reason to set its sights on Bay Area schools.

AWOD began in California as an agreement with the San Francisco Unified School District. To tailor the curriculum, the ADL promised to convene local activist groups as partners. In April 1988, ADL officials recruited one

---

censorship of information, and favoring Palestinian narratives by portraying them "in a romanticized light, as determined resisters" as well as reporting PLO data (which the ADL claimed was exaggerated) on casualties and refugees. ADL report reprinted in Landrum R. Bolling, *Reporters Under Fire: US Media Coverage of Conflicts in Lebanon and Central America* (Routledge, 2019); Nepon, *Justice, Justice Shall You Pursue*, 23, 28.

52. Pamela E. Pennock, *The Rise of the Arab American Left: Activists, Allies, and Their Fight Against Imperialism and Racism, 1960s–1980s* (University of North Carolina Press, 2017), 212, 224.

53. Anti-Defamation League, "Target USA: The Arab Propaganda Offensive," 1975.

54. See chapter 4 for a discussion of this ADL undertaking.

hundred local civil rights groups and government agencies to create a new nonprofit organization. Its purpose was to vet AWOD curriculum and contribute television content. The ADL initially called the group "the Greater San Francisco Civil Rights Coalition," optimistically naming it after the Boston coalition whose deep historical relationships had made AWOD successful there.[55] The invention did not suit the local groups. Instead, the ADL's project went forward as Bay Area United (BAU), a formal organization cochaired by the ADL regional director and a representative from suburban Concord's city government. BAU members were groups covering a vast array of racial and economic justice issues, as well as city and county officials and human rights agencies' staff. They were to participate in a year-long plan that mirrored Boston's program, featuring television programming with local station KGO-TV, to which they could submit material for PSAs about their own concerns.[56] The AWOD study guide would be written by someone chosen by the ADL, and input would be solicited from local organizations on the draft.[57] The program would work with every school district in the greater Bay Area and train three thousand teachers.[58]

From among this group, a few leading organizations emerged to take on the work. Among them was Community United Against Violence (CUAV), which had formed in 1979 to combat attacks on queer communities, mostly by white supremacists, youths, and police. Its roots were in queer street life—early meeting minutes show the directors struggling to balance the demands of running a nonprofit against the countercultural norms of queer community—and as it matured, it had carried along commitments to representing community needs regardless of whether they distressed political leaders.[59] CUAV's ally, activist Fred Persily, joined BAU on behalf of the Contra Costa Human Rights Commission. Lindsey Jang represented Break the Silence, a coalition to combat anti-Asian violence, which formed in 1982 after the murder of Vincent Chin by laid-off auto workers in supposed revenge for the loss of jobs to the

55. Anti-Defamation League to Diane Christenson, June 1, 1988, Box 33, Folder 11, CUAV records, GLBT Historical Society.

56. Handwritten meeting notes, unsigned, n.d. (June 1988, Jill Tregor?), Box 33, Folder 11, CUAV records, GLBT Historical Society.

57. Handwritten meeting notes reflecting meeting with ADL staffers Ron Berman, Amy Schoenblum, and Richard Hirschhaut, n.d., unsigned (Jill Tregor), Box 33, Folder 11, CUAV records, GLBT Historical Society.

58. Handwritten meeting notes, unsigned, n.d. (June 1988, Jill Tregor?).

59. CUAV Board of Directors meeting minutes 1978–83; 1984–86, Box 1, Folder 1–32; Box 3, Folder 1–25, CUAV records, GLBT Historical Society.

Japanese auto industry.[60] Another group was not recruited by the ADL, but, with the support of participating groups, demanded to participate: NAJDA, Women Concerned About the Middle East.[61] No Black community groups participated, although some were listed as BAU members.

The steering committee members were interested in the possibility that AWOD could address the violence they collectively faced. They were also keenly aware of the ADL's efforts to discount the racial politics of Palestine, its attacks on Arab communities, and its habit of campaigning on antisemitism at the expense of other communities. But circumstances demanded their participation. "If a program was going to end up in the San Francisco Unified School District because the ADL was offering it, and SFUSD was willing to say yes to them, we didn't want to miss an opportunity to influence that. Neither Break the Silence Coalition Against Anti-Asian Violence nor Community United Against Violence had that kind of access on our own," CUAV director Jill Tregor explained. Indeed, they understood that they were already negotiating with the ADL, whether they accepted or refused the offer: "Even though many of us had a strongly negative position against their work, we could not ignore them without being tainted by accusations of antisemitism. There weren't visible alternative Jewish organizations that were working in the field of hate violence that we could align ourselves with instead.... We mostly tried to ignore the ADL."[62] Finally, as the groups faced daily crises of violence, they calculated that they could not afford to leave the subject to the ADL. Tregor said flatly, "We didn't trust that the ADL's curriculum wouldn't just spread more hate."[63]

Although the local groups joined BAU under these constraints, the groups' skepticism led them to press for accountability. At a meeting early in

60. Michael Chang, "Bridging the Gap: The Role of Asian American Public Interest Organizations in the Pursuit of Legal and Social Remedies to Anti-Asian Hate Crimes," *Asian American Law Journal* 7, no. 6 (2000): 139–60.

61. Author interview with Jill Tregor, April 19, 2018. NAJDA representatives Audrey Shabbas had already been targeted by the ADL: as a subject of spying, which she did not yet know, and in 1984, when the ADL had forced the San Jose Art Museum to cancel her planned exhibition on Saudi culture. Shabbas recollects this incident in a memorial post for Middle East scholar Elizabeth Fernea, whose work was to be shown in the exhibition. "In Memoriam: Elizabeth Warnock Fernea" (Shabbas comment), *ShelfLife@Texas* (blog), December 5, 2008, https://web.archive.org/web/20150413202532/http://sites.utexas.edu /shelflife/2008/12/04/in-memoriam-elizabeth-warnock-fernea/.

62. Author interview with Jill Tregor.

63. Author interview with Jill Tregor.

the process, the ADL described the successes of Boston that would now be transferred to California.[64] As Tregor listened, she jotted down questions: "Who are we teaching, what happened in Boston, why are we here today? . . . Boston [has] higher anti-Asian violence now (post AWOD) than possibly anywhere."[65] The ADL did not answer questions. Instead, it alternately dismissed, postponed, and ignored calls for information and a group role in decision-making. The ADL's promises of collaborative curriculum development also did not materialize. The local organizers worried particularly because the ADL discussed a teacher study guide that had been drafted (presumably by ADL staff), but had not allowed them to see it. By August 1988 the steering groups were already seeking workarounds that might let them be heard and contribute ideas. Finding the Central Pacific ADL director Richard Hirschhaut inaccessible, they met with Ron Berman, the regional ADL lay president. He agreed to facilitate getting their ideas to Hirschhaut to influence AWOD decisions. Rather than making the process more collaborative, Tregor noted, this reaffirmed the ADL's total control.[66]

When BAU participants did see the study guide, their assessment worsened. Break the Silence, NAJDA, and CUAV discussed the situation, and in October CUAV wrote to ADL staff with their complaints. They echoed earlier antiracist organizers' conflicts with the ADL. CUAV's community organizer at the time, Lester Olmsted-Rose, penned the letter. "First, there is a highly ethnocentric view expressed in the guide. Remember, white folks didn't discover America, and it was not a vast, empty land when we came here," he wrote. "The guide presumes that asians, native americans, latinos, and others are outside the dominant culture." The letter gestured also to the ADL's move to exonerate the liberal state and to declare "prejudice" an aberration from an otherwise fair and equal society. The curriculum, he wrote, "has a propensity to isolate the problems of hate and prejudice. . . . The guide doesn't do enough to challenge the prejudice in the 'white middle class,' focusing instead on skinheads, nazis, and organized hate groups. Speaking from our experience at CUAV, hate violence comes, overwhelmingly, from the 'mainstream.'"

64. A World of Difference meeting agenda and minutes of prior meeting, n.d. (before July 1988), Box 33, Folder 11, CUAV records, GLBT Historical Society.

65. Handwritten meeting notes, unsigned, n.d. (June 1988, Jill Tregor?).

66. Handwritten meeting notes reflecting meeting with ADL staffers Ron Berman, Amy Schoenblum, and Richard Hirschhaut, n.d. and unsigned (Jill Tregor), Box 33, Folder 11, CUAV records, GLBT Historical Society.

Even worse, as Tregor had feared, the curriculum itself was a vehicle for racist ideas: As Olmstead-Rose described, it contained "numerous references, phrases, and implications offensive to people included under the 'race, religion, ethnicity' headings."[67] The letter was not the end of the community's objections. Lindsey Jang called the ADL's coverage of Japanese internment "horrifying in its brevity . . . disrespectful" and noted that none of the guides' material had come from Asian writers. About the ADL's co-optation of Asian voices, he complained: "They didn't allow people to speak for themselves . . . there is a difference about someone talking about you than talking for yourself."[68] NAJDA director Audrey Shabbas noted that a section on Muslim and Middle Eastern peoples featured an Iranian child who deserved welcome because she had been persecuted at home for her interest in America, which reaffirmed Islamophobic stereotypes rather than undoing them.[69] The BAU steering committee also found that no content on LGBTQ or AIDS discrimination had been included (despite the ADL's "reasonably good record on gay and lesbian issues"), and none on disability-related discrimination. Persily had raised the need to include gay and lesbian issues at the first meeting and had failed more than once to find a satisfactory answer.[70]

Perhaps most foreign to the ADL's education staff was the demand to teach about queer lives. It was new, and, as ADL staff pointed out, not an accepted topic for teaching or a settled area of rights. It was catalyzed by organizing to stop the stigmatization of HIV/AIDS, which was not only driving anti-queer violence but blocking research and treatment to stop the virus. The ADL was not a supporter of AIDS organizing or of the rights of people with HIV/AIDS. Still, calls to the ADL for the inclusion of material on gay, lesbian, and AIDS-related discrimination were soon echoed in other major cities where AWOD was rolling out. In June 1988 New York City's mayor, Ed Koch, wrote to the New York ADL to say that a New York City anti-bias program that left out sexual orientation would be "ironic and indeed incomprehensible."[71] In August, ACT UP/Boston wrote to Zakim

67. Lester Olmsted-Rose to Amy Schoenbaum, October 26, 1988, Box 33, Folder 11, CUAV records, GLBT Historical Society.

68. Lindsey Jang, quoted in Kingston, "Together We Can Make a Difference."

69. Bay Area United Steering Committee, resignation letter—draft, Box 33, Folder 11, CUAV records, GLBT Historical Society.

70. A World of Difference meeting agenda and minutes of prior meeting (before July 1988), Box 33, Folder 11, CUAV records, GLBT Historical Society.

71. Koch followed this impassioned paragraph with an assurance that he would not punish the ADL for refusing to address the queer community's concerns: "I hope that you reconsider

making the same complaint about AWOD, this time in the context of protesting the New England ADL's plans to honor the right-wing, homophobic Cardinal Bernard Law.[72] In October, Los Angeles gay activists met with AWOD staff to contest the total absence of sexual orientation and AIDS from AWOD's media campaign, and in January 1989 ACT UP/LA protested the launch of the school program.[73] Representatives of San Francisco's gay synagogue, Sha'ar Zahav, announced in frustration that the ADL did not "comprehend the nature of prejudice."[74] CUAV's director began sending information about the conflict to Kevin Berrill at the National Gay and Lesbian Task Force (NGLTF) and soon added requests for backup.[75] NGLTF organizers began to negotiate with ADL national director Abe Foxman, raising community complaints about AWOD to the national level.

In response to these complaints, Hirschhaut and the ADL's national AWOD chair Caren Keller Niss insisted that AWOD covered only "racial, ethnic, and religious" matters. A local paper quoted a "genuinely perplexed" Keller Niss. She said: "It is not a matter of saying to the gay community we are not going to include your issues, (but) the special things that you want are not applicable to race and religious issues." But as BAU members pressed, the ADL's rationales came into sharper focus. They told the reporter that covering gay issues would dilute their discussions of prejudice, and further, that

your position. Even if you don't, I applaud your efforts and wish you well." Koch was a devoted supporter of Israel; presumably he had other business with the ADL, which was a core member among New York–based Israel advocacy organizations. Mayor Ed Koch to Carol [*sic*] Lister, June 24, 1988, MS Lesbian Herstory Archives: Subject Files: Part 6: Spinsters-Youth Folder No. 15080, Archives of Sexuality and Gender, https://link-gale-com.i.ezproxy.nypl.org/apps /doc/DJBBRF161390396/AHSI?u=nypl&sid=bookmark-AHSI&xid=42996e18&pg=28, accessed January 9, 2019; Jonathan Soffer, *Ed Koch and the Rebuilding of New York City* (Columbia University Press, 2012), 82–87.

72. ACT UP/Boston to Leonard Zakim, August 24, 1988, Box 106, Folder 6, Series II, Field Files: Civil Rights Organizations: ADL, 1984–90, National Gay and Lesbian Task Force records, #7301, Cornell University Library.

73. ACT UP/Los Angeles, "A World of Indifference," press release, January 16, 1989, Box 5, Folder 6, ACT UP/Los Angeles Records, Coll 2011-010, ONE Archives, University of Southern California, Los Angeles.

74. Kingston, "Together We Can Make a Difference."

75. Jill Tregor and Lester Olmsted-Rose to the editor of the *Bay Area Reporter*, August 23, 1988; and Jill Tregor and Lester Olmsted-Rose to Eva Paterson and members of the Coalition on Civil Rights, October 27, 1988, sent to Kevin Berrill with a note from Olmsted-Rose, Box 106, Folder 7, Series II, Field Files: Civil Rights Organizations: ADL: Education Project: "A World of Difference," 1988–91, National Gay and Lesbian Task Force records, #7301, Cornell University.

AWOD was a private program over which the ADL held control.[76] They told BAU members that according to ADL national policy—which superseded BAU's authority—the study guides could not be made "controversial" and in fact specifically excluded gay, lesbian, and disability issues.[77] In later discussions with the NGLTF, they added more pointedly that sexual orientation content would prevent them from accessing schools, prime-time media spots, and backer funding.[78] In short, because "tolerance" of queer people was not a well-established American value, they would not include it.

As BAU steering group members came to understand the ADL's refusals as ideology and policy, they talked about quitting the coalition. They acknowledged to each other, and occasionally to the ADL, that they were being used to promote a program that fundamentally excluded them. They noted, too, that the ADL viewed queer identity as "political," Middle Eastern identities intolerable, and the Nazi Holocaust as a central story that eclipsed others' experiences of racist violence.[79] Hirschhaut had argued to them that the connections and exposure they could get from participating in AWOD were benefit enough, which they found both worrisome and insulting.[80] (This argument ran again later through the ADL's dealings with NGLTF on hate crimes bills: that excluding lesbian and gay content so that bills could pass was ultimately good for the gay community.)[81] For the moment, the BAU steering group stayed: They were unwilling to hand over the region's antiracism education to the ADL. Instead, the Bay Area AWOD planning devolved into open conflict in which community groups leveraged one institution after another

76. Kingston, "Together We Can Make a Difference."

77. Handwritten NGLTF meeting notes reflecting meeting with ADL staffers Ron Berman, Amy Schoenblum, and Richard Hirschhaut, n.d., unsigned, Box 33, Folder 11, CUAV records, GLBT Historical Society; Note from Lester Olmsted-Rose to Carmen [Vasquez, San Francisco Human Rights Commission], November 8, 1988, Box 33, Folder 11, CUAV records, GLBT Historical Society.

78. Handwritten meeting notes, unsigned, n.d., Box 106, Folder 7, Series II, Field Files: Civil Rights Organizations: ADL: Education Project: "A World of Difference," 1988–91, National Gay and Lesbian Task Force records, #7301, Cornell University Library.

79. Bay Area United resignation letter (n.d., April 1989?), handwritten draft, likely authored by Tregor, Box 33, Folder 11, CUAV records, GLBT Historical Society.

80. Letter from Jill Tregor, Lindsey Jang, Fred Persily, Audrey Shabbas, and Robin Wu to Interested Parties, April 5, 1989, Box 106, Folder 7, Series II, Field Files: Civil Rights Organizations: ADL: Education Project: "A World of Difference," 1988–1991, National Gay and Lesbian Task Force records, #7301, Cornell University Library.

81. Kevin Berrill to Charney V. Bromberg, February 7, 1989, Box 106, Folder 7, Series II, Field Files: Civil Rights Organizations: ADL, 1981–91, National Gay and Lesbian Task Force records, #7301, Cornell University.

(and also direct action) to pressure the ADL. BAU asked the San Francisco Human Rights Commission to take up its complaints with the ADL, which it did in a November 1988 letter calling for inclusion of "sexual orientation, gender, and disability"—but not addressing race.[82] The Bay Area Network of Gay and Lesbian Educators (BANGLE) reached out to a sympathetic assistant superintendent in charge of curriculum and also tried on its own to get the ADL to distribute pamphlets to its trainees on the impact of homophobia on students.[83] The ADL stonewalled and delayed, then refused on the grounds that BANGLE should have asked sooner and that the materials would have to be approved by AWOD participating organizations.[84] Outraged, BANGLE went to the teacher training in striped suits with pink triangles so that they resembled gay World War II concentration camp prisoners, and distributed their materials. Adding to the trouble, BAU representatives encountered an AWOD exhibit displaying "materials from the Israeli embassy and a brand new ADL publication, *A Pocket Guide to the PLO.*"[85]

BAU groups raised the alarm among other community groups and in the media, and more organizations began to weigh in. The AIDS National Interfaith Network, a national coalition of church hierarchies, major Jewish organizations, and AIDS policy watchdogs set out to "clarify" with the ADL and take unspecified action.[86] The National Gay and Lesbian Task Force, already working with the ADL on national hate crimes advocacy, tried a collegial approach with Abe Foxman. Writing to him in December 1988, NGLTF's director Jeffrey Levi deployed a host of arguments: He cited statistics on the relevance of anti-gay bias to broader anti-bias efforts and flattered the ADL by recalling its past instances of support for gay rights. Levi even offered a personal reflection on the meaning to him, in his personal capacity as a gay

82. Human Rights Commission of the City and County of San Francisco, Minutes of the Meeting of Thursday, November 10, 1988, Box 33, Folder 11, CUAV records, GLBT Historical Society.

83. Handwritten pink memo (unsigned, likely Jill Tregor), November 1988?, Box 33, Folder 11, CUAV records, GLBT Historical Society.

84. It is unclear whether "participating organizations" meant the Bay Area United steering committee, which had been battling the ADL to include just such material; or whether Hirschhaut told Birle that each school would have to approve the use of gay/lesbian materials. Robert Birle to AWOD participants, February 11, 1989, Box 33, Folder 11, CUAV records, GLBT Historical Society.

85. Audrey Shabbas, "Coalition Raises Doubts About ADL," *Washington Report on Middle East Affairs*, June 1989.

86. Rev. Jeremy Landau to Lester Olmsted-Rose, November 7, 1988, Box 33, Folder 11, CUAV records, GLBT Historical Society.

Jewish person, of writing to the ADL on the anniversary of Kristallnacht.[87] Bay Area United steering committee members wrote to AWOD's funders and program participants laying out the problems of exclusion.

None of these tactics succeeded. Hirschhaut's ADL office turned to two strategies to push back. It accused gay groups of "endangering the real benefit that 'AWOD' is providing to so many people" and entirely ignored the charges of racism in its texts.[88] At the same time, it engaged in a gaslighting campaign. Staff put off activist queries by referring to a decision supposedly made at a meeting they missed, and pretended there was an "agreement" to "include" gay and lesbian issues, by which they meant simply listing CUAV as a local resource and adding a sentence in the guide to say that AWOD's discussion of prejudice *could* be applied to issues not directly raised there. ADL staff wrote a four-page letter to the *Bay Area Reporter* listing their bona fides on gay rights and implying that gay and lesbian groups should stop being concerned with themselves and stand up for others. Hirschhaut chided gay groups for their purported selfishness by using the words of the Jewish sage Hillel, often invoked in the wake of the Nazi genocide as a reminder of the need for solidarity with marginalized groups. Hirschhaut suggested that gay and lesbian advocates ask themselves, "If I am only for myself, then who am I?"[89]

In April 1989, one year after the formation of Bay Area United, the five remaining members of the steering committee finally quit. Their letter revisited the omissions in the curriculum and the racism of its existing content: "The study guide did not adequately treat even the groups it targeted. The section on the internment of Japanese Americans during World War II glosses over the issues and its treatment of an Iranian child reinforces negative stereotypes of Muslim and Eastern Peoples. . . . We no longer consider our continued efforts to make the project work anything other than an exercise in futility."[90] With BAU's withdrawal, ironically, public critiques of AWOD's racism disappeared in California. (At least one other challenge emerged in 1992, in Denver, on the basis of excluding Arab representation.

87. Jeffrey Levi to Abe Foxman, November 9, 1988, Box 33, Folder 11, CUAV records, GLBT Historical Society.

88. Richard Hirschhaut and Ron Berman to the *Bay Area Reporter*, December 29, 1988, Box 33, Folder 11, CUAV records, GLBT Historical Society.

89. Hirschhaut and Berman to the *Bay Area Reporter*, December 29, 1988.

90. Letter from Tregor et al. to Interested Parties, April 5, 1989.

That challenge was similarly held off with bureaucratic maneuvering.)[91] While Bay Area activism around homophobia, racism, and colonialism were tightly connected, the nationally networked gay challenge to AWOD was led by single-issue groups, primarily the NGLTF with support from the new Gay and Lesbian Alliance Against Defamation (GLAAD).[92] ACT UP chapters fought AWOD; they also periodically criticized the ADL for its embrace of right-wingers who embodied a range of ills including sexism, union-busting, and imperialism.[93] Although the NGLTF's directors had been alerted to concerns about materials on Arabs and Asians in AWOD, these issues never appeared on their agenda for moving the ADL.[94]

In fact, although the AWOD conflict was often quite hostile, it was a bridge for the NGLTF's relationship with the ADL. Its organizers had been petitioning the ADL since 1984, as states began to adopt hate crimes legislation, for its support to make anti-gay violence a recognized issue and including sexual orientation in the statutes. In cordial letters responding to NGLTF queries from 1984 to 1988, from a variety of ADL national and regional offices, ADL leaders refused to stake out any public position on sexual orientation. Instead, they offered generalized opposition to violence and hate groups—sometimes positioning itself as an ally of the NGLTF but never asserting a policy demand. In 1984, ADL director Nathan Perlmutter wrote to the US Commission on Civil Rights ostensibly in support of the NGLTF's proposal to study anti-gay violence: "The most awful stain left by bigotry on American history—and its most grievous affront against our country's ideals—is the record of violence committed by haters against the hated, whose 'guilt' and vulnerability has been that they are 'different.' . . . Americans as individuals, however stereotyped as 'different,' have a basic

91. Records of this battle are preserved in the Allan Solomonow papers, 1944–2016 [bulk: 1960–2009], Ms. Coll. 1247, Kislak Center for Special Collections, Rare Books and Manuscripts, University of Pennsylvania.

92. GLAAD/LA to Kevin Berrill, January 1990 (sender name illegible), Box 106, Folder 7, Series II, Field Files: Civil Rights Organizations: ADL: Education Project: "A World of Difference," 1988–91, National Gay and Lesbian Task Force records, #7301, Cornell University.

93. See Joe Ferson, "Jewish Group Honors Cardinal Law; 5 Gay-Rights Supporters Arrested," *Boston Globe*, October 7, 1988.

94. Kevin Berrill, handwritten call notes, "SF/LA A World of Difference," n.d., Box 106, Folder 7, Series II, p. 35, Field Files: Civil Rights Organizations: ADL: Education Project: "A World of Difference," 1988–91, National Gay and Lesbian Task Force records, #7301, Cornell University.

right to be free from societal violence."[95] Despite these oblique overtures, the refusal to name anti-queer violence was steadfast. Two years later, in 1986, Perlmutter's deputy, civil rights director Justin Finger, responded to yet another request for recognition. Kevin Berrill had asked the ADL to issue a resolution condemning anti-gay violence. The answer was less than warm. Instead of the resolution, Finger pointed to a two-year-old letter that Perlmutter had written to the US Commission on Civil Rights as "the official policy of ADL on the subject" and told Berrill he was "free to use it."[96]

The NGLTF's decision to cultivate the ADL as a national partner is evident across this period, in spite of the ADL's regular refusals and broken promises. The ADL's occasional movement toward inclusion, and the encouragement of some ADL staff members who advocated from within, kept the NGLTF hopeful.[97] Adding urgency, the NGLTF was developing a national legislative strategy, the emerging Hate Crimes Statistics Act, for which it needed the ADL's support.[98] Berrill tried one ADL director after another between 1984 and 1990, conducting the NGLTF's research using the ADL's own statistics as a model, and asking them to use their national platform to communicate that anti-gay attacks were a problem commensurate with racial, ethnic, and religiously targeted violence.[99] The ADL quietly adopted

95. Nathan Perlmutter to Kevin Berrill, December 20, 1984, Box 106, Folder 6, Series II, Field Files: Civil Rights Organizations: ADL, 1984–90, National Gay and Lesbian Task Force records, #7301, Cornell University.

96. Justin Finger to Kevin Berrill, June 4, 1986, Box 106, Folder 6, Series II, Field Files: Civil Rights Organizations: ADL, 1984–90, National Gay and Lesbian Task Force records, #7301, Cornell University.

97. Kevin Berrill to Jill Kahn, November 14, 1989, Box 106, Folder 6, Series II, Field Files: Civil Rights Organizations: ADL, 1984–90, National Gay and Lesbian Task Force records, #7301, Cornell University.

98. Kevin Berrill to Jess Hordes, February 9, 1987, in which Berrill notes that it would be impossible to pass a federal bill to collect data on anti-gay hate crimes if they were not included in a broader set of identity categories. Box 106, Folder 6, Series II, Field Files: Civil Rights Organizations: ADL, 1984–90, National Gay and Lesbian Task Force records, #7301, Cornell University.

99. Following the initial 1984 letter that secured the ADL endorsement of the NGLTF's grant application, pleas from Berrill on this subject went to Justin Finger, director of the ADL's Civil Rights Division (June 4, 1986); Jess Hordes (February 2, 1987); ADL counsel Steven Freeman (May 18, 1987); Justin Finger, now the ADL's associate national director (September 4, 1987); and again Steven Freeman (January 1, 1988). Later letters did not directly address the ADL's federal work but rather the ADL's refusal to honor its commitments to inclusion in state-level work that would lay the groundwork for pending federal legislation. These include letters to Charney V. Bromberg (February 7, 1989); Leonard Zakim (July 7, 1989); and Jeffrey Ross (November 15, 1989). Each letter, except possibly the

internal policy on gay inclusion as early as 1986, when its advisory national commission of local leaders adopted a resolution that the ADL would (or should) support legislation "such as the New York City ordinance" that bars sexual orientation discrimination in employment, housing, and public accommodations.[100] But six months later, the ADL was still refusing to support federal data collection on anti-gay violence, fearing that mentioning sexual orientation would render the proposed federal bill "controversial."[101] Apparently disinterested in the crisis of violence generated by AIDS backlash, it did not relent until the NGLTF presented a laundry list of endorsers, including Congressman John Conyers, the ACLU, the American Jewish Congress, the Religious Action Center, the Lutheran Council, and the American Psychological Association. In September 1987 the ADL finally agreed to write a letter in support of the inclusive bill, HR 3193.[102] A few months later it published its own major report on white supremacist violence, *Hate Groups in America*, without any reference to skinheads' habitual, ideological violence against queers.[103]

Finally in July 1988 the ADL national director acceded to the NGLTF's prodding to add sexual orientation to the ADL's model statute for state legislative campaigns.[104] The move was tactical, rather than conveying real support. At the same moment, the influential New England ADL announced it would honor Cardinal Bernard Law, a vocal opponent of gay rights and AIDS

last, produced a renewed refusal by the ADL. Box 106, Folder 6, Series II, Field Files: Civil Rights Organizations: ADL, 1984–90, National Gay and Lesbian Task Force records, #7301, Cornell University.

100. Memo from Justin Finger to Kevin Berrill, describing resolution of June 5, 1986, dated June 18, 1986, Box 106, Folder 6, Series II, Field Files: Civil Rights Organizations: ADL, 1984–90, National Gay and Lesbian Task Force records, #7301, Cornell University.

101. Kevin Berrill to Jess Hordes, February 9, 1987, Box 106, Folder 6, Series II, Field Files: Civil Rights Organizations: ADL, 1984–90, National Gay and Lesbian Task Force records, #7301, Cornell University.

102. US Congress, Hate Crimes Statistics Act, HR 3193, 100th Cong., 1st sess., introduced in House on August 7, 1987.

103. Anti-Defamation League of B'nai B'rith, *Hate Groups in America: A Record of Bigotry and Violence* (1988).

104. National Gay and Lesbian Task Force, "Anti-Defamation League Model Statute Addresses Anti-Gay Violence: NGLTF State Action Lobby Initiates National Campaign for Legislation to Combat Hate Crimes," press release, Box 46, Folder 62, Series II, Field Files: Anti-Violence Project: Press Releases: ADL Model Statute Addresses Anti-Gay Violence 1988, National Gay and Lesbian Task Force records, #7301, Cornell University.

care, and, activists charged, a proponent of anti-gay violence.[105] In the same month, perhaps hoping to induce the NGLTF to smooth gay community outrage over Cardinal Law, the ADL's Midwest director informed Berrill that the ADL would endorse Missouri and Chicago hate crimes legislation that included sexual orientation. A few months later, though, the NGLTF noted in outrage that the ADL's Missouri director had refused to include sexual orientation in his proposed legislation, claiming he "forgot," despite having been overheard by an ACLU lobbyist telling "the Senate sponsor to put 'anything' in the bill but sexual orientation." The ADL had similarly betrayed gay activists in Florida and Washington.[106] In July 1989, Zakim announced that the New England ADL would honor the public service of another right-wing Catholic figure, Boston University president John Silber, yielding protests and mockery from the Boston University Gay and Lesbian Alliance and local gay activists.[107] Once again, another ADL office—the national office—invited Kevin Berrill to be a featured speaker (along with Zakim) at its conference on campus bigotry.[108]

This long game played out alongside the ADL's confrontations over AWOD with Bay Area United, and with gay and AIDS groups in Los

105. ACT UP/Boston (Thomas Reeves) to Leonard Zakim, August 24, 1988, Box 106, Folder 6, Series II, Field Files: Civil Rights Organizations: ADL, 1984–90, National Gay and Lesbian Task Force records, #7301, Cornell University.

106. Kevin Berrill to Charney V. Bromberg, February 7, 1989, Box 106, Folder 6, Series II, Field Files: Civil Rights Organizations: ADL, 1984–90, National Gay and Lesbian Task Force records, #7301, Cornell University.

107. A Boston gay organizer sent Zakim a list of Silber's objectionable positions: supporting US aid to El Salvador without concern for its civil rights record; refusing to divest from South Africa, and opposing the African National Congress; supporting ROTC and proposed cutting financial aid to male students who refuse to register for the draft; denying tenure to women professors at Boston University and suggesting that married women's entry to the workforce harmed families; refusing to add sexual orientation to BU hiring and admissions policies, and "equat[ing] such protections with condoning bestiality"; calling anti-AIDS/safer-sex campaigns "immoral, with no merit whatsoever"; and union-busting, pursuing a court ruling preventing the faculty union from collective bargaining. In response to Zakim's insistence that the ADL stood "opposed to bigotry in all its forms," Boston gay and lesbian activists formed a group specifically to protest the ADL, the Committee to Fight Bigotry in All Its Forms. Warren B- to Leonard Zakim, June 26, 1989; and the Committee to Fight Bigotry in All Its Forms to David Rose, Box 106, Folder 6, Series II, Field Files: Civil Rights Organizations: ADL, 1984–90, National Gay and Lesbian Task Force records, #7301, Cornell University.

108. Abe Foxman to Kevin Berrill, August 16, 1989, Box 106, Folder 6, Series II, Field Files: Civil Rights Organizations: ADL, 1984–90, National Gay and Lesbian Task Force records, #7301, Cornell University.

Angeles. As the NGLTF and gay political actors in San Francisco, Los Angeles, and New York organized political officials to push the ADL on anti-bias education, the ADL got an education in the emergent power, political access, and moral authority that gay and lesbian organizations might add to its campaigns. In New York, Mayor Koch followed up his letter calling on the ADL to include sexual orientation by dispatching Lee Hudson, his gay liaison, to the NGLTF's meetings with ADL leadership; so did Governor Mario Cuomo, whose adviser Ginny Apuzzo had been the NGLTF's founding director. In a memo outlining the prospects for moving the Los Angeles ADL to gay inclusion, attorney and GLAAD/LA cofounder Dean Hansell noted that the ADL's liaison "was astonished for example when I described to him the size and scope of the operations of the Gay and Lesbian Community Services Center."[109]

Conversely, queer political leadership would not press the ADL on the questions of race that troubled the implementation of AWOD. CUAV and grassroots queer groups were accountable to their friends and partners in the antiracist, anti-imperialist Bay Area left, but the queer leaders who worked in electoral politics were much less obliged. In San Francisco, the city's Human Rights Commission in December 1988 called on the ADL to add sexual orientation, women, and people with disabilities. Once the queer content had been added, no further objections to the program were made.[110] The critique that AWOD "taught racism rather than diminishing it" was laid aside by the lesbian and gay commissioners who had been CUAV's route for challenging the ADL, as they had been laid aside by the NGTLF and GLAAD, the single-issue gay organizations that had organized enough political force to move the ADL. In fact, the ADL's conquest of CUAV and its transnational antiracist alliances cleared the path for a partnership with gay and lesbian advocacy. In an ironic turn, the ADL's reluctant adoption of lesbian and gay topics now made it appear as a *progressive* actor in political culture.

109. Memo from Dean Hansell to Interested Persons, "Background to the ADL's A World of Difference Campaign," October 22, 1989, Box 106, Folder 7, Series II, Field Files: Civil Rights Organizations: ADL: Education Project: "A World of Difference," 1988–91, National Gay and Lesbian Task Force records, #7301, Cornell University.

110. Larry Martin, "The ADL Should Change Its Policy," *Bay Area Reporter*, December 22, 1988.

SIX

Hate Crimes and Hegemony

THE '80S AND '90S

IN OCTOBER 2023, AS ISRAELI air strikes pounded Gaza and Israeli offi-cials called for exterminating Palestinians, hundreds of thousands of people took to the streets in protests across the United States. In the months that followed, a quickly growing mass movement in the United States demanded an end to the unfolding genocide and named Zionism as a structure of racist violence. The ADL counted each protest as an antisemitic act.[1] Accordingly, it reported a staggering jump in antisemitic incidents. Interviewed on a CNN news segment, ADL CEO Jonathan Greenblatt grimly likened condi-tions in the United States to Nazi Germany: "Many of us did not expect to see these events unfolding right here in America," he lamented.[2] The ADL viewed the protests not just as a threat against Jews, but as an attack on democracy and the United States itself. One day earlier the ADL and the Brandeis Center, its partner in the emerging tactic of lawfare (like warfare, but using law as a weapon), had proposed that student anti-genocide protests might amount to material support for terrorism.[3] CNN news anchor Kasie

---

1. The new emphasis on Zionism as the subject of mass protest was reflected in the repres-sive backlash by universities against such protest. See Carrie Zaremba, "US Universities Spent the Summer Strategizing to Suppress Student Activism. Here Is Their Plan," *Mondoweiss,* September 2, 2024; Emmaia Gelman, "Encampments and the Unshackling of Study," *Newsletter of the Middle East and North Africa Politics Section of APSA* 7, no. 2 (Fall 2024).

2. Jonathan Greenblatt, interview by Kasie Hunt, "Antisemitic Incidents in Russia and at US College Campuses Cause Alarm," CNN, October 31, 2023, https://www.cnn .com/videos/world/2023/10/30/exp-antisemitism-cornell-russia-greenblatt-hunt-intv -103011aseg1-cnni-world.cnn.

3. Jonathan Greenblatt, Alyza D. Lewin, and Kenneth L. Marcus, "ADL and LDB Letter Regarding SJP on College Campuses," October 25, 2023, https://brandeiscenter.com/wp-content/uploads/2023/12/ADL-LDB-Letter-re-SJP-10-25-23-1.pdf. On the rise of lawfare for

Hunt looked shellshocked. "You found that it's risen nearly 400 percent since October 7 compared to the same period last year," she said, "and *last* year was the highest year on record."[4] In fact, the annual statistics had grown nearly continuously for many years. ADL's 2022 report had announced a 36 percent "dramatic increase" and "significant surge" in antisemitic incidents.[5] Before *that*, the ADL had reported a 34 percent surge and record-breaking numbers of incidents in 2021. Counting backward from any point, the history of year-over-year increases in antisemitic incidents suggested that US Jews should exist in a state of terror. As the ADL reported the numbers each year, media outlets habitually amplified them.[6]

Not unusually, then, news outlets carried the ADL's warning about a surge of antisemitism that month, often carrying the details of sensational claims. The fact that the statistics were "preliminary"—based on reports that were unconfirmed—was set aside and reporters rarely questioned the ADL's characterization of protests as anti-Jewish. When key cases that had grabbed headlines were later debunked, news outlets did not issue corrections or revisit their reporting. A case at Cooper Union turned out to be a misrepresentation. Tabloids had falsely reported that Jewish students in the library had been locked in for protection from an "antisemitic mob" during an anti-genocide protest, but in fact police had locked library doors to keep protesters away from administrators' offices.[7] A case at Cornell University seemed to be a badly conceived false flag: A student who posted violent threats against Jewish students said he had hoped they would generate sympathy for Israel. On-the-ground reporting about protests by college newspapers and investigative journalists repeatedly debunked claims that anti-Zionist protests were anti-Jewish. In a granular investigation by *Jewish Currents* in June 2024, reporters found

<hr>

suppressing and criminalizing support for Palestinian liberation and anti-Zionist organizing, see Kay Guinane, *The Alarming Rise of Lawfare to Suppress Civil Society: The Case of Palestine and Israel* (Charity and Security Network), 2021, https://charityandsecurity.org/wp-content/uploads/2021/09/The-Alarming-Rise-of-Lawfare-to-Suppress-Civil-Society.pdf.

4. Greenblatt, interview by Hunt.

5. Anti-Defamation League, *Audit of Antisemitic Incidents 2022*, March 3, 2023.

6. See Ann Marie Awad, "The Difficult Business of Accurately Tracking Anti-Semitism and Hate Crimes in Colorado," Colorado Public Radio, October 30, 2018.

7. Rachel Treisman, "A Former Cornell Student Is Sentenced to 21 Months for Threatening to Kill Jews," NPR, August 13, 2024; Ed Shanahan and Maria Cramer, "Israel-Hamas War Protest Leads to Tense Scene at Cooper Union Library," *New York Times*, October 26, 2023; Joshua Rhett Miller, "Jewish Students Reveal What Happened at Cooper Union Protest," *New York Post*, October 26, 2023.

over one thousand incidents listed that were not actually antisemitic incidents, and conversely that the ADL undercounted antisemitism on the right.[8] Finally, many observers noted that the ADL did not count smears and attacks against anti-Zionist Jews, including those perpetrated by the ADL itself.

Until 2021, ADL statistics were virtually never critically examined by journalists or researchers. In 2021, *Jewish Currents* magazine published the first journalistic investigation of the ADL's statistics in forty years. Journalist Mari Cohen found the ADL's data opaque, often unverifiable, and "conflating weighty incidents with trivial ones—and encouraging others to do the same." Despite those findings, ADL reports continued to be treated as authoritative. Journalism and research called for quotable data on hate crimes, antisemitism, and white nationalism. Those who questioned the data ran the risk of seeming to deny the crisis and refuse those calls. In a circular effect, the reports themselves generated real fears of antisemitism, as well as supercharging data collection and policing efforts. As news outlets picked up the story, they affirmed the ADL's credibility as the watchdog who sounded the alarm.[9] This *antisemitism industrial complex*, as John Harfouch and

8. Mari Cohen, "A Closer Look at the 'Uptick' in Antisemitism," *Jewish Currents*, May 27, 2021; Shane Burley and Naomi Bennett, "Examining the ADL's Antisemitism Audit," *Jewish Currents*, June 17, 2024.

9. So compelling is the idea of unsafety that the ADL has declared that it is dangerous if it does *not* identify surges in antisemitism, or simply has substituted other statistics. Beginning in 2009, national hate crimes statistics and ADL antisemitism statistics declined together for several years. ADL leaders expressed discomfort with the reduction; they seemed to doubt the success of their own efforts to combat antisemitism. The ADL's California legislative director Nancy Appel explained, "When I see high numbers, in a way I find it encouraging because it says to me there's more awareness . . . low reporting means low awareness." In 2011, the ADL's own data showed no increase. However, speaking to state and NGO officials at the Organization for Security and Co-operation with Europe, ADL regional director Robert Trestan cherry-picked and mischaracterized an antisemitism statistic from a different law enforcement dataset, presumably the FBI's Uniform Crime Reporting (UCR). "Data reported by American law enforcement consistently shows that Jews continue to be the number one target of hate crimes in the United States," Trestan warned, emphasizing "a renewed call for action." In reality, UCR data showed about 12 percent of reported hate crimes targeting Jews, while half of the incidents targeted people of color. (Racist incidents are heavily undercounted.) Another 20 percent targeted LGBTQ people. ADL reports often highlight that among *religiously* targeted hate crimes, anti-Jewish hate crimes are predominant. This is a claim that lends itself to sensational reporting, since it does not convey that religiously targeted hate crimes are a small slice of the total. Perhaps that statistic is what Trestan intended to cite. FBI, "Hate Crimes Statistics 2011, Table 1," https://ucr.fbi .gov/hate-crime/2011/tables/table-1, accessed May 7, 2025. On comparisons in statistics, see Emmaia Gelman, "Astroturf Antisemitism Watchdogs," *Jadaliyya*, April 13, 2024.

Heike Schotten have called it, has historically mobilized fear, political will, and vast resources, including the continuous flow of billions of dollars in US funding and weaponry to the Israeli military.[10] By 2025, in the context of the anti-Palestinian genocide, the ADL's data had served as leverage for bills and policies to restrict protest; drive arrests and deportations for political speech; defund public education; strip nonprofit groups of their protected tax status; and drive investment capital to Israel-supporting corporations.[11] These effects have their origin in the 1980s, in the ADL's efforts to address the changing conditions of its work.

At the end of the 1970s, political and cultural ground was shifting beneath the ADL. The entry of much of US Jewry into middle- and upper-class whiteness—the pathway that Progressive Era Jewish elites had intended—had paradoxically made Jewish organizations less important to them. Nationally, the ADL was viewed as an authority on white nationalism, as Suall's Fact-Finding Department reported the rise of groups like the Ku Klux Klan and Christian Identity churches.[12] Nonetheless, its status as a civil rights agency had been damaged by its breaks with Black organizations in the preceding decade, and those fractures were compounded by the Jewish public's loss of interest in civil rights struggle. This was a problem for its Israel advocacy. While other members of the Israel lobby made the geopolitical and strategic case for US investment in Israel, the ADL constructed moral arguments. It drew heavily on racial liberalism, including claims that the Israeli state was a place of equality and progress. ("The Palestinian tourist ... is curious to see all of Israel," the *ADL Bulletin* reported without irony in 1971. "The bustle and modernity of Tel Aviv amazes him. . . . [He] is amazed to learn that Arab and Israeli workers receive equal treatment.")[13] Similarly, it argued that opposition to Zionism in the United States and Europe arose from leftist racial intolerance. But Israel, too, was increasingly disconnected

10. John Harfouch and C. Heike Schotten, "Sayegh's Critique of Zionism and the IHRA Definition: Notes Toward a Theory of the Antisemitism Industrial Complex," *Journal for the Critical Study of Zionism* 1, no. 1 (Fall 2024); Emmaia Gelman, "Astroturf Antisemitism Watchdogs."

11. See, for instance, Felice Gelman, "The ADL's War on Socially Conscious Investing Is in Service to Israel and the New Oligarchy," *Mondoweiss*, March 17, 2025; Amira Jarmakani and Emmaia Gelman, "Zionist Organizations' Latest Strategy to Criminalize Palestine Advocacy: Weaponizing Civil Rights," *Mondoweiss*, September 24, 2024.

12. Irwin Suall, "The Ku Klux Klan: 1978," *Facts*, March 1978; *Jewish Ledger*, "ADL Survey—Klan Membership on Increase," May 12, 1978.

13. Michael Salomon, "Israel's Arab Tourists," *ADL Bulletin*, November 1971.

from discourses of racial justice and was getting harder to defend to US audiences. It was now recognizable as a military power, prosecuting wars and invasions, and as a racial state. Following Israel's 1967 war victory and the 1968 anticolonial uprisings that had swept the globe, "new heroes emerged, replacing those of the World [War] II era. . . . [T]oday the Arab Palestinians, not the Jews, are perceived as the 'new oppressed.'"[14]

The ADL was not only intent on polishing its reputation as a civil rights agency; it also needed to reorganize Jews into its work. Defending and resourcing the Israeli state had become a central priority for the ADL. Major Jewish organizations had been working to leverage Jewish communal interest in Israel's welfare following the 1967 war. Activating political donors and voting blocs, they had fostered a booming congressional support for Israel, sufficient to override objections from other corners of the federal administration.[15] When Israeli voters jettisoned Labor Zionist leadership in 1977 in favor of a right-wing government, the veneer of racial liberalism was cracked. Along with it, the supposed "Jewish consensus" on Israel began to fray. As Marjorie Feld writes, dissent against the unquestioning Zionism that mainstream organizations demanded had never been absent, but it had not been organized as "a child of the 'establishment'" until a quarter century after the founding of the state.[16] In 1973 a small multichapter group formed, Breira, with about 1,500 members, including the local leadership of some major Jewish institutions. Rather than oppose Zionism, they tried to hold it accountable to its liberal claims, calling for an Israeli society "based upon the principles of justice, peace, and civil liberties" and advocating US pressure on Israeli officials to enact it. Mirroring the tactics of its McCarthy-era purge of leftists, the ADL threatened to fire employees who supported Breira, and the major Jewish organizations collaborated to force it out of operation.[17] Suppressing Breira did not mend the fracture, though. In 1979 the Jewish Community Relations Council warned, as the Carter administration warmed to Palestinian calls for rights, that the "'biggest problem' may be 'erosion' of support [for Israel]

14. Anti-Defamation League of B'nai B'rith, "Middle East Opinion Trends in France and Great Britain," *Facts* 23, no. 1 (October 1976).

15. John J. Mearsheimer and Stephen M. Walt, *The Israel Lobby and US Foreign Policy* (Farrar, Straus and Giroux, 2008), 26.

16. Breira, "Factual and Other Errors in 'Why Breira' by Joseph Shattan," April 1977, as quoted in Marjorie Feld, *The Threshold of Dissent* (New York University Press, 2024), 144–46.

17. Feld, *Threshold of Dissent*, 144.

within the American Jewish community."[18] They were right: New Jewish Agenda (NJA) formed in 1980, larger and further to the left, in response to the election of Reagan and the participation of major Jewish organizations in the national rise of the right. With forty-five national chapters and five thousand members, NJA's appearance suggested that the long-running discipline of elite leadership could be challenged, and that such a challenge would be animated by objections to Israel.[19] The crisis of dissent expanded further in 1982, as the massacre of Palestinian refugees at the Sabra and Shatila refugee camps engendered more outrage and calls to hold Israel accountable.

The ADL's new director, Nathan Perlmutter, a neoconservative and strategic ally of the Reagan administration, set out to regather the moral and representational authority of major Jewish organizations and to construct a new imperative for Americans to act as protectors of Israel. His method, building on the ADL's work to define *The New Anti-Semitism*, was to elevate antisemitism as an American crisis. Perlmutter had been around the ADL for a long time, joining first in 1949 as civil rights director in the Mountain States office, then as director of the Florida and New York regions. After a term as associate national director at the American Jewish Committee, and then at Brandeis University with "special responsibility for race relations and political tensions," Perlmutter rejoined the ADL as assistant national director in 1973. In 1979 he took over as director.[20] Perlmutter was a vital centrist who, in the long tradition of the ADL, viewed civil rights struggle as an instrument of law and order. He had supported Black civil rights calls, for instance, partly out of fear that Black communities' frustrated dreams would empower "militant demagogues."[21] At the same time, his hostility toward Black organizing was freely expressed. He walked back the ADL's own research finding that Black nationalism was not hostile to Jews, finding that it had "rationalized" Black antisemitism and "came squeamishly close to justifying it."[22] He felt no obligation to Arab civil rights and instead held

18. Feld, *Threshold of Dissent*.

19. Ezra Berkley Nepon, *Justice, Justice Shall You Pursue* (Thread Makes Blanket Press, 2012), 28.

20. Perlmutter started at the ADL in 1949, directing regional work and fundraising. Perlmutter, "Biographical Questionnaire," n.d., 1976–85, Nathan Perlmutter (1923–87) Papers, Box 10, Folder 4, American Jewish Historical Society.

21. George Southworth, "Miami Losing Top Fighter for Civil Rights," *Miami Herald*, April 22, 1964.

22. Nathan Perlmutter and Ruth Ann Perlmutter, *The Real Anti-Semitism in America* (Arbor House, 1982), 86.

that Arabs were inherently hostile to democracy. In the interest of shoring up support for Israel and militating against the left, he strongly advocated for a Jewish embrace of the Christian Right.[23]

Perlmutter's view of antisemitism was similarly calculated. He did not actually see anti-Jewish hostility as a problem, and neither did he see any structural exclusion of Jews. "[Our] priorities are no longer the kind of anti-Semitism that used to stalk us. We have long won the battle against that kind of anti-Semitism," he told the ADL's oral historian in 1985.[24] Instead, Perlmutter's perspective was ideological. Expanding on the previous leaders' idea that Jewishness and Americanism were aligned and entwined, Perlmutter took a global view that conceived of Jewishness as fundamentally Western—reaffirming European Zionism's erasures of Jewish histories in Asia and Africa—and Jews' well-being as entwined with Western imperial strength. As such, he focused on what he saw as broad, long-term threats to Western order: the Cold War bugbears of anticolonialism, Black liberationism, and communism, and the Orientalist specter of "Muslim hostility." Rather than danger from antisemitism itself, he explained, his concern was "danger to the status of our free world and our democracy all of which impinge on Jewish security."[25] At the same time, Perlmutter presciently saw that the *idea* of imminent antisemitism could be a lever for political will and material support for the larger project of shoring up the West.

Two factors made the specter of antisemitism a powerful tool, as Perlmutter saw it. The first was the capacity of US Jewry for worry about being marginalized, whether or not their worries were well founded. "No matter their organizational deliberations may be taking place in the posh baroque ambience of the Waldorf-Astoria or . . . the tropical languor of Palm Beach, they worry," he wrote. Rather than facts, it was personal impressions that registered on what he called "the Jews' Richter scale." The second factor was the expectation that government, institutions, and the public would be willing to provide protection against the things that Jews worried about.[26] Civil rights was the US civic religion; its core tenet was that marginalized groups should be uplifted into equality and protected against those who try

23. Perlmutter and Perlmutter, *Real Anti-Semitism in America*, 170.

24. Nathan Perlmutter, "Vol Ib: Perlmutter, Nathan, 1985–1987," Box 1, Folder 1, MS-365, p. 84, B'nai B'rith Anti-Defamation League Oral Histories, American Jewish Archives, Cincinnati, Ohio.

25. Perlmutter, "Vol Ib: Perlmutter," 84.

26. Perlmutter and Perlmutter, *Real Anti-Semitism in America*, 103.

to diminish them. The imperative to be vigilant against Nazism added special significance to antisemitism; showing antisemitism as a problem could be expected to invoke a mobilization to redress it. On the other hand, Perlmutter recognized that *civil rights* was defined by concerns about white privilege and persistent anti-Black racism, and that the concerns of a white, middle- to upper-class Jewish population were not primary in that framework. His view was that this was an unfortunate reflection of "fashion" that lent undue weight to Black voices on race relations. "Nobody says, let's meet with the Poles. You know why?," Perlmutter asked. "Because they are not a fashionable minority, they are not all over the media."[27] The fashion of opposing anti-Black racism had superseded reason in US culture, he complained, and was reinforced in government contracts that induced powerful societal institutions—universities, corporations—to focus too much on fostering racial equality.[28] Affirmative action particularly outraged him; he called it "a racial quota system" and "a virulent form of racism," but affirmative action illustrated for him the power of racial sympathy as a potential technology that could direct material support to other projects, including Israel.[29] Perlmutter was bitter but practical. He set out to convert concern for antisemitism into a force: to construct Jews as *subjects of remedy*.

The ADL launched its *Annual Audit of Anti-Semitic Incidents* just as Perlmutter was promoted to lead the organization. In 1979 the first report appeared as an assemblage of data gleaned from newspaper reports and other sources. By the second annual report, the data already showed a spike. "There was a sharp increase in reported anti-Semitic episodes, including assaults and vandalism," read the press release's lede. (In later pages, the report noted that the increase might have been due to heightened reporting; nonetheless, politicians and press simply reported it as a spike in antisemitic acts.)[30] Undertaking the audits was, in part, a response to trouble over the 1967 ADL study *Protest and Prejudice: A Study of Belief in the Black Community*, which had seemed to undermine the finding of Black antisemitism. Criticism from the right had troubled the idea of quantification, especially from survey data.

27. Perlmutter, "Vol Ib: Perlmutter," 102.

28. Perlmutter and Perlmutter, *Real Anti-Semitism in America*, 109–10.

29. Nathan Perlmutter to Edwin Meese, December 16, 1983, Digital Record, James W. Cicconi Files, Box 3, Ronald Reagan Library, www.reaganlibrary.gov/public/digitallibrary /smof/cos/cicconi/box-3/40-94-6914307-003-006-2016.pdf.

30. In its first year, the report appeared as an article in the *ADL Bulletin*; in 1980 and thereafter it was published as a freestanding report: *1980 Audit of Anti-Semitic Episodes*, 1980.

"Anti-Semitism has no commonly accepted boiling or freezing point; no standard weights or intervals have been assigned to religious anti-Semitism, political anti-Semitism, economic anti-Semitism, authoritarianism, or ethnocentrism," wrote historian Lucy Davidowicz in *Commentary*, in 1970. If a survey detected an insular wish to live only among one's own group, or even a belief in racist tropes, what impact of those ideas could be discerned on Jewish or US life? And could people's motivations really be read through incidents or remarks? Davidowicz noted, for instance, that surveys ascribed "antisemitism" to respondents who disapproved of intermarriage between Jews and Christians, when in fact Jewish respondents disfavored it.[31] Where the sociological studies had tried to wrestle numbers from amorphous attitudes, the audits purported to measure something more tangible: acts. Additionally, they proposed the need for vigilance toward every small instance, preempting questions about whether they measured acts that mattered. Their logic drew heavily on post–World War II analysis of Nazi totalitarianism as a psychological phenomenon, which considered antisemitism to be forever latent and always possibly reemerging.[32] The 1960 "swastika epidemic" was their evidence: "If such things were possible, what else was?" argued Charles Glock and Harold Quinley in the final study of ADL's series. "Could anything about anti-Semitism in America be taken for granted?"[33]

Seeking scientific grounding just as the ADL's survey project had, the audits purported to provide hard data and a concrete form of measurement. In practice, though, they created a new abstraction, converting local events—rich in contexts of local history and relationships—into undifferentiated data points that painted a worrisome bigger picture. Abstraction changed the way incidents were understood. While some incidents were clearly antisemitic, many were ambiguous and others clearly misconstrued. Often enough, Jewish communities disagreed with the ADL's assessment that attacks on

31. Lucy S. Dawidowicz, "Can Anti-Semitism Be Measured?," *Commentary*, June 1970. See also pollster Tom Smith's contention that many of these polls' questions were unusable because of their "violation of norms of politeness and their often absolutist phrasing." Tom W. Smith, *Ethnic Images: GSS Topical Report No. 19*, National Opinion Research Center at the University of Chicago, December 1990.

32. On latency, see Stuart Svonkin, *Jews Against Prejudice: American Jews and the Fight for Civil Liberties* (Columbia University Press, 1997), 116. On the intent to record every small act, see Clara S. Lewis, "Tough on Hate? Addressing Hate Crimes in a Post-Difference Society" (PhD diss., George Washington University, 2010), 42.

33. Harold Earl Quinley and Charles Young Glock, *Anti-Semitism in America* (Transaction Publishers, 1979), xxxv.

their spaces reflected antisemitism. Contrary to Perlmutter's vision of Jewish worry, local communities' response was to seek context and understanding. They sifted through the particulars of each incident to ascertain causes, distinguish between mischief, harassment, or violence, and reflect on whether the incident really meant any change in their status. These dissonances dotted the newspapers as they reported on events counted by the ADL as antisemitic incidents. In Long Island, New York, antisemitic and KKK graffiti was spray-painted on a high school, while nearby a bomb threat was phoned in to a Zionist parade. These events were so inconsistent with Jews' understanding of their local community that they were presumed to be pranks in poor taste.[34] In suburban Westchester County, New York, a "four-month spate of anti-Semitic incidents" in 1988 included swastika graffiti and broken windows. County career politicians swiftly moved to train police on bias crimes and promised a six-month study and "a central reporting system similar to the one that exists for child abuse." But local rabbis were unhappy, the *New York Times* reported. "'The press was absolutely crummy with us in Yorktown,' [Rabbi Leonard Schofer] said, by reporting on the incident 'but ignoring the fact that the community turned out to say the guy's a kook, an outcast, and we don't want any part of it.'" Another rabbi had decided not even to report broken windows in his synagogue, having determined that they were probably not an antisemitic attack. "We can't turn our back on these things, but there is such a thing as overstating a problem ... we don't want to put labels where we don't want them to apply," he said. As other religious institutions had also been attacked, their leaders contemplated whether the incidents reflected hostility to authority, rather than racism.[35]

Nonetheless, as antisemitism became a subject of increasing police action and media coverage, local voices were not the narrators. Responding to elevated statistics in 1980, a New Jersey ADL official and Perlmutter gave assessments that were diametrically opposed. The New Jersey office coordinator genially calmed a *New York Times* reporter who had come to investigate the crisis. "The profile of the swastika-dauber invariably turns out to be a 13-to-17-year-old acting under the influence of someone slightly older," he said. "They are basically good middle-class kids."[36] Conversely, Perlmutter rang out a warning: "The sheer statistics of anti-Jewish incidents suggest that there

34. *New York Times*, "Answering Anti-Semitism with a Lesson," January 4, 1981.
35. *New York Times*, "County Acts to Stem Crimes of Bias," May 22, 1988.
36. John T. McQuiston, "Anti-Semitic Vandals in Suburbs Are Causing Increasing Concern," *New York Times*, November 5, 1980.

is a high quotient of anti-Semitism and anti-Jewish hostility which still exists just beneath the surface of American life."[37] Centralizing the message, ADL national leadership shaped a simplified narrative of Jewish victimhood and always-latent antisemitism, easily summoned.

As soon as they were published, the audits were vehicles for Perlmutter's effort to transform antisemitism into an ideological lever for other projects. Throughout the 1980s and mid-1990s the audits' data gestured to white nationalist perpetrators or, even more commonly, teenage mischief-makers. This finding was matched by ADL reporting on the growing ranks of white nationalists on the whole. The narrative pages of the same reports, though, developed a pastiche portrait of threat that often held Arabs, communists, and Third World resistance movements responsible. Additionally, the audits began to conflate overall numbers of incidents, most of which were vandalism or comments, with violence. A 1981 report, for instance, merged all violence and verbal incidents across the United States into a single category that included bodily assaults, mail or phone threats to Jews and Jewish institutions, and harassment.[38] The reporting was unspecific but still gestured to a scientific approach, suggesting that the ADL held more detailed data in its own files. Alongside the numbers, the ADL proffered unrelated analysis, succinctly packaged for citation and lent authority by its presentation alongside the statistics. The 1981 report noted that in all but two instances involving arrests, the perpetrators had been youths; two additional arrests had been at KKK/neo-Nazi events. The analysis section, though, linked the entire incident tally to anti-Zionism and Third World anticolonialism. It explained:

> [T]he rise of anti-Semitic incidents may be just the "tip of an iceberg." . . . Many dangers to Jewish security, springing from these deep roots, are perceived in the present milieu in American society. . . . There has been an injection of anti-Semitism into debates on US foreign policy. A world-wide campaign of anti-Semitic propaganda has been conducted by the Soviet Union, various Arab regimes, and some Third World countries, exemplified in a

37. Anti-Defamation League, *1980 Audit of Anti-Semitic Episodes*, 1980.

38. "The 1981 ADL Audit records 974 episodes of anti-Semitic vandalism reported to ADL's 27 regional offices around the country. These took place in 31 states and the District of Columbia. The 1981 total is more than two-and-a-half times that of 1980 when 377 episodes were reported in 28 states and the District of Columbia. In 1978 there were 49 episodes, and 120 in 1979. The number of assaults, mail and phone threats, and harassments of Jews and Jewish institutions reported in 1981 was more than triple the 1980 figure. There were 350 in 1981 compared with 112 in 1980. Anti-Defamation League, *1981 Audit of Anti-Semitic Incidents*, 1982.

number of United Nations resolutions including that equating "Zionism" and racism. And a continuing peril confronts the State of Israel with whose destiny the fate of Jews everywhere is inextricably linked. Episodes of anti-Semitic vandalism or harassment against Jews are not, in short, the only measure of anti-Semitism in our society.[39]

Although the ADL's antagonism to the left was long-standing, its call to look away from right-wing threats constituted a shift. Perlmutter crystallized the new approach in his 1982 book-length polemic, *The Real Anti-Semitism in America*. The book eviscerated the ADL's prior fifteen years of research on antisemitism, called for alliances with the right, and asserted the importance of supporting Israel over all other political aims.[40] Ignoring the ADL's many denunciations of the left as antisemitic, Perlmutter charged the ADL's sociologists with being "alert in one direction" in their findings of the right as the site of white supremacy, Christian nationalism, and "preservationist" antisemitism, while rationalizing Black antisemitism as a product of economic conflict or (in a more patronizing vein) lack of education: "Not a word, however—in 1979!—about left-wing extremism. . . . [A] decade of inner-city riots, campus takeovers and international left-wing anti-Semitism and totalitarianism, none of which was examined in 'Politics and Prejudice'! Violence launched from the right, it would seem, is extremism. From the left, it is social protest. To Jews, scapegoated by both, the difference is without a distinction." Perlmutter demanded, too, that Jews stop opposing the right, particularly Christian fundamentalists, and instead build alliances. The domestic issues on which Jewish liberalism had opposed Christian fundamentalism could be traded for support of Israel. "Jews can live with restricted abortions . . . Jews can live without ERA. . . . Prayers in the public schools . . . would not . . . mean the death of the Bill of Rights or seriously impact Jewish life. . . . Banned pornography is not . . . a setback to Jews as would be the alienation of allies who oppose . . . a PLO-dominated state on Israel's borders."[41]

The exhortation to get in step with the right was not only utilitarian. Perlmutter instructed Jews that they truly belonged there. Jews in the United States (and in Latin American countries that Jews had "helped modernize") were now as a group "light years removed from the proletariat of which they

39. Anti-Defamation League, *1981 Audit of Anti-Semitic Incidents*, 7–8.

40. Perlmutter had been a regional director when the antisemitism study was launched by the national ADL leadership.

41. Perlmutter and Perlmutter, *Real Anti-Semitism in America*, 171.

were only yesteryear members." Jews who remained attached to the left, or who still wanted to make common cause with antiracist popular movements, were targets of scathing scorn. "[They] may be the second most self-destructive species known to man," he jibed, "the first being the lemming."[42] Better bedfellows were the Christian Right, who supported Israel even if they were antisemitic. To bring them closer, Perlmutter set out to unwrite critiques of Christian conservatism, many of which had been written by the ADL itself. "[R]arely has a religious persuasion been as broadly smeared as have fundamentalists," he wrote. "As excoriations of Zionism have served to camouflage raw anti-Semitism, so have swollen hyperboles descriptive of the Moral Majority the Religious Roundtable beclouded the image of fundamentalists."[43]

While ADL's audits and fact-finding continued to report on white supremacist groups, its work in the field was increasingly conditioned by its strategic commitments to the right—and other organizers took notice. Perlmutter's era as ADL director coincided with the US farm crisis, a turgid period in the development of white nationalist groups, particularly the Christian Identity church and Posse Comitatus. Rural communities were especially ripe for recruitment in the mid-1980s, as family farms were consumed by foreclosure and transferred to corporate landholders, and farmers came to view themselves as an exploited and devalued minority. Conspiracy theories blaming "international" communists and Jews were mixed with seeds of truth about, for instance, the predatory nature of banking.[44] Seizing on the farmers' disaffection, white supremacist groups were successful in spreading antisemitic disinformation.[45] Daniel Levitas, a researcher and organizer with PrairieFire Rural Action, recounted that in the Midwest in 1985–86, organizations including the North American Farm Alliance, PrairieFire, the Center for Democratic Renewal (formerly the National Anti-Klan Network), the American Jewish Committee, and the National Council of Churches met the crisis with a variety of strategies to advocate for small farmers and prevent white nationalists from recruiting them. With a sense of urgency they tried all routes, from legal interventions in foreclosure to stem

---

42. Perlmutter and Perlmutter, *Real Anti-Semitism in America*, 138–39.

43. Perlmutter and Perlmutter, *Real Anti-Semitism in America*, 176.

44. See James N. Leiker, "Rage of the Rural Minority: The High Plains Farm Crisis and Farmer Activism in Colorado and Kansas," *Great Plains Quarterly* 39, no. 3 (2019): 265–90.

45. Daniel Levitas, *The Terrorist Next Door: The Militia Movement and the Radical Right* (Macmillan, 2004), 253.

the loss of farms, to supporting the presidential campaign of Jesse Jackson with its promise of multiracial solidarities.

To the frustration and surprise of Midwestern organizers, they found the ADL undermining their efforts to combat white nationalism. ADL officials repeatedly argued—in national press, Jewish newspapers, the *ADL Bulletin*, and internal memos—that other groups were exaggerating the problem. Indeed, Perlmutter accused them of "shrilly cry[ing] wolf."[46] In Levitas's analysis, the ADL was not just misinterpreting the situation, but deliberately obscuring it. In autumn 1985, the ADL commissioned a Harris poll of Iowa and Nebraska farmers, and it was published in 1986. To the organizational staffers who read the document, it painted an alarming picture of farm belt resentments morphing into antisemitic mythologies. Levitas wrote that "fully 42 percent of respondents agreed with the view that 'Jews should quit complaining about what happened to them in Nazi Germany,'" and right-wing populist groups were familiar to between a quarter and half of respondents.[47] Rather than raise the usual alarm, ADL leaders were uncharacteristically silent about those findings, and outlandishly minimized others. Perlmutter's analysis was reproduced in the *New York Times*, which wrote that "*only* 27 percent agreed with a statement that farmers had been exploited by 'international Jewish bankers,'" a startling statistic, presented as nothing unusual (emphasis mine). Other Jewish organizations that had earlier been content to ignore or "quarantine" white nationalists did see the emergency and mounted a response. Following the polling, the Union of American Hebrew Congregations, Women's American ORT, several Jewish community relations councils, and the American Jewish Committee launched a concerted project of Jewish advocacy for farmers that included face-to-face meetings with rural communities, raising relief funds, and lobbying for a moratorium on farm foreclosures.[48] The ADL did not join in.

The apparent contradiction in the ADL's' approach to the farmers reflected its leadership's neoconservative strategies, as Levitas recognized, as well as a

46. See Levitas, *Terrorist Next Door*, 253; *Jewish Ledger*, "Farm Belt Anti-Semitism 'Exaggerated': Poll," March 20, 1986.

47. The 1985 Harris poll was published in 1986, but I was not able to locate a copy. Louis Harris, *A Study of Anti-Semitism in Rural Iowa and Nebraska* (Anti-Defamation League of B'nai B'rith, February 1986); Levitas, *Terrorist Next Door*, 254.

48. Walter Ruby, "Planting Seeds of Hatred: Farm Crisis: As Families Fight to Cope Extremists Make a Pitch," *Jewish Exponent*, January 9, 1987; Susan Birnbaum, "Jews to Help Farmers in Trouble," *JTA Daily News Bulletin*, November 10, 1986, 4.

dose of resentment that other groups were leading the charge in rural areas. Perlmutter and Suall were committed to portraying US culture as inherently democratic and anti-extreme, downplaying the need to continue civil rights struggles, and forging alliances with the pro-Israel Christian Right. Beyond those ideological aims, Perlmutter's ADL was tactically allied with Reagan, and it made little sense to trade that alliance for the chance to join farmers in criticizing Reaganite economic policies that exacerbated farm foreclosures. Similarly, as the ADL forged alliances with the pro-Israel Christian Right and urged other Jewish groups to do the same, it made little sense to denounce right-wing churches.[49] Perhaps most significant was the belief that Suall expressed to Levitas in 1986, just as he had to researchers Chip Berlet and Russ Bellant: "The principal struggle in defense of Jewish security in the United States today does not concern the radical right." Instead, what mattered was the ideological and political battle against the transnational left.

Accordingly, although the ADL continued to produce reporting on the white right—and to identify itself as the leading US organization keeping track of white groups—it increasingly offered its alliances and approval to right wingers and overt antisemites. The ADL seemed immune to the criticism these connections provoked. In Boston, the ADL honored Cardinal Bernard Law, a tyrannical figure of the Religious Right, and Boston University president John Silber, who had opposed the anti-Apartheid movement, denounced married women's presence in the workplace, and busted his faculty union. Local organizers became so frustrated that they formed an organization specifically to protest the ADL, the Committee to Fight Bigotry in All Its Forms.[50] In a syndicated column in 1991, Jewish news commentator Sheldon Engelmayer chronicled a further handful of repressive figures whose reputations the ADL had laundered with awards and endorsements in the context, he intimated, of political deal-making. Nonetheless, neoconservatives still claimed to support what Perlmutter called "genuine civil rights."[51] As a result, the ADL was still publicly perceived as an antiracist agency. Engelmayer summarized: "The ADL . . . does not admit it has a bias against the left. . . . Many in the media accept that claim. Thus when the

49. Levitas, *Terrorist Next Door*, 250–51.
50. This conflict between Boston queer organizers and the ADL is discussed in more detail in chapter 5.
51. Perlmutter to Meese, December 16, 1983.

ADL says or does something to benefit the right, it is reported by the media as something extraordinary."[52]

The launch of the *Annual Audits* reaffirmed the ADL as an authority on white nationalism just as a new US crisis of racist violence emerged. People of color, Indigenous people, and queers rose up to demand protection against the attacks, and the neoconservative ADL was incongruously thrust into the leadership of the resulting political movement: the demand to make *hate crime* a distinct subject of policing. Throughout the 1980s, Perlmutter, Suall, and Perlmutter's like-minded successor Abe Foxman would shape the demand for hate crimes protections into a tool for directing attention back toward "intergroup hostility" and colorblindness and away from structural racism. It would rewrite the meanings of race and rights. As in the Progressive Era, the ADL was again in the position of representing groups whose core demands it actually opposed and whose identities it hoped to reshape in a conservative mode. Hate crimes policy proved a vehicle for this discipline.

In 1979 in Greensboro, North Carolina, members of the Ku Klux Klan murdered five antiracism marchers in a drive-by shooting. Although racism was a constant current of US life, the Greensboro massacre heralded a period of overt and spectacular racist attacks by white nationalists, which merged with concerns about violence over segregated neighborhood turf, school busing programs, jobs, and other tensions.[53] The attacks in turn became the subject of a newly heightened national discourse, a moral panic that the spread of racial hatred threatened the pluralistic character of the United States. News outlets widely covered the expansion of the Klan and other white power groups, which had grown in size and established paramilitary training camps. Individual acts of violence targeted Black and brown people, each aimed at displacing them from jobs and communities—or killing them. As the attacks continued, communities noted that law enforcement agencies widely refused to address them. The specter of escalating racist violence, and the crumbling of any expectation of state protection, engendered terror. Althea T. L. Simmons, NAACP Washington bureau director, testified to

52. Sheldon Engelmayer, "ADL's Supposed Shift to the Right: Is It No Longer a Clear Voice?," *Kansas City Jewish Chronicle*, August 23, 1991.

53. On the Greensboro massacre and the development of white nationalist violence in the post–Vietnam War era, see Kathleen Belew, *Bring the War Home: The White Power Movement and Paramilitary America* (Harvard University Press, 2018), chap. 2.

Congress in 1980: "There is a state of hysteria in the black community arising from the resurgence of the Klan and other terrorist groups and the numerous wanton killings of blacks in various areas of the country. . . . There is a strong feeling among our people that we are entering into a period that could duplicate that of the post-Reconstruction era, in which hard-won gains of blacks were taken from them, often with the aid of Klan-perpetrated or inspired physical violence."[54]

The violence and fears alike reflected a sense of disunity and deterioration across the political spectrum. The promises of the civil rights movement were unfulfilled. At the same time, many white workers had lost their grip on prosperity. Economic downturn had been precipitated by the 1970s oil crisis and the 1980s flight of manufacturing to cheaper labor markets, and the politics of white grievance were ascendant. Much of the discourse about white nationalist violence centered on white male workers' loss of status through class changes: not only through the disappearance of good jobs, but through affirmative action that reduced white men's access to those jobs. Resentments mounted against feminism, multiculturalism, and counterculture movements, which had disrupted traditional authority.[55] Political crises had destabilized the imagined meanings of the United States, including deep rifts over the Vietnam War followed by defeat and the advent of the farm crisis. Historian Kathleen Belew writes that white people feared change in the "very meaning of American identity," which in turn catalyzed white nationalist organizing.[56]

Despite agreeing that racist violence presented a crisis, the disparate organizations confronting it did not agree on solutions to the crisis or what the crisis actually *was*. The search for concrete information and ways to intervene characterized many institutions' responses. Media outlets trying to document the crisis were drawn to the ADL's data; if there were no solid answers, at least they could quantify racist incidents. The Southern Poverty Law Center filed legal actions against the Klan. The National Anti-Klan Network mounted protests demanding that the Justice Department prosecute white nationalist violence. State officials sought administrative ways to

54. US Congress, *Increasing Violence Against Minorities: Hearing Before the Subcommittee on Crime of the Committee on the Judiciary*, House of Representatives, 96th Cong., 2nd Session, December 9, 1980, p. 117.

55. On the narration of white rights under siege, see Daniel Martinez HoSang, *Racial Propositions: Ballot Initiatives and the Making of Postwar California* (University of California Press, 2010), 24; Belew, *Bring the War Home*, 2–4.

56. Belew, *Bring the War Home*, 2.

interfere: changing parade permit rules, increasing the criminal penalties for cross burnings and violations committed "while wearing a hood, mask, or other device," and banning paramilitary training. The responses revealed different analyses of the problem at hand: Media presented white nationalism as a kind of foreign object irritating regular American life, while others contemplated whether "hate groups" were the problem or symptoms of more significant ills.[57] In reports to the US Commission on Civil Rights in 1981 and 1982, state officials pointed to discrimination in housing, employment, and education that created racial disparity, and white middle-class resentment about Black advancement.[58] They also took note of the different conditions that produced racist violence in each place. In West Virginia, officials pointed to entrenched segregation and government foot-dragging in implementing gender, disability, and Indigenous rights.[59] In Michigan, officials said the rollback of state investments in civil rights had signaled "a conservative trend . . . of people who say, 'You've had enough,' as far as minorities and women are concerned, 'You've had your day, now give some back.'"[60] In Georgia, the site of much of the Klan's expansion, officials did find the KKK itself to be the problem.[61] But this context-specific, historical analysis was not received as a road map for addressing racism. Instead it seemed an unsatisfy-

57. See, for instance, *New York Times*, "How the Klans Are Organized," September 13, 1981; *New York Times*, "Arms Training by Klan Cited in Suit," June 7, 1984; *New York Times*, "Anti-Klan Group Plans Action Against Racism," February 2, 1981.

58. According to the 1983 US Civil Rights Commission's *Intimidation and Violence: Racial and Religious Bigotry in America*, the states responding were Michigan, Connecticut, West Virginia, New Jersey, and Georgia. I have not been able to locate New Jersey's "brief statement" or West Virginia's report. New Jersey's statement is quoted in the 1983 document. I use West Virginia's 1981 advisory committee report, prepared before the call to examine "hate violence," to reflect that committee's perspective.

59. West Virginia's report situated the battle over civil rights in suburban America in the late 1970s, a change of venue after the urban riots of the prior decade: "Banners were raised, not in the name of a war against poverty, but in the name of property owners brandishing Proposition 13 as their weapon against high taxes, and big government. Campaigns were mounted against affirmative action and against equal rights for women." West Virginia Advisory Committee to the US Commission on Civil Rights, *Achieving Change*, US Commission on Civil Rights, January 1981, iv.

60. Michigan Advisory Committee to the US Commission on Civil Rights, *Hate Groups in Michigan: A Sham or a Shame*, US Commission on Civil Rights, March 1982, 17.

61. Georgia's report consisted of testimony from a hearing on the issue of hate groups, rather than study. Its recommendations reflected a summary of speakers' calls for action. Georgia State Advisory Committee to the US Commission on Civil Rights, *Perceptions of Hate Group Activity in Georgia*, US Commission on Civil Rights, December 1982.

ing answer for the new, national problem labeled *hate.* Officials were frustrated to know so little about white nationalist groups, or about psychological factors that might lead people to abandon pluralism.[62] A raft of state commissions and committees formed to study the problem, and an infrastructure began to grow up around the problem of white nationalism, violence, and hate. The effort to assess whether there was a major new problem had helped to construct one. In the process, local insights into the structures of racism were submerged.

The urgency of formalizing *hate* as a matter for law enforcement was driven by the concerns and advocacy of Black, brown, and queer communities that were unfolding in legislative campaigns throughout the 1980s and breaking into federal policy with the 1990 passage of the Hate Crimes Statistics Act. Antiracist and anti-homophobic demands were not compelling enough. Sufficient leverage to realize policy change on a wide scale, though, did lie with whiter and more conservative institutions: It depended on tapping into the political will for law and order. A 1978 law that was a precursor to hate crimes laws, for instance, used the image of a racist killer as a rationale to expand the state's death penalty. Its advocates conjured an image of "a killer who murders a citizen in cold blood because of his race or religion or nationality." The NAACP opposed the bill, while the State Sheriffs' Association campaigned for it. Californians passed it in a landslide.[63]

In 1980, as the desperate call rose for public officials to do something about racist violence, the ADL became its leading legislative advocate. In political-historical terms, opposing Nazis was the presumed purview of Jewish groups, and opposing US white nationalist organizing was already the ADL's established turf. As the ADL took up the work, the lawmakers with whom they partnered were already working on parallel efforts to create new penalties for religious vandalism. The first two federal bills were proposed in 1981: one by New York Rep. Mario Biaggi, a former police officer, and the

---

62. Connecticut submitted a particularly dramatic 107-page report expressing deep anxiety about this gap in knowledge, filled with unanswered questions, borrowed hypotheses, and laments about the lack of conclusive evidence. Connecticut Advisory Committee to the US Commission on Civil Rights, *Hate Groups and Acts of Bigotry: Connecticut's Response,* US Commission on Civil Rights, October 1982.

63. March Fong Eu, *California Voters Pamphlet,* Office of the Secretary of State, California, 1978, p. 34; Ballotpedia, "California Proposition 7, Expand Death Penalty and Life Imprisonment for Murders Initiative (1978)," https://ballotpedia.org/California_Proposition_7,_Expand_Death_Penalty_and_Life_Imprisonment_for_Murders_Initiative_(1978), accessed June 2, 2025.

other by California Rep. Bobbi Fiedler, a Reagan Republican who had just risen to office as an opponent of school desegregation busing. Their bills, and the religious vandalism bills that followed between 1981 and 1988, were geared almost exclusively toward antisemitism; their focus on the exercise of religion, rather than opposition to racism, meant they had a more conservative bent.[64] Biaggi's was a law-and-order bill calling for life imprisonment on some offenses, and for which his rationale was the ADL *Annual Audit*'s finding of a large spike in numbers (likely a false reading, as the ADL had noted).[65] Conservatives like Fiedler had anxiously perceived "anti-religious acts" as symptoms of loss of respect for authority, a narrative threaded through Reagan administration policies. Initially, they were not successful; although Jewish institutions had the relationships to get bills introduced, religious vandalism did not mobilize enough political will to get bills passed. However, when the ADL merged the call for religious vandalism statutes with antiracist framings, it unlocked a major force.

As states turned to legislation to contain racist violence, early efforts were shaped by communities' insights into racism itself. Combating racism still meant recognizing and opposing the uses of violence to strip people, primarily people of color, of their political power, resources, and geographic communities. In 1979 Massachusetts introduced a state civil rights bill establishing a new offense: racial harassment. Proponents cited the need to protect "basic rights [denied through violence to people of color], such as living where they choose, . . . using public transportation, . . . going to school, . . . [and] access to all parts of the city."[66] It passed quickly into law in 1980. The Massachusetts bill was driven by the American Civil Liberties Union (ACLU) as a response to ongoing turf-based violence arising from ethnic and racial community conflicts and white communities' efforts to maintain control over city resources; perhaps for this reason ethno-religious groups like the ADL did

64. An early call for the laws later termed "religious vandalism statutes" was made in New York City in 1976 by Chuck Schumer, then an Assembly representative. Federal bills were first proposed in 1981; California representative Bobbi Fiedler (former leader of the California anti-busing campaign) introduced HR 2394 in that year targeting the desecration of graces or religious structures or the placement of antireligious symbols "on the property of another." Eleanor Blau, "Legislator Decries Synagogue Arson," *New York Times*, March 23, 1976.

65. *Rhode Island Herald*, "Bills Seek to Reverse Rise in Anti-Semitism," March 12, 1981.

66. *Boston Globe*, "Massachusetts' Own Civil Rights Law," November 7, 1979.

not join in.[67] In 1981, Oregon and Washington state legislatures followed suit with their own racial harassment laws. The Northwest laws, in contrast to the law in Massachusetts, were motivated by catastrophic acts of violence primarily against Black people and their property: The home of a Black corrections officer had been firebombed; a Black man was doused with gasoline; Black families had been stalked at their homes with death threats.[68] Police first refused to intervene; later, police were perpetrators, spreading opossum corpses in front of a local Black-owned restaurant.[69] In each case, the campaigns to pass racial harassment laws recognized the material effects of anti-Black violence and were spurred by specific instances of dispossession. White nationalist messaging had targeted Jews as well: In November 1980, a Portland neighborhood was stickered with anti-Jewish messages reading "Gas a Jew for Jesus, Nuke the [N*****], White Power." Here again, the local Jewish community leadership distinguished such antisemitic "name-calling" from what they understood as the "persecution" of their Black neighbors.[70] The materiality of violence, its effect in stripping away not just psychological peace but communities' ability to exist and engage in daily life, was what mattered.

Something shifted, though, as the legislative machinery geared up to respond to catastrophic anti-Black violence. In February 1981, Oregon's Republican governor Victor Atiyeh proposed a racial harassment law that would fine perpetrators up to $12,500 and carry a felony charge, both serious penalties. "Racial harassment" was a term that meant the shocking attacks of the preceding months. "Nothing defiles humanity as much as outrageous acts of racism. That such terrorism could happen [in] Oregon today is a sobering reminder of the dormant seed of bigotry," he told the legislature in January 1981. "But, when that [covert] bigotry is manifested in malicious and

67. I find no record of ADL participation in efforts to win the Massachusetts civil rights law. The bill had been championed by the ACLU for several years and was expected to fail as it had each year, until at the last moment the Boston Police commissioner endorsed it. *Boston Globe*, "Voices from Our City: Racism in Boston," December 14, 1980; Lonnie Isabel, "Mass. Rights Bill Described as Important Tool," *Boston Globe*, November 8, 1979; *Boston Globe*, "Massachusetts' Own Civil Rights Law."

68. Alan K. Ota, "Racial Harassment Incidents Increasing in Oregon," *Sunday Oregonian*, December 21, 1980.

69. Julie Tripp, "Racial Threats Plague Milwaukee-Area Family," *Sunday Oregonian*, August 17, 1980; Alan K. Ota, "Black Publisher, Leader Ask Firing of Officers," *Oregonian*, March 20, 1981.

70. This distinction is made by Laurie Rogoway, director of the American Jewish Committee in Portland, quoted in Julie Tripp, "Law Urged to Counter Racial Acts," *Oregonian*, February 21, 1981. Antisemitic "name-calling" was generally in the form of graffiti.

wanton racial harassment . . . when citizens fear for the safety of their lives and property . . . then we must be prepared to do more than sit back and call those depraved persons who are responsible 'cowards' and 'bullies.'"[71] As it moved through an off-the-record negotiation process, though, progressive elected officials began to denounce it. They called it a sweetheart bill laden with other interests, and "an outrageous scam" perpetrated on minority voters that "would allow minorities to believe the state was taking action in their behalf." Presciently, they noted that it meant that a "black person could be arrested for calling a white policeman a 'honky' in certain circumstances."[72] Their concerns were not addressed; they did not appear in local press until after the bill had been passed.

The amended Oregon racial harassment bill passed in June 1981. Whatever had taken place in the closed proceedings, it had substantially moved away from Atiyeh's speech. Instead the new law sutured racial violence to religious vandalism, referring to them jointly as "intimidation . . . by reason of the race, color, religion, or national origin of another person" and papering over the community's efforts to distinguish between name-calling and violence.[73] The ADL was ready to catch and harness the wave. By December, it had drafted model state legislation on "intimidation," which was included as an appendix in the 1981 *Annual Audit*. Eight states had already passed racial harassment bills that took a variety of approaches but, animated by intense racial violence, they did not all elevate the small acts that the ADL wanted to recognize. "Some have opted only for increased penalties; others have developed new categories of offenses to punish those who 'terrorize or intimidate' individuals because of their ethnic, religious or racial background. Our

71. Governor Victor G. Atiyeh, "Legislative Message, 1981 (January)," Records of Governor Victor G. Atiyeh Administration, January 8, 1979, to January 12, 1987, Oregon State Archives.

72. Two Democratic state senators, Gretchen Kafoury and Margie Hendrikson, opposed the bill as a whitewash that did not seriously address racism and bigotry. *The Oregonian*, the state newspaper of record, reported on their objections only after the passage of the bill. Foster Church, "Harassment Bill Passes over Protests of 2 Liberals," June 20, 1981.

73. State newspaper reporting on the bill referred only to racial harassment, suggesting that the bill's final language was developed out of the public eye. Black communities had identified police racism as a contributing factor in racist violence, but the bill did not address it. White supremacists also targeted queers with direct, repeated violence, but calls for hate crimes legislation to cover anti-queer violence were denied. Atiyeh threatened to veto his own bill if queers were included. Oregon State Archives, "Listing of Legislative Records in Oregon State Archives Pertaining to House Bill 2479, 1981," Oregon State Archives; *Oregonian*, "Gay Political Leader Urges Alternative to Reagan Plan," May 16, 1981.

'model' bill, therefore, seeks to provide state legislators with a single comprehensive, yet constitutionally sound approach to this growing problem," the report read. The model statute did that work. As it provided a tool kit for meeting the emergency of racist violence, it hitched along language that elevated religious vandalism, too, as a threat "just beneath the surface of American life" and turned attention from race to the broader, flattening terms of "race, color, religion, or national origin."[74]

Hate crimes laws were not just one more area of advocacy for the ADL. Rather, they constructed an entire new policy domain, as sociologists Valerie Jenness and Ryken Grattet describe a field in which a wide set of political actors develops a shared set of "cultural logics, theories, frameworks, and ideologies" and, through them, produces policy. The project, and the infrastructure that enabled it, were quite specific to the ADL. "The key organization responsible for creating and promoting the legal concept of hate crime, the Anti-Defamation League, is the most powerful domestic-policy-oriented Jewish organization in the United States," write Jenness and Grattet, historicizing the emergence of the domain. The fact that the ADL was already understood as a partner of state actors on civil rights and intolerance—as well as its ability to provide data, advise on legislative language, lobby, and narrate issues in the press, all on a regional and national scale—uniquely positioned it to introduce the hate frame and propel it

74. Within the ADL's Civil Rights Division, the language of "religious vandalism" alone still defined the issue for staff. In 1986, the division issued an internal paper in an effort to decide whether they should take over the Maryland Jewish Advocacy Center (JAC) as a civil litigation center to support victims of attacks to seek compensation. The report debated trying to use federal law that provided remedy only for attacks based on race. Jewish victims of crimes had not so far claimed that they weren't white. JAC had lost a 1984 test case in which it argued that the victim was *perceived* as "racially distinct." The ADL memo queried whether "it would be a bad precedent to argue for the applicability of a racial discrimination statute to a class of Jewish plaintiffs" either because of the implied racialization, or because of the appearance of trying to find profit in a protection that did not pertain to them. The ADL's reasons for declining help illuminate why hate crimes law was an important solution. They were wary of the optics of JAC's plan to rely on racial discrimination statutes, and the optics of lost cases. Their preferred pathway was to work with law enforcement, which had produced good results for the ADL if not for people of color facing violence. Anti-Defamation League, *1981 Audit of Anti-Semitic Incidents*, 5–7; Anti-Defamation League, *Countering Anti-Semitic Vandalism: Civil Litigation and the Jewish Advocacy Center*, September 1986, ADL Nearprint files, Box 4, American Jewish Archives.

forward.[75] By 1988, thirty states had adopted some version of such a law, many with the ADL's involvement; by the mid-1990s, nearly all states had done the same.[76] The ADL was a leader of a new, national cultural/political approach to racial anxieties, much as the audits had made it a national narrator of local Jewish communities' experiences.

The renewed focus on white supremacists and the KKK in the 1980s provided the ADL with a platform for this work. It imbued the ADL with current authority on matters of race, and helped position it as a necessary state partner in protecting democracy. In the 1970s the FBI had greatly reduced its monitoring of white nationalist groups, due in part to challenges asserting that white nationalist organizing was constitutionally protected speech, while the ADL had continued to surveil them as a latent threat, periodically updating reports in *Facts* and the *ADL Bulletin*.[77] It was that vigilance, as Suall described it, that had permitted the ADL to "notice some blips on our radar screen" in 1975 that intimated a resurgence.[78] In 1976 and 1977 its documentation of new activities and increasing membership led the public and law enforcement alike to comprehend the growth of the Klan as an emergency.[79] This prescience, as well as the ADL's granular reporting on leading figures and internal practices, meant that policymakers and media turned to the ADL for expertise. News reports on the KKK overwhelmingly cited the ADL as a singular authoritative source; soon, reports would regularly cite the ADL on hate crimes more generally.

The construction of *hate* as a national problem was catalyzed by the state model legislation campaigns and by frustration with the US Department of Justice's refusal to address it as a federal matter. The federal campaign began

75. Former NGLTF director Urvashi Vaid likewise cites the ADL as a key player (1985–90) in passing the HCSA, along with the ACLU, People for the American Way, and NAACP. Valerie Jenness and Ryken Grattet, *Making Hate a Crime: From Social Movement to Law Enforcement* (Russell Sage Foundation, 2004), 6, 48, 171; Urvashi Vaid, *Virtual Equality: The Mainstreaming of Gay and Lesbian Liberation* (Anchor Books, 1995), 141.

76. Ryken Grattet et al., "The Homogenization and Differentiation of Hate Crime Law in the United States, 1978 to 1995: Innovation and Diffusion in the Criminalization of Bigotry," *American Sociological Review* 63, no. 2 (1998): 132–33.

77. See, for instance, Dwayne Walls, "The Dormant Klan," *ADL Bulletin*, September 1970, 3; Charles F. Wittenstein, "It's Not the Same Old Klan," *ADL Bulletin*, October 1973, 3; *ADL Bulletin*, "The Klan Again," May 1975, 2.

78. Aryeh Neier, "Surveillance by the FBI," *Index on Censorship* 10, no. 2, April 1, 1981, 45–46; US Congress, *Increasing Violence Against Minorities*, 78.

79. See, for instance, Associated Press, "Klan Making Comeback, Anti-Defamation League Claims," in *Santa Cruz Sentinel*, November 18, 1977.

with a proposal simply to measure hate crimes: the Hate Crimes Statistics Act (HCSA). Despite a sense of urgency to intervene in violence, the problem defined as *hate* had defied the kind of measurement that would underwrite meaningful solutions. Connecticut Rep. Barbara Kennelly set out the problem: "Are crimes of hate a significant problem in this country? Are we in the midst of an upsurge in violence against particular racial, religious, or ethnic groups? Or is the problem confined to a few areas of the country where racial and ethnic tensions run high? I honestly don't know. Neither does anyone else."[80] More than just numbers, Kennelly wanted to distinguish between different kinds of violence. "The slaying of a spouse in a domestic quarrel and the murder of a black person because of racial hatred are both recorded as homicides ... [but] they don't have the same root causes. And they shouldn't be treated the same way."[81] In 1985, the ADL and a coalition of antiracist organizations, including the NAACP, ACLU, People for the American Way, and the National Organization of Black Law Enforcement Executives, along with the American Jewish Committee, the Lutheran Council, and the National Gay and Lesbian Task Force, began a five-year push to pass the HCSA.[82]

The conversation had begun in the federal arena at the same time as spectacles of violence had mobilized local action, in 1980. Much of this violence was described in terms of *terror*. The idea of *terror* had gained salience through the 1970s as a description of attacks on Western imperial power, seen as emanating from the Middle East. It had entered public discourse through the shock of the People's Front for the Liberation of Palestine attack on the 1972 Munich Olympics, and it had crystallized with the Iran hostage crisis of 1979–81, at the same time that white nationalism became a legible threat.

80. Testimony by Barbara Kennelly to US Congress, *Hate Crime Statistics Act: Hearing Before the Subcommittee on Criminal Justice of the Committee on the Judiciary, House of Representatives*, March 21, 1985, p. 21.

81. US Congress, *Hate Crime Statistics Act: Hearing Before the Subcommittee on Criminal Justice of the Committee on the Judiciary*, House of Representatives, March 21, 1985, p. 20.

82. Urvashi Vaid notes that "credit for the Hate Crimes Act ... belongs to a small number of gay and straight people." She lists the ADL, the ACLU legislative office, the NAACP, People for the American Way, congressional representatives John Conyers and Barney Frank, and Senator Paul Simon. A draft letter in the NGLTF files from Morton Halperin to David Brody lists the AJC and the influential Lutheran Council, among others, as early drivers of the queer-inclusive version (whose endorsements paved the way for the ADL's own). Vaid, *Virtual Equality*, 404n14. See draft letter from Morton Halperin to David Brody, Box 106, Folder 6, Series II, Field Files: Civil Rights Organizations: ADL, 1984–90, National Gay and Lesbian Task Force records, #7301, Cornell University.

Melani McAlister writes that the construction of *terror*, fueled by television coverage, constructed a moral geography that posited a dangerous and illiberal Middle East (except Israel) against an innocent West.[83] *Domestic* white nationalist violence both violated the moral sense of the United States as a place of safety and liberalism and echoed the circulating discourse of attack on the nation. Further, it was armed and organized. An ADL investigation had found an increase in paramilitary training camps, while the Klan was so entrenched in the US military that it had been using army printshops to publish materials, and uniformed soldiers had participated in Klan rallies as guards.[84] The years 1979 and 1980 saw dozens of racist sniper shootings, among other instances of racist violence. Under the caption "The Body Count," journalists at *Black Enterprise* magazine mapped at least twenty-five shootings and the murders of abducted Black children in seven states. In Fort Wayne, Indiana, a white supremacist serial killer shot Vernon Jordan, director of the National Urban League; the shooter had already been "involved" in eleven racially motivated murders the same year. Others included the Greensboro massacre, and a Ku Klux Klan attack in which four Black women were shot.[85] Adding to the urgency was the sense that quotidian racism was resurgent in American culture. It appeared in fights over busing and control of schools, and blame and outrage over economic losses.

In an extraordinary project to get to the bottom of this upwelling of violence, Michigan Rep. John Conyers launched a series of congressional hearings in 1980. By the time they concluded in 1988 he had conducted nine hearings, most stretching over multiple days. At the outset, "hate crime" did not yet exist as a legal category or even as a discrete social problem as a subject of advocacy. Instead, Conyers's subcommittee set for itself a task of confronting a problem not fully understood, characterized by the rise of "hate groups" and a "dangerous psychological climate" in which racism was normalized.[86]

83. Melani McAlister, *Epic Encounters: Culture, Media, and US Interests in the Middle East Since 1945* (University of California Press, 2005), 199–200.

84. US Congress, *Increasing Violence Against Minorities*.

85. The shootings, if not the other forms of racist violence, were the subject of inquiries by media and legislators, who struggled to aggregate and make sense of information about the attacks. Isaiah J. Poole and Miles White, "A Plot to Kill?," *Black Enterprise*, January 1981; Testimony of Drew S. Days III, US Congress, *Increasing Violence Against Minorities*, pp. 89–94.

86. US Congress, *Racially Motivated Violence: Hearings Before the Subcommittee on Criminal Justice of the Committee on the Judiciary*, House of Representatives, 97th Cong., 1st Session, March 4, June 3, and November 12, 1981, p. 4.

Neither Conyers nor many of the advocates and scholars who testified accepted *hate* as an independent phenomenon; instead, Conyers gathered testimony from those who studied systems and conditions of violence. Advocates from the NAACP to the National Organization of Black Law Enforcement Executives brought to Congress an analysis of white supremacist violence as a multifaceted problem embedded in the state. As they saw it, it encompassed police violence and impunity, structural denials of access to housing, education, and employment, and the embrace of racism by Reagan and earlier presidential administrations.

The inaugural hearing included four leftist movement lawyers, two political science professors, and the ADL's fact-finding director Irwin Suall, who testified as an expert on white supremacist groups. By 1988, the subcommittee had heard from a vast crew of race theorists, antiracist activists, radical lawyers, federal and state civil rights bodies, law enforcement, and Black, Indigenous, Chinese, Japanese, Southeast Asian, Arab, Puerto Rican, Muslim, queer, women's, and Jewish rights organizations. This unruly process produced a rich record of knowledge on racist violence and its relation to the history of the United States itself. Witnesses rejected the race-liberal claim that racist violence was an aberration, but rather pointed to the lethal policing of communities of color as a way that the state constructed them as normal, necessary subjects of violence.[87] When witnesses turned their attention to white nationalists, they interrogated power as a driver of the anger that motivated violence; not a single witness suggested the existence of abstract prejudice. Racist and anti-gay violence were described as a project of dispossession.[88] White nationalist ideology was reprehensible, but what made it matter was white nationalists' use of violence to deny people the ability to

87. Testimony of Kenneth Clark to US Congress, *Racially Motivated Violence: Hearings Before the Subcommittee on Criminal Justice of the Committee on the Judiciary*, House of Representatives, 97th Cong., 1st Session, March 4, June 3, and November 12, 1981, p. 6.

88. Legal scholar Denise Carty-Bennia presented an extensive legal history in 1981. Conyers's questioning of scholarly witnesses in later hearings, including the 1988 hiring on racially motivated violence, continued to reflect Reconstruction as a framing event for understanding such violence and the state's obligation and intention to intervene. Written testimony by Carty-Bennia to US Congress, *Racially Motivated Violence: Hearings Before the Subcommittee on Criminal Justice of the Committee on the Judiciary*, House of Representatives, 97th Cong., 1st Session, March 4, June 3, and November 12, 1981; US Congress, *Ethnically Motivated Violence Against Arab-Americans*, 40–42.

live out their citizenship, compounding denials already embedded in the state.[89] The hearings sketched an intensely political violence.

While the call for hate crimes laws responded to the inaction of law enforcement, religious vandalism bills addressed a very different kind of problem. Hate crimes laws were intended to force civil rights back onto the agenda of a disinterested state. Although Justice Department officials claimed that they were prosecuting the Klan's federal crimes, they separately asserted that federal law did not criminalize the use of racial violence by individuals, including "acts of terror" or murder, to limit the exercise of citizenship.[90] To advocates, this failure reflected a broader abandonment of race-based civil rights commitments. They needed another tool to induce federal agencies to regulate violence in the immediate crisis. But religious vandalism bills were more straightforwardly aimed at increasing discipline. At least ten such bills were introduced between 1981 and 1988, when a law was finally passed.[91] Rep. Dan Glickman of Kansas (whose staff overlapped with the ADL) proposed a 1985 bill criminalizing the destruction of religious property in fairly simple terms.[92] At a hearing on "crimes against religious practices and property," presided over by Conyers, the American Jewish Committee and five white congressional representatives gave the only testimony. The

89. The incommensurability of racist violence with full citizenship is taken up in discussions across hearings. Witnesses drew parallels between 1980s violence and projects to scuttle Reconstruction; noted the broad national failure to respond to the recommendations of the Kerner Commission report; and identified the refusal of law enforcement to intervene in violence as a contributing element of violence. See, for instance, testimony of Denise S. Carty-Bennia to US Congress, *Racially Motivated Violence*, 1981, pp. 102–7; Statement of Fred R. Harris to US Congress, *Racially Motivated Violence*, 1988, pp. 117–18.

90. See testimony of Victoria Toensing to US Congress, *Crimes Against Religious Practices and Property: Hearings Before the Subcommittee on Criminal Justice of the Committee on the Judiciary*, House of Representatives, 99th Cong., 1st session, May 16 and June 19, 1985, pp. 26–44.

91. Sponsors of legislation on religious vandalism and religious bigotry came from a variety of political positions: staunchly conservative Republicans (New York's Al D'Amato and California's Bobbi Fiedler) and a relatively conservative machine Democrat (New York's Mario Biaggi, who was indicted on corruption charges within a few years) introduced three such bills, all in pursuit of elevating antisemitism. Several more were proposed by Rep. Dan Glickman of Kansas, almost certainly in collaboration with the ADL and also motivated by antisemitism, as his congressional testimony affirms. A progressive Democrat, Rep. Barbara Kennelly of Connecticut, whose advocacy included anti-Black, antisemitic, and white nationalist activity broadly, proposed an early version of the HCSA.

92. Rep. Glickman's in-house counsel Michael Lieberman became the ADL's Midwest regional director in 1982.

vandalism addressed in the bill was characterized as outrageous but neither epidemic nor dispossessive. Indeed, Glickman noted that Jewish communities weren't interested in the bill: "There seems to be some reticence—it's not formal—among some Jewish groups that perhaps we ought to leave well enough alone, that the States can handle this matter, why make it a big Federal issue, why play the issue out in the press more than it is."[93] As the two threads progressively merged, legislators struggled to expand their scope beyond antisemitism, the presumptive religious subject of "racial and religious bigotry," and to describe religious identity in terms that aligned with race.

Despite advocates' calls for solutions to the problems underlying racist violence, a more simplistic approach—legislating on *hate*—gathered force, in part because more meaningful solutions simply called for too much change. Given the Reagan administration's disinterest, convincing the Department of Justice to enforce civil rights laws seemed a distant hope. Beyond that, solutions called for altering core US systems, and ultimately redistributing power. Advocates sought to shift the normalization of police killings of Black people as the maintenance of "law and order" in geographies and economies defined by racism. Indigenous groups called for redress of settler violence, as when white fishermen shot at them while trying to claim waterways, and when police treated them as intruders in white communities.[94] Queer advocates, while primarily calling for law enforcement to intervene in anti-gay and anti-lesbian violence, called also for the uprooting of puritanical narratives and a culture of disposability.[95] Conyers, too, was anxious to go to the root. "Legislators are frequently operating in a vacuum," he commented to sociologist M. Harvey Brenner during a 1981 hearing. "Why don't the

93. US Congress, *Crimes Against Religious Practices and Property*, p. 64.

94. Testimony of Kenneth B. Clark to US Congress, *Racially Motivated Violence*, House of Representatives, 97th Cong., 1st Session, March 4, June 3, and November 12, 1981, p. 6; Statements of Christine Griffin and James M. Janetta to US Congress, *Anti-Indian Violence: Hearings Before the Subcommittee on Civil and Constitutional Rights of the Committee on the Judiciary*, House of Representatives, 100th Cong., 2nd Session, May 4 and 18, 1988, pp. 21–22, 139.

95. On the National Gay and Lesbian Task Force's use of anti-Black and "terror" framings of anti-queer violence, see Christina B. Hanhardt, *Safe Space: Gay Neighborhood History and the Politics of Violence* (Duke University Press, 2013), 176. On calls for shifts in heteronormative culture, see prepared statement of Steven L. Kendall to US Congress, *Anti-Gay Violence: Hearing Before the Subcommittee on Criminal Justice of the Committee on the Judiciary*, House of Representatives, 99th Cong., 2nd Session, October 9, 1986, p. 221.

national organizations . . . come forward in a more organized way to help the Government and the lawmakers make decisions on the basis of something more than 'gut' reactions to increases in crime?" Racial violence was beyond legislative solutions, Brenner answered. "It lies within the social and economic fabric and unless that is in some way reconstructed we shall be living with this problem."[96] Witnesses kept returning to that message throughout eight years of hearings.

As media, advocates, and legislators articulated racist violence as a crisis, it took on the shape of moral panic. As Stuart Hall et al. explain, moral panics arise around sensational events—such as the Greensboro massacre, the Oregon arsons, the Long Island bomb threats, the Boston turf wars—that are narrated as a singular, immediate social problem. As reporting on violence continued, the idea of "an epidemic of hate" driven by personal biases became the crisis to which legislators were responding. Elevated to the level of nationally recognized crisis, the notion of *hate* became a cipher that permitted marginalized groups to make violence against them *matter*; to be a call to action.[97] If the United States promised racial equality and a modicum of safety, the targets of violence found it hard to get. "There has been a real feeling . . . that we are not wanted," Kim Oanh Cook told Congress, testifying on behalf of Southeast Asian refugees. Because Asian refugees were so marginal, Cook explained, even their experiences of racism were invisible, so no remedies were forthcoming. "A refugee who has been hit, beaten, and discriminated against . . . he doesn't know the ABCs of documentation." The counting of hate crimes offered an unmissable chance to be legible. "[A]mong localities who have shown the foresight to collect statistics on such attacks, an alarming, increasing wave of hate crimes has been reported," Rep. Norman

96. US Congress, *Racially Motivated Violence: Hearings Before the Subcommittee on Criminal Justice of the Committee on the Judiciary*, House of Representatives, 97th Cong., 1st Session, March 4, June 3, and November 12, 1981, 24.

97. The construction of hate violence as an "epidemic" arose from gay and lesbian advocates' efforts to document violence, particularly the National Gay and Lesbian Task Force, and to place it in relation to the ongoing AIDS epidemic. It was then applied to other spheres, including violence against women and various racial and ethnic groups. (See, for instance, Center for Democratic Renewal, *When Hate Groups Come to Town: A Handbook of Effective Community Responses* [1992], 33–34. The first edition was published in 1987.) For a critique of the term "epidemic" to construct hate as a pervasive social problem, see James B. Jacobs and Jessica S. Henry, "The Social Construction of a Hate Crime Epidemic," *Journal of Criminal Law and Criminology* 86, no. 2 (1996): 367.

Y. Mineta testified at the same hearing. "Our society can no longer ignore the widespread, and often unrecognized, incidence of harassment and violence against Americans of Asian ancestry."[98] Despite the fact that antiracist organizers and scholars had identified political-historical state structures underlying the crisis, and despite the highly local contexts for violence, these were overshadowed by the much simpler idea of *hate*.

For Perlmutter's ADL, boiling the problem down to individual bias had the benefit of putting religious vandalism and racial violence under a single umbrella, placing antisemitism alongside "fashionable" anti-Blackness. Proposing them as a form of *terror* redirected blame away from the structures of state and capital. In addition, the hate frame marginalized the conceptions of racism, and race itself, that Perlmutter and other neoconservatives found objectionable; it was colorblind. It moved sharply away from the ideas that Perlmutter had denounced as "fashionable"—that race was a structure, and racism should be resolved by redistributive measures, whether community control of schools, affirmative action, or anticolonial rebellion. ADL leaders did not believe that the social and economic fabric ought to be reconstructed at all. Instead, they regularly affirmed that the United States was a model of democracy and egalitarianism; "bias" was an aberration. While marginalized groups saw police as perpetrators of violence against them, the ADL's complaint was that law enforcement was not empowered *enough*. "[S]ituations people encounter every day, slurs written on doors or in cemeteries . . . don't get investigated because they are third degree misdemeanors," explained Michael Lieberman, director of the ADL's Civil Rights Policy Planning Center and former staffer for Rep. Dan Glickman during his efforts for a federal religious vandalism law.[99] They needed to escalate the criminality of small acts. Focusing on individual bad actors and adding penalties made the hate frame appealing to conservative advocates for law and order, too. Gathering police groups, victims' rights groups, and an array of agencies and officials along with antiracist and queer rights advocates, the call for hate

98. Testimonies of Kim Oanh Cook and Hon. Norman Y. Mineta to US Congress, *Anti-Asian Violence: Oversight Hearing Before the Subcommittee on Criminal Justice of the Committee on the Judiciary*, House of Representatives, 100th Cong., 1st Session, November 10, 1983, pp. 3, 101–2.

99. Lieberman quoted in Clara S. Lewis, *Tough on Hate? The Cultural Politics of Hate Crimes* (Rutgers University Press, 2013), 30.

crimes laws amassed a broad base.[100] What had begun as an effort to intervene in racism had become a program to escalate policing.

In 1990, HCSA's passage into federal law announced *hate* and *hate crime* as a national law enforcement framework. The adoption of the hate frame accomplished Perlmutter's aims. It flew the banner of civil rights, with the ADL in its lead. It stripped anti-Black and other repressive violences of their specificity and helped to dehistoricize them. It also stripped antisemitism of its specificity, as it conflated small, casual acts with the intense violence experienced by Jews in specific places and in particular historic moments. In doing so, it likened Jewishness to Blackness and a host of other marginalized identities, rewriting them together as targets of hate and *subjects of remedy*. Fulfilling the call that Forster and Epstein had laid out in *The New Anti-Semitism*, it applied to US Jewry the imperative protections owed to structurally marginalized groups, without regard to the community's placement in a broader power structure. The reorganization of the landscape of civil rights allowed the embarrassing rift between Jewish- and Black-led organizations to recede from memory. As acting *against hate* became a staple of community advocacy, groups associated with racial justice and queer rights increasingly collaborated with the ADL and often saw the partnership as logistically essential.[101] News outlets, too, escalated their coverage of antisemitism, crowding out other coverage of Jewish life and, eventually, other forms of racism. In 1980, antisemitism stories quadrupled in proportion to total news, and steadily filled that space throughout the decade. In earlier years, such stories had a minuscule presence in newspaper reporting, even while the ADL's jaunty books had reached a mass audience. Now, in addition to attending to domestic incidents, coverage of Middle Eastern politics increasingly discussed them as a site of anti-Jewish intolerance.[102] At the same time, US foreign policy discourse on Zionism, Israel, and the Middle East were increas-

100. Jenness and Grattet note that the call for hate crimes legislation brought conservative groups from the victims' rights movement into the campaign that civil rights organizations had created. Those groups, too, had been campaigning for approaches to criminal justice that focused on individuals and deemphasized structural contexts. Jenness and Grattet, *Making Hate a Crime*, 30–31.

101. Hanhardt, *Safe Space*, 170.

102. This assessment is based on Factiva data using term searches between 1979 and 1990.

ingly articulated in terms of antisemitism and the need for US foreign policy to defend against it.

In polarity with Epstein, Forster, and Perlmutter's move to re-narrate Jewishness as a marginalized like-race identity and in that way extend protections to Zionism, the ADL also worked to re-narrate Arab identity as *political* and therefore attackable. Since 1956, when Forster and Epstein's book *Cross-Currents* had portrayed the Klan and the Arab League as "overlapping forces," ADL public relations strategy had entailed using US white nationalism as an allegory for its denunciations of Palestinian politics. Conversely, it had chided and dismissed mentions of Palestinian rights in connection with civil rights. In the lead-up to the 1975 UN vote on Resolution 3379, the "Zionism is racism" resolution, ADL leaders re-upped this strategy. "Is not the participation of the PLO in this debate like having the Ku Klux Klan or the Symbionese Revolutionary Army debating on the floor of the United States Congress?," demanded Stuart Lewengrub, the ADL's southeast regional director.[103] As Arab and Black political connections were built through the work of organizers like attorney Abdeen Jabara, who worked with Conyers, and Jesse Jackson's Operation PUSH, the ADL and other Zionist groups more insistently used the Klan as a glyph for Palestinians. When President Jimmy Carter, explaining the importance of optics in negotiations on Palestinian rights, used the civil rights movement as an analogy, major Jewish institutions reared up. In a rhetorical twist, Arnold Forster denounced Carter's comment not as anti-Jewish, but as anti-Black. It was the "worst insult," Forster fumed, "to suggest that the PLO is akin to the civil rights movement. . . . The president was comparing organized murderers with the best of America."[104]

The developments of the latter part of the 1970s further escalated Zionist worries about Black-Arab solidarities and their potential weight in the US political arena. Following the election of Menachem Begin as prime minister of Israel in 1977, Carter called for the PLO to be part of peace negotiations—in other words, for Israeli-Arab negotiations over Palestine to at last include

103. Arnold Forster and Benjamin R. Epstein, *Cross-Currents* (Doubleday, 1956), 143, 164; Stuart Lewengrub, "UN Vote on PLO," Letter to the Editor, *Atlanta Constitution*, October 28, 1974.

104. William Raspberry, "A Costly Omission of Context," *The Record*, August 14, 1979.

Palestinians. The Conference of Presidents of Major American Jewish Organizations immediately responded by likening it to a demand for "civil rights leaders (in the American south) to negotiate with the Ku Klux Klan."[105] Shortly afterward, Carter's UN ambassador, the former civil rights leader Andrew Young, met secretly with PLO officials. Israeli officials leaked news of the meeting; presumably the Israeli Mossad had been surveilling the PLO. Although the purpose of the meeting had been to delay a call for Palestinian statehood, not support it, Young was forced to resign from his ambassador post. Once again, Israel and its demands became a subject of outrage in Black political spheres. The events called "for a reassessment of black relations with the White House, the Jewish community and traditional attitudes towards Israel and the Arab world," as Richard Hatcher, the mayor of Gary, Indiana, commented.[106] It also escalated other grievances: Jewish institutions' opposition to affirmative action, their defense of Israel's continuing trade with Apartheid South Africa, and the feeling that Jewish communities had abandoned civil rights efforts just at the moment when Black communities began demanding real power.[107]

The ADL's response, like that of major Jewish institutions collectively, mixed chiding and cajoling aimed at Black audiences in a litany of statements packed with references to civil rights and the Klan.[108] ADL national chairman Maxwell E. Greenberg took a stern line in October, as Young's resignation still reverberated. After insisting that the ADL's positions on South Africa and affirmative action did not contradict its commitments to civil rights, he attacked from the other direction: He charged Jesse Jackson, Young's political heir apparent, with contributing to the racial violence of hate groups. "Let me

105. Robert Kaiser, "US Jews Expect Clash with Carter," *Jerusalem Post*, October 5, 1977.

106. Paul Delaney, "Leaders Try to Halt a Black-Jewish Rift," *New York Times*, August 19, 1979.

107. *Chicago Jewish Post and Opinion*, "Small Meetings Being Held; Barrage by Blacks Continue," August 24, 1979; David M. Alpern, Kim Willensen, and Thomas M. DeFrank, "The Black Backlash," *Newsweek*, August 27, 1979; Sid Cassese, "Jews Pledge Black Support," *Newsday*, August 25, 1979.

108. The collective approach is illustrated in a statement by the Jewish Community Relations Council, representing over a hundred groups, issued shortly after Young's resignation. The statement primly pledged to overlook the harsh criticisms that Black leaders had levied against Jewish organizations and repeated commitments to the demands of civil rights movement projects—"full employment, fair housing, integrated quality education, health care and equitable solutions to inflation and the energy crisis." Affirmative action was conspicuously absent. In presenting the statement to press, the JCRC's leader again denounced the PLO as "like the Klan." Cassese, "Jews Pledge Black Support."

be clear. As a private citizen, the Rev. Jesse Jackson has the right to sit down and talk to anyone—Arafat, Charlie Manson, Josef Mengele, or the head of the Ku Klux Klan, but by doing so he gives murderers and bigots added credibility . . . he tacitly approves the murder of . . . Arab and Jewish women and children."[109]

The ADL's leadership on hate crimes advocacy provided it another important platform for placing Arabs and Arabness outside of the sphere of *civil rights*. As it prepared to launch the audits, the ADL's opposition to Arab American organizing took a tactical turn toward *hate*. "ADL Reports 50 Anti-Jewish Incidents at Some 31 Campuses Around the US," the *Detroit Jewish News* announced, reporting on a 1979 ADL survey of universities conducted with Hillel. Although the framing gestured to the growing national conversation on racial hostility, the story noted that one-fifth of incidents identified were labeled "political" and covered anti-Zionist events. (Doubling down on the ADL's opposition to affirmative action, the report complained that twenty-three universities were still using admissions policies geared toward bringing in students of color.)[110] Suall's testimony at Conyers's 1980 hearing on "increasing violence against minorities" further hinted at the emerging project. At that hearing, Conyers presumed that Suall's subject would be white power groups. After presenting a portrait of the Klan, though, Suall surprised him by adding that leftist groups, particularly Palestinian ones, posed a parallel "serious potential threat to innocent American citizens." Suall claimed that the PLO had violently attacked Jews and Israelis inside the United States, and he likened the PLO to the Ku Klux Klan. Understanding the claim as a smear, Conyers tartly but diplomatically pressed Suall to specify when this had happened; Suall had no answer. No such incidents had been documented. "There have been acts against Jews and Israelis in the United States. In not all cases were the culprits found," Suall demurred. "The acts were conducted in such a manner that in my judgment the PLO was very likely involved." Conyers warned: "You don't want to be irresponsible, so let's leave the subject at that."[111]

109. Maxwell E. Greenberg, "A Commentary: Jewish Point of View," *Michigan Chronicle*, October 20, 1979.

110. *Detroit Jewish News*, "ADL Reports 50 Anti-Jewish Incidents at Some 31 Campuses Around the US," June 22, 1979.

111. US Congress, *Increasing Violence Against Minorities*, 85; Pamela E. Pennock, *The Rise of the Arab American Left: Activists, Allies, and Their Fight Against Imperialism and Racism, 1960s–1980s* (University of North Carolina Press, 2016), 207–21.

Beyond the PLO, the ADL was concerned about Arab Americans' progress in establishing a place in domestic ethnic politics. Arab American political organizing had been galvanized over the prior long decade, in large part by the 1967 war and the wave of emigrants and students it sent to the United States.[112] Additionally the FBI's Operation Boulder—the first War on Terror–style program of surveillance, interrogation, and deportation of Arabs and Iranians in the United States (1972–75)—mobilized resistance against such "political racism" and intimidation.[113] The circumstances of organizing Palestinian resistance across dispersion gave it an inherently transnational character, and student movements and scholarship theorizing Arab and Palestinian experience under colonization and the Western gaze established its ties with Third World radicalisms.[114] In the 1970s, Arab American politics developed beyond campuses and also took the shape of participation in the US mainstream. Like the ADL, organizations like the Palestine Human Rights Campaign spoke in the language of civil rights, and the American-Arab Anti-Discrimination Committee embraced Americanism as the framework for its calls for inclusion. They built relationships both with Black radicals who understood anti-Arab and anti-Palestinian discrimination as the product of imperialism, and also with civil rights organizers who were receptive to the groups' newer, more liberal frame. Additionally, like the ADL and its partners in what had emerged as the Israel lobby, they collectively began to form a countervailing Arab lobby, registering opinions and interests with presidents and policymakers.[115] By the 1980s the Arab American Institute (AAI) was shepherding Arab issues and voters to the national electoral sphere through Jackson's campaign, and the American-Arab Anti-Discrimination Committee was conducting anti-defamation work along much the same lines as the ADL, through incident reports and public relations work.

For the ADL, Arab American community organizing constituted an emergency. Since 1969, the ADL and other Zionist organizations had charged that Arab university students in the United States were an insurgent Cold War threat: a conduit for Third Worldist ideas and Arab League intrusions

112. Pennock, *Rise of the Arab American Left*, 47–49.
113. Pennock, *Rise of the Arab American Left*, 143, 153.
114. Alex Lubin, *Geographies of Liberation: The Making of an Afro-Arab Political Imaginary* (University of North Carolina Press, 2014), 113.
115. Pennock, *Rise of the Arab American Left*, 202–5.

into US politics, as Pamela Pennock writes.[116] "There is growing evidence of an effort to mobilize the Arab-American community, numbering more than a million citizens, for political action and lobbying," warned ADL research director Jerome Bakst in 1975. If American public opinion shifted, he wrote, it would mean the withdrawal of US support for Israel, and Israel's demise.[117] That year the ADL published a 118-page report, *Target USA: The Arab Propaganda Offensive*. It argued that the Arab League was conducting "economic warfare" that involved recruiting global allies by offering access to lucrative Arab markets, siphoning up "the world's wealth" and spreading petrodollar-funded "global [anti-Israel] propaganda" in "carefully detailed master plans."[118] Without irony, the report cast Arab American politics—closely modeled on Zionist politics—as a foreign influence conspiracy: "A key ingredient in the Arab propaganda game plan is an effort to mobilize the approximately one million Americans of Arab extraction, many residing in key political states and cities, into a unified, activist and ethnically oriented force that would work in political campaigns and serve as an effective lobbying instrument to influence Congressional votes on Middle Eastern issues." The targets of this distinctly ADL-like outreach, the ADL fretted, included churches, organized labor, Black Americans, universities, and media. It complained particularly bitterly about the extensive list of Jewish activists who advocated for Palestinian rights "from their anti-war, 'pro-peace,' 'anti-establishment' or New Left viewpoints."[119] It worried about the development of Middle East Studies programs at US universities, which it viewed as propaganda outlets that could be funded by foreign states.

Throughout the 1970s and into the 1980s, Arab American political organizations developed beyond the milieu of student movements and the left: forging space in the arena of liberal politics and developing strategies in electoral politics.[120] As they established their place in ethnic representational politics, they faced both broad cultural opposition and targeted political attack. Jack Shaheen's 1984 study *TV Arabs* documented mass media stereotypes that produced a broad cultural anti-Arabness that in many ways paralleled antisemitism. It was grounded in notions of foreignness, conspiracy,

116. Pennock, *Rise of the Arab American Left*, 55, 145.
117. David Young, "Arabs, Jews Wage War on the Propaganda Front," *Chicago Tribune*, July 27, 1975.
118. Anti-Defamation League, *Target USA: The Arab Propaganda Offensive*, 1975, 5.
119. Anti-Defamation League, *Target USA*, 9, 19.
120. Pennock, *Rise of the Arab American Left*, 204–22.

wealth, and racialized bodies—and violence—linked with the narrative of *terror* circulating through US foreign policy discourse.[121] In a more direct attack, the ADL set out to discredit and isolate Arab American organizations and leading figures, and was joined in this effort by AIPAC. In 1983 the ADL circulated another blacklist of Arab American political groups, academics, and organizers (along with Jewish and Iranian groups) identifying them as "pro-Arab sympathizers" and antisemites. The ADL's complaint was that Arab Americans were affecting public opinion on Israel. "Pro-Arab propagandists make their point well," read an introductory note to a campus version of the blacklist. "Israel is depicted as a 'militaristic,' 'brutal,' and 'oppressive' nation. . . . The ultimate goal of these anti-Israel, pro-Arab propagandists is to sway Americans from their historically strong support for Israel." That version of the blacklist was stamped "Confidential" because, according to Boston ADL director Leonard Zakim's cover letter, "it easily could be misconstrued." It was mailed to "several dozen campus Jewish leaders," presumably students and faculty, and possibly administrators, with the request that they submit information on anyone else who should be on the list. AIPAC produced a second list of "enemies of Israel" at the same time, written by an ADL staffer who moved between the two organizations.[122]

Arab American communities were also being subjected to intense violence. A series of bombings, murders, and violent assaults targeted Arab and Muslim community groups across the US: in Boston, New York, Philadelphia, Washington, DC, Detroit, Houston, San Francisco, among other cities and suburbs. The Jewish Defense League—a Zionist, Jewish supremacist, FBI-designated "domestic terror organization"—was widely believed to be carrying out the most egregious anti-Arab violence. In October 1985 a bombing killed Alex Odeh, the director of the San Francisco regional American-Arab Anti-Discrimination Committee, at his office. In that year and the next, according to the committee's *Harassment and Violence Log Sheet*, a Houston mosque was bombed, and the office of the United Palestinian Appeal relief agency was destroyed by arson. Homes were set on fire, and beatings and rapes were threatened in anonymous phone calls. A woman dating a Palestinian man was raped, assaulted with a lead pipe, and a Star of David

121. Jack G. Shaheen, *The TV Arab* (Popular Press, 1984), 12.

122. Leonard Zakim to Campus Jewish Leaders, November 1983, in Lee O'Brien, *American Jewish Organizations and Israel* (Institute for Palestine Studies, 1986), 180. Former ADL staffer Amy Goott moved to AIPAC in 1982, tasked with tracking the increasingly significant "Arab lobby."

carved on her chest. Two Muslim scholars of Islamic Studies had been hacked to death in their home in Cheltenham, Pennsylvania.[123]

Describing these conditions in 1986, Arab American Institute director James Zogby laid out how anti-Arab violence was integrated with the ADL's delegitimization of Arab citizenship and membership in the US polity. The bombings, fires, and murders followed where the ADL and AIPAC had vilified Arab Americans and where Arabs had been frozen out of political power structures. Victims of violence were "terroriz[ed] into submission," Zogby wrote, because the FBI failed to prosecute any case, the community was unable to gain political support, and ADL and its partners had successfully cast anti-Arab violence as a rational response to Arab politics. "In pointing out these connections," Zogby wrote, "I am not suggesting that AIPAC, the ADL and the JDL [Jewish Defense League] are collaborators. They do, however, share a common political agenda, and their tactics in fact converge to create a personal and a political threat to the civil rights of Arab Americans and their organizations."[124]

When these violent acts and assaults on Arab American political organizing entered the discourse on *hate*, the ADL suddenly appeared as an antagonist. Conyers added it to the agenda in 1986, with a hearing on "ethnically motivated violence against Arab-Americans." An American Jewish Committee witness stood in for the major Jewish organizations. Had ADL staff appeared, it would have been an uncomfortable confrontation: Zogby described to Congress eighteen specific instances when efforts to access the electoral process had been stymied by the blacklists or reputational threats promulgated by the ADL. In one instance, Arab Americans had been entirely disinvited from all White House briefings for ethnic groups' representatives after Jewish press reported that "two PLO supporters"—Zogby and another organizational leader—had attended such a meeting. Another took place in New York state, where the local ADL had told the Democratic Party leadership that an Arab candidate was a "Libyan agent" and should not get the party's endorsement. In another, Arab Americans had fundraised for Philadelphia mayoral candidate W. Wilson Goode in 1983, but then Goode's

123. American-Arab Anti-Discrimination Committee, "ADC Harassment and Violence Log Sheet," reprinted in US Congress, *Ethnically Motivated Violence Against Arab-Americans*, House of Representatives, 99th Cong., 2nd Session, July 16, 1986, pp. 61–70.

124. Statement by Dr. James Zogby to US Congress, *Ethnically Motivated Violence Against Arab-Americans*, House of Representatives, 99th Cong., 2nd Session, July 16, 1986, p. 134.

opponent had accused him of accepting foreign money, echoing the allegations circulated by the ADL and AIPAC. Not only had Goode returned the money, but after his election he had refused to meet with Arab American constituents. "In each instance," Zogby testified, "we have found essentially the same 'blacklists' being circulated and re-circulated to congressmen, newspaper editorial boards and political campaigns, with a deliberate attempt to ruin political careers and deny Arab Americans their political rights."[125]

After the first three witnesses—Arab American members of Congress Nick Joe Rahall and Mary Rose Oakar, and former senator James Abourezk—had described a tidal wave of racist and misogynist violence, American Jewish Committee executive vice president David Gordis sat to testify. He assured the panel that the AJC opposed anti-Arab violence and "attempted to counter ethnic stereotyping of any and all ethnic groups, including Arab Americans." On the other hand, Gordis hedged, "we do not know for certain that these particular acts were ethnically motivated." Rather, Arab Americans and their organizations were guilty of "encouraging terrorism" through their support for the PLO and working against the US national interest by opposing Israel; it was political animus toward those acts that produced anti-Arab violence, not racism. Given the *Zionist* nature of anti-Arab violence, Gordis bluntly proposed that it did not belong in the category of hate crimes at all, and that Arab Americans were making a disingenuous claim. If animus toward Arabs was political, they were not owed protection: They could not be *subjects of remedy*. "Any campaign against stereotyping or violence must not be a pretext for a campaign, the real purpose of which is to defame another group or another country," Gordis concluded.[126] In a discourse of *hate* whose job was to flatten the experience of "difference" into a simple set of rights—the right to policing above all—no politics or history could be admissible. *Hate* did not need to be violent or dispossessive to draw down the carceral protection of the state; instead, it had to make no sense at all. Such arguments casting anti-Arab violence as retribution, making *opposition* to anti-Palestinian racism impermissible in US civil rights discourse, would build and reverberate over the next decades.

As organizing for hate crimes legislation heated up with the formalization of a Hate Crimes Bill Coalition in 1987—gathering the ADL, American Jewish Committee, victims' rights groups, and the National Gay and Lesbian

125. US Congress, *Ethnically Motivated Violence Against Arab-Americans*, 139.
126. US Congress, *Ethnically Motivated Violence Against Arab-Americans*, 40–42.

Task Force—the Palestinian First Intifada began. It was an uprising against what Rabea Eghbariah has defined conceptually as *Nakba*: a dominative structure of ongoing conquest, dispossession, occupation, criminalization, societal fracture, and catastrophic violence for the purpose of denying self-determination to Palestinians.[127] In crucial ways, it echoed the shapes of racial violence that animated the call for hate crimes laws. But rather than sparking discourse on anti-Arab racism or *hate*, the Intifada was used in US discourse to connect Palestinians and *terror*.[128] The ADL had associated *terror* with Nazi persecution of Jews, and in 1965 it was central in Forster and Epstein's renewed reporting on the Klan. In those contexts, *terror* meant an overpowering, all-surrounding racial violence. But its engagement with *terror* as a matter of US national security interest had strictly to do with anti-Palestinianism. Forster, having rushed to Israel to report after the 1967 war, sent home reports of "Arab terrorists" as an offshoot of Arab League armies, driven by evil thoughts and beholden to the Soviet Union and the international anti-Western left, who flouted the purported peace that Israel had constructed in the region.[129] The construction of Jews as *subjects of remedy* united the two frames. It stitched together US empire as a civilizing, settling project, and the United States itself as a safe harbor against racism and intolerance, protected by police. Arabness was incommensurable.

Within a few months of October 7, 2023, the imperative to "stand against hate"—to extend protections not to Jews, but to Zionist Jews and the Israeli state—had become an open-ended demand for securitization.[130] By summer, dozens of campuses had invited hundreds of police forces to brutalize students who had set up tent encampments to call for their universities to divest

127. Rabea Eghbariah, "Toward Nakba as a Legal Concept," *Columbia Law Review* 124, no. 4 (2024): 964–66, 988.

128. Darryl Li, *Anti-Palestinian at the Core: The Origins and Growing Dangers of US Antiterrorism Law* (Center for Constitutional Rights and Palestine Legal, 2024).

129. See, for instance, Arnold Forster, "Report from Israel: The Soviet-Arab Axis," *ADL Bulletin*, September 1968, 1–2; Arnold Forster, "Report from Israel: Arab Terrorists," *ADL Bulletin*, January 1969, 3; Jerome Bakst, "The Radical Left and Al Fatah," *ADL Bulletin*, September, 1969, 1–2.

130. Amira Jarmakani, "On the Move from 'Zionism Is Racism' to 'Antisemitism Is Racism,'" *Battling the IHRA Definition*, podcast by the Institute for the Critical Study of Zionism, August 15, 2024, https://criticalzionismstudies.org/amira-jarmakani-on-the-move-from-zionism-is-racism-to-antisemitism-is-racism/.

from weapons manufacturing. Continually, President Joe Biden denounced Palestine solidarity protests as *hate* and repeated his commitment to "the safety of the Jewish people" by promising virtually limitless weaponry to Israel, which the International Criminal Court had charged with ongoing genocide. In 2025, as Trump moved to fulfill his promise to "deport millions" by snatching Mahmoud Khalil, Leqaa Kordia, Rumeysa Ozturk, and many other students, fighting antisemitism was the rationale. The frames of *terror* and *hate* rest on closely shared conceptual ground. But *terror* vastly scales up the carceral resources, and, as legal theorist Shirin Sinnar writes, it deploys them in the domain of secretive, repressive policy. "By design, the mandates of security agencies do not prioritize civil rights, racial justice, or the concerns of subordinated communities," Sinnar explains. In other words, this "protection" grows a police state.[131] As Hall et al. theorize moral panic, the "solution" is more repression and leaves in place the underlying structures that produced the original problem: racism, economic exploitation, explosive tension between colonized and colonizer. Indeed, those structures are reinforced and renaturalized, as people come to believe that they have provided safety. Those calling for change at the root seem "out there," marginal, extreme.[132]

These are the enticements that Perlmutter envisioned as the spoils of "Jewish worry." Together, *hate* and *terror* suture law and order and the national interest to support for Israel, suppression of the anticolonial left, and the criminalization of the ADL's own opponents—Jewish, Palestinian, and Black especially. Perlmutter could not have known that his efforts to leverage the power of *subjects of remedy* would be so successful or that they would meet a world increasingly in rebellion against Western hegemony.

131. Shirin Sinnar, "Hate Crimes, Terrorism, and the Framing of White Supremacist Violence," *California Law Review* 110 (April 2022): 527, 545.

132. Stuart Hall et al., *Policing the Crisis: Mugging, the State, and Law and Order* (Pan Macmillan, 1978), 201.

Epilogue

IN 2009, THE ISRAELI DOCUMENTARY *Defamation* made a small splash.
It was warmly reviewed on National Public Radio's website and in the *Boston
Globe*, and given a scant two paragraphs by the *New York Times*, which called
it "disorganized and somewhat annoying . . . another day on the Op-Ed page."[1]
In the film, Anti-Defamation League national director Abe Foxman grants
filmmaker Yoav Shamir inside access to ADL offices—knowing little about
him except that Shamir is Israeli—including meetings with state leaders in
Israel and Europe and a March of the Living concentration camp tour for
Israeli high schoolers. The film's titillating tension comes as ADL leaders and
Israeli high school students insist that a terrifying crisis of antisemitism is
underway. The viewer sees that no such crisis exists, and that the ADL is comi-
cally struggling to produce one. ADL leaders meet to discuss "a spike in anti-
semitic and racist activities." They tell Shamir, "We're flooded every day with
these things all over the country," but they cannot point to any incidents. The
students on their journey through concentration camp sites report that "everyone knows that Jews are hated, we were raised like that." In the moment,
though, the antisemitism they experience is imagined, fueled by the assertions
of their teachers and Israeli security officers that they will constantly encounter hatred and danger once they leave Israel. In a village square, an elderly man
asks some Israeli teenagers in Polish: "Where are you from? Israel?" The students, who do not understand Polish, presume they are under attack: "He said
we're bitches!" "I understood that!," they say, amping up each other's panic.[2]

---

1. Neil Genzlinger, "The Past in the Present," *New York Times*, November 20, 2009.

2. Yoav Shamir, dir., *Defamation* (First Run Features, 2009), posted September 5, 2023, by
Yoav Shamir Films, YouTube, 1:31:40, https://www.youtube.com/watch?v=CTAjc1OSrmY.

For the viewer the crisis deflates, while the students continue to live it as an intense shared fantasy.

For the ADL, though, the film makes stark that the antisemitism discourse that is perpetuated through the students is also a currency within and between states—and that the ADL is a critical defender and driver of it. Foxman goes to Rome, where he is chauffeured to his meeting with the Pope. Chatting in the lush backseat, he reflects that heads of state understand the ADL as a lever puller in US politics. "It's their perception of the power of Jewish community," he says, "that we can make a difference in Washington." It is also a lever *provider* for Israel: Shamir reports that the ADL is the Israeli government's main source for information about antisemitism worldwide. Antisemitism concerns—spikes—become leverage in recruiting support for Israel and preventing Palestinians from gaining support in places that may also support Israeli capital interests: trade in arms, tech, and other interests. (The ADL's invocations of "crises in antisemitism" have escalated at moments when Israel has faced a rising Palestine solidarity movement and abated as criticism receded, as Amira Jarmakani has noted.)[3] *Defamation* shows the circular nature of the ADL's stewardship of the currency. States seek out the ADL as an access point to US politics because of its leverage, and the ADL uses those connections to preserve the discourse. In one striking scene, Ukrainian officials meet with the ADL because they need US protection against Russian aggression. In return for unspecified support, Foxman demands in obliquely threatening terms that they downplay the 1932–33 Holodomor ("death inflicted by starvation," in which Stalin imposed a famine killing 3.9 million Ukrainians) making sure never to suggest comparisons to the Nazi Holocaust. "I understood your message," says the Ukrainian emissary.

But as the ADL's history shows, advocating for Israel is not entirely the point. In a longue-durée project with ideological and political features—call it settler colonialism, Cold War imperialism, Western hegemony—Zionism is only a later, crystallizing expression. Many activists and scholars have traced the motivations of the US state-capital apparatus for defending Israel, uncovering mutually advancing relationships in areas like tech, policing, and capital.[4] However, the progress through history of the *hate* frame, and its

3. Amira Jarmakani, "IHRA: The Soft Power of Epistemic Violence," in *The Anti-Defamation League: A Critical Reader*, ed. Heike Schotten and Emmaia Gelman (Pluto Press, 2026).

4. See Maya Wind, *Towers of Ivory and Steel: How Israeli Universities Deny Palestinian Freedom* (Verso, 2024).

concatenations with *terror* and *antisemitism*, lay out a more extensive and existential shared project.

As Jarmakani explains, what is at stake in refusing to acknowledge ongoing processes of Israeli conquest, dispossession, and extraction—in insisting that anti-Zionism is irrational *hate*—is a denial and erasure of the racial regime itself and the foreclosure of dissent against it. It obscures how the idea of *subjects of remedy* is co-opted as the tool of a social movement from above: a move to protect those who have power and are supportive of power, not to redistribute it more fairly. The hate frame, rather than protecting marginalized groups, has in practice extended its protections primarily to white people and has disproportionately been used to imprison Black, brown, and queer people, as Dean Spade documents.[5] (One often cited example is the 1995 *Mitchell* case, in which Black teenagers who had just seen the film *Mississippi Burning*—a historical film about white supremacist violence and US government complicity—assaulted a white teenager. The attack was deemed a racial hate crime.)[6] Applied now to states themselves, the hate frame absurdly posits resistance to domination by police, military, and capital forces as a kind of intolerance. The territorial expansionism of the US and Israeli states, visited on Palestinians with the starkest articulations of intent at racial killing and societal erasure, is cast as defense of Jews against antisemitism and defense of democracy against illiberal insurgency.[7] This, indeed, is an age-old rationale of colonialism (and neoconservative democracy promotion): that those who oppose its expansion are backward and unsuited for self-determination.[8]

The concatenation of *hate* with *terror* converted this carceral machinery into a fully militarized force. As Shirin Sinnar writes, as white supremacist violence escalated in the 2010s with incidents including the 2015 massacre of

<hr>

5. Dean Spade, *Normal Life: Administrative Violence, Critical Trans Politics, and the Limits of Law* (Duke University Press, 2015), 44–47.

6. Shirin Sinnar, "Hate Crimes, Terrorism, and the Framing of White Supremacist Violence," *California Law Review* 110 (April 2022): 513.

7. Al-Haq, "A Registry of Israeli Genocidal Statements on Gaza," April 6, 2025, https:// www.alhaq.org/FAI-Unit/26257.html, accessed August 25, 2025; Law for Palestine, "Law for Palestine Releases Database with 500+ Instances of Israeli Incitement to Genocide— Continuously Updated," January 4, 2024, https://law4palestine.org/law-for-palestine-releases -database-with-500-instances-of-israeli-incitement-to-genocide-continuously-updated/.

8. Amira Jarmakani, "From 'Zionism Is Racism' to 'Antisemitism Is Racism,'" paper presented at Battling the "IHRA Definition": Theory and Activism Conference, October 14, 2023, Santa Cruz, California.

congregants at Charleston, South Carolina's Emanuel AME Church, racist violence was increasingly reconceived as *terror*, a threat to the nation. That move was especially easy because *hate* names a purportedly irrational hostility, portraying domestic white nationalism as a foreign object within the United States. The redefinition of racial violence as "domestic terrorism" also allowed the application of the label of *terror* to the overly broad, undifferentiated conflicts gathered under the hate frame. Where *hate* already conflated antiracist resistance with the rejection of tolerance, integration, and individual rights, its conflation with *terror* resistance proposed antiracist resistance as an assault on the democratic underpinnings of the liberal state. In the era of mass resistance under the banner of Black Lives Matter, beginning in 2016 prosecutors pushed the boundaries of hate crimes law to prosecute political protest, as seen in efforts to counter antiracist protest by adding "blue lives"—police officers—to the list of groups protected against *hate*.[9] In 2025, Columbia University and New York University similarly moved to counter protests to stop the genocide of Palestinians by adding "Zionist" to the list. These expansions have increasingly recategorized resistance to racist and repressive state structures as *terror*. As Sinnar notes, *terror* is not a racial justice framework, but rather a national security framework that brings vast legal exemptions from rights and public scrutiny. By design, it aims to preempt and repress challenges to state order.[10] *Hate* and *terror* take over the work that *communism* has done, per Charisse Burden-Stelly, tarring movements to intervene in racism as attacks on democracy, state, and people—particularly movements that aim to transfer power away from its centers in whiteness and the West.

Following *hate* and *terror*, *antisemitism* became a third term stripped of its contexts in history and structural power, and added to the chain of weaponized race-liberal protections. Extending the project that launched with the 1974 publication of *The New Anti-Semitism*, in 2016 the International Holocaust Remembrance Alliance (IHRA) "working definition of antisemitism" was adopted by the IHRA plenary body, along with eleven examples of possible forms of antisemitism. Although not formally part of the definition,

9. See India Thusi, "Blue Lives & the Permanence of Racism," *Cornell Law Review Online* 105 (2020): 14.

10. Sinnar, "Hate Crimes, Terrorism, and the Framing of White Supremacist Violence," 492–93. On the political conditions that have historically accompanied white power organizing, see also Kathleen Belew, *Bring the War Home: The White Power Movement and Paramilitary America* (Harvard University Press, 2018).

the examples became the politically operative text. Seven of them set out claims that criticism of Israel and Zionism, discussions of the racist nature of Zionism, and historical comparisons to other racial regimes—Nazis in particular—all constituted antisemitism.[11] Zionist institutions have escalated antisemitism discourse when Israel needs support. Sean Malloy notes that the IHRA definition was a response to the success of the Boycott, Divestment, Sanctions (BDS) movement. It also pushed back on US-based Black and Indigenous movements, which, in partnership with Palestinians, had unraveled notions of Zionism as a racial liberation project.[12] Zionist organizations, often led by the ADL, began advocating for institutions, state and city legislators, and federal bodies to adopt the IHRA definition as policy. They met with mixed success: It failed repeatedly as legislation in Congress as the Anti-Semitism Awareness Act, but was imposed as a rule in other areas, including US Department of Education policy under the first Trump administration, and embraced (less formally) in the Biden White House Strategy to Combat Antisemitism. As localities and universities adopted it, the IHRA definition created a strange set of material impacts, from disallowing boycotts of Israel to denying FEMA funds to disaster victims.

Increasingly, though, the IHRA definition became the basis for identifying anti-Jewish *hate*, sutured to the notion of *hate as terror* that had emerged to categorize white nationalism as a domestic threat to national security. In 2022, the ADL's audit first used the term "antisemitic terrorism" to describe an emerging threat, linked to white nationalism but "integrated across ideologies," an invocation easily transferrable to the ADL's other projects. In October 2023 it called on university presidents to "urgently" investigate whether chapters of Students for Justice in Palestine, whose calls for an end to Israeli colonization in Palestine it had long declared "antisemitic,"

11. Jamie Stern-Weiner, *The Politics of a Definition: How the IHRA Working Definition of Antisemitism Is Being Misrepresented* (Free Speech on Israel, 2021), https://www.documentcloud.org/documents/20689366-stern-weiner-j-fsoi-the-politics-of-a-definition/.

12. Sean Malloy, "From the 'New Antisemitism' to the IHRA Definition," *Journal for the Critical Study of Zionism* 1, no. 1 (Fall 2024). On the ADL's analysis of the effectiveness of Black Lives Matter, No Dakota Access Pipeline (NoDAPL), and queer movements in delegitimating Zionism, see Anti-Defamation League and Reut Institute, *The Frustrating 20X Question: Why Is It Still Growing?*, January 2017, https://www.jewishpublicaffairs.org/wp-content/uploads/sites/10/2015/09/The-20X-Question-Strategic-Framework-vs-DLG-and-BDS-By-Reut-Group-and-ADL.pdf.

were violating anti-terror laws. On March 9, 2025, one day after Columbia student leader Mahmoud Khalil was abducted by ICE agents, targeted for his prominent role in student organizing against the Israeli genocide in Gaza, the ADL cheered his arrest, propagating the charge that he had "demonize[d] America" and harassed and intimidated Jews—and that his political organizing constituted terrorism.[13] As critics noted, although white nationalism and indeed fascism was taking hold throughout this period, ADL leadership evinced little concern. Instead, it sought to leverage fascist power where useful—as in its endorsement of ICE's arrests of Palestinian student organizers—and made uneven gestures against right-wing racism, quietly publishing data on white nationalist disinformation campaigns, for example, while publicly exonerating Elon Musk after his Nazi salute.[14] In this move from a flattened conception of racial conflict as *hate* to the *terror* of challenges to the racial state, the ADL gestured back to the Americanism of its founding. Jonathan Greenblatt declared: "There is a straight line, there's a throughline, from Occupy Wall Street to BLM [Black Lives Matter] to 'defund the police' to 'river to the sea.' They are the same people, these are the same kind of nihilists . . . promoting a kind of anarchy. . . . [They're] frothing at the mouth, looking like they just came out of Mosul. . . . They're not just opposed to Jews, although they are. . . . They're opposed to the West, they're opposed to capitalism, they're opposed to America."[15]

In 2023 a journalist at the Jewish *Forward*, Arno Rosenfeld, noticed a shift in the landscape of Jewish institutions. For a hundred years or so, three defense organizations—the Anti-Defamation League, and American Jewish Committee, and at one point the American Jewish Congress—had been the

13. ADL (@ADL), "We firmly believe there should be swift and severe consequences for those who provide material support to foreign terrorist organizations, incite violence in support of terrorist activities, or conceal their identities in order to harass and intimidate Jewish individuals," Twitter (now X), March 10, 2025, https://x.com/ADL/status/1898918587437338827. Quoted text is in the quote-tweeted thread. Columbia Jewish Alumni Association (@CU_JewishAlumni), "4/ No one forced Khalil to barge onto campus, disrupt learning, or take over buildings. No one forced him to lead mobs that demonize America, or harass and intimidate Jews. This was his choice," Twitter (now X), March 9, 2025, https://x.com/CU_JewishAlumni/status/1898819033291780554.

14. Anti-Defamation League Center on Extremism, "Mis- and Disinformation Trends and Tactics to Watch in 2025," February 6, 2025, https://www.adl.org/resources/article/mis-and-disinformation-trends-and-tactics-watch-2025.

15. Arno Rosenfeld, "Exclusive: ADL Chief Compares Student Protesters to ISIS and al-Qaeda in Address to Republican Officials," *The Forward*, June 6, 2025, https://forward.com/news/726133/greenblatt-adl-protesters-terrorists/.

central address for Jewish communal efforts to oppose antisemitism. Now, fairly suddenly, new "anti-antisemitism groups" were proliferating. Out of curiosity he began keeping a list. By Rosenfeld's count, around three dozen such groups had launched in the preceding decade.[16] Many used "antisemitism" in their names and as a keyword in their advocacy, but almost all were primarily focused on support for the Israeli state—especially on combating the BDS movement. Throughout the period when new groups were forming, white nationalists' influence was quickly spreading, from the Charlottesville militias who had chanted "Jews will not replace us" to corporate boardrooms and elected offices. But the antisemitism groups mostly ignored white nationalists; their focus was on the Palestine liberation movement and the left. By 2024, Rosenfeld counted sixty-five new watchdog groups. Alongside them, a set of right-wing organizations was also growing, including groups like the Jewish Institute for Liberal Values (later renamed the North American Values Institute) and the Alliance for Constructive Ethnic Studies, who used *opposing antisemitism* as their rationale for campaigns against critical race theory and "woke ideology."[17] Some were megadonor-funded, like the Foundation to Combat Antisemitism, undertaking multimillion-dollar public relations campaigns in urban centers. Some were well connected, like the Academic Engagement Network, which was ushered into meetings with highly placed political officials and university heads almost as soon as it was created. Antisemitism watchdogs were quite suddenly an institutional ecology.

The Gaza genocide began shortly after Rosenfeld published his list. As a massive resistance movement rose in the United States, led mostly by Palestinians, Jews, and students of color, a parallel movement of Zionist organizations rose to counter it.[18] The ADL, American Jewish Committee, the Conference of Presidents of Major American Jewish Organizations all

16. Rosenfeld's list contained forty-eight entries in June 2023. About a quarter of them appeared to be defunct at the time. Arno Rosenfeld, "Jewish Defense Organizations," https://principled-haddock-800.notion.site/Jewish-defense-organizations-ee9091c9d57c4347978538a41dbabaob, updated February 1, 2025, accessed June 4, 2025.

17. See David Bernstein, "How Critical Social Justice Ideology Fuels Antisemitism," *eJewishPhilanthropy*, September 3, 2021, https://ejewishphilanthropy.com/critical-social-justice-antisemitism/; and Alliance for Constructive Ethnic Studies, "Jewish Community Concerns," https://www.calethstudies.org/ethnic-studies-jewish-community, accessed June 4, 2025.

18. On Zionist organizations as a movement from above, see Hil Aked, *Friends of Israel: The Backlash Against Palestine Solidarity* (Verso, 2023).

rose to denounce the movement against genocide as antisemitic. But it was the proliferation of watchdog groups that made the movement powerful. To frame discussion of Israeli colonialism and Palestinian freedom as "anti-Jewish hate," they united a diffuse set of tactics: megadonors, corporate advertising, lawfare, civil rights complaints—and astroturfing, working through dozens of small, opaque organizations simulating a grassroots movement. The work of weaponized antisemitism discourse was repressive. It brought police violence to campuses, aligned "opponents of antisemitism" with MAGA thugs, underwrote restrictive policies on protests and teaching—locked-down campuses, curriculum checks. As the Trump regime came into place, the repression that Zionist antisemitism watchdogs had demanded became the toolbox for its instantiation of fascism.

In fact, the watchdogs were operating levers that the ADL had built. Since the campaigns of the 1980s, a vast anti-hate complex had arisen, with antisemitism as a central node. The complex spanned laws, public and private funding streams, police units, school task forces, nonprofits, and media beats. The ADL had become an essential organization within it, providing services, guidance, research, and validation. The new watchdogs stepped into these roles.[19] In a mode reminiscent of the Institute for American Democracy billboards (the organization created by the ADL and American Jewish Committee for anonymity), public relations projects like JewBelong dotted US cities with billboards that decried antisemitism, concatenating Palestinian calls for rights with Nazi persecution of Jews; they invoked Americans' duty to fight it with references to the Nazi Holocaust, the civil rights movement, feminism, and other appeals coded in progressive rhetoric, and indeed echoing Progressive Era instruction on good liberal citizenship. Echoing the ADL's role as a vehicle for complaint and demands for remedy, groups like Mothers Against College Antisemitism offered an infrastructure for targeting universities, media outlets, or elected officials; they recruited complainants. Their complaints became the basis for lawfare and civil rights action. Once the crisis had been established, they offered advising services to campus administrators, legislators, CEOs: how to avoid being antisemitic, how to avoid the fiscal risk of being sued for being antisemitic. The projects of *opposing antisemitism* in this weaponized mode include redefining key ideas about

19. This section is drawn from an article initially published in *Jadaliyya*. See Emmaia Gelman, "Astroturf Antisemitism Watchdogs," *Jadaliyya*, April 13, 2024, https://www .jadaliyya.com/Details/45918.

race, colonialism, and power, including "indigeneity" so that it can refer to European Jews, "settler colonialism" to assert that Israel cannot be counted as a settler project, and "white," and safety.

As flattened notions of race and rights have lent power to a new wave of global imperialism, the ADL has remained involved, even central. But a new set of organizations, fueled by megadonors, tech oligarchy, and militarized carceral power has inhabited the complexes that the ADL built. If the ADL's history is illuminated through its conflicts with antiracist and anticolonial resistance, those conflicts are setting fires on a vastly wider terrain.

ACKNOWLEDGMENTS

Reading empire's history against the grain is necessarily collective work. Over the years I collected a very, very long list of acknowledgments. At the time of writing, it is too dangerous to publish such lists, but I know every name.

I am so grateful to the collective and community of the Institute for the Critical Study of Zionism, whose rigor, generosity, and ethical refusal to separate research from struggles against state violence have guided me. Brave and principled scholars whose homes are in Faculty and Staff for Justice in Palestine, the American Studies Association, Middle East Studies Association, American Historical Association, American Association of University Professors, AAUP-AFT Local 6741, UC Ethnic Studies Faculty Council, and more: thank you.

Grassroots organizing communities provided the frameworks that made this research possible, and sustained me in it. Abdeen Jabara, legendary organizer of Arab American communities for half a century, supported the book from start to finish with stories, food, and love. The scholars, journalists, and organizers researching the Anti-Defamation League and surrounding organizations have been a well of insight and research-sharing, as have organizers in the Palestinian Youth Movement, Queers Against Israeli Apartheid, NYU's Grad Student Organizing Committee (GSOC-UAW Local 2110), #CancelPinkwashing at CreatingChange, Jewish Voice for Peace, #DropTheADL, and #DropTheADLfromSchools. New York City's queer, HIV/AIDS, sex worker, housing, and Palestine solidarity movements taught me about rigorous research into institutions that deal in claims about rights and the incisive power of knowledge from below. Many comrades' ideas are here in this text, and it is especially guided by the memories of Bob Kohler, Tarlach Mac Niallais, Nikita Price, Mel Stevens, and Sylvia Rivera.

Wonderful people who chronicle queer and antiracist histories, Zionist and Cold War shenanigans, and liberation movements have been central to this book. They include Susie Day, Bill Dobbs, Marjorie Feld, Keith Feldman, Christina Hanhardt, Taher Herzallah, Abdeen Jabara, Arun Kundnani, Rosza Lang/Levitsky, Brooke

Lober, Rachel Mattson, J. F. Mulligan, Nora Lester Murad, Ezra Berkley Nepon, Donna Nevel, Phan Nguyen, Loubna Qutami, Sarah Schulman, David Sheen, Abba Solomon, Louisa Solomon, Dean Spade, Laura Whitehorn, Will Youmans, Omar Zahzah, and Dorothy Zellner. Jill Tregor and Hallie Rosen were incredibly generous with their time and trust. Conversations with journalists Mari Cohen, Alex Kane, and Arno Rosenfeld substantially shaped the book. Editors who published earlier pieces of this research helped me understand how to write about it, including Arielle Angel, Crystal Mun-hye Baik, Nora Caplan-Bricker, Christine Hong, Adam Horowitz, Matt Lord, and Anjali Nath. Thanks to the many archivists who helped, especially good souls at the Freedom Archives, Jacob Rader Marcus Center of the American Jewish Archives, NYU Special Collections, and the Oregon State Archives.

This book's first life as a dissertation is owed to Lisa Duggan, who championed it, and Gayatri Gopinath, Alex Lubin, Jasbir Puar, and Andrew Ross, who guided it to completion. Many generous people gave close critical readings of sections of this book, shared expertise and improvements, and encouraged me, including A. J. Bauer, Lila Corwin Berman, Paul Buhle, Jessie Daniels, Max Greenberg, Abdeen Jabara, Shaul Magid, Jodi Melamed, Jeremy Menchik, Heike Schotten, and the Right-Wing Studies Working Group. I am deeply indebted to the editors and team at the University of California Press, especially Niels Hooper for believing in the project from the start and Julie Van Pelt and Leah Caldwell for careful and supportive editing.

This book was written over much of my children's lives. The NYC public school educators whose antiracist teaching helped them comprehend my project and the beloved carers who supported our family made this book possible. So have our chosen and just-lucky family, including our perfect Tagine. My parents, Felice and Yoram Gelman, have been beyond supportive, role models, and comrades. To my partner Staci Smith, a zillion stars of love and thanks for getting us here. To our kids, who are everything, thank you for everything.

BIBLIOGRAPHY

ACT UP/Boston. ACT UP/Boston to Leonard Zakim, August 24, 1988. Box 106, Folder 6, Series II. Field Files: Civil Rights Organizations: ADL, 1981–90. National Gay and Lesbian Task Force records, #7301. Cornell University.

ACT UP/Los Angeles. "A World of Indifference." Press release, January 16, 1989. ACT UP/Los Angeles Records, Coll 2011-010. ONE Archives, University of Southern California.

ADL Bulletin. Advertisements. September 1953.

ADL Bulletin. "The Klan Again." May 1975, 2.

Ahmad, Eqbal. *Terrorism: Theirs & Ours.* Seven Stories Press, 1998.

Aked, Hil. *Friends of Israel: The Backlash Against Palestine Solidarity.* Verso, 2023.

ALA Bulletin. "Unity Bookmark." Vol. 43, no. 4 (1949): 144.

Alliance for Constructive Ethnic Studies. "Jewish Community." https://www.calethstudies.org/ethnic-studies-jewish-community. Accessed June 4, 2025.

Allport, Gordon W. *ABC's of Scapegoating.* Anti-Defamation League of B'nai B'rith, 1948.

Alpern, David M., Kim Willensen, and Thomas M. DeFrank. "The Black Backlash." *Newsweek,* August 27, 1979.

Alvarez, William A., Morton M. Rosenthal, and Richard Silverstein. "Letters to the Times: Sandinistas and Anti-Semitism." *Los Angeles Times,* April 8, 1985.

American Israelite. "To Head ADL's Awards Dinner." October 28, 1976.

American Jewish Committee. "American Jewish Committee: Press Release." January 17, 1962. https://web.archive.org/web/20200715223130/http://www.ajcarchives.org/AJC_DATA/Files/619.PDF.

American Jewish World. "Ashamed of Negro Bias, Rustin Says." December 30, 1966.

American Jewish World. "NCRAC Formulates Guidelines for US Jewry." July 2, 1965.

American Jewish World. "'The Negro and Anti-Semitism' Will Be Discussed by Negro and Jewish Leaders on the WNBC-TV 'Open Mind' Program Sunday." Photo caption. June 3, 1966.

American Jewish Year Book. "United States: Civic and Political." Vol. 51 (1950): 116–19.

American Muslims for Palestine. "Drop the ADL." https://www.ampalestine.org/organize/campaigns/drop-adl.

Anderson, Jervis. *Bayard Rustin: Troubles I've Seen.* HarperCollins, 1997.

Anti-Defamation League. *Audit of Antisemitic Incidents 2022.* March 3, 2023.

Anti-Defamation League. "Backgrounder: Hamas." October 10, 2023. https://www.adl.org/resources/backgrounder/hamas.

Anti-Defamation League. "Who Are the Primary Groups Behind the US Anti-Israel Rallies?" October 20, 2023. https://www.adl.org/resources/blog/who-are-primary-groups-behind-us-anti-israel-rallies. Accessed November 14, 2023.

Anti-Defamation League and Reut Institute. *The Frustrating 20X Question: Why Is It Still Growing?* January 2017.

Anti-Defamation League of B'nai B'rith. *The Anti-Semitism of Black Demagogues and Extremists.* 1992.

Anti-Defamation League of B'nai B'rith. "Anti-Semitism in the New York City Schools Controversy." January 1969. Dore Schary Papers, Box 153, Folder 14. Wisconsin Historical Society.

Anti-Defamation League of B'nai B'rith. *Countering Anti-Semitic Vandalism: Civil Litigation and the Jewish Advocacy Center.* September 1986. ADL Nearprint files, Box 4, American Jewish Archives.

Anti-Defamation League of B'nai B'rith. "Danger on the Left." *Facts,* November 1972. Reprinted in Congressional Record, Extension of Remarks, February 8, 1973.

Anti-Defamation League of B'nai B'rith. *Facts,* June 1946.

Anti-Defamation League of B'nai B'rith. *Fireside Discussion Group of the Anti-Defamation League B'nai B'rith.* Anti-Defamation League, 1939.

Anti-Defamation League of B'nai B'rith. "Freedom of Press." Poster, 2007. Palestine Poster Project. https://www.palestineposterproject.org/posters/freedom-press-0.

Anti-Defamation League of B'nai B'rith. *Hate Groups in America: A Record of Bigotry and Violence.* 1988.

Anti-Defamation League of B'nai B'rith. *Hitler's Communism Unmasked.* Fireside Discussion Group of the Anti-Defamation League, 1938.

Anti-Defamation League of B'nai B'rith. "Middle East Opinion Trends in France and Great Britain." *Facts* 23, no. 1 (October 1976).

Anti-Defamation League of B'nai B'rith. "The Most Unbelievable Nonsense." *ADL Bulletin,* November 1975.

Anti-Defamation League of B'nai B'rith. *1980 Audit of Anti-Semitic Episodes.* 1980.

Anti-Defamation League of B'nai B'rith. *Not the Work of a Day: The Story of the Anti-Defamation League of B'nai B'rith.* 1965.

Anti-Defamation League of B'nai B'rith. "Only Israel." Poster, 2007. Palestine Poster Project. https://www.palestineposterproject.org/posters/only-israel-1.

Anti-Defamation League of B'nai B'rith. *Primer on Communism.* 1951.

Anti-Defamation League of B'nai B'rith. *Public Human Relations Agencies; 1957 Directory.* 1957.

Anti-Defamation League of B'nai B'rith. *Report of Anti-Defamation League B'nai B'rith*. 1920.

Anti-Defamation League of B'nai B'rith. *Report of Anti-Defamation League B'nai B'rith*. 1959.

Anti-Defamation League of B'nai B'rith v. American Italian Anti-Defamation League, Inc. 283 N.Y.S.2d 828, 54 Misc.2d 830 (N.Y. Sup. Ct. 1967). https://case-law.vlex.com/vid/anti-defamation-league-of-886991762.

Asare, Abena Ampofoa. "The Silencing of Fred Dube." *Boston Review*, January 18, 2024.

Askin, Steve. "Unteaching Racism." *Black Enterprise*, March 1982.

Associated Press. "Klan Making Comeback, Anti-Defamation League Claims." *Santa Cruz Sentinel*, November 18, 1977.

Atiyeh, Victor G. "Legislative Message, 1981 (January)." Records of Governor Victor G. Atiyeh Administration, January 8, 1979, to January 12, 1987, Oregon State Archives.

Awad, Ann Marie. "The Difficult Business of Accurately Tracking Anti-Semitism and Hate Crimes in Colorado." Colorado Public Radio, October 30, 2018.

B-, Warren. Warren B- to Leonard Zakim. June 26, 1989. Box 106, Folder 6, Series II. Field Files: Civil Rights Organizations: ADL, 1981–90.

Back, Adina. "Blacks, Jews and the Struggle to Integrate Brooklyn's Junior High School 258: A Cold War Story." *Journal of American Ethnic History* 20, no. 2 (2001).

Bahbah, Bishara. *Israel and Latin America: The Military Connection*. 1986.

Bakst, Jerome. "The Radical Left and Al Fatah." *ADL Bulletin*, September 1969, 1–2.

Baldwin, James. "Negroes Are Anti-Semitic Because They're Anti-White." *New York Times Magazine*, April 9, 1967.

Balint, Benjamin. *Running Commentary: The Contentious Magazine That Transformed the Jewish Left into the Neoconservative Right*. PublicAffairs, 2010.

Ballotpedia. "California Proposition 7, Expand Death Penalty and Life Imprisonment for Murders Initiative (1978)." https://ballotpedia.org/California_Proposition_7,_Expand_Death_Penalty_and_Life_Imprisonment_for_Murders_Initiative_(1978).

Baltimore Sun. "Anti-Defamation League Offices Raided by Police Spy Data Sought in San Francisco." April 9, 1993.

Barnouw, Erik. *The Image Empire: A History of Broadcasting in the United States*, Vol. 3, *From 1953*. Oxford University Press, 1970.

Barron, Andrea. "Referenda on the Palestinian Question in Four US Cities." *Journal of Palestine Studies* 18, no. 4 (1989): 71–83.

Barry, Tom, and Deb Preusch. *AIFLD in Central America: Agents as Organizers*. Resource Center, 1990.

Bar-Siman-Tov, Yaacov. "The United States and Israel Since 1948: A 'Special Relationship'?" *Diplomatic History* 22, no. 2 (1998): 231–62.

Bawardi, Hani J. *The Making of Arab Americans: From Syrian Nationalism to US Citizenship*. University of Texas Press, 2014.

Bay Area United Steering Committee. Resignation letter—draft, n.d. Box 33, Folder 11, Community United Against Violence records. GLBT Historical Society.

Bay Area Veterans of the Civil Rights Movement. "MFDP Challenge to the Democratic Convention," n.d. Civil Rights Movement Archive. https://www.crmvet.org/info/mfdp_atlantic.pdf. Accessed December 3, 2024.

Bazyler, Michael J., and Julia Y Scheppach. "The Strange and Curious History of the Law Used to Prosecute Adolf Eichmann." *Loyola of Los Angeles International and Comparative Law Review* 34, no. 3 (2012).

Becklund, Laurie. "Sandinistas Are Anti-Semitic, Group Says." *Los Angeles Times*, March 14, 1985.

Belew, Kathleen. *Bring the War Home: The White Power Movement and Paramilitary America*. Harvard University Press, 2018.

Belth, Nathan. "Vol Va: Belth, Nathan C., 1985–1987," n.d. B'nai B'rith Anti-Defamation League Oral Histories. American Jewish Archives, Cincinnati, Ohio.

Ben-Daniel, Tallie. "Branding Israel: Queer Markets and Politics in San Francisco and Tel Aviv." PhD diss., University of California, Davis, 2014.

Berkman, Matthew. "Coercive Consensus: Jewish Federations, Ethnic Representation, and the Roots of American Pro-Israel Politics." PhD diss., University of Pennsylvania, 2018.

Berlet, Chip. *Trumping Democracy: From Reagan to the Alt-Right*. Routledge, 2019.

Berlet, Chip, and Matthew N. Lyons. "Repression and Ideology: The Legacy of Discredited Centrist/Extremist Theory." *Police Misconduct and Civil Rights Law Report* 5, nos. 13–14 (1998).

Berman, Lila Corwin. *The American Jewish Philanthropic Complex: The History of a Multibillion-Dollar Institution*. Princeton University Press, 2020.

Bernstein, David. "How Critical Social Justice Ideology Fuels Antisemitism." *eJewishPhilanthropy*, September 3, 2021.

Berrill, Kevin. Kevin Berrill to Charney V. Bromberg, February 7, 1989. Box 106, Folder 6, Series II. Field Files: Civil Rights Organizations: ADL, 1981–90. National Gay and Lesbian Task Force records, #7301. Cornell University.

Berrill, Kevin. Handwritten Call Notes, "SF/LA A World of Difference," n.d. Box 106, Folder 7, Series II. Field Files: Civil Rights Organizations: ADL: Education Project: "A World of Difference," 1988–91. National Gay and Lesbian Task Force records, #7301. Cornell University.

Berrill, Kevin. Kevin Berrill to Jeffrey Ross, November 15, 1989. Box 106, Folder 6, Series II. Field Files: Civil Rights Organizations: ADL, 1981–90. National Gay and Lesbian Task Force records, #7301. Cornell University.

Berrill, Kevin. Kevin Berrill to Jess Hordes, February 9, 1987. Box 106, Folder 6, Series II. Field Files: Civil Rights Organizations: ADL, 1981–90. National Gay and Lesbian Task Force records, #7301. Cornell University.

Berrill, Kevin. Kevin Berrill to Jill Kahn, November 14, 1989. Box 106, Folder 6, Series II. Field Files: Civil Rights Organizations: ADL, 1981–90. National Gay and Lesbian Task Force records, #7301. Cornell University.

Berrill, Kevin. Kevin Berrill to Justin Finger, June 4, 1986. Box 106, Folder 6, Series II. Field Files: Civil Rights Organizations: ADL, 1981–90. National Gay and Lesbian Task Force records, #7301. Cornell University.

Berrill, Kevin. Kevin Berrill to Justin Finger, September 4, 1987. Box 106, Folder 6, Series II. Field Files: Civil Rights Organizations: ADL, 1981–90. National Gay and Lesbian Task Force records, #7301. Cornell University.

Berrill, Kevin. Kevin Berrill to Leonard Zakim, July 7, 1989. Box 106, Folder 6, Series II. Field Files: Civil Rights Organizations: ADL, 1981–90. National Gay and Lesbian Task Force records, #7301. Cornell University.

Berrill, Kevin. Kevin Berrill to Steven Freeman, May 18, 1987. Box 106, Folder 6, Series II. Field Files: Civil Rights Organizations: ADL, 1981–90. National Gay and Lesbian Task Force records, #7301. Cornell University.

Berrill, Kevin. Kevin Berrill to Steven Freeman, January 2, 1988. Box 106, Folder 6, Series II. Field Files: Civil Rights Organizations: ADL, 1981–90. National Gay and Lesbian Task Force records, #7301. Cornell University.

Berube, Maurice R. "'Democratic Socialists' and the Schools." *New Politics* (Summer 1969): 57–63.

Biden, Joseph. "Remarks by President Biden on the Terrorist Attacks in Israel." The White House, October 10, 2023. https://bidenwhitehouse.archives.gov/briefing-room/speeches-remarks/2024/05/07/remarks-by-president-biden-at-the-u-s-holocaust-memorial-museums-annual-days-of-remembrance-ceremony/.

Biondi, Martha. *To Stand and Fight: The Struggle for Civil Rights in Postwar New York City.* Harvard University Press, 2006.

Birle, Robert. Robert Birle to AWOD participants, February 11, 1989. Box 33, Folder 11, Community United Against Violence records. GLBT Historical Society.

Birnbaum, Susan. "Jews to Help Farmers in Trouble." *JTA Daily News Bulletin*, November 10, 1986, 4.

Blau, Eleanor. "Legislator Decries Synagogue Arson." *New York Times*, March 23, 1976.

Blythe, June. "Can Public Relations Help Reduce Prejudice?" *Public Opinion Quarterly* 11, no. 3 (1947): 342–60.

B'nai B'rith. *Not the Work of a Day: The Story of the Anti-Defamation League of B'nai B'rith.* New York, 1965.

B'nai B'rith Messenger. "As We Were Saying." July 2, 1965.

Boggs, Grace Lee. *Living for Change.* University of Minnesota Press, 2016.

Bolling, Landrum R. *Reporters Under Fire: US Media Coverage of Conflicts in Lebanon and Central America.* Routledge, 2019.

Boston Globe. "Bread of Affliction." March 29, 1985.

Boston Globe. "Massachusetts' Own Civil Rights Law." November 7, 1979.

Boston Globe. "Voices from Our City: Racism in Boston." December 14, 1980.

Bourdieu, Pierre. *The Logic of Practice.* Stanford University Press, 1990.

Boyce, Travis D., and Winsome M. Chunnu, eds. *Historicizing Fear: Ignorance, Vilification, and Othering.* University Press of Colorado, 2019.

Boyer, Sandy. "Here's Who the AFL-CIO Is Funding in South Africa." *Labor Notes*, December 1986.

Branch, Taylor. *Parting the Waters: America in the King Years, 1954–63.* Simon and Schuster, 1989.

Brier, Stephen. "The Ideological and Organizational Origins of the United Federation of Teachers' Opposition to the Community Control Movement in the New York City Public Schools, 1960–1968." *Labour/Le Travail*, no. 73 (Spring 2014): 179–93.

Broadcasting. "Do-It-Yourself Movement: Stations into Syndication." June 30, 1980.

Brodkin, Karen. *How Jews Became White Folks and What That Says About Race in America.* Rutgers University Press, 1998.

Brody, David. "American Jewry, the Refugees, and Immigration Restriction (1932–1942)." *Publications of the American Jewish Historical Society* 45, no. 4 (1956): 219–47.

Brown, Wendy. *States of Injury: Power and Freedom in Late Modernity.* Princeton University Press, 1995.

Burden-Stelly, Charisse. *Black Scare/Red Scare: Theorizing Capitalist Racism in the United States.* University of Chicago Press, 2023.

Bureau of National Affairs. "Affirmative Action Today: A Legal and Political Analysis." 1985.

Burke, Kenyon C. "A Trip To Israel." *Negro History Bulletin* 33, no. 4 (1970): 94–96.

Burley, Shane, and Naomi Bennett. "Examining the ADL's Antisemitism Audit." *Jewish Currents*, June 17, 2024.

Butler, Donald R. Donald T. Butler to Robert Mullin and Concord city councilmembers, December 4, 1986. Box 33, Folder 11, Community United Against Violence records. GLBT Historical Society.

Cable, Umayyah. "Compulsory Zionism and Palestinian Existence: A Genealogy." *Journal of Palestine Studies* 51, no. 2 (2022): 66–71.

Caplovitz, David, and Candace Rogers. *Swastika 1960: The Epidemic of Anti-Semitic Vandalism in America.* Anti-Defamation League of B'nai B'rith, 1961.

Carmichael, Stokely, and Charles V. Hamilton. *Black Power: The Politics of Liberation in America.* Vintage Books, 1967.

The Carolinian. "Black Editors, Publishers, Plan 10-Day-Stay in Israel." November 22, 1969.

Carson, Clayborne. *The Eyes on the Prize: Civil Rights Reader: Documents, Speeches, and Firsthand Accounts from the Black Freedom Struggle, 1954–1990.* Penguin Books, 1991.

Case, Riley B. *Evangelical and Methodist: A Popular History.* Abingdon Press, 2004.

Center for American Progress. "52 Harms in 52 Weeks." January 10, 2018. https://www.americanprogress.org/article/52-harms-52-weeks/.

Center for Democratic Renewal. *When Hate Groups Come to Town: A Handbook of Effective Community Responses.* 1992 [1987].

Ceplair, Larry. *Anti-Communism in Twentieth-Century America: A Critical History.* Praeger, 2011.

Chicago Jewish Post and Opinion. "Small Meetings Being Held; Barrage by Blacks Continue." August 24, 1979.

Christenson, Diane. Diane Christenson to Community United Against Violence staffer, June 1, 1988. Box 33, Folder 11, CUAV records. GLBT Historical Society.

Chua, Charmaine. "Abolition Is a Constant Struggle: Five Lessons from Minneapolis." *Theory & Event* 23, no. 5 (2020): S-127–47.

Church, Foster. "Harassment Bill Passes over Protests of 2 Liberals." *The Oregonian*, June 20, 1981.

Cobban, Helena. "The US-Israeli Relationship in the Reagan Era." *Conflict Quarterly*, Spring 1989, 15.

Code Pink. "Drop the ADL Action Guide." https://www.boughtbyzionism.org/expeladlguide.

Cohen, Naomi W. *Not Free to Desist: The American Jewish Committee, 1906–1966.* Jewish Publication Society of America, 1972.

Columbia Broadcasting System (CBS). "Dinner with the President (November 23, 1953-CBS)." Posted November 16, 2019, by Free The Kinescopes!, YouTube, 1:03:56. https://www.youtube.com/watch?v=-8_d2_yDxEU.

Committee to Fight Bigotry in All Its Forms. Committee to Fight Bigotry in All Its Forms to David Rose, n.d. Box 106, Folder 6, Series II. Field Files: Civil Rights Organizations: ADL, 1981–90. National Gay and Lesbian Task Force records, #7301. Cornell University.

Community United Against Violence. A World of Difference. Meeting Agenda and Minutes of Prior Meeting, n.d. [before July 1988]. Box 33, Folder 11, CUAV records. GLBT Historical Society.

Community United Against Violence. Handwritten draft BAU resignation letter, n.d. [April 1989?], likely authored by Tregor. Box 33, Folder 11, CUAV records. GLBT Historical Society.

Community United Against Violence. Handwritten meeting notes reflecting meeting with ADL staffers Ron Berman, Amy Schoenblum, and Richard Hirschhaut, n.d. and unsigned. Box 33, Folder 11, CUAV records. GLBT Historical Society.

Community United Against Violence. Handwritten meeting notes, unsigned, n.d. [June 1988, Jill Tregor?]. Box 33, Folder 11, CUAV records. GLBT Historical Society.

Community United Against Violence. Handwritten pink memo, n.d. [November 1988?]. Box 33, Folder 11, CUAV records. GLBT Historical Society.

Community United Against Violence Board of Directors. Meeting minutes 1978–83; 1984–86. Box 1, Folder 1–32; Box 3, Folder 1–25, Community United Against Violence records. GLBT Historical Society.

Cox, John M. *Circles of Resistance: Jewish, Leftist, and Youth Dissidence in Nazi Germany.* Peter Lang, 2009.

Cox, Laurence, and Alf Gunvald Nilsen. "'At the Heart of Society Burns the Fire of Social Movements': What Would a Marxist Theory of Social Movements Look Like?" In *Tenth International Conference on Alternative Futures and Popular Protest: A Selection of Papers from the Conference*, edited by Colin Barker and Mike Tyldesley. Manchester Metropolitan University, 2005.

Cox, Oliver C. *Caste, Class, & Race: A Study in Social Dynamics.* Monthly Review Press, 1959.

Crary, Ryland W., and Gerald L. Steibel. *How You Can Teach About Communism.* Anti-Defamation League of B'nai B'rith, 1951.

Decter, Moshe. *The Profile of Communism: A Fact-by-Fact Primer.* Collier Books, 1961.

Decter, Moshe. *"To Serve, to Teach, to Leave": The Story of Israel's Development Assistance Program in Black Africa.* American Jewish Congress, 1977.

Deeb, Lara, and Jessica Winegar. *Anthropology's Politics: Disciplining the Middle East.* Stanford University Press, 2015.

Delaney, Paul. "Leaders Try to Halt a Black-Jewish Rift." *New York Times*, August 19, 1979.

Delmont, Matthew. *Half American: The Epic Story of African Americans Fighting World War II at Home and Abroad.* Penguin Random House, 2022.

Detroit Jewish News. "ADL Reports 50 Anti-Jewish Incidents at Some 31 Campuses Around the US." June 22, 1979.

Detroit Jewish News. "Conclave Experts Disagree on Roots of Anti-Semitism." May 8, 1964.

Deutsch, Michael E., and Erica Thompson. "Secrets and Lies: The Persecution of Muhammad Salah (Part II)." *Journal of Palestine Studies* 38, no. 1 (Autumn 2008): 25–53.

Diamond, Sara. *Roads to Dominion: Right-Wing Movements and Political Power in the United States.* Guilford Press, 1995.

Diner, Hasia R. *The Jews of the United States, 1654 to 2000.* University of California Press, 2006.

Diner, Hasia R. "Oscar Handlin: A Jewish Historian." *Journal of American Ethnic History* 32, no. 3 (2013): 53–61.

Diner, Hasia R. *A Time for Gathering: The Second Migration, 1820–1880.* John Hopkins University Press, 1995.

Dinnerstein, Leonard. *The Leo Frank Case.* University of Georgia Press, 2008.

Dinnerstein, Leonard. *Uneasy at Home: Antisemitism and the American Jewish Experience.* Columbia University Press, 1987.

Dollinger, Marc. *Black Power, Jewish Politics: Reinventing the Alliance in the 1960s.* Brandeis University Press, 2018.

Drop the ADL from Schools. "Open Letter to Educators: The ADL Is Not a Social Justice Partner." https://droptheadlfromschools.org/.

Drucker, Peter. *Max Shachtman and His Left: A Socialist's Odyssey Through the "American Century."* Globe Pequot Press, 1993.

Dudziak, Mary. *Cold War Civil Rights: Race and the Image of American Democracy.* Princeton University Press, 2000.

Duggan, Lisa. *The Twilight of Equality? Neoliberalism, Cultural Politics, and the Attack on Democracy.* Beacon Press, 2003.

Dunbar-Ortiz, Roxanne. *An Indigenous Peoples' History of the United States.* Beacon Press, 2014.

Ebony. "The Ku Klux Klan." October 1979.

Eghbariah, Rabea. "Toward Nakba as a Legal Concept." *Columbia Law Review* 124, no. 4 (2024): 887–992.

Ehrlich, Howard J. "The Swastika Epidemic of 1959–1960: Anti-Semitism and Community Characteristics." *Social Problems* 9, no. 3 (1962): 264–72.

Ehrman, John. *The Rise of Neoconservatism: Intellectuals and Foreign Affairs, 1945–1994.* Yale University Press, 1995.

18 Million Rising. "TAAF: Drop the ADL! Community Letter." May 2, 2024. https://www.18millionrising.org/2024/dropadl-letter/.

Eisenstadt, Peter, ed. *Black Conservatism: Essays in Intellectual and Political History.* Routledge, 1999.

Elazar, Daniel Judah. *Community and Polity: The Organizational Dynamics of American Jewry.* Jewish Publication Society, 1995.

Elia, Nada. *Greater Than the Sum of Our Parts: Feminism, Inter/Nationalism, and Palestine.* Pluto Press, 2023.

Elrazik, Adnan Abed, Riyad Amin, and Uri Davis. "Problems of Palestinians in Israel: Land, Work, Education." *Journal of Palestine Studies* 7, no. 3 (Spring 1978): 31–54.

Engelmayer, Sheldon. "ADL's Supposed Shift to the Right: Is It No Longer a Clear Voice?" *Kansas City Jewish Chronicle*, August 23, 1991.

English Journal. "Report and Summary: NCTE High School Section Election." Vol. 43, no. 3 (1954): 155–60.

Epstein, Benjamin R. "The Miracle." *ADL Bulletin*, September 1967, 2.

Epstein, Benjamin R. "Negro Anti-Semitism." *American Israelite*, March 27, 1969.

Epstein, Benjamin R. "Vol Ia: Epstein, Benjamin R., 1985–1987," n.d. Box 1, Folder 1. B'nai B'rith Anti-Defamation League Oral Histories. American Jewish Archives, Cincinnati, Ohio.

Epstein, Benjamin R., and Arnold Forster. *Some of My Best Friends . . .* Farrar, Straus and Cudahy, 1962.

Epstein, Melech. *Jewish Labor in U.S.A.: An Industrial, Political and Cultural History of the Jewish Labor Movement.* Ktav Publishing House, 1969.

Estraikh, Gennady. "Professing Leninist Yiddishkayt: The Decline of American Yiddish Communism." *American Jewish History* 96, no. 1 (2010): 33–60.

Eu, March Fong. *California Voters Pamphlet.* Office of the Secretary of State, California, 1978.

FBI. *Incidents, Offenses, Victims, and Known Offenders by Bias Motivation, 2011.* https://ucr.fbi.gov/hate-crime/2011/tables/table-1. Accessed May 7, 2025.

FBI. Memo from FBI Director to SAC Atlanta et al.: Liaison with the Anti-Defamation League of B'nai B'rith, January 17, 1968. File 1199215-000 --- 100-IP-16164 --- Section 1, p. 5. The FBI and the Anti-Defamation League. Israel Lobby Archive, Institute for Research: Middle Eastern Policy. https://www.israellobby.org/adl/.

FBI. Memo from SAC San Francisco to FBI Director (subject redacted), March 15, 1993. File 1199215-0-65X-LA-153918-Section1, pp. 27–30. FBI Investigates the ADL for Espionage. Israel Lobby Archive, Institute for Research: Middle Eastern Policy. https://www.israellobby.org/ADL-FBI.

Feitlowitz, Marguerite. *A Lexicon of Terror: Argentina and the Legacies of Torture.* Oxford University Press, 1998.

Feld, Marjorie. *The Threshold of Dissent.* New York University Press, 2024.

Feldman, Keith P. *A Shadow over Palestine: The Imperial Life of Race in America.* University of Minnesota Press, 2015.

Fineberg, S. Andhil. *The Rosenberg Case: Fact and Fiction.* Oceana, 1953.

Finger, Justin. Justin Finger to Kevin Berrill, June 4, 1986. Box 106, Folder 6, Series II. Field Files: Civil Rights Organizations: ADL, 1981–90. National Gay and Lesbian Task Force records, #7301. Cornell University.

Finger, Justin. Memo from Justin Finger to Kevin Berrill describing resolution of June 5, 1986, dated June 18, 1986. Box 106, Folder 6, Series II. Field Files: Civil Rights Organizations: ADL, 1981–90. National Gay and Lesbian Task Force records, #7301. Cornell University.

Fischbach, Michael R. *Black Power and Palestine: Transnational Countries of Color.* Stanford University Press, 2023.

Fischbach, Michael R. *The Movement and the Middle East: How the Arab-Israeli Conflict Divided the American Left.* Stanford University Press, 2019.

Forster, Arnold. "The Jerusalem Dig." *Dateline Israel.* Produced by Zev Furst and Igal Efrati, Israel Film Service, 1975. https://jfc.org.il/en/news_journal/108804-2/.

Forster, Arnold. *A Measure of Freedom: An Anti-Defamation League Report.* Doubleday, 1950.

Forster, Arnold. *Report from Israel.* Anti-Defamation League, 1968.

Forster, Arnold. "Report from Israel: Arab Terrorists." *ADL Bulletin,* January 1969, 3.

Forster, Arnold. "Report from Israel: The Soviet-Arab Axis." *ADL Bulletin,* September 1968, 1–2.

Forster, Arnold. "Roots of Terrorism." *Dateline Israel.* Directed by Gideon Hausner, September 9, 1979. Original: open reel tape, id. 13, Box 207. WSB collection, Manuscript Collection No. 663. Stuart A. Rose Manuscript, Archives, and Rare Book Library.

Forster, Arnold. *Square One: A Memoir.* D. I. Fine, 1988.

Forster, Arnold. "The Truth About Arabs." *ADL Bulletin,* June 1964.

Forster, Arnold, and Benjamin R. Epstein. *Cross-Currents.* Doubleday, 1956.

Forster, Arnold, and Benjamin R. Epstein. *The New Anti-Semitism.* McGraw-Hill, 1974.

Forster, Arnold, and Benjamin R. Epstein. *The Trouble-Makers: An Anti-Defamation League Report.* 1952.

Foxman, Abe. Abe Foxman to Kevin Berrill, August 16, 1989. Box 106, Folder 6, Series II. Field Files: Civil Rights Organizations: ADL, 1981–90. National Gay and Lesbian Task Force records, #7301. Cornell University.

Friedman, Milton. "McCarthyism Viewed as Peril to Democratic Institutions by ADL." *American Jewish World,* December 11, 1953.

Friedman, Murray. *The Neoconservative Revolution: Jewish Intellectuals and the Shaping of Public Policy.* Cambridge University Press, 2005.

Friedman, Murray. "A New Direction for American Jews." *Commentary* 72, no. 6 (1981): 37–44.

Friedman, Murray. *What Went Wrong? The Creation & Collapse of the Black-Jewish Alliance*. Simon and Schuster, 1994.

Friedman, Robert I. "How the Anti-Defamation League Turned the Notion of Human Rights on Its Head, Spying on Progressives and Funneling Information to Law Enforcement." *Village Voice*, May 11, 1993.

Friedman, Robert I. "The Jewish Thought Police." *Village Voice*, July 27, 1993.

Gabler, Neal. *Winchell: Gossip, Power, and the Culture of Celebrity*. Knopf Doubleday, 1995.

Gay and Lesbian Alliance Against Defamation/Los Angeles (GLAAD/LA). GLAAD/LA (sender illegible) to Kevin Berrill, January 1990. Box 106, Folder 7, Series II. Field Files: Civil Rights Organizations: ADL: Education Project: "A World of Difference," 1988–91. National Gay and Lesbian Task Force records, #7301. Cornell University.

Gelbspan, Ross. "4 Boston Firms to Show Data on Minority Hiring." *Boston Globe*, May 24, 1986.

Gelman, Emmaia. "Astroturf Antisemitism Watchdogs." *Jadaliyya*, April 13, 2024.

Gelman, Emmaia. "Encampments and the Unshackling of Study." *Newsletter of the Middle East and North Africa Politics Section of APSA* 7, no. 2 (Fall 2024).

Gelman, Emmaia. "The World Upside-Down: Zionist Institutions, Civil Rights Talk, and the New Cold War on Ethnic Studies." *Critical Ethnic Studies* 8, no. 2 (2023).

Gelman, Felice. "The ADL's War on Socially Conscious Investing Is in Service to Israel and the New Oligarchy." *Mondoweiss*, March 17, 2025

Genzlinger, Neil. "The Past in the Present." *New York Times*, November 20, 2009.

Gerson, Mark. *The Neoconservative Vision: From the Cold War to the Culture Wars*. Madison Books, 1996.

Gilbert, Lauren. "'A Very Ticklish Problem': The AJC Response to the Rosenberg Trial & Execution." *The Word: The CJH Blog*, April 27, 2023. https://blog.cjh.org /index.php/2023/04/25/a-very-ticklish-problem-the-ajc-response-to-the-rosenberg-trial-execution/.

Gilmore, Ruth Wilson. *Golden Gulag: Prisons, Surplus, Crisis, and Opposition in Globalizing California*. University of California Press, 2007.

Glock, Charles Y., Gertrude Jaeger Selznick, and Joe L. Spaeth. *The Apathetic Majority: A Study Based on Public Responses to the Eichmann Trial*. Harper & Row, 1966.

Goldberg, J.J. *Jewish Power*. Addison Wesley Publishing Company, 1996.

Goldstein, Eric L. *The Price of Whiteness: Jews, Race, and American Identity*. Princeton University Press, 2019.

Gordon, Jane Anna. *Why They Couldn't Wait: A Critique of the Black-Jewish Conflict over Community Control in Ocean Hill-Brownsville, 1967–1971*. Psychology Press, 2001.

Gordon, Leah N. *From Power to Prejudice: The Rise of Racial Individualism in Mid-Century America*. University of Chicago Press, 2016.

Grandin, Greg. *Empire's Workshop*. Metropolitan Books, 2006.

Graubard, Seymour. "Vol IIa: Graubard, Seymour, 1985–1987," n.d. Box 1, Folder 1. B'nai B'rith Anti-Defamation League Oral Histories. American Jewish Archives, Cincinnati, Ohio.

Greenberg, Cheryl Lynn. *Troubling the Waters: Black-Jewish Relations in the American Century.* Princeton University Press, 2010.

Greenberg, Maxwell E. "A Commentary: Jewish Point of View." *Michigan Chronicle*, October 20, 1979.

Greenberg, Maxwell E. "Vol IIc: Greenberg, Maxwell E., 1985–1987," n.d. Box 1, Folder 1, MS-365. B'nai B'rith Anti-Defamation League Oral Histories. American Jewish Archives, Cincinnati, Ohio.

Greenblatt, Jonathan. "Antisemitic Incidents in Russia & at US College Campuses Cause Alarm." CNN interview by Kasie Hunt. October 31, 2023. https://www.cnn.com/videos/world/2023/10/30/exp-antisemitism-cornell-russia-greenblatt-hunt-intv-10301asegi-cnni-world.cnn.

Greenblatt, Jonathan. "Eyes on the Prize: In Pursuit of Racial Justice, Stick to the Facts and Avoid the Fiction." *Medium*, August 4, 2016. https://jonathan-g.medium.com/eyes-on-the-prize-in-pursuit-of-racial-justice-stick-to-the-facts-and-avoid-the-fiction-5a5486a5cb4e.

Grier, George W., and Eunice S. Grier. *Equality and Beyond: Housing Segregation and the Goals of the Great Society.* Quadrangle Books, 1966.

Grosjean, Pauline, Federico Masera, and Hasin Yousaf. "Inflammatory Political Campaigns and Racial Bias in Policing." *Quarterly Journal of Economics* 138, no. 1 (2023): 413–63.

Guinane, Kay. *The Alarming Rise of Lawfare to Suppress Civil Society: The Case of Palestine and Israel.* Charity and Security Network, 2021. https://charityandsecurity.org/wp-content/uploads/2021/09/The-Alarming-Rise-of-Lawfare-to-Suppress-Civil-Society.pdf.

Gurock, Jeffrey S. *Central European Jews in America, 1840–1880: Migration and Advancement.* Routledge, 1998.

Hall, Stuart, Chas Critcher, Tony Jefferson, Brian Roberts, and John Clarke. *Policing the Crisis: Mugging, the State, and Law and Order.* Pan Macmillan, 1978.

Halley, Janet E. "'Like Race' Arguments." In *What's Left of Theory? New Work on the Politics of Literary Theory*, edited by Judith Butler, John Guillory, and Kendall Thomas. Routledge, 2000.

Halperin, Morton. Draft letter from Morton Halperin to David Brody, n.d. Box 106, Folder 6, Series II. Field Files: Civil Rights Organizations: ADL, 1981–90. National Gay and Lesbian Task Force records, #7301. Cornell University.

Handlin, Oscar. "Freedom or Authority in Group Life? Voluntary Agreements Work, Our Experience Teaches Us." *Commentary Magazine*, December 1, 1952.

Handlin, Oscar. "The Study of Man: Prejudice and Capitalist Exploitation." *Commentary Magazine*, July 1, 1948.

Handlin, Oscar, and Mary Flug Handlin. *Danger in Discord: Origins of Anti-Semitism in the United States.* Anti-Defamation League of B'nai B'rith, 1948.

Hanhardt, Christina B. *Safe Space: Gay Neighborhood History and the Politics of Violence*. Duke University Press, 2013.

Hansell, Dean. Memo from Dean Hansell to Interested Persons. "Background to the ADL's A World of Difference Campaign," October 22, 1989. Box 106, Folder 7, Series II. Field Files: Civil Rights Organizations: ADL: Education Project: "A World of Difference," 1988–91. National Gay and Lesbian Task Force records, #7301. Cornell University.

Harap, Louis. "ADL Reports on Anti-Semitism." *Jewish Life*, June 1950.

Harap, Louis. "From the Four Corners." *Jewish Life*, February 1952.

Harfouch, John, and C. Heike Schotten. "Sayegh's Critique of Zionism and the IHRA Definition: Notes Toward a Theory of the Antisemitism Industrial Complex." *Journal for the Critical Study of Zionism* 1, no. 1 (Fall 2024).

Haritaworn, Jin, Adi Kuntsman, and Silvia Posocco, eds. *Queer Necropolitics*. Routledge, 2014.

Harris, Cheryl I. "Whiteness as Property." *Harvard Law Review* 106, no. 8 (1993): 1707–91.

Harris, Louis. *A Study of Anti-Semitism in Rural Iowa and Nebraska*. Anti-Defamation League of B'nai B'rith, February 1986.

Harvey, David. *The Enigma of Capital and the Crises of Capitalism*. Profile, 2010.

Heard, Alex. *The Eyes of Willie McGee: A Tragedy of Race, Sex, and Secrets in the Jim Crow South*. Harper Collins, 2011.

Heer, Jeet. "Why the Anti-Defamation League Loves Certain Bigots." *The Nation*, November 20, 2023.

Henry, Kevin Lawrence, DeMarcus Jenkins, Mark White, and Carl D. Greer. "Conjuring the Devil: Historicizing Attacks on Critical Race Theory." *Thresholds* 46, no. 1 (2023).

Herald Tribune. "B'nai B'rith Says Arabs Help Foment Bias in US." March 11, 1956.

Hilbink, Thomas M. "Filling the Void: The Lawyers Constitutional Defense Committee and the 1964 Freedom Summer." *SSRN Electronic Journal* (1993).

Hirschhaut, Richard, and Ron Berman. Hirschaut and Berman to the *Bay Area Reporter*, December 19, 1988. Box 33, Folder 11. Community United Against Violence records. GLBT Historical Society.

Hobson, Emily K. *Lavender and Red: Liberation and Solidarity in the Gay and Lesbian Left*. University of California Press, 2016.

Hoffman, Bruce. "The PLO and Israel in Central America: The Geopolitical Dimension." *Terrorism and Political Violence* 1, no. 4 (1989): 482–515.

Hoffman, Paul. "Socialists at Parley Hail Their Golda." *New York Times*, June 28, 1972.

Hoover, Ken. "Anti-Defamation League Raided by S. F. Cops." *San Francisco Chronicle*, April 9, 1993.

Horn, Ariana. "Paved with Good Intentions: The Rise and Fall of the 'Human Relations' Movement in Milwaukee, 1934–1980." PhD diss., University of Wisconsin-Madison, 2015.

Horne, Gerald. "Who Lost the Cold War? Africans and African Americans." *Diplomatic History* 20, no. 4 (1996): 613–26.

HoSang, Daniel Martinez. *Racial Propositions: Ballot Initiatives and the Making of Postwar California.* University of California Press, 2010.

Hutt, Jacob, and Alex Kane. "How the ADL's Israel Advocacy Undermines Its Civil Rights Work." *Jewish Currents*, February 8, 2021. https://jewishcurrents.org/how-the-adls-israel-advocacy-undermines-its-civil-rights-work/.

Indiana Jewish Post and Opinion. "Negroes Seem Likely to Jump on Jews Next." April 16, 1965.

Isabel, Lonnie. "Mass. Rights Bill Described as Important Tool." *Boston Globe*, November 8, 1979.

Jabara, Abdeen. "The Anti-Defamation League: Civil Rights and Wrongs." *Covert Action*, no. 45 (Summer 1993).

Jacob, Abel. "Israel's Military Aid to Africa, 1960–66." *Journal of Modern African Studies* 9, no. 2 (1971): 165–87.

Jacobson, Matthew Frye. *Roots Too: White Ethnic Revival in Post-Civil Rights America.* Harvard University Press, 2006.

Jarmakani, Amira. "Amira Jarmakani on the Move from 'Zionism Is Racism' to 'Antisemitism Is Racism.'" *Battling the IHRA Definition.* Podcast by the Institute for the Critical Study of Zionism. August 15, 2024. https://criticalzionismstudies.org/amira-jarmakani-on-the-move-from-zionism-is-racism-to-antisemitism-is-racism/.

Jarmakani, Amira. "From 'Zionism Is Racism' to 'Antisemitism Is Racism.'" Paper presented at Battling the "IHRA Definition": Theory and Activism Conference, October 14, 2023, Santa Cruz, CA.

Jarmakani, Amira, and Emmaia Gelman. "Zionist Organizations' Latest Strategy to Criminalize Palestine Advocacy: Weaponizing Civil Rights." *Mondoweiss*, September 24, 2024. https://mondoweiss.net/2024/09/zionist-organizations-latest-strategy-to-criminalize-palestine-advocacy-weaponizing-civil-rights/.

Jenness, Valerie, and Ryken Grattet. *Making Hate a Crime: From Social Movement to Law Enforcement.* Russell Sage Foundation, 2004.

Jessup, David. David Jessup Papers, ca. 1970–96. Emory University Library.

Jewish Advocate. "ADL Board to Meet March 17." March 11, 1971, 17.

Jewish Currents. "Envisioning Solidarity." January 6, 2020. https://jewishcurrents.org/envisioning-solidarity.

Jewish Herald. "Confirm Deal Between Velde and Top 'Defense' Organizations." October 9, 1953.

Jewish Ledger. "ADL Survey—Klan Membership on Increase." May 12, 1978.

Jewish Life. "The Harap Testimony." September 1953.

Jewish Life. "Memorandum of the ADL." September 1953.

Jewish Telegraphic Agency. "ADL Announces New Radio Series on Israel." July 22, 1976.

Jewish Telegraphic Agency. "ADL Names First Negro Executive as Urban Affairs Unit Director." August 23, 1968.

Jewish Telegraphic Agency. "Anti-Defamation League Reports Discrimination in 781 Clubs in US." January 15, 1962.

Jewish Telegraphic Agency. "New Report Charges Anti-Semitic Campaign by Sandinistas." June 25, 1986.

Jewish Telegraphic Agency. "Randolph Initiates Committee of Black Americans to Support Israel." April 28, 1975.

Jewish Voice for Peace. "Fight Antisemitism, Reject the ADL." https://www.jewishvoiceforpeace.org/resource/reject-the-adl-landing/.

Johnson, Willard. "A National Strategy for Intergroup Education." *Social Science* 22, no. 1 (1947): 35–39.

Kaiser, Robert. "US Jews Expect Clash with Carter." *Jerusalem Post*, October 5, 1977.

Kaplan, Amy. *Our American Israel: The Story of an Entangled Alliance.* Harvard University Press, 2018.

Keene, Louis. "Every Time Donald Trump Has Accused American Jews of Disloyalty." *The Forward*, March 19, 2024.

Kelley, Robin D. G. *Freedom Dreams: The Black Radical Imagination.* Beacon Press, 2003.

Kelley, Robin D. G. *Race Rebels: Culture, Politics, and the Black Working Class.* Free Press, 1996.

Kennedy, Edward M. "Interview with Edward M. Kennedy." Conducted by James Sterling Young. May 31, 2007. Edward M. Kennedy Oral History Project, Miller Center, University of Virginia.

Kenney, Charles. "The Inner Circles; King's Rainbow: Black, White, Male, Female." *Boston Globe,* October 20, 1983.

Kibler, M. Alison. *Censoring Racial Ridicule: Irish, Jewish, and African American Struggles over Race and Representation, 1890–1930.* University of North Carolina Press, 2015.

Kifner, John. "Echoes of a New York Waterloo." *New York Times*, December 22, 1996.

King, Bill. "The Origins of Neoconservative Support for Democracy Promotion, 1960–1991." MA thesis, University of Calgary, 2007.

King, Martin Luther, Jr. "Negroes, Jews, Israel, and Anti-Semitism." *Jewish Currents* 22, no. 1 (238) (1968): 7–9.

Kirman, Joseph M. "Major Programs of the B'nai B'rith Anti-Defamation League: 1945–1965." PhD diss., New York University, 1967.

Klarlund, Susan E. "The Origins of Racism: The Critical Theory of Oliver C. Cox." *Mid-American Review of Sociology* 18, no. 1/2 (1994): 85–92.

Klehr, Harvey. *Far Left of Center: The American Radical Left Today.* Transaction, 1988.

Klepper, David, and Lori Hinnant. "George Soros Conspiracy Theories Surge as Protests Sweep US." AP News, June 21, 2020.

Klurfeld, Herman. *Winchell, His Life and Times.* Praeger, 1976.

Knopf, Terry Ann. *The Golden Age of Boston Television.* University Press of New England, 2017.

Koch, Edward, to Carol [*sic*] Lister. June 24, 1988. MS Lesbian Herstory Archives: Subject Files: Part 6: Spinsters-Youth Folder No. 15080. Archives of Sexuality and Gender. https://link-gale-com.i.ezproxy.nypl.org/apps/doc/DJBBRF161390396 /AHSI?u=nypl&sid=bookmark-AHSI&xid=42996e18&pg=28. Accessed January 9, 2019.

Koffman, David S. *The Jews' Indian: Colonialism, Pluralism, and Belonging in America*. Rutgers University Press, 2019.

Kolack, Sol. "Vol VIb: Kolack, Sol B., 1985–1987," n.d. Box 1, Folder 1. B'nai B'rith Anti-Defamation League Oral Histories. American Jewish Archives, Cincinnati, Ohio.

Kotzin, Daniel P. *Judah L. Magnes: An American Jewish Nonconformist*. Syracuse University Press, 2010.

Kruglanski, Arie W., and Wolfgang Stroebe. *Handbook of the History of Social Psychology*. Taylor and Francis Group, 2011.

Labor Notes. "Reagan Funds AFL-CIO's South Africa Activities." August 1986.

Labor Notes. "South African Unionists Tell AFL-CIO 'No Trade Union Imperialism!'" December 1986.

Landau, Rev. Jeremy. Rev. Jeremy Landau to Lester Olmsted-Rose, November 7, 1988. Box 33, Folder 11, Community United Against Violence records. GLBT Historical Society.

Lavinsky, Larry M. "Defunis v. Odegaard: The 'Non-Decision' with a Message." *Columbia Law Review* 75, no. 3 (1975): 520.

Lee, Felicia R. "Intolerance Will Be Topic for Students." *New York Times*, September 18, 1989.

Leiker, James N. "Rage of the Rural Minority: The High Plains Farm Crisis and Farmer Activism in Colorado and Kansas." *Great Plains Quarterly* 39, no. 3 (2019): 265–90.

Levey, Zach. "Israel's Strategy in Africa, 1961–67." *International Journal of Middle East Studies* 36, no. 1 (2004): 71–87.

Levi, Jeffrey. Jeffrey Levi to Abe Foxman, November 9, 1988. Box 33, Folder 11, Community United Against Violence records. GLBT Historical Society.

Levin, Geoffery P. "Before the New Antisemitism: Arab Critics of Zionism and American Jewish Politics, 1917–1974." *American Jewish History* 105, no. 1 (2021): 103–26.

Levine, Mike. "'No Blame?' ABC News Finds 54 Cases Invoking 'Trump' in Connection with Violence, Threats, Alleged Assaults." ABC News, May 30, 2020. https://abcnews.go.com/Politics/blame-abc-news-finds-17-cases-invoking-trump/story?id=58912889. Accessed February 7, 2024.

Levitas, Daniel. *The Terrorist Next Door: The Militia Movement and the Radical Right*. Macmillan, 2004.

Lewengrub, Stuart. "UN Vote on PLO." Letter to the editor. *Atlanta Constitution*, October 28, 1974.

Lewis, Clara S. "Tough on Hate? Addressing Hate Crimes in a Post-Difference Society." PhD diss., George Washington University, 2010. https://scholarspace .library.gwu.edu/downloads/2n49t171b.

Lewis, Clara S. *Tough on Hate? The Cultural Politics of Hate Crimes.* Rutgers University Press, 2013.

Lewis, David Levering. "Parallels and Divergences: Assimilationist Strategies of Afro-American and Jewish Elites from 1910 to the Early 1930s." *Journal of American History* 71, no. 3 (1984): 543–64.

Li, Darryl. *Anti-Palestinian at the Core: The Origins and Growing Dangers of US Antiterrorism Law.* Center for Constitutional Rights and Palestine Legal, 2024.

Liebman, Arthur. "The Ties That Bind: The Jewish Support for the Left in the United States." *American Jewish Historical Quarterly* 66, no. 2 (1976): 285–321.

Life. "Voices of Defeat." Vol. 12, no. 5 (1942).

Lilienthal, Alfred M. *What Price Israel.* Henry Regnery Company, 1953.

Lipset, Seymour Martin, and Everett Carll Ladd Jr. "Jewish Academics in the United States: Their Achievements, Culture, and Politics." *American Jewish Year Book,* 1971.

Lipsitz, George. *The Possessive Investment in Whiteness.* Temple University Press, 1998.

Livingston, Sigmund. *Facts About Fictions Concerning the Jew.* Anti-Defamation League of B'nai B'rith, 1938.

Livingston, Sigmund. *Must Men Hate?* Harper and Brothers, 1944.

Lubin, Alex. *Geographies of Liberation: The Making of an Afro-Arab Political Imaginary.* University of North Carolina Press, 2014.

Lynn, Denise. "Before the Central Park Five, There Was the Trenton Six." African American Intellectual History Society, July 3, 2019. https://www.aaihs.org /before-the-central-park-five-there-was-the-trenton-six/.

Lynn, Denise. "Losing Willie McGee." African American Intellectual History Society, July 6, 2020. https://www.aaihs.org/losing-willie-mcgee/.

MacDonald, Fred J. "The Cold War as Entertainment in 'Fifties Television." *Journal of Popular Film and Television* 7, no. 1 (1978): 3–31.

Makdisi, Saree. *Tolerance Is a Wasteland: Palestine and the Culture of Denial.* University of California Press, 2022.

Makdisi, Ussama. "Beyond the Palestine Exception." *Critical Times* 8, no. 1 (2025): 1–32.

Malloy, Sean. "From the 'New Antisemitism' to the IHRA Definition." *Journal for the Critical Study of Zionism* 1, no. 1 (Fall 2024). https://criticalzionismstudies .org/from-the-new-antisemitism-to-the-ihra-definition/.

Mann, Thomas J. "Oliver C. Cox and the Political Economy of Racial Capitalism." *Dialectical Anthropology* 46, no. 1 (2022): 85–102.

Marable, Manning. "A. Philip Randolph and the Foundations of Black American Socialism." In *Workers' Struggles, Past and Present,* edited by James Green. Temple University Press, 1983.

Mariaschin, Dan. Memorandum from Dan Mariaschin to Nathan Perlmutter. Administrative Staff Meeting, June 5, 1981, June 16, 1981. Nathan Perlmutter (1923–87) Papers, Box 11, Folder 7. American Jewish Historical Society.

Martin, Charles H. "Internationalizing 'the American Dilemma': The Civil Rights Congress and the 1951 Genocide Petition to the United Nations." *Journal of American Ethnic History* 16, no. 4 (1997): 35–61.

Martin, Larry. "The ADL Should Change Its Policy." *Bay Area Reporter*, December 22, 1988.

Marx, Gary T. *Protest and Prejudice: A Study of Belief in the Black Community.* Greenwood Press, 1967.

Masco, Joseph. *The Theater of Operations: National Security Affect from the Cold War to the War on Terror.* Duke University Press, 2014.

McAlister, Melani. *Epic Encounters: Culture, Media, and US Interests in the Middle East Since 1945.* University of California Press, 2005.

McQuiston, John T. "Anti-Semitic Vandals in Suburbs Are Causing Increasing Concern." *New York Times*, November 5, 1980.

McReynolds, David. "The Evitability of War, Revolution, Socialism." *On the Wilder Side* (blog). September 2009. https://www.onthewilderside.com /2009/09/11/david-mcreynolds-comments-on-war-revolution-and-socialism/.

Mearsheimer, John J., and Stephen M. Walt. *The Israel Lobby and US Foreign Policy.* Farrar, Straus and Giroux, 2008.

Melamed, Jodi. *Represent and Destroy: Rationalizing Violence in the New Racial Capitalism.* University of Minnesota Press, 2011.

Melnick, Jeffrey. *Black-Jewish Relations on Trial: Leo Frank and Jim Conley in the New South.* University Press of Mississippi, 2000.

Menchik, Jeremy. *The Missionary Impulse in World Politics: Democracy Promotion at the End of American Liberal Imperialism.* Forthcoming.

Miller, Alexander F. "Vol Vb: Miller, Alexander F., 1985–1987," n.d. Box 1, Folder 1. B'nai B'rith Anti-Defamation League Oral Histories. American Jewish Archives, Cincinnati, Ohio.

Miller, Jake C. "Black Viewpoints on the Mid-East Conflict." *Journal of Palestine Studies* 10, no. 2 (1981): 37–49.

Miller, Stuart. "The Author of 'The Iron Wall' Sees a 'Sinister' Precedent Behind Israel's Actions in Gaza." *Los Angeles Times*, November 27, 2023.

Milwaukee Star Times. "Black Americans Committee Condemns Boycott." October 16, 1975.

Mitchell, Vernay. "Curriculum and Instruction to Reduce Racial Conflict." *ERIC/ CUE Digest,* no. 64 (n.d.).

Mittleman, Alan, Robert A. Licht, and Jonathan D. Sarna, eds. *Jewish Polity and American Civil Society: Communal Agencies and Religious Movements in the American Public Sphere.* Rowman and Littlefield, 2002.

Molina, Natalia. *Relational Formations of Race: Theory, Method, and Practice.* University of California Press, 2019.

Moore, Deborah D. *B'nai B'rith and the Challenge of Ethnic Leadership.* State University of New York Press, 1981.

Movement for Black Lives. "Invest-Divest." 2016. https://web.archive.org /web/20160801231555/https://policy.m4bl.org/invest-divest/.

Movement for Black Lives. *A Vision for Black Lives: Policy Demands for Black Power, Freedom, & Justice.* 2016. https://web.archive.org/web/20160801231434/https:// policy.m4bl.org/platform/.

Moynihan, Daniel P. "The Professors and the Poor." *Commentary*, August 1968.

Myrdal, Gunnar. *An American Dilemma*. Harper and Brothers, 1944.

Najjar, Orayb Aref. "'Dear Israeli Chief-Censor . . . Sincerely Yours, the Palestinian Editor-in-Chief': Censorship, Negotiation and Procedural Justice." *Studies in Cultures, Organizations and Societies* 5, no. 2 (1999): 297–330.

National Association for the Advancement of Colored People (NAACP). "NAACP Education Chief Says Klan Is Not an Aberration." Press release, October 28, 1981. Box 106, Folder 6, Series II. Field Files: Civil Rights Organizations: ADL, 1984–90. National Gay and Lesbian Task Force records, #7301. Cornell University.

National Center for Transgender Equality. "The Discrimination Administration." https://transequality.org/the-discrimination-administration. Accessed February 7, 2024.

National Gay and Lesbian Task Force. "Anti-Defamation League Model Statute Addresses Anti-Gay Violence: NGLTF State Action Lobby Initiates National Campaign for Legislation to Combat Hate Crimes." Press release. Box 46, Folder 62, Series II. Field Files: Anti-Violence Project: Press Releases: ADL Model Statute Addresses Anti-Gay Violence 1988. National Gay and Lesbian Task Force records, #7301. Cornell University.

National Gay and Lesbian Task Force. Handwritten meeting notes, unsigned, n.d. Box 106, Folder 7, Series II. Field Files: Civil Rights Organizations: ADL: Education Project: "A World of Difference," 1988–91. National Gay and Lesbian Task Force records, #7301. Cornell University.

Nazarian, Sharon. "By Rejecting Jews, Intersectionality Betrays Itself." Anti-Defamation League, January 25, 2018. https://www.adl.org/news/op-ed/by-rejecting-jews-intersectionality-betrays-itself.

Neier, Aryeh. "Surveillance by the FBI." *Index on Censorship* 10, no. 2 (April 1, 1981): 45–46.

Nepon, Ezra Berkley. *Justice, Justice Shall You Pursue*. Thread Makes Blanket Press, 2012.

Neusner, Jacob. *American Judaism, Adventure in Modernity: An Anthological Essay*. KTAV Publishing House Inc., 1978.

Newfield, Mayer U. "Vol IVb: Newfield, Mayer U., 1985–1987," n.d. Box 1, Folder 1. B'nai B'rith Anti-Defamation League Oral Histories. American Jewish Archives, Cincinnati, Ohio.

New York Post. "Jewish Students Reveal What Happened at Cooper Union Protest." October 26, 2023.

New York Times. "Anti-Klan Group Plans Action Against Racism." February 2, 1981.

New York Times. "Arms Training by Klan Cited in Suit." June 7, 1984.

New York Times. "County Acts to Stem Crimes of Bias." May 22, 1988.

New York Times. "A Dealer in Art and, Some Say, a Dealer in Secret Police Data." April 25, 1993.

New York Times. "Germans Accused of Anti-Semitism; B'nai B'rith Mission Asks US to Continue Its Program of Democratic Education." July 20, 1954.

New York Times. "How the Klans Are Organized." September 13, 1981.

Nichols, L. B. Office memorandum, US Government, from Mr. L. B. Nichols to M. A. Jones. "Subject: Herman Edelsberg; Henry E. Schultz; Arnold Forster; Judge David A. Rose Anti-Defamation League of B'nai B'rith meeting with director 10:30 A.M., 6-21-54." June 22, 1954. Anti Defamation League -- HQ 100-530, 70. https://archive.org/details/AntiDefamationLeagueHQ100530/page/n69.

Novick, Peter. *The Holocaust in American Life*. Houghton Mifflin Harcourt, 2000.

O'Brien, Lee. *American Jewish Organizations and Israel*. Institute for Palestine Studies, 1986.

Olmsted-Rose, Lester. Note from Lester Olmsted-Rose to Amy Schoenbaum, October 26, 1988. Box 33, Folder 11, Community United Against Violence records. GLBT Historical Society.

Olmsted-Rose, Lester. Note from Lester Olmsted-Rose to Carmen [Vasquez], November 8, 1088. Box 33, Folder 11, Community United Against Violence records. GLBT Historical Society.

Oregon State Archives. "Listing of Legislative Records in Oregon State Archives Pertaining to House Bill 2479, 1981."

Oregonian. "Gay Political Leader Urges Alternative to Reagan Plan." May 16, 1981.

Oregonian. "Law Urged to Counter Racial Acts." February 21, 1981.

Ota, Alan K. "Racial Harassment Incidents Increasing in Oregon." *Sunday Oregonian*, December 21, 1980.

Pate, Glenn S. *Prejudice Reduction and the Findings of Research*. 1995. ERIC Database, Institute of Education Sciences within the US Department of Education. https://files.eric.ed.gov/fulltext/ED383803.pdf.

Peabody Awards. "A World of Difference WCVB-TV." https://peabodyawards.com/award-profile/a-world-of-difference/. Accessed March 22, 2018.

Pee, Robert. *Democracy Promotion, National Security and Strategy: Foreign Policy Under the Reagan Administration*. Taylor and Francis Group, 2015.

Pennock, Pamela E. *The Rise of the Arab American Left: Activists, Allies, and Their Fight Against Imperialism and Racism, 1960s–1980s*. University of North Carolina Press, 2016.

Perkins, Tom. "Anti-Defamation League Ramps Up Lobbying to Promote Controversial Definition of Antisemitism." *The Guardian*, May 16, 2024.

Perlmutter, Nathan. "Biographical Questionnaire," n.d., 1976–85. Nathan Perlmutter (1923–87) Papers, Box 10, Folder 4. American Jewish Historical Society.

Perlmutter, Nathan. Nathan Perlmutter to Edwin Meese, December 16, 1983. Digital record. James W. Cicconi Files, Box 3. Ronald Reagan Library. https://www.reaganlibrary.gov/public/digitallibrary/smof/cos/cicconi/box-3/40-94-6914307-003-006-2016.pdf.

Perlmutter, Nathan. Nathan Perlmutter to Kevin Berrill, December 20, 1984. Box 106, Folder 6, Series II. Field Files: Civil Rights Organizations: ADL, 1981–90. National Gay and Lesbian Task Force records, #7301. Cornell University.

Perlmutter, Nathan. "Vol Ib: Perlmutter, Nathan, 1985–1987," n.d. Box 1, Folder 1, MS-365. B'nai B'rith Anti-Defamation League Oral Histories. American Jewish Archives, Cincinnati, Ohio.

Perlmutter, Nathan, and Ruth Ann Perlmutter. *The Real Anti-Semitism in America.* Arbor House, 1982.

Perlstein, Daniel. "The Dead End of Despair: Bayard Rustin, the 1968 New York School Crisis, and the Struggle for Racial Justice." *Afro-Americans in New York Life and History* 31, no. 2 (July 2007).

Perlstein, Daniel Hiram. *Justice, Justice: School Politics and the Eclipse of Liberalism.* Peter Lang, 2004.

Phillips, Maya. "I Grew Up with Soviet Communism; Now as a Trustee I See It Embedded in California's Ethnic Studies." *California Globe*, September 14, 2024. https://californiaglobe.com/fr/i-grew-up-with-soviet-communism-now-as-a-trustee-i-see-it-embedded-in-californias-ethnic-studies/.

Podair, Jerald E. *The Strike That Changed New York: Blacks, Whites, and the Ocean Hill-Brownsville Crisis.* Yale University Press, 2004.

Poinsett, Alex. "Battle to Control Black Schools: National Drive Mounts for Ghetto Self-Determination in Education." *Ebony* 24, no. 7 (1969): 44–54.

Porter, Jack Nusan, and Peter Dreier. *Jewish Radicalism: A Selected Anthology.* Grove, 1973.

Powell, Julie M. "Making 'The Case Against the "Reds"': Racializing Communism, 1919–1920." In *Historicizing Fear*, edited by Travis D. Boyce and Winsome M. Chunnu. University Press of Colorado, 2019.

Presner, Todd Samuel. "'Clear Heads, Solid Stomachs, and Hard Muscles': Max Nordau and the Aesthetics of Jewish Regeneration." *Modernism/Modernity* 10, no. 2 (2003): 269–96.

Pritchett, Wendell E. *Brownsville, Brooklyn: Blacks, Jews, and the Changing Face of the Ghetto.* University of Chicago Press, 2003.

Quinley, Harold Earl, and Charles Young Glock. *Anti-Semitism in America.* Transaction Publishers, 1979.

Raab, Earl, and Seymour Martin Lipset. *Prejudice and Society.* Anti-Defamation League of B'nai B'rith, 1959.

Raphael, Marc Lee, ed. *Understanding American Jewish Philanthropy.* Ktav Publishing, 1979.

Raspberry, William. "A Costly Omission of Context." *The Record*, August 14, 1979.

Rastegar, Mitra. *Tolerance and Risk: How US Liberalism Racializes Muslims.* University of Minnesota Press, 2021.

Record, Wilson, and Nat Hentoff, eds. *Black Anti-Semitism and Jewish Racism.* Richard W. Baron, 1969.

Reid, Alexander. "Bias in Nicaragua Reported by Jews." *New York Times*, March 20, 1986.

Rhode Island Herald. "Bills Seek to Reverse Rise in Anti-Semitism." March 12, 1981, 1.

Richards, Yevette. *Conversations with Maida Springer: A Personal History of Labor, Race, and International Relations.* University of Pittsburgh Press, 2004.

Richman, Jackson, and Sean Savage. "Proposed Anti-Israel Ethnic-Studies Curriculum in California Has Jewish Community on Alert." Jewish News Syndicate, August 2, 2019.

Rickford, Russell John. *We Are an African People: Independent Education, Black Power, and the Radical Imagination.* Oxford University Press, 2016.

Robinson, Cedric J. *Black Marxism: The Making of the Black Radical Tradition.* University of North Carolina Press, 2021 [1983].

Robinson, William I. *A Faustian Bargain: US Intervention in the Nicaraguan Elections and American Foreign Policy in the Post-Cold War Era.* Westview Press, 1992.

Rodríguez, Dylan. *White Reconstruction: Domestic Warfare and the Logics of Genocide.* Fordham University Press, 2020.

Rogers, David. *110 Livingston: Politics and Bureaucracy in the New York City Schools.* Random House, 1968.

Rogin, Michael. *Blackface, White Noise: Jewish Immigrants in the Hollywood Melting Pot.* University of California Press, 1996.

Rosen, A. Office Memorandum, US Government, from A. Rosen to E. A. Tamm. Subject: Antidefmation League, May 18, 1948. File 1199215-000 --- 100-HQ-530 --- Section 7, p. 171. The FBI and the Anti-Defamation League, Israel Lobby Archive, Institute for Research: Middle Eastern Policy. https://www.israellobby.org/adl/.

Rosenfeld, Arno. "Jewish Defense Organizations." https://principled-haddock-800.notion.site/Jewish-defense-organizations-ee9091c9d57c4347978538a41dbabaob.

Rosenthal, Morton M. "The Threatened Jews of Argentina: Extremist Nationalist Groups and Arab Propagandists Are Natural Allies in an Organized Anti-Semitic Campaign." *ADL Bulletin*, March 1971. Reprinted in Proceedings and Debates of the 92nd Cong., 1st Session, Congressional Record 117, pp. 8259–9468.

Ross, Jack. *The Socialist Party of America: A Complete History.* Potomac Books, 2015.

Roucek, Joseph S., and Bernard Eisenberg, eds. *America's Ethnic Politics.* Greenwood Press, 1982.

Ruby, Walter. "Planting Seeds of Hatred: Farm Crisis: As Families Fight to Cope Extremists Make a Pitch." *Jewish Exponent*, January 9, 1987.

Rustin, Bayard. "The Anatomy of Frustration." Anti-Defamation League of B'nai B'rith, 1968.

Rustin, Bayard. "Black Links to Israel." *Wichita Times*, April 20, 1972.

Rustin, Bayard. "From Protest to Politics: The Future of the Civil Rights Movement." *Commentary*, February 1965.

Sachar, Howard Morley. *A History of the Jews in America.* Vintage Books, 1993.

Salaita, Steven. *Israel's Dead Soul.* Temple University Press, 2011.

Salomon, Michael. "Israel's Arab Tourists." *ADL Bulletin*, November 1971.

Sarna, Jonathan D., ed. *The American Jewish Experience.* Holmes and Meier, 1986.

Sayegh, Fayez. "Authors of 'Cross-Currents' Willing to Prove Their Truthfulness." Radio Reports Inc. Radio transcript, April 13–14, 1956. Fayez A. Sayegh Collection. University of Utah.

Sayegh, Fayez. "Dr. Sayegh Mentioned in Interview with Authors of Cross-

Currents." Radio Reports Inc. Radio transcript, WMCA, March 14, 1956, 2–3. Fayez A. Sayegh Collection, Box 60, Folder 1, J. University of Utah.

Sayegh, Fayez. Memo from Fayez Sayegh, March 14, 1956. Fayez A. Sayegh Collection. University of Utah.

Sayegh, Fayez. "Sayegh Challenges Authors of Cross-Currents." Radio Reports Inc. Radio transcript, March 15–16, 1956. Fayez A. Sayegh Collection. University of Utah.

Schappes, Morris U., and Louis Harap. "Open Letter to the Jewish People of the United States." *Jewish Life*, September 1953.

Schary, Dore, and Benjamin R. Epstein. *Report of the Anti-Defamation League, 1964*. Anti-Defamation League of B'nai B'rith, 1964.

Schlesinger, Arthur, Jr. "Not Left, Not Right, but a Vital Center." *New York Times Magazine*, April 4, 1948.

Schlesinger, Arthur M. *The Vital Center: The Politics of Freedom*. Riverside Press, 1949.

Schmidt, Leigh E. "Pluralism, Secularism, and Religion in Modern American History." *Modern American History* 1, no. 1 (2018): 87–91.

Schotten, Heike, and Emmaia Gelman, eds. *The Anti-Defamation League: A Critical Reader*. Pluto Press, 2026.

Schuhrke, Jeff. *Blue-Collar Empire: The Untold Story of US Labor's Global Anticommunist Crusade*. Verso, 2024.

Schultz, Henry Edward. "Chairman's Report to ADL National Commission." 1960. Anti-Defamation League of B'nai B'rith Race Relations Work Records, Box 2, Folder 1, Amistad Research Center.

Schultz, Henry Edward, and Benjamin R Epstein. *Report of the Anti-Defamation League 1962*. Anti-Defamation League of B'nai B'rith, 1962.

Scipes, Kim. *AFL-CIO's Secret War Against Developing Country Workers: Solidarity or Sabotage?* Lexington Books, 2011.

Segal, Al. "Al Segal Speaks on in Place of Speeches." *Jewish Post* (Indiana), August 15, 1947.

Segev, Tom. *1967: Israel, the War, and the Year That Transformed the Middle East*. Macmillan, 2007.

Segre, Itai. "Israel and the Contras: A Buried History." Master's thesis, University of Chicago, 2023. https://knowledge.uchicago.edu/record/7213.

The Sentinel. "Is Negro Condemning Jew for Becoming 'White Christian'?" September 28, 1967.

The Sentinel. "Report: McCarthy Slurs Jews; Calls Them 'Slick.'" February 21, 1952.

Shaheen, Jack G. *The TV Arab*. Popular Press, 1984.

Shamir, Yoav, dir. *Defamation*. First Run Features, 2009. Posted September 5, 2023, by Yoav Shamir Films, YouTube, 1:31:40. https://www.youtube.com/watch?v=CTAjc1OSrmY.

Shanahan, Ed, and Maria Cramer. "Israel-Hamas War Protest Leads to Tense Scene at Cooper Union Library." *New York Times*, October 26, 2023.

Shanker, Albert. "Interview with Albert Shanker, conducted by Blackside, Inc. on November 15, 1988 for Eyes on the Prize II: America at the Racial Crossroads,

1965–mid 1980s." Washington University Libraries, Film and Media Archive, Henry Hampton Collection.

ShelfLife@Texas (blog). "In Memoriam: Elizabeth Warnock Fernea." December 5, 2008, https://web.archive.org/web/20150413202532/http://sites.utexas.edu/shelflife/2008/12/04/in-memoriam-elizabeth-warnock-fernea/.

Shohat, Ella. *On the Arab-Jew, Palestine, and Other Displacements: Selected Writings of Ella Shohat.* Pluto Press, 2017.

Silverstein, Ken, and Alexander Cockburn. "Big Labor's Goon Squads." *Counterpunch* 2, no. 18, October 15, 1995.

Sims, Beth. *Workers of the World Undermined: American Labor's Role in US Foreign Policy.* South End Press, 1992.

Sinnar, Shirin. "Hate Crimes, Terrorism, and the Framing of White Supremacist Violence." *California Law Review* 110 (April 2022).

Sitkoff, Harvard. "Harry Truman and the Election of 1948: The Coming of Age of Civil Rights in American Politics." *Journal of Southern History* 37, no. 4 (1971): 597–616.

Smith, David. "Donald Trump's Rhetoric Has Stoked Antisemitism and Hatred, Experts Warn." *The Guardian,* October 29, 2018.

Smith, Tom W. *Ethnic Images: GSS Topical Report No. 19.* National Opinion Research Center, University of Chicago, December 1990.

Soffer, Jonathan. *Ed Koch and the Rebuilding of New York City.* Columbia University Press, 2012.

Southworth, George. "Miami Losing Top Fighter for Civil Rights." *Miami Herald,* April 22, 1964.

Spade, Dean. *Normal Life: Administrative Violence, Critical Trans Politics, and the Limits of Law.* Duke University Press, 2015.

Staub, Michael. *Torn at the Roots: The Crisis of Jewish Liberalism in Postwar America.* Columbia University Press, 2004.

Steele, Richard W. "The War on Intolerance: The Reformulation of American Nationalism, 1939–1941." *Journal of American Ethnic History* 9, no. 1 (1989): 9–35.

Steinfels, Peter. *The Neoconservatives: The Origins of a Movement.* Simon and Schuster, 2013.

Stern-Weiner, Jamie. *The Politics of a Definition: How the IHRA Working Definition of Antisemitism Is Being Misrepresented.* Free Speech on Israel, 2021.

Stork, Joe. "The American New Left and Palestine." *Journal of Palestine Studies* 2, no. 1 (1972): 64–69.

Suall, Irwin. *The American Ultras: The Extreme Right and the Military-Industrial Complex.* New America, 1962. http://hdl.handle.net/2027/mdp.39015074199046.

Suall, Irwin. "The Ku Klux Klan: 1978." *Facts,* March 1978.

Svonkin, Stuart. *Jews Against Prejudice: American Jews and the Fight for Civil Liberties.* Columbia University Press, 1997.

Táíwò, Olúfẹ́mi O. *Elite Capture: How the Powerful Took Over Identity Politics (And Everything Else).* Haymarket Books, 2022.

Tanenbaum, Marc H. "Is Nicaragua Anti-Semitic?" Press release, American Jewish Committee. October 14, 1983.

Tatour, Lana, and Ronit Lentin. *Race and the Question of Palestine*. Stanford University Press, 2025.

Teltsch, Kathleen. "S.N.C.C. Criticized for Israel Stand; Rights Leaders Score Attack on Jews as 'Anti-Semitism.'" *New York Times*, August 16, 1967.

ThamesTv. "1960s New York | Crisis in the City | Teachers Strikes | Racial Tension | John Lindsay | 1968." Originally aired July 11, 1968. Posted April 3, 2022, YouTube. https://www.youtube.com/watch?v=RRTQsFpH7P8.

Thomas, Michael. *American Policy Toward Israel: The Power and Limits of Beliefs*. Routledge, 2007.

Thusi, India. "Blue Lives & the Permanence of Racism." *Cornell Law Review Online* 105 (2020): 14.

Time. "The Black and the Jew: A Falling Out of Allies." January 31, 1969.

Time. "Nation: With Sorrow and Anger." September 3, 1979.

Tregor, Jill, Lindsey Jang, Fred Persily, Audrey Shabbas, and Robin Wu to Interested Parties. April 5, 1989. Box 33, Folder 11, Community United Against Violence records. GLBT Historical Society.

Tregor, Jill, and Lester Olmsted-Rose. Jill Tregor and Lester Olmsted-Rose to Eva Paterson and members of the Coalition on Civil Rights, October 27, 1988. Sent to Kevin Berrill with a note from Olmsted-Rose. Box 106, Folder 7, Series II. Field Files: Civil Rights Organizations: ADL: Education Project: "A World of Difference," 1988–91. National Gay and Lesbian Task Force records, #7301. Cornell University.

Tregor, Jill, and Lester Olmsted-Rose. Letter to the editor of the *Bay Area Reporter*, August 23, 1988. Box 106, Folder 7, Series II. Field Files: Civil Rights Organizations: ADL: Education Project: "A World of Difference," 1988–91. National Gay and Lesbian Task Force records, #7301. Cornell University.

Treisman, Rachel. "A Former Cornell Student Is Sentenced to 21 Months for Threatening to Kill Jews." NPR, August 13, 2024.

Tripp, Julie. "Racial Threats Plague Milwaukie-Area Family." *Sunday Oregonian*, August 17, 1980.

Umemoto, Karen. "'On Strike!' San Francisco State College Strike, 1968–69: The Role of Asian American Students." *Amerasia Journal* 15, no. 1 (1989): 3–41.

UNESCO. Records of the General Conference, Eighteenth Session Paris. October 17–23, 1974. https://en.unesco.org/inclusivepolicylab/system/files/teams/discussion/2022/2/UNESCO%20Records%201974.pdf.

Upadhyaya, Kayla Kumari. "ACT UP NY Calls on GLAAD to Oppose Genocide, Drop the ADL." *Autostraddle*, May 13, 2024. https://www.autostraddle.com/act-up-ny-calls-on-glaad-to-oppose-genocide-drop-the-adl/.

Urofsky, Melvin I. "American Jewish Leadership." *American Jewish History* 70, no. 4 (1981): 401–19.

US Campaign for Palestinian Rights. "The ADL Is Not An Ally! #DropTheADL." September 14, 2022. https://uscpr.org/campaigns/drop-the-adl/.

US Commission on Civil Rights. *Achieving Change: A Report/Prepared by the West Virginia Advisory Committee to the US Commission on Civil Rights.* 1981.

US Commission on Civil Rights. *Hate Groups and Acts of Bigotry: Connecticut's Response.* October 1982.

US Commission on Civil Rights. *Hate Groups in Michigan: A Sham or a Shame.* March 1982.

US Commission on Civil Rights. *Perceptions of Hate Group Activity in Georgia.* December 1982.

US Congress. *Anti-Gay Violence: Hearing Before the Subcommittee on Criminal Justice of the Committee on the Judiciary.* House of Representatives, 99th Cong., 2nd Session, October 9, 1986.

US Congress. *Anti-Indian Violence: Hearings Before the Subcommittee on Civil and Constitutional Rights of the Committee on the Judiciary.* House of Representatives, 100th Cong., 2nd Session, May 4 and 18, 1988.

US Congress. *Crimes Against Religious Practices and Property: Hearings Before the Subcommittee on Criminal Justice of the Committee on the Judiciary.* House of Representatives, 99th Cong., 1st Session, May 16 and June 19, 1985.

US Congress. *Ethnically Motivated Violence Against Arab-Americans: Hearing Before the Subcommittee on Criminal Justice of the Committee on the Judiciary.* House of Representatives, 99th Cong., 2nd Session, July 16, 1986.

US Congress. *Hate Crime Statistics Act: Hearing Before the Subcommittee on Criminal Justice of the Committee on the Judiciary.* House of Representatives, 99th Cong., 1st Session, March 21, 1985.

US Congress. *Hate Crimes Statistics Act*, HR 3193. 100th Cong., 1st session, introduced in House August 7, 1987.

US Congress. *Increasing Violence Against Minorities: Hearing Before the Subcommittee on Crime of the Committee on the Judiciary.* House of Representatives, 96th Cong., 2nd Session, December 9, 1980.

US Congress. *Racially Motivated Violence: Hearings Before the Subcommittee on Criminal Justice of the Committee on the Judiciary.* House of Representatives, 97th Cong., 1st Session, March 4, June 3, and November 12, 1981.

Vaid, Urvashi. *Virtual Equality: The Mainstreaming of Gay and Lesbian Liberation.* Anchor Books, 1995.

Vaïsse, Justin. *Neoconservatism: The Biography of a Movement.* Harvard University Press, 2010.

Verbeeten, David. *The Politics of Nonassimilation: The American Jewish Left in the Twentieth Century.* Cornell University Press, 2017.

Von Eschen, Penny M. *Race Against Empire: Black Americans and Anticolonialism, 1937–1957.* Cornell University Press, 1997.

Waldman, Lester J. "Vol Vc: Waldman, Lester J., 1985–1987," n.d. Box 1, Folder 1, MS-365. B'nai B'rith Anti-Defamation League Oral Histories. American Jewish Archives, Cincinnati, Ohio.

Walls, Dwayne. "The Dormant Klan." *ADL Bulletin*, September 1970, 3.

Weisbord, Robert G., and Arthur Stein. *Bittersweet Encounter: The Afro-American and the American Jew*. Negro Universities Press, 1970.

Whetstone, Lauren MacKenzie. "An Evaluation of Prejudice Reduction Program for Children." PhD diss., Claremont Graduate University, 1991.

Whitfield, Stephen J. *The Culture of the Cold War*. John Hopkins University Press, 1996.

Whitlock, Kay. "Reconsidering Hate: Policy & Politics at the Intersection." Political Research Associates, June 1, 2012.

Wides, Sonia Chajet. "In Monumental Vote, NEA Teachers Join Chorus Against ADL." *In These Times*, August 21, 2025. https://inthesetimes.com/article/in-monumental-vote-nea-teachers-join-chorus-against-adl.

Williams, Robin M. *The Reduction of Intergroup Tensions: A Survey of Research on Problems of Ethnic, Racial, and Religious Group Relations*. Social Science Research Network, 1947.

Winant, Howard. *The World Is a Ghetto: Race and Democracy Since World War II*. Basic Books, 2001.

Wind, Maya. *Towers of Ivory and Steel: How Israeli Universities Deny Palestinian Freedom*. Verso, 2024.

Witcher, Gregory "Rev. Stith Turns Down Invitation to Head PUSH." *Boston Globe*, February 11, 1985.

Wittenstein, Charles F. "It's Not the Same Old Klan." *ADL Bulletin*, October 1973, 3.

Young, David. "Arabs, Jews Wage War on the Propaganda Front." *Chicago Tribune*, July 27, 1975.

Zakim, Leonard. Letter to Campus Jewish Leaders, November 1983. File 111983_ADL_pro-Arab_Sympathizers, Criminal investigation and successful civil lawsuits against the ADL over privacy right violations - 1992–1993. Israel Lobby Archive, Institute for Research: Middle East Policy. http://www.israellobby.org/ADL-CA.

Zeitz, Joshua Michael. "'If I Am Not for Myself . . .': The American Jewish Establishment in the Aftermath of the Six Day War." *American Jewish History* 88, no. 2 (2000): 253–86.

Zerndt, Emily A. "The House That Propaganda Built: Historicizing the Democracy Promotion Efforts and Measurement Tools of Freedom House." PhD diss., Western Michigan University, 2016.

Zhulina, Alisa. "Performing Philanthropy from Andrew Carnegie to Bill Gates." *Performance Research* 23, no. 6 (2018): 50–57.

Zukerman, William. *Jewish Newsletter*, March 26, 1956. Fayez A. Sayegh Collection. University of Utah.

INDEX

Humphrey, Hubert, 92, 93
Hunt, Kasie, 219–20

IAAA (Institute for Arab American
    Affairs), 105
ICE agents, abductions by, 266
identity, logics of, 27
identity politics, US: ADL and, 2, 14;
    campaign Judaism, 14; donor class and,
    57; neoliberalism and, 4; New Left
    replaced by, 171; single-issue, 4
IHRA (International Holocaust Remem-
    brance Alliance), 8, 27
imperial state: ADL and, 65; ADL defense
    of, 24, 120
inclusion: Arab inclusion, 254; conceptions
    of difference and, 68; Eastern European
    Jewish immigrants and, 23; as group
    demand, 18; inversion and weaponiza-
    tion of language of, 64; Jewish inclu-
    sion, 32–33, 132, 133; repression in
    defending, 65n6; whiteness as position
    of, 33, 78, 132
income taxation, 57
Independent Socialist League, 162
Indian Removal Act of 1830, 34
indigeneity, 269; discussions of racist state
    violence expanding to, 10; mass move-
    ment against Gaza genocide and, 9; US
    Jewish identity formation in opposition
    to, 34–37
Indigenous people: discrimination experi-
    ences, 200; Indigenous movement, 265;
    Indigenous experiences of colonization
    and decolonization, 63; national belong-
    ing and, 35–36; protest of, 10, 34; vet-
    eran's burial at Arlington, 93n96
individual freedom: capitalism and, 5; Jews
    commitment to, 46
industrialization, state-capital formation
    and, 54
industry: Jews commitment to, 46; state-
    building for purposes of, 4–5
inequality: economic inequality, 18;
    increase after World War II, 117; non-
    discrimination and, 6n10. *See also*
    residential segregation
inheritance, race and, 5

Institute for American Democracy (IAD),
    78–79, 78n49, 268
Institute for Arab American Affairs
    (IAAA), 105
Institute for Free Labor Development,
    180
Institute on Religion and Democracy,
    180
institutional racism, concept of, 5
integration: accommodating of, 126; ADL
    position on, 128–29; failed efforts of,
    123; American Jewish Committee and,
    130; as opposite of racism, 116; rejection
    of, 117, 124, 125, 264
intercessor (*shtadlan*) model, 42, 46, 54, 85,
    93n98
intergroup relations: ADL expansion in
    field of, 82; ADL involvement in, 84, 88;
    collapse of field of, 116; conflict, 69;
    democratic values and, 72, 81n62;
    "Dinner with the President" event,
    92–93n96; as ideological project, 71;
    institutions of, 73; intellectual infra-
    structure for, 72; Jewish groups turning
    to, 70n24; racial state and, 77; scholar-
    ship on, 83–84
intergroup relations movement: ADL and,
    74–76; defense organizations and, 71;
    roots in war efforts, 74–75
intergroup relations organizations: ADL
    as, 25; community organizing and,
    69–70; culture work and, 69–70;
    education and, 69–70; health depart-
    ments and, 72; legal advocacy and,
    69–70
International Holocaust Remembrance
    Alliance (IHRA), 27; working defini-
    tion of antisemitism, 8, 27, 264–65
internationalism, 127, 148
International Workers Order, 100, 105
intersectionality, term usage, 12
Intifada, Palestinian: First, 203, 259; Sec-
    ond, 259
intolerance: fears about Black nationalist
    intolerance, 125; forms of, 76; tolerance
    of, 71. *See also* tolerance
Iran hostage crisis, 243
Irving, Kyrie, 29